OSF®/DCE
Administration Guide—
Core Components

Revision 1.1

Open Software Foundation

Prentice Hall PTR, Upper Saddle River, New Jersey 07458

This book was formatted with troff

 Published by Prentice Hall P T R
A Division of Simon & Schuster
Upper Saddle River, New Jersey 07458

Printed in the United States of America
10   9   8   7   6   5

ISBN   0-13-185844-0

Prentice-Hall International (UK) Limited, *London*
Prentice-Hall of Australia Pty. Limited, *Sydney*
Prentice-Hall Canada Inc., *Toronto*
Prentice-Hall Hispanoamericana, S.A., *Mexico*
Prentice-Hall of India Private Limited, *New Delhi*
Prentice-Hall of Japan, Inc., *Tokyo*
Simon & Schuster Asia Pte. Ltd., *Singapore*
Editora Prentice-Hall do Brasil, Ltda., *Rio de Janeiro*

Contents

Part 1. The DCE Control Program

Part 2. DCE Administration Tasks

Part 3. DCE Host and Application Administration

Part 4. Cell Directory Service

Part 5. DCE Distributed Time Service

Contents

Part 6. DCE Security Service

List of Figures

Contents

List of Tables

Preface

The *OSF DCE Administration Guide* provides concepts and procedures that enable you to manage the OSF® Distributed Computing Environment (DCE). Basic OSF DCE® terms are introduced throughout the guide. A glossary for all of the DCE documentation is provided in the *Introduction to OSF DCE*. The *Introduction to OSF DCE* helps you to gain a high-level understanding of the DCE technologies and describes the documentation set that supports DCE.

Audience

This guide is written for system and network administrators who have previously administered a UNIX environment.

Applicability

This is Revision 1.1 of this guide. It applies to the OSF DCE Version 1.1 offering and related updates. (See your software license for details.)

Purpose

The purpose of this guide is to help system and network administrators to plan, configure, and manage DCE. After reading the guide, you will understand what the system administrator needs to do to plan for DCE. Once you have built the DCE source code on your system, use this guide to assist you in installing executable files and configuring DCE. The *OSF DCE Release Notes* contain instructions for installing and building DCE source code.

Document Usage

The *OSF DCE Administration Guide* consists of two books, each of which is divided into parts, as follows:

- The *OSF DCE Administration Guide—Introduction*
  - Part 1. Introduction to DCE Administration
  - Part 2. Configuring and Starting Up DCE
- The *OSF DCE Administration Guide—Core Components*
  - Part 1. The DCE Control Program
  - Part 2. DCE Administration Tasks
  - Part 3. DCE Host and Application Administration
  - Part 4. DCE Cell Directory Service
  - Part 5. DCE Distributed Time Service
  - Part 6. DCE Security Service

Related Documents

For additional information about the Distributed Computing Environment, refer to the following documents:

- *Introduction to OSF DCE*
- *OSF DCE Command Reference*
- *OSF DCE Application Development Reference*
- *OSF DCE Application Development Guide—Introduction and Style Guide*
- *OSF DCE Application Development Guide—Core Components*
- *OSF DCE Application Development Guide—Directory Services*
- *OSF DCE DFS Administration Guide and Reference*
- *OSF DCE GDS Administration Guide and Reference*
- *OSF DCE Problem Determination Guide*
- *OSF DCE Porting and Testing Guide*
- *Application Environment Specification/Distributed Computing*
- *OSF DCE Release Notes*

For a detailed description of OSF DCE documentation, see the *Introduction to OSF DCE*.

Typographic and Keying Conventions

This guide uses the following typographic conventions:

Bold **Bold** words or characters represent system elements that you must use literally, such as commands, options, and pathnames.

Italic *Italic* words or characters represent variable values that you must supply. *Italic* type is also used to introduce a new DCE term.

`Constant width`	Examples and information that the system displays appear in `constant width` typeface.
[ ]	Brackets enclose optional items in format and syntax descriptions.
{ }	Braces enclose a list from which you must choose an item in format and syntax descriptions.
|	A vertical bar separates items in a list of choices.
< >	Angle brackets enclose the name of a key on the keyboard.
...	Horizontal ellipsis points indicate that you can repeat the preceding item one or more times.

This guide uses the following keying conventions:

<Ctrl-*x*> or ^*x*	The notation **<Ctrl-*x*>** or ^*x* followed by the name of a key indicates a control character sequence. For example, **<Ctrl-c>** means that you hold down the control key while pressing **<c>**.
<Return>	The notation **<Return>** refers to the key on your terminal or workstation that is labeled with the word Return or Enter, or with a left arrow.

Problem Reporting

If you have any problems with the software or documentation, please contact your software vendor's customer service department.

Pathnames of Directories and Files in DCE Documentation

For a list of the pathnames for directories and files referred to in this guide, see the *OSF DCE Administration Guide—Introduction* and the *OSF DCE Porting and Testing Guide*.

Part 1

The DCE Control Program

Chapter 1

DCE Control Program Introduction

DCE is an integrated set of services that supports the development and execution of distributed applications between heterogeneous networked computers. Each DCE environment (called a *cell*) maintains at least the following core DCE services:

- DCE Threads

- DCE Host Services

- DCE Cell Directory Service

- DCE Time Service

- DCE Security Service

With the exception of DCE Threads, all of the core services require administration in one way or another. Some services, such as CDS and the DCE Security Service, usually need more managing than, say, the DCE Time Service, which after you have set it up needs practically no intervention. If your DCE cell consists of just a few computers and their users, you could probably manage the naming, time, and security needs of users, programs, and host systems by logging into individual hosts to perform any necessary administration tasks. But most cells will consist of many, perhaps hundreds or even thousands, of computers and their users.

Consequently, the core services in such large cells will likely be extensive and complex, with some services being replicated or even partitioned across multiple heterogeneous systems. Some services, such as the DCE host services, will exist on every computer in the cell. Such large-scale operations demand an administrative interface that provides consistent and uniform access to DCE administration functions, wherever they reside, from any and every point in the cell. This means that administrative operations must work consistently and predictably regardless of the platform on which they execute.

The DCE control program (**dcecp**) available with DCE Version 1.1 fills this need, providing consistent, portable, extensible, and secure access to nearly all DCE administration functions from any point in a DCE cell. The DCE control program implements most of the operations previously performed by using various component control programs.

The DCE control program further streamlines administration by providing a number of *task objects* for performing complex DCE operations. For example, adding a host to a cell requires adding a host principal to the registry, adding the principal to various security groups and organizations, creating an account, placing host information in CDS and probably setting some ACLs on CDS directories. All of these operations can be accomplished using a single task object.

1.1 Flexible, Portable, and Extensible Administration

The DCE control program is built on a portable command language called Tcl (pronounced "tickle"), which stands for Tool Command Language developed by John K. Ousterhout at the University of California at Berkeley, California. Most computers provide a command language of some sort to give users a flexible and extensible way to access and use system capabilities. For instance, many UNIX systems offer shell language interpreters, and Digital Equipment Corporation's OpenVMS operating system offers the Digital Command Language (DCL). But these command languages aren't always portable. Commands and scripts based on one command language might not work in other command language environments.

Tcl, on the other hand, is a platform-independent command language that runs on every system where DCE Version 1.1 is installed. A Tcl command interpreter and the DCE control program that uses it are provided as part of the DCE Version 1.1 software.

Note: The DCE implementation of the Tcl command interpreter is called the *DCE control program language*. From now on we'll refer just to the DCE control program language. The Tcl command interpreter is designed expressly to support the DCE control program language. You will likely have difficulty if you try to execute generic (not DCE) Tcl scripts using the **dcecp** command interpreter.

The availability of both the DCE control program and the DCE control program language offer important benefits to DCE administrators:

- You can perform virtually all routine DCE operations from within a single administrative interface.

- Most DCE administrative operations are consistently and uniformly executed from any DCE Version 1.1 platform, allowing administrators to manage just about all DCE operations from any DCE Version 1.1 system in the cell. DCE Version 1.1 platforms that are not UNIX systems might not handle all DCE control program file operations.

- The DCE control program provides administration *objects* with names like **clearinghouse**, **principal**, and **endpoint**. This direct approach makes DCE administration intuitive and consistent. While for now this has only the appearance of being object oriented, it is an important step toward a true object-oriented administration interface.

- *Task objects* (high-level **dcecp** scripts that perform complex DCE operations) reduce the training requirements for DCE administrators. One needn't be a DCE guru to perform routine DCE administrative tasks.

- You can adapt the supplied task objects to new uses or write new task objects or scripts by using the **dcecp** operations along with more general commands provided within Tcl.

- The **dcecp** language allows the use of variables, **if** statements, looping functions and other programming operations that let you boost the power of your operations. For instance, looping functions let you repeat operations on multiple objects such as users, servers, or CDS entries.

- Administrators can easily share their tools because scripts can be moved to foreign platforms without change. For instance, enterprises with multiple cells could use **dcecp** scripts to propagate a common cell configuration throughout the enterprise.

The DCE control program is an administrative interface that you can use to manage most aspects of the DCE core components. You can't use **dcecp** to manage every aspect of DCE. First, not all of the existing programs are replaced by **dcecp**. For instance **dcecp** cannot control GDS or DFS. Second, even when **dcecp** replaces a control program such as **cdscp**, not every operation in the control program is necessarily implemented by **dcecp**. Typically unimplemented operations are those that are performed only once or relatively infrequently. OSF plans to implement all DCE operations in **dcecp** eventually. For now, you'll have to use the individual component control programs to perform operations not implemented in **dcecp**.

The chapters in Part 1 discuss how you can use **dcecp** to administer the core services in your DCE environment. We also discuss how to make your operations do more by using Tcl constructs on the command line and by writing your own customized operations as scripts. We don't provide a complete discussion of Tcl or its companion toolkit (called *Tk*) for the X11 window system. For in-depth discussions of these topics, refer to *Tcl and the Tk Toolkit*, John K. Ousterhout, (c)1994, AddisonWesley Publishing Company.

1.2 DCE Administration Objects

A DCE cell consists of many things that need administration. As examples, CDS servers (*clearinghouses*), DTS clocks, and server location information are all entities in a DCE cell that require administration in one way or another. The DCE control program treats all of DCE's administrative entities as individual administration objects.

You operate on an entity by invoking its *object* name with some operation. For example, to check the time of a DTS clock, you invoke the object's name (**clock**) and the desired operation (**show**) as in the following:

```
dcecp> clock show
1994-09-23-10:46:42.016-04:00I-----
dcecp>
```

Each administrative entity in DCE has a corresponding administration object in the DCE control program. As a few examples, you can manage CDS clearinghouse operations in a cell by using the **clearinghouse** object. Manage application servers and their configuration information on DCE hosts by using the **server** object. Compare and manipulate time information using the **utc** object. Administer users in a DCE cell with the **user** object. These examples represent just a few of the **dcecp** administration objects. All of the objects are listed in the **dcecp(8dce)** reference page.

1.3 Using the DCE Control Program

This section provides a quick look at how to start and stop the DCE control program and how to perform operations. Additional information about these topics is contained in the **dcecp** reference pages.

1.3.1 Starting and Stopping the DCE Control Program

You can enter **dcecp** operations directly from your operating system prompt or from within the DCE control program. If you are performing just one or two simple **dcecp** operations, you can invoke them directly at the operating system prompt.

If you will be doing several operations, you can invoke the DCE control program and then enter operations at the **dcecp** prompt. This method offers several advantages.

- It is more efficient for multiple operations because **dcecp** is initialized once rather than for each separate operation.

- The program stores operations in a history facility so they can be recalled and reused.

- You avoid the extra keystrokes needed to precede each operation with the **dcecp** command.

The following example shows how to invoke the DCE control program and perform a **directory** operation:

```
%  dcecp
dcecp>  directory create /.:/hosts/appserver2
dcecp>
```

When you are through using the DCE control program, use the **exit** or **quit** operation to stop the program and return to the operating system prompt. The following example illustrates using the **exit** operation:

```
dcecp>  exit
%
```

1.3.2 Invoking dcecp Operations

If you are performing a single **dcecp** operation, you can invoke it directly from the operating system prompt. Just precede the desired operation with the **dcecp** command and the **-c** (command-line operation) flag, as follows:

```
%  dcecp -c directory list /.:/subsys -simplename
HP applications dce sales eng admin accts
%  dcecp -c cell show
{secservers
 /.../my_cell.goodco.com/subsys/dce/sec/master}
{cdsservers
 /.../my_cell.goodco.com/hosts/krypton}
{dtsservers
 /.../my_cell.goodco.com/hosts/mars}
{hosts
 /.../my_cell.goodco.com/hosts/earth
 /.../my_cell.goodco.com/hosts/jupiter
 /.../my_cell.goodco.com/hosts/kyrpton
 /.../my_cell.goodco.com/hosts/mars
 /.../my_cell.goodco.com/hosts/mercury
 /.../my_cell.goodco.com/hosts/neptune
 /.../my_cell.goodco.com/hosts/pluto
 /.../my_cell.goodco.com/hosts/saturn
 /.../my_cell.goodco.com/hosts/uranus
 /.../my_cell.goodco.com/hosts/venus}
%
```

You can also enter some limited multiple operations using the ; (semicolon) as a command separator and enclosing the operations in "" (double quotes). The following example adds a principal to the registry and then checks that the principal is added:

% dcecp -c "principal create S_Preska ; principal show S_Preska"
```
{fullname {}}
{uid 28}
{uuid 0000001c-dc77-21cd-b700-0000c08adf56}
{alias no}
{quota unlimited}
%
```

Be careful entering multiple operations via the **dcecp** command with the **-c** option because operation results return to the **dcecp** interpreter, not to the shell. An operation like the following returns the results of just the last operation (**group list users**) to the shell:

% dcecp -c "group list staff; group list managers; group list users"
```
/.../ward_cell.osf.org/P_Pestana
/.../ward_cell.osf.org/R_Parsons
/.../ward_cell.osf.org/L_Jones
/.../ward_cell.osf.org/S_Preska
/.../ward_cell.osf.org/N_Long
/.../ward_cell.osf.org/D_Witt
/.../ward_cell.osf.org/C_Pilat
     .
     .
     .
%
```

To invoke a **dcecp** script, omit the **-c** argument but include the name of the script. The following example invokes a script that lists the names of all hosts in the cell in alphabetical order:

```
% dcecp list_hosts
earth
jupiter
krypton
mars
mercury
neptune
planets
pluto
saturn
uranus
venus
%
```

When you want to invoke complex or multiple operations, you might want to invoke operations from within **dcecp**. The program provides a convenient history facility and a command-line editing capability that is useful for recalling and reusing previous operations. The following example operations invoke the **dcecp** program and add a new user to a DCE cell:

```
% dcecp
dcecp> principal create J_Jones
dcecp> group add users -member J_Jones
dcecp> organization add staff -member J_Jones
dcecp> account create J_Jones -group users -organization staff \
> -password change.me -mypwd mxyzptlk
dcecp>
```

All **dcecp** object, operation, and option names can be abbreviated to the shortest unique string when used interactively. These names have been chosen with this in mind so that unique abbreviations are usually not more than one or two characters.

Avoid using object or command abbreviations within scripts as this limits a script's portability. Users defining their own commands could alter the uniqueness of abbreviations, resulting in ambiguous command names or object names.

1.4 Doing More with dcecp

The DCE control program accepts commands ranging from simple to complex, with more complex commands offering greater strength and versatility. Although simple commands are the easiest to compose, they are also limited, usually to performing one operation on a single object. So while it's always possible to enter simple commands, you'll probably find that, at times, you want to repeat operations over several or even many objects, or to perform some operation only under certain conditions. For instance you might want to add some entry to a CDS directory only if some other specified entry already exists in CDS. The DCE control program makes this possible by utilizing Tcl's built-in commands that imitate elements commonly found in numerous programming and shell languages.

The DCE control program contains many C-like constructs that control command execution. Some examples are **if** statements for conditional execution, looping commands such as **while**, **for**, and **foreach** used to repeat operations under various conditions, a **case** command for testing values against various patterns, and **proc** for writing your own customized commands.

The DCE control program also includes other syntactic elements such as "" (quotes), { } (braces), [ ] (brackets), and \ (backslash), which it uses to group elements together and for controlling interpretation of special characters.

Although many features are designed for use in scripts, you'll probably find yourself using some constructs and elements (particularly quotes, braces, brackets, and backslashes) in interactive operations as well. You'll need to decide when it makes sense to perform operations interactively or to use a script. In general, complexity and potential for reuse can help you decide.

Now let's look at a couple of simple examples that illustrate some DCE control program and Tcl basics. Some **dcecp** operations can be very straightforward like

dcecp> **account modify N_Long -expdate 1996-06-30**

This operation lets you change information in the DCE Security Service registry. Here, we're changing the account expiration date for the principal (**N_Long**) named in the command line. While it's relatively simple to execute this operation for one or two principals, it's more difficult to change the account expiration date for many principals.

Imagine that your organization employs six temporary workers and the project they're associated with has been extended for three months. Rather than execute the **account modify** operation six times, you can use a **dcecp** **foreach** command to loop (repeat) an action for each item of a list:

```
dcecp>  foreach i {N_Long L_Jones P_Sawyer
>  D_Witt M_Dougherty S_Preska} {
>  account modify $i -expdate 1996-06-30 }
dcecp>
```

In the example, the **foreach** looping command has three arguments: a variable, a list, and the body. The variable **i** substitutes sequentially for each item in the list (**N_Long**, **L_Jones**, and so on). The **foreach** command executes the body (**account modify $i -expdate 1996-06-30**)) for each item in the list. The **$i** variable in the body takes on the value of each principal name in the list, in turn, until all items in the list have been used. See Section 2.9.2 for more detailed information about looping commands.

This example illustrates several other important syntax rules. The DCE control program uses { } (braces) to determine where command arguments, such as the script body, begin and end. For example, the **foreach** command has three arguments: a variable name, a list, and a script body. Normally, command arguments are separated by spaces. To prevent **dcecp** from incorrectly interpreting the spaces between list elements as argument separators, we use braces to enclose the list and disable special interpretation of the spaces. Thus, all of the list elements appear as one argument. Similarly, we use braces to enclose the individual elements in the script body.

Braces also help **dcecp** determine whether a command is complete; incomplete commands will have more opening than closing braces. The lack of a closing brace at the end of the first line signals **dcecp** that more command input is coming, so **dcecp** prompts with the secondary prompt (>). Similarly, the opening brace at the end of line 2 signals that you are still not finished entering the command. This lets you wrap lines without using a \ (backslash) line wrap character. The DCE control program executes the command when you press **<Return>** after the closing brace at the end of line 3. Chapter 2 contains more information about braces.

Now assume that, instead of six temporary workers, your organization has fifty temporary workers (all in one group called **temps**) for whom you want to add three-month account extensions. We'll still use the **foreach** command but, rather than write all fifty principals directly in the list, use the **dcecp group list temps** operation to generate a list for you, as follows:

```
dcecp>  foreach i [group list temps] {
>  account modify $i -expdate 1996-06-30 }
dcecp>
```

In this example, we've put the **group list temps** operation in [ ] (brackets). Called *command substitution*, this technique replaces the command inside the brackets with the results returned by that command. The results of the **group list temps** operation produces a valid Tcl list that might look like the following:

```
dcecp>  group list temps
N_Long
L_Jones
P_Sawyer
D_Witt
M_Dougherty
S_Preska
   .
   .
   .
J_Jones
```

Here, we've provided a high-level look at some practical uses of **dcecp**. Of course there's a lot we haven't seen, too. In the next chapter we'll look more closely at some of the **dcecp** operations that you're likely to use for DCE administration. Remember that **dcecp** is based on Tcl, and Tcl has other commands and command variations we won't discuss. So be sure you have access to the standard Tcl publications for detailed information on all of the commands.

1.5 When to Use an Interactive Command or Script

There's no absolute dividing line for when you should enter commands interactively or with a script. In general though, the simpler operations—those that perform one or maybe two tasks—make the best candidates for interactive use. The following examples typify interactive operations:

dcecp> **directory create /.:/printers**

dcecp> **account show w_shakespeare**

dcecp> **server start /.:/hosts/curley/config/srvrconf/BBSserver**

The next example is a little more complicated, so at first you might choose to run this as a script:

```
foreach i [group list temps] {
    account modify $i -expdate 1996-06-30}
```

Saving a frequently used operation as a script (in a file) has its advantages; it can help to automate repetitive or complicated tasks and you can keep it around for possible modification and use in other situations later on. Whichever method you choose, as you become more comfortable using **dcecp** and Tcl, you might find yourself entering fairly complex operations interactively. For information on how to how to create and invoke scripts, refer to Section 1.8.

1.6 Editing Command Lines

We've seen some basic ways to enter interactive **dcecp** commands. But let's say that now you want to edit the command you're entering or that you want to recall and modify a command you entered previously. The DCE control program offers several ways to edit commands. You can edit a current command line by using the command-line editing facility. You can use the **history** command to recall, edit, and reissue a previously used command.

1.6.1 Editing the Current Command Line

You can edit a command line before sending it to the **dcecp** by typing control characters or escape sequences that resemble **ksh** or **emacs** editing commands. A *control character*, shown as **<Ctrl-x>**, where x is a letter, is entered by holding down **<Ctrl>** (or **<Control>**) and pressing the letter key. For example, **<Ctrl-A>** is **<Ctrl>** and **<A>**, pressed at the same time. Enter an *escape sequence* by pressing **<Escape>** followed by one or more characters. In an escape sequence, **<Escape >** is referred to as **ESC**, as in **<ESC f>** for example. Case matters in escape sequences (unlike control characters, which don't distinguish between upper and lower case); **<ESC F>** is not the same as **<ESC f>**.

You can enter an editing command anywhere on the line, not just at the beginning. In addition, a return may also be pressed anywhere on the line, not just at the end.

Most editing commands accept a repeat count, n, where n is a number. Enter a repeat count by pressing **<Escape>**, the number, and then the command to execute. For example, **<ESC 4> <Ctrl-f>** moves forward four characters. Some of the descriptions that follow are marked with [n] to identify commands that accept a repeat count.

The following control characters are accepted:

<Ctrl-A>	Move to the beginning of the line
<Ctrl-B>	Move left (backward) [n]
<Ctrl-D>	Delete character [n]
<Ctrl-E>	Move to end of line
<Ctrl-F>	Move right (forward) [n]
<Ctrl-G>	Ring the bell
<Ctrl-H>	Delete character before cursor (**<Backspace>**) [n]
<Ctrl-I>	Complete filename (**<Tab>**); see following text
<Ctrl-J>	Done with line (**<Return>**)
<Ctrl-K>	Kill to end of line (or column [n])
<Ctrl-L>	Redisplay line

<Ctrl-M>	Done with line (alternate **<Return>**)
<Ctrl-N>	Get next line from history [n]
<Ctrl-P>	Get previous line from history [n]
<Ctrl-R>	Search backward (forward if [n]) through history for text; must start line if text begins with an up arrow
<Ctrl-T>	Transpose characters
<Ctrl-V>	Insert next character, even if it is an edit command
<Ctrl-W>	Wipe to the mark
<Ctrl-X><Ctrl-X>	Exchange current location and mark
<Ctrl-Y>	Yank back last killed text
<Ctrl-[>	Start an escape sequence (**<Escape>**)
<Ctrl-]>c	Move forward to next character c
<Ctrl-?>	Delete character before cursor (**<Delete>**) [n]

The following escape sequences are accepted:

<Escape><Ctrl-H>	Delete previous word (**<Backspace>**) [n]
<ESC DEL>	Delete previous word (**<Delete>**) [n]
<ESC SPC>	Set the mark (**<Spacebar>**); see **<Ctrl-X><Ctrl-X>** and **<Ctrl-Y>**
<ESC .>	Get the last (or [nth]) word from previous line
<ESC ?>	Show possible completions; see following text
<ESC <>	Move to start of history
<ESC >>	Move to end of history
<ESC b>	Move backward a word [n]
<ESC d>	Delete word under cursor [n]
<ESC f>	Move forward a word [n]
<ESC l>	Make word lowercase [n]
<ESC u>	Make word uppercase [n]
<ESC y>	Yank back last killed text

<ESC w>   Make area up to mark yankable

<ESC *nn*>   Set repeat count to the number *nn*

The DCE control program also provides filename completion. Suppose the root directory has the following files in it:

```
bin     vmunix
core    vmunix.old
```

If you type **rm /v** and then press **<Tab>**, the command processor completes as much of the name as possible by adding **munix**. Because the example name is not unique, it beeps. If you press **<Escape>** followed by the ? (question mark), it displays the two choices. The command processor completes the filename when you then enter the period (which makes the name unique) followed by **<Tab>**, as shown in the following:

rm /v<Tab>munix.**<Tab>**old

In this example, the constant width font indicates text automatically entered by the command processor.

1.6.2 Editing Command Lines with the history Command

Sometimes when you're entering interactive commands, you want to recall and reuse a previously entered command. Let's say you list the objects in a CDS directory and then you modify one of the objects. Now you want to list the objects again to verify that your modification took effect. You can use the **history** command to recall, edit, and reissue a previously used command. The history facility saves only interactive commands. Commands issued from scripts aren't saved and can't be recalled.

The **history** command takes various arguments depending on what you want to do. Entering **history** with no arguments lists all the commands (called *events*) entered during the current invocation of **dcecp**, as shown:

```
dcecp> history
      1   principal create wardr -fullname {Ward Rosenberry} \
            -quota unlimited
      2   group add users -member wardr
      3   organization add consultants -member wardr
      4   account create wardr -mypwd mxyptlk -password qwerty \
            -group users -organization consultants
dcecp>
```

Each history event is independent of previous events. This means that, if a recalled command used a variable, its current value may not be the same as when it was first entered. The **history** command itself generates a history event, too.

By default, the history list keeps the 20 most recent commands. You can use the **history keep** command to lengthen or shorten the history list. For example, the following command lengthens the history list to keep the 50 most recent events:

```
dcecp> history keep 50
dcecp>
```

You can specify events in various ways. Positive numbers specify events relative to the earliest event in the list. Negative numbers specify events relative to the most recent command. You can also specify an event by typing characters that match all or part of a previous event.

The history facility lets you reuse previous events in many ways. The following discussion covers just a few of the history commands you can use.

- You can execute a previous command without revision by using the **history redo** command:

```
dcecp> history
        1 directory show /.:/printers
        2 object create /.:/printers/ascii_printer1
        3 object create /.:/printers/ascii_printer2
        4 object create /.:/printers/ascii_printer3
dcecp> history redo directory
directory show /.:/printers
     .
   . [output omitted]
     .
dcecp>
```

You can save the most typing by entering just the unique first characters of words in a history command. For instance, you can enter the **history redo directory** command from the previous example as

```
dcecp> hi r d
directory show /.:/printers

 .
 . [output omitted]
 .
dcecp>
```

Other ways to redo commands include **!!**, which recalls the most recent command, and **!***event number* to recall a specific event.

- You can revise and reexecute a previous command by using the **history substitute** command. A common use of this command is to correct typing mistakes. The command syntax is as follows:

history substitute *old new* [*event number*]

If you omit the *event number*, you'll redo the most recent command. Replace the *old* part of the recalled command with *new* information:

```
dcecp> history
        1 directory show /.:/printers
        2 object create /.:/printers/ascii_printer1
        3 object create /.:/printers/ascii_printer2
        4 object create /.:/printers/ascii_printer3
        5 directory show /.:/printers
dcecp> hi s -2 printer3 printer4
object add /.:/printers/ascii_printer4
dcecp>
```

You can also recall and revise the most recent command by using the *^old^new* syntax familiar to users of the UNIX **csh** shell, as follows:

```
dcecp> ^4^5
object add /.:/printers/ascii_printer5
dcecp>
```

1.7 Using the dcecp Help Facilities

The DCE control program offers help in several ways:

- If you want to see a list of objects provided by the DCE control program, enter **help** at the **dcecp** prompt as shown in the following example:

```
dcecp> help
The general format of all dcecp object operations is as follows:
  dcecp> <object> <verb> [argument] [options]

In addition to all of the standard tcl commands, dcecp supports many commands
to administer DCE objects.  A dcecp object or task represents a DCE entity.
All of the following dcecp objects and tasks require a verb:
account         cdscache        group         organization    user
acl             cell            host          principal       utc
attrlist        cellalias       hostdata      registry        uuid
aud             clearinghouse   keytab        rpcentry        xattrschema
audevents       clock           link          rpcgroup
audfilter       directory       log           rpcprofile
audtrail        dts             name          secval
cdsalias        endpoint        object        server

Miscellaneous commands perform specific functions.  Type 'man <command>' for
more information.  These commands take no verb:
echo      errtext  login    logout   quit      resolve   shell

To list all dcecp objects:                          dcecp> help -verbose
To list all verbs an object supports:               dcecp> <object> help
To list all options for an object operation:        dcecp> <object> help <verb>
For verbose information on a dcecp object:           dcecp> <object> help -verbose
For the manual page on a dcecp object:               dcecp> man <object>
dcecp>
```

- If you just need to know which operations an object supports, use the command

  object **operations**

  which returns a list of the actions you can take on an object. The following example shows how to list the operations available for the **principal** object:

```
dcecp> principal operations
create delete modify show catalog operations help
dcecp>
```

  You can save typing by abbreviating this command to something like **prin oper**.

- Get more detailed help about an object and its operations by using the *object* **help** command. The following example returns a 1-line description of each operation supported by the **principal** object:

```
dcecp> principal help
catalog            View a list of all the names of principals in the registry
create             Create a dce principal
delete             Delete a principal from the registry
modify             Change the information about a principal
rename             Rename the specified principal
show               Returns an attribute list of the specified principal
help               Print summary of command-line options and abort
operations         Return valid operations for command
dcecp>
```

- Get information about available command options by adding an *operation* argument to the *object* **help** command. The following example returns a 1-line description of each option supported by the **principal create** operation:

```
dcecp> principal help create
-alias             Add principal named as an alias of specified uid
-attribute         Attribute list to be assigned to the principal to be added
-fullname          Fullname of the principal to be added
-quota             Quota of the principal to be added
-uid               User Identifier of the principal to be added
-uuid              Orphaned UUID to be adopted by the specified principal
dcecp>
```

- Get help about an object itself by using an *object* **help -verbose** command. The following example returns a description of the **principal** object along with information about how to use the object:

```
dcecp> principal help -verbose
The principal object represents registry principals.  All of
the principal operations take one argument which is a list
of names of principals to act on.  It must be a principal
name, not the name of the database object that contains the
registry information about the principal (i.e., it should
not begin with /.:/sec/principal/).  After this operation
executes, the s(sec) convenience variable is set to the name
of the server that was bound to for the operation.  The value
of the variable before the operation is treated as a hint.
In the registry, each principal has a primary name and a
value for each of the following attributes: alias, fullname,
quota, uid, uuid.
dcecp>
```

- Finally, some POSIX style systems will have reference pages for **dcecp** objects as well as a Tcl summary reference page. Each **dcecp** object has its own reference page that describes the object and the operations available to it. The general syntax for viewing a **dcecp** object reference page is

man *object_name*

The following example shows how to invoke the reference page for the **principal** object. Note that you can use the **man** command from within **dcecp**.

```
dcecp> man principal
  .
  . [output omitted]
  .
dcecp>
```

The **Tcl** reference page summarizes the Tcl built-in commands. You can view the Tcl summary reference page on a UNIX style system by entering

```
dcecp> man Tcl
  .
  . [output omitted]
  .
dcecp>
```

1.8 Customizing dcecp Sessions

The DCE control program includes a number of commands, objects, and task scripts for performing most of the day-to-day DCE administration operations. Nevertheless, as you gain experience using the **dcecp** interface, you may find you want to add new commands and capabilities or to customize some existing ones. The following sections explain how to add scripts and new objects to your **dcecp** session. An object is just a formal implementation of a script that uses the **dcecp** help system and takes the form of *object operation*. Chapters 2 and 3 explain the fundamentals of writing **dcecp** scripts and creating new objects.

1.8.1 Adding Scripts to dcecp Sessions

Once you have written a script, you can make it available to one person or to
everyone who is logged into the host by modifying one or more of the
following files invoked when **dcecp** initializes:

[info library]/init.tcl

> This file is read first and contains standard Tcl initialization
> commands for the host. This affects all instances of **dcecp**
> running on a host. The file contains definitions for the Tcl
> **unknown** command and the **auto_load** facility used for
> initializing all of the **dcecp** objects. Administrators should
> avoid adding **dcecp** customizations to this file.

dcelocal/**init.dcecp**

> This file contains **dcecp**-specific startup information for the
> host. This affects all instances of **dcecp** running on a host.
> The **dcecp** scripts implementing operations and tasks are
> stored in the *dcelocal*/**dcecp** directory. Add customizations in
> the form of procedures to this file to make them available to
> all **dcecp** users on the host.

$HOME/.dcecprc

> This optional file stores user customizations that affect
> individual **dcecp** users (the owners of the **.dcecprc** files).
> Each DCE user can maintain a **.dcecprc** file and store private
> procedures or alias names for operations. Modified **.dcecprc**
> files allow flexible administration in environments with
> multiple administrators. For example, different **.dcecprc** files
> for each administrator could use **dcecp source** commands to
> call specific commands and task scripts that are tailored to
> particular areas of administration.

The rest of this section illustrates a simple task script and shows one way to
make the script available for personal use. Our example begins with the
control program's existing **clock** object that shows the current time.
However, the time is simply a DTS timestamp from the clock on the local
host as in

```
dcecp> clock show
1994-10-03-10:22:59.991-04:00I-----
dcecp>
```

Let's say you create a procedure that gets a timestamp from a DTS server
but also displays the name of the DTS server with the time as in the
following example which invokes a user-created procedure called
show_clock:

```
dcecp> show_clock
Time on mars is             1994-09-30-15:03:43.979-04:00I-----
dcecp>
```

You can make this procedure available to one user by including the
procedure in the user's **.dcecprc** file. The following sample **.dcecprc** file
includes user customizations consisting of the **_dcp_show_clocks** procedure
and an alias that lets you invoke the procedure with the simpler
show_clocks command name. Another procedure called **_dcp_whoami**
shows the current login identity information. Note the order of operations in
the **.dcecprc** file. Procedures are defined at the beginning of the file.
Renaming and invoking the procedures must occur after the procedures are
defined.

```
##
## Start up commands
##
# A simple command to rerun .dcecprc after modifications
proc .d {} {source $HOME/.dcecprc}

# Show your current login name and your current cell name.
proc _dcp_whoami {} {
   global _c _u
   return "You are '$_u' logged into '$_c'."
}
```

```
# Show the time on all of the dts servers running in your cell.
proc _dcp_show_clocks {} {
    set x [directory list /.:/hosts]
    foreach n $x {
        if {[catch {object show $n/dts-entity}] == 0} {
            set index [string last "/" $n]
            set y [string range $n [incr index] end]
            if {[catch {clock show $n/dts-entity} msg] == 0} {
                set i [expr 20 - [string length $y]]
                puts [format "Time on $y is %${i}s %s" " " \
                    [clock show $n/dts-entity]]
            } else {
                set i [expr 20 - [string length $y]]
                puts [format "Time on $y is %${i}s %s" " " \
                    "Server not responding."]
            }
        }
    }
}


# Give some procs usable names
rename _dcp_whoami whoami
rename _dcp_show_clocks show_clocks

# If I am authorized, say so
if {$_u != ""} {
  whoami
}
```

The **rename** command near the end of the file lets you invoke the
_dcp_show_clocks and **_dcp_whoami** procedures using the easier
command names **show_clocks** and **whoami**.

When you start **dcecp**, the last part of this file invokes the **_dcp_whoami**
procedure if you are logged into DCE. If the **_u** convenience variable is set,
the **_dcp_whoami** procedure prints your current login identity as follows:

```
% dcecp
You are 'principal_name' logged into 'cell_name'.
dcecp>
```

1.8.2 Adding New Objects to the DCE Control Program

If you have written a script as a formal **dcecp** object, you can make it available by including the new object in the same directory where other task objects reside. On UNIX systems, this is often *dcelocal*/**dcecp**. As a rule, you should add the new object to each host in the DCE cell. Chapter 3 describes how you can use the **dcecp hostdata** object to copy scripts or other files to every host in a cell.

When you install a new script, you must run the **auto_mkindex** utility to make the new object available to other users on the host. For more information about running the **auto_mkindex** utility, see Chapter 3.

Chapter 2

Using the DCE Control Program Command Language

In Chapter 1, we provided a high-level look at some ways to use the DCE control program to administer your DCE environment. In this chapter, we will discuss some syntax rules and some of the more important commands you'll need to use in composing your **dcecp** administration commands and task scripts.

The **dcecp** command language consists of DCE administration commands like **directory create** and **object modify**, as well as Tcl built-in commands such as **if** and **foreach**. We won't discuss DCE administration commands here. These commands are discussed in sections that deal with administering the particular DCE component. Instead, we will focus on using the more generic syntax rules and built-in commands.

The Tool Command Language (Tcl) on which **dcecp** is based is a general-purpose language that is also used for other applications besides **dcecp**. Although there are many ways you can use Tcl for various purposes, we will limit our discussion to those commands most likely to be used for administering DCE environments. Furthermore, our command discussions don't describe every aspect of individual commands. Rather, they suggest why and how you might use a command in the context of administering a DCE environment. If you're not already familiar with Tcl, you'll likely need to have access to the appropriate Tcl documentation, including the Tcl reference pages, for writing sophisticated commands and task scripts.

2.1 Chapter Preview

This chapter walks you through the basic **dcecp** syntax and then looks at some commands that you're likely to use in interactive commands and task scripts. The discussions will focus on

- Use of variables as an easy way to pass data around in your command or script

- Command substitution as a way to channel the output from one command to the input of another command

- Grouping elements together so that **dcecp** parses commands correctly

- Using lists to sort, find, and reuse information

- Using arithmetic functions in commands and task scripts

- Conditionalizing and controlling your script with **if** statements and loops

- Executing scripts associated with character patterns by using the **case** command

- Synthesizing commands by using **eval**

- Importing operations with **source**

- Creating new **dcecp** commands with **proc**

- Using error and exception information

- Handling strings

- Working with files

- Spawning subprocesses

2.2 Variable Substitution

Like other programming languages, **dcecp** provides shorthand ways to express and use values. Variable substitution is one shorthand method that lets you represent a value—say, the name of an object in a CDS directory—as a variable.

Use the **set** command to establish a value for a variable. For readability, a variable name can consist of any combination of letters, numbers, and _ (underscore) characters. Use "" (quotes) or \ (backslash) to include spaces in variable names (although this is not usually recommended) or values. All of the following examples use valid variable names:

```
set a $i
set CDS_clearinghouse_name cambridge_ch
set DCE_user_1 "William Rosenberry"
```

The following example sets variable *a* to have a value of **7**. The second use of the **set a** command without a value causes **dcecp** to display the current value of the variable:

```
dcecp> set a 7
7
dcecp> set a
7
```

Once you have established a value for a variable using the **dcecp set** command, the variable can be subsequently used elsewhere in your script or interactive command. The DCE control program uses the $ (dollar sign) to trigger insertion of the current value into the command word. A simple example is

```
dcecp> set a 7
7
dcecp> expr $a+2
9
```

Here we first set variable *a* to **7**. In line 2, we use the **expr** command to add 2 to the value of *a* (7). The dollar sign triggers **dcecp** to insert the value 7. The last line shows the return value from the **expr** command.

A more relevant example might be

```
dcecp> set a /.:/sec
/.:/sec
dcecp> object show $a
{RPC_ClassVersion
 {01 00}}
{RPC_ObjectUUIDs
 {06 3b 23 00 72 e5 e0 1d 8c b4 00 00 c0 8a df 56}}
{RPC_Group
 {2f 2e 2e 2e 2f 77 61 72 64 5f 63 65 6c 2e 6f 73 66 2e 6f 72
 67 2f 73 75 62 73 79 73 2f 64 63 65 2f 73 65 63 2f 6d 61 73 74
 65 72 00}}
{CDS_CTS 1994-05-23-17:21:37.481+00:00I0.000/00-00-c0-8a-df-56}
{CDS_UTS 1994-05-23-17:22:36.607+00:00I0.000/00-00-c0-8a-df-56}
{CDS_Class RPC_Group}
{CDS_ClassVersion 1.0}
dcecp>
```

Remove (undefine) a variable by using the **unset** command as in the
following example:

```
dcecp> unset a
dcecp> set a
Error: can't read "a": no such variable
dcecp>
```

2.3 Command Substitution

Command substitution provides a convenient way to express the return
value of one command within another command. This is useful when you
want to use the return value of one command as input to another command.
Use brackets to invoke command substitution. The following example uses
the **expr** command, which we'll discuss shortly. Generally, **expr** performs a
math function, returning the computed value expressed by its arguments, as
shown:

```
dcecp> set a 4
4
dcecp> set b [expr $a+2]
6
dcecp> set b
6
dcecp>
```

A more practical example might use command substitution for a command that returns a long name or a list. Let's recall an example we saw in Chapter 1. In this example, the **[group list temps]** command returns a list to the **foreach** command that performs the **account modify** operation on each element in the list. We'll look more closely at the **foreach** looping command later in this section.

```
dcecp> foreach i [group list users] {
> account modify $i -change {expdate 1995-12-31}}
dcecp>
```

Another practical use of command substitution is to set up a test condition for an **if** statement. We show an example of this usage in Section 2.9.1.

2.4 Grouping Elements and Controlling Interpretation

Programming languages often use symbols such as braces, quotes, and parentheses to operate on selected elements as a group rather than individually. Similarly, **dcecp** uses "" (double quotes) and {} (braces) to group elements into structures called *lists*. A list is a special way to group elements so that **dcecp** can correctly parse commands and other data like return values. We'll discuss lists further later on in the chapter.

The **dcecp** command elements are separated by whitespace: the space, tab, and newline characters. The following **dcecp** command uses space characters to separate its three elements:

```
dcecp> directory create /.:/subsys/comm_services
dcecp>
```

Use either the newline character or the ; (semicolon) to separate commands in a script. The following two examples, which set and then use a variable, are equivalent:

```
dcecp> set a /.:/subsys/comm_services
/.:/subsys/comm_services
dcecp> directory create $a
dcecp>
```

```
dcecp> set a /.:/subsys/comm_services; directory create $a
dcecp>
```

The choice to use braces or quotes to group elements together depends on how you want **dcecp** to interpret special characters like $, [, and {. While braces disable special interpretation of most of these characters, double quotes disable special interpretation of just a few. The backslash character, discussed in Section 2.4.3, offers another way to disable interpretation of special characters. When used together, braces, quotes, and backslashes offer lots of flexibility in composing **dcecp** command strings.

2.4.1 Grouping Elements with Braces

Braces group separate elements to create a new element that consists of everything between a { (left brace) and its corresponding } (right brace). You can also nest braced elements. Each of the following example lists contain three elements:

```
larry moe curly
```

```
1 {3 5 7 11 13} {17 19}
```

```
red {orange yellow {green blue} indigo} violet
```

Braces disable command ([ ]), variable ($), and backslash substitution. While the most important use of braces is to ensure a **dcecp** command has the correct number of arguments, this also provides a convenient way to include special characters in a list. To see how this works, consider the following example:

```
dcecp> set a solution
solution
dcecp> puts $a
solution
dcecp> puts {This is a convenient $a}
This is a convenient $a
```

While the **puts** command is often used for writing to files, when called with only one argument it writes the argument to **stdout**. In our example, the first use of **puts** allows normal interpretation of the variable *a*. The second use of **puts** groups the separate elements into one argument by disabling special interpretation of space characters and the dollar sign.

2.4.2 Grouping Elements with Double Quotes

Like braces, double quotes also group elements together. But unlike braces, double quotes cannot be nested. Furthermore, while braces disable almost all special characters, double quotes disable just a few—spaces, tabs, newlines and semicolons— letting you avoid the potentially awkward use of backslashes in a string of text elements. The most convenient use of double quotes is to allow clean, readable expansion of variables using the dollar sign trigger. For instance, in the following example we set a variable (*a*) to a value that includes spaces:

```
dcecp> set a "XYZ server for /.:/corp/comm_groups"
XYZ server for /.:/corp/comm_groups
dcecp> puts $a
XYZ server for /.:/corp/comm_groups
dcecp>
```

Use of double quotes does not disable command, variable, and backslash substitution. Let's look at a variation of the example used in the Section 2.4.1:

```
dcecp> set a solution
solution
dcecp> puts $a
solution
dcecp> puts "This is a convenient $a."
This is a convenient solution.
dcecp>
```

In this example, the use of quotes with the second **puts** command gathers five elements into a single argument for **puts** by disabling special interpretation of the space characters. However, the quotes don't affect interpretation of the dollar sign.

2.4.3 Including Special Characters with Backslashes

We already know that **dcecp** relies on certain special characters such as spaces, braces, quotes, or dollar signs to control its interpretation of elements. Sometimes, you might want to include one special character in a string, temporarily suspending its special interpretation. The backslash provides a form of substitution that suppresses special interpretation of the character immediately following the backslash.

Use the backslash to insert a nonprinting space character in a string of elements. For instance, each of the following **dcecp** lists have three elements:

```
a b\ c d
a b \{
```

The elements in the first example are **a**, **b c**, and **d**. The elements in the second example are **a**, **b**, and {. A more practical example could use the backslash to include quotes in error messages as shown in the following code fragment:

```
if {[llength $a] < 2} {
    error "Unable to parse \"$element_list\"."
}
```

The following list shows the special characters that you can include in a string of elements by using the backslash character:

\b	Backspace
\t	Tab
\e	Escape
\n	Newline
\r	Carriage-return
\{	Left brace
\}	Right brace
\[	Open bracket
\]	Close bracket
\$	Dollar sign
\ (space)	Space (" ")
\;	Semi-colon
\"	Double quote
****	Backslash
\(newline)	Nothing
\\ddd	Octal value

2.5 Documenting Scripts with Comments

When you are writing scripts, you might want to include some comment lines to remind yourself and others what the script is doing. Use the # (number sign) to insert comments. The DCE control program suppresses interpretation between a number sign and the next newline. You must place the number sign in a position where **dcecp** expects the first character of a command. Both of the following examples are valid:

```
set a 5
# sets a to 5


set a 5 ;# sets a to 5
```

The following example is not valid because the number sign is not positioned where **dcecp** expects the first character of a command:

```
set a 5 # sets a to 5
```

A common use of comments is to document procedures in scripts as in the following sample script fragment:

```
#
# _dcp_cleanup_user_create   - This function undoes changes
# after a failure in one of the user create functions as
# though the operation never occurred.
#

proc _dcp_cleanup_user_create {account_name args} {
```

2.6 Convenience Variables

The DCE control program remembers what you enter as well as command output, and stores certain pieces of that information in convenience variables for reuse in subsequent commands. Using these variables in your interactive commands can reduce typing and help eliminate typing mistakes.

Convenience variables apply only to **dcecp** commands like **directory**, **principal**, **acl**, **account**, and so on. They don't apply to Tcl commands like **for** or **eval**, or UNIX commands like **mv** or **grep**. As an example, the convenience variable **_n** holds the name (the argument) used in the following **principal create** operation. The **principal show** operation retrieves the name by using the **$_n** variable.

```
dcecp> principal create D_Kalivas
dcecp> principal show $_n -all
{fullname {}}
{uid 17}
{uuid 00000011-d957-21cd-8d00-0000c08adf56}
{alias no}
{quota unlimited}
dcecp>
```

While this simple explanation demonstrates the general operation of convenience variables, it understates their usefulness. Most of the convenience variables are intended to aid interactive use, but some can be used in scripts as well, adding flexibility because the information they contain isn't hardcoded in the script. Moreover, as you gain experience with the DCE control program, you will likely find these variables to be indispensible administrative tools.

The DCE control program provides several convenience variables that substitute for previously entered information or command output. All of the convenience variables begin with a _ (underscore) to leave 1-character variable names free for other uses.

The following sections describe the convenience variables. Their order of presentation generally keeps similar or related variables together.

2.6.1 Current Principal (User) Name (_u)

The **_u** convenience variable holds the current simple principal name. The DCE control program sets this variable from the login context inherited from the parent process. You can change its value by performing another **login** operation. Setting it using **set** generates an error.

```
dcecp> puts $_u
cell_admin
```

A practical use of this variable could be in scripts that test for a certain DCE identity before proceeding. On finding an incorrect identity, scripts could prompt for the necessary identity information and perform a **dce_login** operation.

See the cell name variable description in Section 2.6.2 for information about composing fully qualified principal names.

2.6.2 Current Cell Name (_c)

The **_c** convenience variable holds the name of the cell in which the principal is registered. The DCE control program sets this variable from the login context inherited from the parent process. You can change its value by performing another **login** operation. Setting it using **set** generates an error.

```
dcecp> puts $_c
/.../my_cell.goodco.com
dcecp>
```

This variable is generally useful in environments where administrators deal with multiple cells. For example, you could use the **_c** variable as a building block in constructing the current context's fully qualified principal name for use in scripts. Join the cell name and user name variables together with a / (slash) as shown in the following example:

```
dcecp> puts $_c/$_u
/.../my_cell.goodco.com/cell_admin
dcecp>
```

2.6.3 Current Host Name (_h)

The **_h** convenience variable holds the DCE name of the current host. The DCE control program sets this variable when **dcecp** is invoked. Setting it using **set** generates an error.

```
dcecp> puts $_h
hosts/planets
dcecp>
```

The **_h** variable is useful for returning the name of the host to an interactive user. You can also use it with the **_c** variable, as shown, to construct names such as a host principal name in a script:

```
dcecp> puts $_c/$_h/self
/.../my_cell.goodco.com/hosts/planets/self
dcecp>
```

2.6.4 Most Recent Operation Argument Name (_n)

The **_n** variable holds the name or names used as an argument to the most recent control program operation. Most DCE control program objects take a name or a list of names as an argument. Those that don't do so include **endpoint**, **attrlist**, **uuid**, **name**, **utc,** and the miscellaneous **dcecp** commands **dcecp_initInterp**, **login**, **logout**, **errtext**, **quit**, **resolve**, and **shell**.

The name is usually the third argument in a **dcecp** operation, as shown in the following **directory** operation:

```
dcecp> directory create /.:/sales/printers/text_printers
dcecp>
```

Once set, you can use **$_n** in subsequent operations in place of the name argument. For example, you could modify a directory attribute for the **/.:/sales/printers/text_printers** directory created in the preceding example, as follows:

```
dcecp> directory mod $_n -change {CDS_Convergence low}
dcecp>
```

The **_n** variable can also hold a list of names, as when you perform a directory service operation on more than one name. For instance, you could create several directories and then decide to modify an attribute:

```
dcecp> directory create {
> /.:/sales/printers/text_printers
> /.:/sales/printers/graphics_printers
> /.:/sales/printers/colorgraphics_printers }
dcecp>
```

A subsequent directory service operation can simply use the **_n** variable in place of the name or list of names:

```
dcecp> directory modify $_n -change {CDS_convergence high}
dcecp>
```

2.6.5 Parent of _n (_p)

The **_p** variable holds the parent of the name stored in **_n**. The **_n** variable holds the name or list of names used in the argument to the most recent operation (see Section 2.6.4). The **_p** variable holds the name or list of names that are hierarchically above the name in **_n** (closer to the cell root).

One use of the **_p** variable is in traversing up a CDS hierarchy of directories. Another use is showing the *access control list* (ACL) of a parent object. The following operations view the ACLs of a server configuration object and of its parent object (**/.:/hosts/krypton/config/srvrconf**):

```
dcecp> acl show /.:/hosts/krypton/config/srvrconf/video_clip
{appl_admin cdfrwx}
{unauthenticated r}
{any_other r}
dcecp> acl show $_p
{appl_admin criI}
{unauthenticated r}
{any_other r}
dcecp>
```

2.6.6 Last dcecp Object Name (_o)

The **_o** variable holds the name of the **dcecp** object used in the most recent operation. The following example uses the **_o** variable to avoid retyping **account**:

```
dcecp> account show j_wanders
{acctvalid yes}
{client yes}
   .
   .    [output omitted]
   .
{home /}
   .
   .    [output omitted]
   .
{shell {}}
{stdtgtauth yes}
dcecp> $_o modify j_wanders -home /.:/fs/corporate_services/users/j_wanders
dcecp>
```

2.6.7 Last Operation's Return Value (_r)

The **_r** variable holds the return value of the most recent operation. Many **dcecp** commands return multiple lines of output which are in the form of a list.

The following example shows one use of the **_r** convenience variable. The **dts show** command returns multiple lines as a list. The **attrlist getvalues** operation (see the **attrlist(8dce)** reference page) searches through the returned list for the string **toofewservers** and returns its associated value.

```
dcecp> dts show -counters
{creationtime 1994-09-16-07:50:13.067-04:00I-----}
{nointersections 0}
{nointersections 0}
{diffepochs 0}
{toofewservers 1}
{providertimeouts 82}
{badprotocols 0}
{badtimerep 0}
{noglobals 81}
{noresponses 0}
{abrupts 0}
{epochchanges 0}
```

```
{syserrors 0}
{syncs 1574}
{updates 0}
{enables 1}
{disables 0}
{nomemories 0}
{providerfailures 0}
{badlocalservers 0}
{badservers 0}
dcecp> attrlist getvalues $_r -type toofewservers
1
dcecp>
```

2.6.8 DCE Servers to Use (_s(xxx))

The _s(*xxx*) variables hold the names of the DCE servers to use for the next DCE operation. The DCE control program provides four of these variables. Because the variables are not set by **dcecp**, users must set these variables if they want to use them. The variables are as follows:

_s(sec)   This variable holds the name of the security server you want to use for the next registry operation. If you set this to specify a read-only replica and the operation (such as **principal create**) requires a master replica, **dcecp** ignores the variable and tries to bind to the master registry. Registry operations that use the _s(sec) variable include **principal**, **group**, **organization**, **registry**, **account**, and **xattrschema**.

DCE control program operations use the _s(sec) variable in conjunction with the _b(sec) variable, which holds the name of the most recent registry used. A **registry** operation uses the following order to select a security server:

1. Use the server passed as a name argument to the **registry** operation.

2. If the operation lacks a name argument, use the server named in the _s(sec) variable.

3. If the_s(sec) variable has not been set, use the server named in the _b(sec) variable.

4. If the **_b(sec)** variable has not been set (that is, this is the first **registry** operation since **dcecp** was initialized), the service provides an arbitrary server that is suitable for the operation.

_s(cds)　　This variable holds the name of the CDS server you want to use for the next directory service operation. When set, CDS operations attempt to use the specified server. The operation fails if the attempt is unsuccessful such as when the server is unavailable for some reason. To overcome such a failure, you must **unset** this variable or make the server available.

It makes sense to use the **_s(cds)** variable when all of your application needs can be satisfied by the clearinghouse named in the variable. Consider not using the **_s(cds)** variable when name lookups in CDS are likely to traverse directories in several clearinghouses. In this case, you'll get lookup errors because the **_s(cds)** variable limits the lookup operation to using just the named clearinghouse.

_s(dts)　　This variable holds the name of the DTS server you want to use for the next time service operation. When set, DTS operations attempt to use the specified server. The operation fails if the attempt is unsuccessful such as when the server is unavailable for some reason. To overcome such a failure, you must **unset** this variable or make the server available.

One use of this variable is to restrict DTS operations to a single DTS server for monitoring purposes. Normally, time service operations can use any available DTS server.

_s(aud)　　This variable holds the name of the audit daemon you want to use for the audit operation. By default, audit operations affect the local host's audit daemon. You can operate on a remote host's audit daemon by specifying its name as the value of the **_s(aud)** variable, as follows:

```
dcecp> set _s(aud) /.:/hosts/planets/audit-server
/.:/hosts/planets/audit-server
dcecp>
```

When **_s(aud)** is set, audit operations attempts to use the specified audit daemon. The operation fails if the attempt is unsuccessful such as when the specified audit daemon is unavailable for some reason. To overcome such a failure, you must **unset** this variable or make the audit daemon available.

You can specify a DCE server or audit daemon as any of the following:

- A DCE name. An example of a global registry name is **/.../my_cell.goodco.com/subsys/dce/sec/master**. An example of a cell-relative CDS clearinghouse name is **/.:/Paris_CH**.

- The string binding for the host where the server resides. String bindings can represent security servers, DTS servers, and audit daemons. They cannot represent CDS servers. An example of a string binding is **{ncacn_ip_tcp 110.15.22.131}**. The DCE control program resolves the binding to the appropriate service on the host.

- The name of the cell. This form applies only to **registry** operations. For a remote cell, specify a global cell name, for example **/.../my_cell.goodco.com**. For the local cell you can specify the root as **/.:**. These operations use an arbitrary server that is suitable for the operation.

2.6.9 Last Security Server Used (_b(sec))

The **_b(sec)** convenience variable holds the name of the security server used for the most recent **registry** operation. The DCE control program sets this variable based on previous registry operations. Consequently, users can view, but not set, this variable.

One reason to read the value of this variable is to check which registry performed the most recent operation as shown in the following example:

```
dcecp> puts $_b(sec)
/.../my_cell.goodco.com/subsys/dce/sec/master
dcecp>
```

Registry operations use the value of the **_b(sec)** variable in conjunction with the value of the **_s(sec)** variable to determine which security server to use. Refer to Section 2.6.8 for information about the **_s(sec)** variable and how these values work together for registry operations.

2.7 Measuring and Counting with Expressions

The **expr** command offers flexible ways to express and use arithmetic
functions in your scripts. Expressions are useful for things like comparing
numeric information such as the number of elements in a list, setting
thresholds for monitoring purposes, incrementing counters that control your
script's execution, and producing statistical information.

A simple **dcecp** expression is a combination of an operator like + (add) or *
(multiply) and some operands. The **expr** command takes one argument—
the expression—so parentheses or braces may be needed if your expression
has spaces. Use parentheses to control grouping in expressions.
Expressions can also be nested. All of the following are valid expressions:

```
dcecp> expr {2 + 3}
5
dcecp> expr 2+3
5
dcecp> set x 24
24
dcecp> expr ($x-8)*2
32
dcecp> expr $x-(8*2)
8
dcecp> expr $x-8*2
8
dcecp>
```

Be careful using variables in expressions; variables like **$x** must be numeric
strings like 24, not nonnumeric strings like 4*6.

The DCE control program normally treats numbers as decimal integers, but
can read numbers in octal and hexadecimal formats too. Precede a number
with 0 (zero) for octal interpretation, as in 0477. Precede a number with 0x
for hexadecimal interpretation, as in 0x9FF. You can also represent
numbers in floating-point format by using any of the forms specified by the
ANSI C standard (with the exception of the f, F, l, and L suffixes).

The DCE control program also supports numerous mathematical functions
in expressions such as cos, exp, log, tan, sin, and others, by invoking the C
math library functions of the same name.

Here's a partial list of operators you can use with the **expr** command. The list order also denotes precedence. This means, for instance, that **expr** multiplies before adding (2+2*4 equals 10).

-	unary minus
~	bitwise NOT
!	logical NOT
*	multiply
/	divide
%	remainder
+	add
-	subtract
<<	left shift
>>	right shift
<	Boolean less than
<=	Boolean less than or equal
>	Boolean greater than
>=	Boolean greater than or equal
==	Boolean equal
!=	not equal
&	bitwise AND
^	bitwise exclusive OR
|	bitwise OR
&&	logical AND
||	logical OR
a?b:c	if-then-else (as in C).

2.8 Operating on Lists

Lists provide convenient ways to operate on collections of things such as sets of principals, group members, or other objects. Lists are collections of objects entered by you or returned from commands. We've already seen lists in previous examples in this chapter; they're any number of elements separated by spaces, tabs, or newlines. Usually, a list is enclosed in braces.

All of the following are examples of lists:

```
{n_long l_jones p_sawyer d_witt m_dougherty s_preska}
```

```
{{/.:/hosts} {/.:/subsys}}
```

The DCE control program relies on lists to group elements so they can be correctly parsed by the **dcecp** command interpreter. For example, the set command takes two arguments:

set *varName value*

The following **set** command can't be correctly parsed because **dcecp** detects a third argument:

```
dcecp> set a John Hunter
Error: wrong # args: should be "set varName ?newValue?"
dcecp>
```

Use braces, quotes, or backslashes to create a valid list, as follows:

```
dcecp> set a {John Hunter}
John Hunter
dcecp> set a "John Hunter"
John Hunter
dcecp> set a John\ Hunter
John Hunter
dcecp>
```

The commands that operate on lists provide convenient ways to evaluate, select, and act on individual elements or groups of elements in a list. The DCE control program provides a comprehensive set of commands that let you create, modify, search, sort, and convert to and from lists.

For example, the following script returns the last element in a list. The **llength** command returns the number of elements in the list. Our list has four elements so **llength** returns **4**. The **dcecp** program numbers the elements from left to right starting with **0** (zero) so our list with three elements has elements numbered **0**, **1**, **2**, and **3**. The value of variable c is set to the number of the last element in the list (3). Finally the **lindex** command returns element 2 (**f**).

```
dcecp> set a {a b {c d e} f}
a b {c d e} f
dcecp> set b [llength $a]
4
dcecp> set c [expr $b-1]
3
dcecp> lindex $a $c
f
dcecp>
```

The DCE control program provides numerous commands for working with lists. You can join lists together using the **concat** command. Use **linsert** to add elements to an existing list. Extract a range of elements by using **lrange**, replace elements in a list with **lreplace**, and sort list elements in alphabetical (dictionary) order by using **lsort**. The DCE control program also includes an **attrlist** object (see **attrlist(8dce)** for use in manipulating list elements.

Here's an example that lists all child directories in a tree in alphabetic order. The **_r** variable is a **dcecp** convenience variable that holds the output of the last command. In this case, **_r** holds the list of directories returned by the **directory list -simple** command.

```
dcecp> directory list -simple /.:
hosts subsys cell-profile fs lan-profile planets_ch sec sec-v1
dcecp> lsort $_r
cell-profile fs hosts lan-profile planets_ch sec sec-v1 subsys
dcecp>
```

2.9 Controlling Scripts

The DCE control program provides several commands for controlling your script's execution. Commands such as **if**, **while**, **for**, **foreach**, and **case** execute parts of scripts under various conditions. The **break** and **continue** commands can stop execution of part or all of a command script.

2.9.1 Conditionalizing with if Statements

Sometimes, you'll want part of your script to execute only under certain conditions. Use an **if** statement to detect a condition and conditionally perform some operation. The syntax for an **if** statement is

if *test true_body* **else** *false_body*

Let's say you're writing a script that searches through a list of attributes for a particular attribute. An **if** statement could take particular actions depending on whether an attribute exists. The following example script fragment returns an error message if the account name does not exist in the **list_of_group_entries** variable:

```
set list_of_group_entries [group list $group -simplename]
if { [lsearch $list_of_group_entries $account_name] == -1} {
    group add $group -member $account_name
} else {
error "Group \"$group\" already has an entry \
  for \"$account_name\"."
}
```

2.9.2 Controlling Script Execution with Loops

Programming languages use loops to repeat operations as long as specified conditions exist. The DCE control program offers three kinds of loops: **foreach**, **while**, and **for**. The type of loop you use depends on the way conditions are specified.

2.9.2.1 The **foreach** Loop

When you want to perform a given operation on each element in a list, use the **foreach** command. Remember that a list is a colletion of objects, or things enetered by you or returned from a command.

The syntax is

foreach *variable_name list body*

The **foreach** command consists of a list, a script body, and a variable that represents each element of the list, in turn. The command runs the script body on the element represented by the variable and then sets the variable to be the next element in the list.

The following sample **foreach** command could be part of a script that manages hosts in a DCE cell. This script fragment removes the host principal name from the registry if a failure occurs while configuring the host in the cell. The **foreach** command looks at each principal name in the cell. If the **string** commands find the host name listed in the output from **principal catalog**, the script deletes the principal name from the registry.

```
foreach princ [principal catalog -simplename] {
    if {[string match $host_name [string range $princ 0 \
        [expr [string length $host_name] - 1]]] == 1} {
        principal delete $princ
    }
}
```

Keep in mind that loops return their results to the interpreter, not to **stdout**. You need to take extra steps to send the results to **stdout**. The next example uses a **puts** command to send the results of the **foreach** loop to **stdout**:

```
foreach i [group list subsys/dce/dts-servers] {
    puts [principal show $i]
}
```

You can also **append** all the results together into a variable in a script, or you can use **lappend** to append the results as separate list elements, as follows:

```
foreach i [group list subsys/dce/dts-servers] {
  append result [principal show $i]
}
return $result
```

2.9.2.2 The **while** Loop

The **while** loop behaves like the **while** loop in C. It takes two arguments: an expression and a script (called the *body*). When the expression evaluates to nonzero, the **while** command executes the body and then reevaluates the expression, continuing the loop until the expression evaluates to 0. The syntax for a **while** loop is

while *expression body*

The following example procedure uses a **while** loop to search through each element in a list for a pattern. As long as the list size contains more than zero elements (**$size > 0**), the procedure continues looping.

```
proc _dcp_list_find {search_list pattern} {

  set found_items ""
  set size [llength $search_list]

  while { $size > 0 } {
    set size [expr $size - 1]
    set index [lsearch $search_list $pattern]
    if { $index == -1 } {
      return $found_items
    }
    lappend found_items [lindex $search_list $index]
    set search_list [lreplace $search_list $index $index]
  }
}
```

2.9.2.3 The **for** Loop

The **for** loop also behaves just like its C counterpart. Although **for** is more complex than its sibling **while**, **for** keeps all of the loop control information together, making it easier to see what's going on. The **for** command syntax is

for *initial_expression test reinit script_body*

To use **for**, set an initial expression and then test for that condition before executing the script body. After executing the script body, the **for** command reinitializes the initial expression and again tests for the new value, repeating the loop until the test becomes false.

The following example shows a **for** loop that performs an operation a specified number of times and stops. In this example, we create 50 guest principal names in the registry.

```
dcecp>  for {set i 0} {$i < 50} {incr i} {
>  principal create guest$i
>  }
dcecp>
```

2.9.3 Terminating Loops with continue and break

The **continue** and **break** commands terminate loops started with the **while**, **for**, and **foreach** commands.

Use the **continue** command to terminate the current iteration of a loop. For instance, your loop can test for, and selectively ignore, particular elements in a list while continuing to operate on the rest of the elements. Use the **break** command to immediately terminate loop execution.

The following example script fragment is a **foreach** command loop that includes **continue** and **break** commands. The **foreach** command looks through all the DTS servers in a cell until it finds one that is a time-provider. (A time-provider is a special DTS server that receives time from an external time source.) If the first server in the list (created by the **dts catalog** operation) returns output from a **dts show** operation, the **continue** command invokes the next lines in the script which search the output for the **{provider yes}** attribute and value. If the **provider** attribute (examined by the **attrlist getval** operation) is **yes**, the script sets the **server** variable to be the name of that DTS server, and the **break** command terminates the entire **foreach** loop.

```
foreach s [dts catalog] {
    if {[catch {dts show $s} dts_sh_out] != 0} {
        continue
    }
    set p [attrlist getval $dts_sh_out -type provider]
    if {[string match $p "yes"] == 1} {
        set provider "yes"
        set server $s
        break
    }
set provider "no"
}
```

2.9.4 Testing with Patterns Before Execution with case

Some commands return a list such as a list of objects in a directory or a list of servers running on a host system. You can use the **case** command to test a list or string for specific patterns such as the name of a particular object or server. On detecting a specified pattern, the **case** command then executes a script associated with the pattern detected. The syntax for the **case** command is

case *string* **in** *pattern* {*script*} *pattern* {*script*}

The **case** command looks in *string* for *pattern* and executes {*script*}. The word **in** may be omitted. The following example illustrates how the **case** command works:

```
dcecp> set x {one ten twenty}
one ten twenty
dcecp> foreach el $x {case $el in one {puts script1} two {puts script2}}
script1
dcecp>
```

The **case** command first checks in **$x** for the *pattern* **one**. On finding this pattern, the associated script echoes **script 1** on the display. When it finds no more matches, the **case** command ends.

For a more practical example, say you run a **dcecp** command that lists all the servers on a particular system. You could search the list for particular server names and execute a script that appends each name to a particular file, as follows:

```
case $x in server1 {lappend filename1} server2 {lappend filename2}
```

If your list of patterns is lengthy and likely to break across lines, you can prevent newlines from being interpreted as separators by enclosing the entire list of target patterns and scripts in braces. This has the additional benefit of preventing variable and command substitutions in the braced list.

Patterns can include wildcard characters. A ? (question mark) in a search pattern matches any single character in the target pattern. For instance, **?at** matches **bat** and **hat**. A * (asterisk) in a pattern matches any string in the target pattern. For instance, ***at** matches both **bat** and **"three cornered hat"** (note the use of quotes to disable spaces as separators).

You might want a way to execute some default script when no pattern matches are found. The **case** command has a special pattern called *default* whose corresponding script executes when no pattern match is found. You should place the default pattern as the last position in the list:

```
case $x in {
   a {puts "script for case a"}
   b {puts "script for case b"}
   default {puts "run this script if no matches are found"}
}
```

2.10 Creating Commands Dynamically

The **eval** command lets you create scripts as you go along by chaining smaller scripts together. This technique could be useful in a script that records administrator responses to various questions and then constructs a specialized script based on those responses. The syntax is

eval *arg ... arg*

The following example uses variables to hold options and their values for an **account create** operation. The **eval** command ensures that the variables expand and execute properly.

```
dcecp> set mpwd {-mypwd mxyzptlk}
-mypwd mxyzptlk
dcecp> set pwd {-password change.me}
-password change.me
dcecp> set org {-organization guests}
-organization guests
dcecp> set grp {-group guest}
-group guest
dcecp> eval account create guest1 $mpwd $pwd $org $grp
dcecp>
```

Be careful when using variables to construct **eval** commands. An **eval** command like the following can sometimes cause problems within scripts because **dcecp** parses it twice. First, **dcecp** parses the **eval** command and its arguments. Then it again parses the **eval** arguments when they're executed as scripts.

```
dcecp> eval $a $b $c
dcecp>
```

You can avoid some parsing problems by placing braces around the arguments as in this example:

```
dcecp> eval {$a $b $c}
dcecp>
```

To make certain **dcecp** parses your **eval** command correctly, you can invoke the **dcecp list** command to generate a valid list structure:

```
dcecp>  eval [list $a $b $c]
dcecp>
```

2.11 Reading Other Files as dcecp Scripts

The **source** command reads the contents of other files, executing them as **dcecp** scripts. This capability lets you construct higher level scripts by plugging lower level functions together—like building blocks. Because you reuse your scripts rather than duplicate them with potential variations, scripts are more consistent and easy to develop and maintain. The command syntax is

source *filename*

The return value from **source** is the return value from the last command in *filename*.

As a practical example, imagine we have one script that lists entries in CDS subtrees, another script that deletes subtrees, and another script that moves subtrees. One common function needed by all these scripts might be to list every child directory under the root of the subtree. You could write a script that lists every child and name it something like **children_list.dcp**. (The **.dcp** extension is a **dcecp** convention for naming script files.) When any of your scripts need to list all the child directories, simply use the **source** command:

source children_list.dcp

Terminate a **source** command by using the **return** command. The **return** command provides a way for commands like **source** and **proc** to exit in a controlled manner, even when expected or unexpected error conditions occur. Rather than allow error conditions to cause the whole script to exit and fail, the **return** command manages error information and allows the script to continue executing. We discuss the use of **return** with other error-handling techniques in Section 2.14.

2.12 Creating New Commands

The DCE control program provides a powerful and comprehensive set of commands for controlling and monitoring DCE operations. But the exact uses to which DCE is put by end users is unpredictable. Consequently, it's quite likely that some administrators will need additional commands to meet very specific needs. The **proc** command offers an easy way to create additional commands that look and behave just like built-in commands such as **set**, **list**, and **while**. But unlike built-in commands, which are written in C, commands created with **proc** are written using scripts, as follows:

```
dcecp> proc div {x y} {expr $x/$y}
dcecp>
```

The **proc** command takes three arguments: the procedure name, a list of names of procedure arguments, and the **dcecp** script that forms the body of the new procedure. Our new procedure **div** requires two arguments. For example:

```
dcecp> div 12 4
3
dcecp>
```

By default, **proc** assumes all variables are local variables. That is, their names and values are set only within the procedure and they expire when the procedure completes. The following command produces an error because variables *x* and *y* have not been set within the procedure:

```
dcecp> set x 15
15
dcecp> set y 3
3
dcecp> proc div {} {expr $x/$y}
dcecp> div
Error: can't read "x": no such variable
```

You can import global variables (variables defined outside the procedure) by using the **global** command:

```
dcecp> set x 15
dcecp> set y 3
dcecp> proc div {} {
> global x y
> expr $x/$y
> }
dcecp> div
5
dcecp>
```

Once you import a global variable, it persists for the duration of the procedure. Your procedure can change the value of the variable by using **unset** and **set**. The new value will be available for use inside and outside of your procedure, as shown.

You can use the **return** command to make your procedure return immediately. The value of the argument to **return** becomes the procedure's return value.

```
proc find {a} {
    <some pattern matching script that looks for a specific CDS entry>
    if {a != b} {
       return 1
    }
    return 0
}
```

You can design procedures to take either no arguments or variable numbers of arguments. For instance, a procedure with no arguments could simply perform some straightforward operation as in the following example:

```
proc _do_create_group {} {
     global rpcgroupname
     rpcgroup create $rpcgroupname
}
```

You can also specify a default value for an argument by using a nested list structure in the argument list. In the following example, the first argument, *attr*, must be supplied. The second argument, *value*, defaults to 1 if no argument is supplied.

```
proc _attr_show {attr {value "unset"}}  {
    puts "$attr is $value"
}
```

Procedures can call other procedures. The current procedure can import variables from any calling procedure by using the **upvar** command, as shown:

```
upvar level otherVar1 myVar1 otherVar2 myVar2
```

A *level* argument of **1** gets the variable context of the parent procedure. An argument of **2** gets the variable context of parent's parent procedure. You can also specify levels relative to the global context by preceding the *level* argument with **#**. A *level* of **#0** gets global variables. A *level* of **#1** gets variables from a procedure invoked from the global level.

The **otherVar** argument names the variable you want to import. You need to include the **myVar** argument to rename the variable for use in the current procedure. The following example renames the imported variable to **cargs**:

```
upvar 1 local_args cargs
```

Procedures can also execute scripts under the context of parent procedures by using the **uplevel** command. This command offers a convenient way to manage your procedure's context. For instance, rather than import and manipulate numerous variables from a parent procedure, use **uplevel** to connect to them all at once. The syntax is

uplevel *level arg arg arg*

The **uplevel** command is similar to **eval**; it concatenates arguments and executes them as scripts but, unlike **eval**, **uplevel** executes the script in the context specified by *level* rather than the current context. The *level* argument works the same in **uplevel** as it does in **upvar**. Use the parent's context with a *level* argument of **1**. Use the context of a first-level procedure with a *level* argument of **#1**.

If a **proc** command specifies a command name that is already in effect, the new procedure replaces the existing procedure with the same name. Except in unusual cases, you should avoid naming new commands so that they replace existing built-in commands.

You can rename or delete Tcl commands by using the **rename** command. For instance, you could temporarily rename **list** to **list.old** and then use **proc** to create another command called **list**. When you're through using the manufactured **list** command, you could rename **list old** to **list**, restoring the original function of **list** as in the following:

```
rename list list.old
proc list {} {
     <some list operation>
}
rename list.old list
```

Delete a command by omitting the second argument to the **rename** command. The following example deletes the **list** command:

```
rename list
```

2.13 String Manipulation

Many DCE administrative operations return information of some sort. For instance, the **principal show** operation returns information about a principal. Usually this information is in the form of a list, as in the following example:

```
dcecp> principal show R_Parsons
{fullname {}}
{uid 15}
{uuid 0000000f-d6f9-21cd-8d00-0000c08adf56}
{alias no}
{quota unlimited}
{groups users}
dcecp>
```

Although it's fairly easy for an administrator to scan a list and extract the necessary information from it, scripts operate in the dark, feeling their way through information. When scripts search for specific information, they usually ignore the notion of lists, operating instead on the collection of characters (called a **string**) that makes up a list. The DCE control program provides a set of commands to operate on strings, letting you construct, parse, compare, extract values from, and modify strings.

2.13.1 Constructing Strings

Often, scripts need to construct strings for use in other commands or for displaying on the screen for users. The DCE control program provides a **format** command that you use to construct strings for use by your script.

The **format** command substitutes variables where needed. The following example constructs the variable **_dcp_host_entries** by using the **format** command to prepend the cell name string (the **string** type is indicated by %**s**) to the string **/hosts**. The cell name is contained in the **_c** convenience variable.

```
dcecp> set _dcp_host_entries [format "%s/hosts" $_c]
/.../my_cell.goodco.com/hosts
dcecp>
```

The **format** command can also convert arguments between differing forms including decimal, octal, hexadecimal, floating-point, and scientific notation. You can also specify to print or omit signs for signed numbers, right or left justify output, and pad with spaces or zeroes. The following examples convert the integer 8 to its octal equivalent. The second example shifts the output nine character spaces to the right.

```
dcecp> format %1o 8
10
dcecp> format %9o 8
        10
dcecp>
```

2.13.2 Parsing Strings

The DCE control program includes a **scan** command that parses strings and then converts and stores relevant parts of strings in variables. This capability is useful, for instance, when converting information returned by a previous command into data that can be input to another command. The syntax for the **scan** command is as follows:

scan "*string*" "*format*" [*varname* [*varname*]...]

You can specify the *string* literally or by using a variable. The *format* section controls parsing, ignoring blanks and tab characters you might have included in the *format* section for readability. This section consists of one or more conversion specifiers delimited by % (percent sign). Conversion specifiers define which parts of *string* get converted and stored, as well as the type of conversion.

The following example parses the string contained in the variable **_dcp_temp** for a valid floating-point number and stores it in the variable **_dcp_temp2**:

```
if { [scan $_dcp_temp "%f" _dcp_temp2] != 1 } {
   error "Variable \"$_dcp_temp\" is not a \
     valid floating-point number"
}
```

2.13.3 Other String Handling Operations

You can specify one character or a range of characters in a string by using **string index** and **string range**. These commands would be useful for extracting information from a string of predictable length.

The **string index** command has one argument that is the position of one character (counting from left to right beginning with 0 (zero) to be extracted from the string. The **string range** command includes two arguments that are the positions of the leftmost and rightmost characters to be included in the range. The following example illustrates one use of the **string range** command:

```
dcecp> string range {The quick brown fox} 4 9
quick
dcecp>
```

You can determine whether one string is lexicographically (alphabetically) greater than, less than, or equal to another string by using **string compare**. Generally, this operation performs a byte comparison of ASCII codes that make up the string.

Count the number of characters in a string using the **string length** command. Here is an example:

```
dcecp> string length "The quick brown fox"
19
dcecp>
```

Convert characters between uppercase and lowercase by using the **string toupper** and **string tolower** commands. Here is an example:

```
dcecp> string toupper "The quick brown fox"
THE QUICK BROWN FOX
dcecp>
```

Trim specific characters from a string by using the **string trim** command. Remove the leftmost or rightmost characters from a string by using the **string trimleft** and **string trimright** commands.

You can perform pattern-matching operations in any of several ways. Invoke ''glob'' style pattern matching with the **string match** command. This mimics the glob pattern matching capabilities available in **csh**, returning **1** for a match and **0** for no match. More flexible regular expression pattern matching (like that found in **egrep**) can be performed using **regexp** command. You can extend this operation to perform regular expression substitution by using the **regsub** command.

The following example illustrates the use of the **regsub** command. The first argument specifies the search pattern. The second argument is the string to search. The third argument specifies the replacement pattern. The last argument is a variable into which **regsub** places the new string. The command returns **0** if no substitution occurs and **1** if substitution does occur.

```
dcecp> regsub brown "The quick brown fox" blue color
1
dcecp> puts $color
The quick blue fox
```

2.14 Dealing with Errors and Exceptions

The **dcecp** interpreter includes error facilities that return error information when something goes wrong with a **dcecp** script. Error information tells users what went wrong so that they can avoid making the same mistake in the future. Many things can cause **dcecp** errors. For instance, a command might not receive the correct number of arguments, a command might have a typographic error of some kind, or the object of an operation (such as a CDS directory) might be unavailable for some reason.

Here, we discuss three ways of dealing with errors and exceptions:

- Using global error information variables

- Catching exceptions

- Reissuing complex errors

2.14.1 Using Global Error Information Variables

When **dcecp** encounters an error it prints a descriptive message, such as:

```
Error: wrong # args: should be "set varName ?newValue?"
```

In some cases, error messages may be insufficient for determining exactly where a problem occurred. So **dcecp** stores additional error information in a global variable called **errorInfo**. Your script can access and print this information to help you find the error. Generally, it traces the commands that were executing when the error occurred.

The following example shows the kind of information that can be stored in **errorInfo**. Reading backwards, you can determine that the error occurred near line 4 of the script body in the **parseagrs** procedure called from the **_dcp_create_user** procedure of a **user** operation.

```
dcecp> puts $errorInfo
Unknown option "group"
    while executing
"
    invoked from within
"
    ("while" body line 4)
    invoked from within
"
    (procedure "parseargs" line 60)
    invoked from within
"
    (procedure "_dcp_create_user" line 64)
    invoked from within
"
    invoked from within
"
    invoked from within
"
    (procedure "user" line 24)
"
dcecp>
```

In addition, **dcecp** may store another kind of error information in another global variable called **errorCode**. This variable contains a list like the following that can identify other classes of errors.

```
UNIX, ENOENT, "insufficient arguments for filename"
```

The DCE control program sets the **errorCode** variable to NONE if an error produces no useful error information.

2.14.2 Using catch to Trap Errors and Exceptions

Occasionally, you might want to trap some kinds of errors rather than let them terminate an active command. The **catch** command lets you trap and ignore errors so your script can continue processing. Let's say your script wants to rename a command if it exists. However, it's possible that the command name might not exist when you execute the **rename** command.

```
dcecp> rename move move.old
Error: can't rename "move":  command doesn't exist
dcecp>
```

Use **catch** to invoke the **rename** command as a script.

```
dcecp> catch {ren move move.old}
1
dcecp>
```

The **catch** command treats its argument as a script and executes it, returning a **0** on successful execution. If an error occurs, it is caught by the **catch** command which returns a **1**.

You can add a second argument to the **catch** command. This argument is a variable that **catch** modifies to hold the script's return value (on successful completion) or the error message. The syntax for the **catch** command is

catch *command varName*

One use of **catch** in scripts is to invoke other procedures. You can read the following script fragment as follows: "If the **_dcp_create_group** procedure returns unsuccessfully (**!= 0**) then perform the **_dcp_cleanup_-user_create** procedure and display the error stored in the **msg** variable."

```
if {[ catch {_dcp_create_group $group group_created} msg] != 0 } {
    _dcp_cleanup_user_create $element -principal
    error $msg
}
```

Exceptions are a special class of error generated by the **break**, **continue**, and **return** commands. You use the **break** and **continue** commands to terminate loops such as **while**, **for**, and **foreach**, and you use the **return** command to terminate a **proc** or **source** command.

Resulting exceptions can be hard to handle in procedures where loops exist inside (as part of) a more comprehensive command. For instance, a user-written procedure that searches for specific object types in CDS might invoke **foreach** as part of a looping activity to test for the occurrence of particular attributes.

If you use the **break**, **continue**, or **return** commands to manage loop execution or to manage some other nested command (like **case** or **if**, for example), the parent command will not be ready to catch the exception. The parent command will abort and issue an error message as usual. However, the error is associated with the parent command and is difficult to track to the looping command where it actually occurred.

If it's necessary to use a **continue**, **break**, or **return** command to terminate a command that has been called by another command, consider using **catch** to invoke the nested command which, in turn, calls the **continue**, **break**, or **return** command to recover from errors or exceptions. Used this way, the **catch** command keeps the exception within the looping or nested procedure where it's easier to track down.

```
foreach s [server catalog] {
    if {[catch {server show $s} srv_sh_out] != 0} {
        continue
    }
}
```

2.14.3 Reissuing Complex Errors

The **proc** command lets you create procedures or commands that perform very precise operations. For instance, a user-written procedure called **_dcp_get_servers** that retrieves and filters information about running servers could include *nested* commands or procedures that perform various subtasks such as looping through server information looking for certain strings. While use of nested commands or procedures lets you develop comprehensive procedures or commands, they can also produce errors that are difficult to pinpoint if errors aren't passed along properly.

Complex scripts can use the **error** command to reissue errors that have been triggered by some previously executing part of the script. The following script fragment simply prints out a hard coded error message. This use also lets you custom tailor messages to precisely explain error conditions.

```
set dts_cat_out [_dcp_dts_catalog]
if {[llength $dts_cat_out] == 0} {
    error "Unable to find any DTS servers"
}
```

The next script fragment does more, using **catch** to store any error information returned from the **_dcp_create_group** procedure in the **msg** variable. On failure (**!= 0**), the script invokes a cleanup procedure that undoes whatever was done, and then prints out the message stored in the **msg** variable.

```
if {[ catch {_dcp_create_group $group group_created} msg] != 0 } {
    _dcp_cleanup_user_create $element -principal
    error $msg
}
```

This discussion has provided some fairly simple error handling techniques. Note, though, that error handling can be complicated, especially in more complex situations. We encourage you to read more about error handling in other publications that cover more general use of Tcl.

2.15 Working with Files

The DCE control program has several commands for use in reading from and writing to files. Files are useful for things like storing the output of **dcecp** operations for later reference. Here are several useful examples of file manipulation:

- You could run a **server catalog** operation across all of the hosts in a cell and store the results from each host in a host-specific file. Later, you could compare the files to produce a report of server configurations.

- You could detect inactive accounts by running a **dcecp** script that shows the last time each account was logged into, storing this information in a file for later evaluation.

- You could also modify DCE files that aren't manipulated easily by using the **dcecp hostdata** object. For example, you could write a function that added a new attribute to the **cds_attributes** file.

DCE as provided by OSF currently supports file operations only for UNIX systems or for systems that support POSIX system calls. However, some vendor DCE versions may support file operations on other systems.

2.15.1 Specifying Filenames

Specify filenames using customary UNIX rules. For instance, **/opt/dcelocal/dcecp/server_snap.dcecp** refers to a file named **server_snap.dcecp** in a directory called **/opt/dcelocal/dcecp**. You can also refer to files by using relative filenames, for example **~dce_admin/scripts/server_snap.dcecp** and **~/admin/server_snap.dcecp**. You can print the current working directory by using the **pwd** command and set the current working directory by using the **cd** command. The following command sets the current directory to be **~dce_admin/scripts**:

```
dcecp> cd ~dce_admin/scripts
dcecp>
```

You can view a list of files in a directory by using the **glob** command. This command returns a list of filenames that match pattern arguments to the command. Here is an example:

```
dcecp> glob *
help local_lib.dcp
dcecp>
```

You can view lots of other information about files by using the **file** command with various options. The **file** commands can help select a file based on its age, its size, or its permissions (whether it is executable, or readable, or writable by the current user).

2.15.2 Reading and Writing Files

The **dcecp** commands for reading and writing to files look and act like their C language counterparts **fopen**, **fclose**, and so on.

Open a file for reading and writing using the **open** command. The second argument to the **open** command (shown in the following example as **+r**) specifies the file access mode. You can open files for reading, or writing, or both and you can specify whether to replace existing files or to add to them with new information. You can also set the initial access position to the beginning or the end of a file. The default access mode is read-only (the file must already exist).

```
dcecp> open server_snap.dcecp +r
file5
dcecp>
```

The **open** command assigns a file identifier to each file when it is opened. Use the file identifier to refer to files in subsequent commands.

Once a file is opened, you can add lines to a file by using the **puts** command. Normally, **dcecp** waits until it has accumulated sufficient data before writing this information to a file. If you want **dcecp** to immediately write the information to a file, use the **flush** command. Use **gets** to read the next line from a file or use **read** to read a number of bytes or all of the bytes in a file. The following example writes a list of all principals in a file named **prins**:

```
dcecp> open prins w+
file8
dcecp> puts file8 [principal catalog]
dcecp> close file8
dcecp>
```

Sometimes, you don't want to start reading or writing at the first line of a file. The DCE control program provides several commands that set the access position so you don't have to advance through every line in the file. These commands will produce an error if you use them for devices like terminals or other sequential devices that don't support random access. Use the **seek** command to set the access point in a file. Specify the offset as a number of bytes from the origin, which can be the beginning or end of the file or the current position. Use a negative number to move toward the beginning of the file, as in the following example which moves back 16 bytes from the current access position.

```
dcecp> seek file5 -16 current
dcecp>
```

You can determine the current access position by using the **tell** command. Save the return value in a variable so you can go back to that position in the file later on.

Finally, you can close a file by using the **close** command, as follows:

```
dcecp> close file5
dcecp>
```

2.16 Spawning Subprocesses

Using subprocesses to execute commands offers several convenient solutions to some complex scripting or special administrative needs. Subprocesses can provide

- Access to operating system commands
- A way to establish synchronous, orderly execution
- Methods for streamlining complex or sophisticated scripts

2.16.1 Running Operating System Commands from a Script

Although the DCE control program is versatile, there are times when you may want your script to use operating system commands to accomplish some simple (or even not-so-simple) operation. The **exec** command provides a way for scripts to perform external commands by forking a subprocess in which the command executes. The following example uses the **exec** command to retrieve the local host name which is then established as a *hostname* variable and subsequently used in the script.

```
dcecp>  set hostname [exec hostname]
myhost
dcecp>  directory list /.:/hosts/$hostname -simple
cds-clerk cds-server dts-entity profile self
dcecp>
```

The **exec** command normally returns the results of the operation performed in the subprocess. However, you can use UNIX redirection symbols (<, <<, and >) to redirect standard input or standard output. You can also use the | (vertical bar) to pipe the output through filters such as **nroff**, **sort**, or **grep**.

When used alone, the **exec** command is synchronous, meaning that the external command completes before the script continues executing. But when a subprocess will take a long time to complete, for instance when you synchronize directories in a CDS cell, you can use the **exec** command with a & (ampersand) to push a subprocess into the background. The following example uses the *exec* command to send previously collected output to a printer. This lets your script continue without having to wait for the **print** command to complete.

```
dcecp>  exec lpr output.log &
dcecp>
```

## Chapter 3

Writing Scripts and dcecp Objects

The DCE control program supplies a number of *objects* that offer administrative access to each manageable component in a DCE cell. For instance, the **principal** object lets administrators manage principal information in the DCE Security Service registry database. Similarly, the **rpcgroup** object lets administrators manage group information in CDS.

Some DCE operations affect multiple components as when several operations must be performed to add a new user to a DCE cell. To meet this need, the DCE control program provides *task objects* which let administrators operate on multiple components with a single operation. For instance, the **user** task object performs several operations that include creating principal information in the registry, adding the principal to an organization and to relevant groups, creating a CDS directory for the user, and so on. Task objects look and behave just like other **dcecp** objects, implementing the same help system used by other **dcecp** objects. However, task objects are written using the **dcecp** language instead of the C programming language. This makes it easy for administrators to extend or customize existing scripts.

While the DCE control program provides task objects to handle some multicomponent operations, variations in cell configurations and differences in the ways administrators manage their cells make it impractical for the supplied DCE task objects to satisfy all the needs of every DCE cell. For instance, some cells may use DFS or GDS components, or a cell may implement a cell directory naming scheme that differs from the standard OSF DCE implementation. Alternatively, some DCE implementations could have specialized administrative components, such as services or repositories, that need distinct **dcecp** objects for managing them.

To accommodate a cell's specific needs, the DCE control program language lets administrators create their own scripts. Administrators can also extend or modify existing task objects or they can create new task objects to manage specialized components in a DCE cell. This chapter provides information for extending, modifying, or creating the following kinds of dcecp scripts:

- Informal administration scripts

- Formal task objects

3.1 Informal Administration Scripts

Informal administration scripts let administrators store multiple operations in a file and replay them whenever necessary. Informal scripts are useful for operations that take only one or two arguments or that just perform simple tasks. Furthermore, the script's precise behavior and output can be custom tailored to the needs of its author. While informal scripts can be shared among administrators in a cell, they are typically included just in the author's **.dcecprc** file.

Scripts generally consist of one or more procedures created with the **proc** command. This lets you invoke the scripted operation by simply typing the procedure's name at the **dcecp** prompt.

The following simple script prints information about your current cell and login identity:

```
# Show your current login name and your current cell name.
proc _dcp_whoami {} {
  global _c _u
  puts stdout "You are '$_u' logged into '$_c'."
}
```

This script can be included in your **.dcecprc** file either directly or by using the **source** command and keeping the actual script in an external file. The second method lets other administrators include your same script by simply pointing to it with **source** commands in their **.dcecprc** files. This method also keeps your **.dcecprc** file uncluttered, making it easier for others to understand what is going on. Alternatively, you can place the script or a pointer in the **init.dcecp** file. Changes to this file are available to all users on a host. For more information about the **init.dcecp** file and the **.dcecprc** file, see Section 1.8 of Chapter 1. The following is an example of the **source** command in a **.dcecprc** file:

```
source /usr/users/wardr/dcecp/local_lib.dcp
```

The **.dcp** filename extension is a convention for naming files used by the DCE control program. Another convention precedes procedure names with **_dcp**, as in **_dcp_whoami**. Many **dcecp** procedures adhere to this convention to distinguish their names from user-created procedures that do not need to use this convention. If you find procedure names like **_dcp_whoami** hard to remember or type, you can rename them. For instance, you could rename the procedure to **whoami** by using the **rename** command in the **.dcecprc** file, as follows:

```
rename _dcp_whoami whoami
```

Restart **dcecp** to pick up any changes. Now you can enter **whoami** at the DCE control program prompt, as follows:

```
dcecp> whoami
You are 'cell_admin' logged into '/.../my_cell.goodco.com'.
dcecp>
```

By chaining operations together, you can create scripts that do more. For example, the following script lists all the hosts in a DCE cell. Then it checks whether each host has an object entry in CDS for a dts-entity. (This would indicate that a DTS server is available on the host.) For each host with an object entry for a dts-entity, the script does a **clock show** operation which returns the time on that host. The script prints the information on the display, formatting it for readability, and continues looping through all the hosts in the cell until all host entries have been checked.

Make the **_dcp_show_clocks** procedure available to your **dcecp** session in the same way as the simpler script described previously.

```
# Show the time on all of the dts servers running in your cell.
proc _dcp_show_clocks {} {
    set x [directory list /.:/hosts]
    foreach n $x {
        if {[catch {object show $n/dts-entity}] == 0} {
            set index [string last "/" $n]
            set y [string range $n [incr index] end]
            if {[catch {clock show $n/dts-entity} msg] == 0} {
                set i [expr 20 - [string length $y]]
                puts [format "Time on $y is %${i}s %s" " " \
                    [clock show $n/dts-entity]]
            } else {
                set i [expr 20 - [string length $y]]
                puts [format "Time on $y is %${i}s %s" " " \
                    "Server not responding."]
            }
        }
    }
}
```

3.2 Formal Task Objects

Some DCE environments might have special administration needs that
aren't strictly addressed by the standard DCE control program objects.
While you could write and distribute informal scripts to meet this
administration need, you would likely need to document their operation in
some way. More importantly, though, a complicated operation might
require the use of numerous options to precisely control the script's
behavior. Rather than invent your own mechanisms to provide help
information and handle complicated argument parsing operations, you could
rely on the existing help system and the **parseargs** facility utilized by other
formal task objects supplied with **dcecp**. This approach makes your script
consistent with other **dcecp** objects.

Formal task objects build on the idea of the informal scripts presented
previously with some important additions:

- An argument table at the beginning of the script defines operations as separate procedures within the script. An argument table can also define available options. A **parseargs** procedure is called to parse the arguments and options passed to the script when it is invoked.

- Help information for each operation is placed in the argument tables in the script. Other script users can get this information by using standard **dcecp help** operations.

- Extensive error control is included because you cannnot predict or control the conditions in which the script executes.

The rest of this section shows the general structures and conventions used in a formal task object. To aid our explanation, we use the **dcecp user** task object supplied with the DCE control program.

3.2.1 A Model for Task Objects

This section examines the parts of the **user** task object that should be emulated in other task objects that you create for use with the DCE control program. Adhering to the basic model ensures that your task object will look and behave consistently with other parts of **dcecp**.

For efficiency and readability, the example does not include all of the procedures contained in the **user** task object. Furthermore, we have omitted some repetitive parts of the included procedures, replacing the omitted parts with vertical ellipses in the code examples. The entire **user** task object is contained in *dcelocal*/**dcecp**.

Name your object after the entity on which it operates rather than as a verb such as "show" or "modify." DCE control program objects are named for the DCE entity on which they operate. Primitive objects like **rpcentry** and **principal** objects operate on single manageable DCE entities. Task objects operate at a higher level, generally invoking several primitive objects to achieve their goal. The authors of the user task object contrived a higher-level entity—a *user*—as a manageable object.

The **user** object begins with the top level **proc** command and its argument table that defines the procedures and operations provided by the **user** object. Use this syntax to define separate procedures in this argument table:

verb **command function_call** *procedure_name* "*helptext_string*"

The call to the **parseargs** procedure (defined in a separate file called **parseargs.dcp**) returns the name of the internal procedure that is to be called along with its arguments. The **parseargs** procedure is explained in Section 3.2.2.

```
# proc user - This procedure is the front end for the user task
# scripts.  All argument checking for the provided switches is done
# in the individual functions.
#

proc user { args } {
   set arg_table {
      {create command function_call _dcp_create_user
         "Create a DCE user" }
      {delete command function_call _dcp_delete_user
         "Delete a DCE user"}
      {show    command function_call _dcp_show_user
         "Show the attributes of a DCE user"}
      {help    help  help_list
         "Print summary of command-line options and abort"}
      {operations operations operation_list
         "Return valid operations for command."}}

   set verbose_prose
"This object allows the manipulation of a DCE user.  A user is
represented as a principal and account with membership in a group and
organization as well as having a directory in the CDS namespace.  A user
may be created, deleted or have attribute information returned.  The
argument is a list of either relative or fully qualified principal names.
All fixed attributes of the principal and account object may be specified
when creating a user.  The -force option to the create verb allows the
group or organization for that user to be created if necessary.  The user
is provided a directory in the CDS namespace, with the appropriate ACLs.
Access to create a user requires the correct ACLs on principal, group and
organization directories within the registry and the clearinghouse and
users directory in the CDS namespace."

   set local_args $args

   parseargs $arg_table local_args -found_one

   if { [info local help_prose ] > 0 } { return $help_prose }

   if { [info local function_call ] > 0 } {
     return [$function_call local_args]
   } else {
     error "\"user\" object requires a verb to form a command."
   }

}
```

The next part of the script examines a procedure that takes many options or attributes as input: the **_dcp_create_user** procedure. While this procedure relies on numerous lower-level procedures to do the actual work of creating a user, the example begins by showing just one of the lower-level procedures, **_dcp_create_principal_entry**.

Then the script continues with the **_dcp_create_user** procedure. Notice that the name of this procedure (and all lower-level procedures) begins with an underscore. That's because the Tcl **info** command is frequently used to return the names of all procedures. This convention distinguishes these internal procedure names from procedures like **user**, which are documented procedures. Furthermore, the **_dcp** part of the name distinguishes **dcecp** procedures from other Tcl procedures on a host.

The **_dcp_create_user** procedure has an argument table defining its available options. This argument table differs from the script's initial argument table in that it lacks the **command** keyword and the **function_call** variable that define separate procedures in the script.

Next it initializes variables entered either as options or as attributes in a list. A **process_attribute_list** procedure (at the end of the example) actually parses attributes that have been passed as a list. Then it does the work of creating the user information in the registry and in CDS. Near the end, the cleanup procedure **_dcp_cleanup_user_create** can undo a failed user create operation.

```
  .
  . [several low-level procedures omitted]
  .


#
# This procedure creates a principal in the current registry _s(sec)
# if that principal does not yet exist.
#

proc _dcp_create_principal_entry { principal_name princ_args} {

    set list_of_principals [principal catalog]
    if { [lsearch $list_of_principals $principal_name] == -1} {
      if { [llength $princ_args ] != 0 } {
        principal create $principal_name -attribute $princ_args
      } else
    } else {
      error "Principal \"$principal_name\" already exists."
    }
}
```

```
#
# proc _dcp_create_user - This procedure actually creates a DCE user.
# Several steps are performed.  If the principal does not exist
# a new one is created.  If the groups do not exist and a -force switch is
# set, then two new groups will be added.  The user will be added to the
# groups.  The account will then be created.  An entry in the CDS
# namespace will then be created with the appropriate ACL's.
#

proc _dcp_create_user { local_args } {
  set arg_table {
    {-alias string alias
          "Add principal named as an alias of specified uid."}
    {-attribute string attribute_list
          "Provide attributes in an attribute list format."}
    {-client string client
          "Can the account principal be a client."}
    {-description string descr
          "A general description of the account."}
    {-dupkey string dupkey
          "Can the accounts's principal have duplicate keys."}
    {-expdate string expdate
          "When does the account expire."}

  . [repetitive elements omitted]


    {-uid integer uid
        "User Identifier of the principal to be added."}}

#
# Initializing some variables.
#
    upvar 1 local_args cargs
    set local_args $cargs
    set account_args ""
    set princ_args ""
    set group_args ""
    set force 0

    parseargs $arg_table local_args -no_leftovers

    if { [info local help_prose ] > 0 } { return }

    if { [llength $local_args] > 1 } {
      error "Unrecognized argument [lindex $local_args 1]."
    } elseif { [llength $local_args] == 0 } { error "No user name."
    } else { set account_name $local_args }
```


OSF DCE Administration Guide—Core Components

```
#
#  If parseargs returned attributes in a list instead of options,
#  create an attribute list.  Then call process_attribute_list to
#  parse the list.
#
    if { [info local attribute_list] > 0} {
        set pile_of_attributes "alias client descr dupkey expdate\
        forwadabletkt fullname force group home organization maxtktlife \
        maxtktrenew mypwd password postdatedtkt proxiabletkt pwdvalid \
        renewabletkt server quota shell stdgtauth"
        process_attribute_list attribute_list $pile_of_attributes
    }
#
# If user entered attributes as options rather than in a list,
# check for attribute options.
#
    if { [info local group] > 0} {
      set account_args [format "%s {%s %s}" $account_args group $group]
    } else { error "No group name specified." }

    if { [info local organization] > 0} {
      set account_args [format "%s {%s %s}" $account_args organiz \
          $organization]
    } else { error "No organization name specified." }

    if { [info local password] > 0} {
      set account_args [format "%s {%s %s}" $account_args password \
          $password]
    } else { error "No password specified." }

    if { [info local mypwd] > 0 } {
      set account_args [format "%s {%s %s}" $account_args mypwd $mypwd]
    } else { error "No admin password specified." }
#
# principal and group operations both use the principal's fullname
#
    if { [info local fullname] > 0 } {
      set princ_args [format "%s {%s {%s}}" $princ_args fullname \
          $fullname]
      set group_args [format "%s {%s {%s}}" $group_args fullname \
          $fullname]
    }

    if { [info local uid] > 0 } {
      set princ_args [format "%s {%s %s}" $princ_args uid $uid]
    }
    .
    . [repetitive elements omitted]
    .
```

```
    if { [info local stdtgtauth] > 0 } {
       set account_args [format "%s {%s %s}" $account_args stdtgtauth \
          $stdtgtauth]
    }
#
# set variables if entered as attributes in an attribute list
#
    set account_name [lindex $account_name 0]
    set group_created 0
    set org_created 0
    set group_arg ""
    set org_arg ""
#
# do the work - create principal, do group and organization
# operations, create the account, and create directory in CDS
#
    foreach element $account_name {
       set clup_user "_dcp_cleanup_user_create $element -principal"

       _dcp_create_principal_entry $element $princ_args

       if { $force == 1 } {
          if {[ catch {_dcp_create_group $group group_created} \
             msg] != 0 } {
             _dcp_cleanup_user_create $element -principal
             error $msg
          }
          if { $group_created == 1 } {
             set group_arg "-group group"
          }
          if {[ catch {_dcp_create_org $organization org_created} \
             msg] != 0 } {
             set clup_user [concat $clup_user $group_arg]
             eval $clup_user
             error $msg
          }
          if { $org_created == 1 } {
             set org_arg "-org organization"
          }
       }
       set clup_user [concat $clup_user $group_arg $org_arg]
       if {[catch {_dcp_add_group_entry $group  $element} msg] != 0} {
          eval $clup_user
          error $msg
       }

       if {[catch {_dcp_add_org_entry $organization $element} msg] != 0 } {
           eval $clup_user
          error $msg
       }
```

```
    if {[catch {_dcp_add_account_entry $element $account_args} \
        msg] != 0} {
        eval $clup_user
        error $msg
    }

    if {[catch {_dcp_add_namespace_entry $element} msg] != 0} {
        eval $clup_user
        error $msg
    }
}
set _n $account_name
return
}


#
# _dcp_cleanup_user_create  - This function undoes changes after a
# failure in one of the user create functions as though the operation
# never occurred
#

proc _dcp_cleanup_user_create {account_name args} {

    if { [lsearch $args -principal] != -1 } {
        principal delete $account_name
    }
    if { [lsearch $args -group] != -1 } {
        upvar 1 group clean_group
        group delete $clean_group
    }
    if { [lsearch $args -org] != -1 } {
        upvar 1 organization clean_org
        organization delete $clean_org
    }
}


#
# process_attribute_list - Takes an attribute_list and parses out the
#                          appropriate attributes contained in the
#                          pile_of_attributes variable
#

proc process_attribute_list {attribute_list pile_of_attributes} {

    foreach element $pile_of_attributes { upvar 1 $element _dcp_$element }

    upvar 1 attribute_list _dcp_attribute_list

    set _dcp_attribute_list [check_list_list $_dcp_attribute_list]
```

```
        foreach element $_dcp_attribute_list {
            if { [llength $element] != 2 } {
                error "Incorrect attribute list element
            }
            set attribute_name [lindex $element 0]
            set attribute_value [lindex $element 1]
            set _dcp_attr_name [info vars _dcp_$attribute_name*]
            if {[llength $_dcp_attr_name] > 1} {
                error                   "Ambiguous attribute
            }
            set [set _dcp_attr_name] $attribute_value
        }
    }

proc check_list_list {attribute_list} {

    set not_list_list 0
    set i 1

    foreach element $attribute_list {
        if {[llength $element] != 2 && [llength $attribute_list] < 3} {
            if {$i == 1} {
                return [format "{%s}" $attribute_list]
            }
        }
        incr i
    }

    return $attribute_list
}
```

The next procedure we discuss in the **user** task object is one that takes a
single optional argument and returns lots of output information: the
_dcp_show_user procedure. This procedure returns the results of **principal
show**, **principal catalog**, and **account show** operations.

```
#
#_dcp_show_user - This procedure shows the principal and account
#                 attribute lists for a specified user.
#

proc _dcp_show_user {local_args} {

    upvar 1 local_args cargs
    set local_args $cargs

    parseargs "" local_args -no_leftovers

    if { [info local help_prose ] > 0 } { return }
```

```
if { [llength $local_args] > 1 } {
  error "Unrecognized argument [lindex $local_args 1]."
} elseif { [llength $local_args] == 0 } { error "No user name."
} else { set account_name $local_args }

# Take the first element of the account_name in order to
# eliminate list nesting.

set account_name [lindex $account_name 0]
set _dcp_principals [principal catalog -simplename]

# Show each account that has been requested.

foreach element $account_name {
   if { [lsearch $_dcp_principals $element] == -1 } {
      error "User \"$element\" does not exist."
   } else {
      set _dcp_user_attributes [principal show $element]
   }

   set _dcp_accounts [account catalog -simplename]
   if { [lsearch $_dcp_accounts $element] == -1 } {
      error "User \"$element\" does not exist."
   } else {
      set _dcp_user_attributes [format "%s\n%s" \
         $_dcp_user_attributes [account show $element -all]]
   }
}
return $_dcp_user_attributes

}
```

3.2.2 Using the parseargs Procedure

Task objects and scripts that take arguments or options can call the **parseargs** procedure to parse arguments passed along with the object or script invocation. The **parseargs** procedure is a script in a separate file that provides a convenient and reusable method for argument parsing within a **dcecp** script. The basic syntax is

parseargs *parse_options local_args args*

The procedure relies on arguments passed to it by the calling script. The **parseargs** procedure requires the following inputs:

parse_options   the argument table (**arg_table**) describing the parsing options. The *parse_options* argument can consist of five elements, as in the script's top-level argument table, or four elements as in lower-level argument tables for called procedures within a script. The two syntaxes for *parse_options* are

verb **command** *variable command_name* "*help string*"

or

-options type variable "*help string*"

verb   Provides top-level parsing. Typically an operation contains an object and a verb. The verb portion generally calls another procedure.

command   A keyword indicating that the procedure being defined is a verb of an object.

variable   The name of the variable that holds the value of the option. When parsing verbs, the variable is named **function call**. When parsing options, the variable is named for the option being parsed. For example, if the option name is **-alias**, the variable is named **alias**.

command_name   The procedure name to store in the variable.

help string   The string that describes the use of the verb or option.

-options   The actual string value of the option to be parsed such as **-attribute** or **-mypwd**.

type	The type of variable to be associated with **-option**. Acceptable types are **integer**, **string**, **float**, **boolean**, **command**, and **help**.
local_args	The arguments to be parsed. The **parseargs** procedure extracts all of the recognized entries into a list and resets **local_args** with the values that were not parsed (or not parsable). For instance, a top-level command like **user create** includes options that are parsed later when the procedure implementing the **create** operation is invoked within the script.
args	One of two flags:

-found_one	Tells the parser to return when one procedure argument has been found. In **user create**, for example, the parser would return after one **create** command had been found and processed.
-no_leftovers	Looks for extra options and generates an error if one is found.

3.2.3 Invoking Task Objects

Once your task object is written (and tested), you need to make it available for use. If your script is intended just for your personal use, you can include it in your **.dcecprc** file and invoke it as described in Section 3.1.

Formal task objects require a few steps to make them behave like other **dcecp** objects.

1. Log in as **root** and copy the finished script into the *dcelocal*/**dcecp** directory and set the file permissions to executable.

2. Start the DCE control program and run the **auto_mkindex** utility. This creates information that informs the DCE control program about all available objects. With root privileges, run the following command in the directory where the task objects reside. On UNIX systems, this is often the *dcelocal*/**dcecp** directory.

```
%  dcecp
dcecp>  auto_mkindex /opt/dcelocal/dcecp *.dcp
dcecp>
```

3. To include the new task object name in the **dcecp** help screen, edit the file **/opt/dcelocal/dcecp/help.dcp**. This file is displayed in response to the **dcecp help** operation.

You need to make this file available on each DCE host where the script will be executed. Generally this means copying the file to each host's **/opt/dcelocal/dcecp** directory and then running the **auto_mkindex** utility on the files in the directory. You might want to place the object name in the **/opt/dcelocal/dcecp/help.dcp** file as well.

As a convenience, you could write a script that uses the DCE control program's **hostdata** object to create the file on each host. The script could then run the **auto_mkindex** utility using the **hostdata** object's postprocessor attribute. Chapter 9 contains information on using the **dcecp hostdata** object.

Part 2

DCE Administration Tasks

Chapter 4

DCE Administration Task Objects

This part of the *OSF DCE Administration Guide—Core Components* discusses the purpose and use of DCE administration task objects provided with DCE Version 1.1. Generally, these special **dcecp** objects perform routine high-level administration tasks by combining several lower-level operations.

Often, a single task object uses or affects multiple DCE services. For example, one of the task objects, the **host** object, can configure a host computer into a DCE cell. This task adds specific kinds of information to the DCE Security Service, the Cell Directory Service, and the DCE host daemon services. Because a single invocation of the **host** object can perform multiple steps, it shields DCE administrators from some of the lower-level administration details that would otherwise have to be attended to by using several lower-level **dcecp** administration objects.

While we discuss the task objects at a high level, you'll need to keep in mind that there is often more going on that we're only hinting at. In these cases, we'll point out where to go in this guide for more detailed information. Usually you'll be directed to the corresponding lower-level discussion in the relevant component's part of this guide.

4.1 Using Task Objects to Simplify DCE Administration

Individual DCE control program objects operate on very specific pieces of information in DCE. For example, the **group** object operates solely on security groups in the DCE Security Service registry database. The **group** object enables administrators to create and delete security groups, add and remove members from security groups, rename the groups, and so on. Such precise control is necessary because it allows you to custom tailor DCE to meet very specific needs or circumstances.

While such control might be necessary when configuring a new cell or fixing some access control problem, it can overwhelm routine DCE administration tasks. As an example, let's look at the minimum steps needed to add a new user to a DCE cell:

1. Use the **principal** object to create a principal name for the user.

2. Use the **group** object to add the principal to a security group.

3. Use the **organization** object to add the principal to a security organization.

4. Use the **account** object to create an account for the principal.

5. Use the **directory** object to create a directory for the principal in CDS.

6. Use the **acl** object to give the principal access to the CDS directory.

Performing these six steps probably wouldn't pose any problems in a small cell with 15 or 20 users. But consider a cell with more, perhaps a hundred or maybe even a thousand or more users, and the need to automate this and other administration tasks becomes evident.

To meet this administration need, the DCE control program includes several administration *task objects* for performing some routine DCE administration tasks. Here, we're using the term *task* to mean doing something that requires multiple steps, such as when adding a user consists of performing six lower-level operations.

One of the task objects is the **user** object that you can use to add and remove user information in your DCE environment. For instance, a single invocation of the **user** object can perform all six of the previously mentioned steps needed to correctly add a new user to your DCE environment. You can also use this same task object to delete the user from your environment.

The task objects are implemented as **dcecp** scripts by using the DCE control program language, which means that you can extend the scripts or change their behavior according to your needs. For instance, the default implementation of the **user** task object does not operate on any GDS or DFS information. If your DCE environment includes these extended services, you might want to add some GDS or DFS operations to the script. Part 1 of this guide explains how to use the DCE control program language to write and modify a **dcecp** task object.

4.2 Looking Beyond the Tools

Although you use the task objects to perform various administrative operations, your most important focus is on the elements or entities that you're managing. Each of four task objects provided with DCE enables you to manage a specific element or entity in your DCE cell. The elements are as follows:

A DCE cell	You can test whether a cell is running, show general information about available services in a cell, and back up security and CDS information by using the **cell** task object.
Cell name	You can create and manage cell alias names, which are needed for changing a cell's name or registering a cell in multiple global directory services. These operations use the **cellalias** task object.
DCE hosts	You can configure and remove DCE hosts in a cell, show information about hosts in a cell, and start and stop DCE processes on hosts in a cell by using the **host** task object.
DCE users	You can add and remove users and show information about users in a DCE cell with the **user** task object.

The remaining chapters in this part discusses how to manage these DCE elements by using the default implementations of the four **dcecp** task objects provided with DCE Version 1.1.

Chapter 5

Managing a DCE Cell

From a cell administrator's point of view, a DCE cell consists of a set of networked services that supports the execution of distributed applications. This simple statement, however, doesn't really say anything about what services are currently available in your cell. In fact, the exact number of DCE servers and their locations differs from cell to cell. Even in the same cell, host and network outages and reconfigurations affect service availability.

Although you could use various service-related **dcecp** objects to test whether and where services are available in a cell, it would be cumbersome. Instead, the DCE control program provides a **cell** task object that conveniently lists configured DCE servers and tests whether services are available. It can also back up critical data maintained by the DCE Security Service and CDS.

5.1 Showing All Configured DCE Servers and DCE Hosts

Some DCE cells may be relatively stable, with few DCE hosts or DCE servers being added or removed. Other cells can be quite dynamic, with hosts and DCE servers being added, removed, or moved weekly or even daily. In this environment, tracking the locations of DCE resources can be difficult, so the **cell** task object has a **show** operation that scans various databases in the cell returning the names of configured DCE servers and DCE hosts.

One use of a **cell show** command could be to track performance problems. For example, maybe many new hosts and users have been added, but the number or location of CDS or security servers hasn't grown accordingly. Or perhaps you've just been hired to administer a new cell and you want to see what your cell consists of.

To show configured DCE servers and hosts in a cell, enter a **cell show** operation. The command returns a list of servers grouped by type, along with a list of DCE hosts, as follows:

secservers Each value is the name of a security server.

cdsservers Each value is the name of a machine running a CDS server. The name is the simple name found under **/.:/hosts**. A clearinghouse must be configured on that machine.

dtsservers Each value is the name of a DTS server in the cell.

hosts Each value is the name of a host in the cell, including machines mentioned previously as servers. This is simply the return value of a **directory list /.:/hosts** operation.

The following example shows the names of all the configured DCE servers and hosts in the local cell:

```
dcecp> cell show
{secservers
 /.../my_cell.goodco.com/subsys/dce/sec/master}
{cdsservers
 /.../my_cell.goodco.com/hosts/earth}
{dtsservers
 /.../my_cell.goodco.com/hosts/krypton}
{hosts
 /.../my_cell.goodco.com/hosts/earth
 /.../my_cell.goodco.com/hosts/jupiter
 /.../my_cell.goodco.com/hosts/krypton
 /.../my_cell.goodco.com/hosts/mars
 /.../my_cell.goodco.com/hosts/mercury
 /.../my_cell.goodco.com/hosts/neptune
 /.../my_cell.goodco.com/hosts/pluto
 /.../my_cell.goodco.com/hosts/saturn
 /.../my_cell.goodco.com/hosts/uranus
 /.../my_cell.goodco.com/hosts/venus}
```

If you have the necessary permission, you can show the configured DCE servers and hosts in another cell by including that cell's name as an argument as shown in the following example:

```
dcecp> cell show /.../their_cell.goodco.com
{secservers
 /.../their_cell.goodco.com/subsys/dce/sec/master}
{cdsserver
 /.../their_cell.goodco.com/gold}
{dtsservers
 /.../their_cell.goodco.com/hosts/silver/dts-entity}
{hosts
 /.../their_cell.goodco.com/hosts/brass
 /.../their_cell.goodco.com/hosts/bronze
 /.../their_cell.goodco.com/hosts/copper
 /.../their_cell.goodco.com/hosts/gold
 /.../their_cell.goodco.com/hosts/iron
 /.../their_cell.goodco.com/hosts/mercury
 /.../their_cell.goodco.com/hosts/silver
 /.../their_cell.goodco.com/hosts/steel
 /.../their_cell.goodco.com/hosts/tin}
```

5.2 Testing Cell Operation

When client-server communication problems occur, it's easy to suspect that one or more DCE services is not operating in the cell. You can easily test whether a cell's DCE services are running by invoking a **cell ping** operation.

If called with no option, the **cell ping** operation performs a **server ping** operation on the master security server, on the CDS server that has a master clearinghouse, and all the DTS servers in the cell. Use the **-replicas** option to test CDS and security service replicas as well as the masters. The **-clients** option tests every DCE host in the cell by looping though the **/.:/hosts** directory in CDS and performing a **host ping**, with each host name as an argument.

In case of failure, the operation generates an error and returns a list of servers or hosts that could not be contacted. For any successes, the operation returns the message **DCE Services Available**. For successes with the **-clients** option, the message is **DCE Clients Available**.

The following example pings the names of all the configured master DCE servers in the local cell:

```
dcecp> cell ping
DCE services available
```

The following example pings the names of all the configured DCE hosts in the local cell. Depending on the size of a cell and timeout values set, this command can take a long time (from several to many minutes) to complete.

```
dcecp> cell ping -clients
DCE clients available
```

If you have the necessary permission, you can ping the configured DCE servers and hosts in another cell by including that cell's name as an argument as shown in the following example:

```
dcecp> cell ping /.../their_cell.goodco.com
DCE services available
```

5.3 Backing Up the Security Service Registry and CDS

As organizations increasingly depend on DCE cells for their day-to-day operations, they can't afford to lose the cell's directory and security data. Organizations generally rely on regular backup schemes to prevent the loss of this and other critical data. But backing up these DCE databases by using traditional backup methods can cause security holes in your cell if the archives aren't properly protected.

Fortunately, DCE includes features that let you back up these essential databases to destinations of your choosing. Once you've begun using the DCE mechanism to back up CDS and security data, you can redirect your traditional backup program to ignore these DCE databases.

The **cell backup** operation backs up the master security database and each clearinghouse with master replicas in the cell. This operation requires that a **dced** program is running on each of the server hosts being backed up.

Prepare a cell for regular backup operations by setting up an Extended Registry Attribute (ERA) that can specify a backup destination (typically a tape archive). Then add the new attribute to the principals for the master DCE Security Service registry database and all CDS clearinghouses with master replicas that you want to back up. To do this, follow these steps:

1. Create an ERA as a string that specifies a backup destination. Name the ERA **/.:/sec/xattrschema/bckp_dest** and the type **pringstring**. Select the ACL manager named **principal** and set its four permission bits to **r** (read), **m** (manage), **r** (read), and **D** (Delete) as shown in the following command:

    ```
    dcecp>  xattrschema create /.:/sec/xattrschema/bckp_dest \
               -encoding printstring -aclmgr {principal r m r D}
    ```

2. Add the new ERA (**bckp_dest**) to the principal **dce-rgy** (the DCE Security Service registry database). Set the value to be the **tar** filename or the device that is the backup destination:

    ```
    dcecp>  principal modify dce-rgy \
               -add {bckp_dest tarfilename_or_device}
    ```

3. Add the new ERA (**bckp_dest**) to the principal **/.:/hosts/**_hostname_**/cds-server** (the CDS server). Set the value to be the **tar** filename or the device that is the backup destination:

dcecp> **principal modify /.:/hosts/**_hostname_**/cds-server \
-add {bckp_dest** _tarfilename_or_device_**}**

Now, whenever you want to back up your registry database or CDS database, just invoke a **cell backup** operation as follows:

dcecp> **cell backup**

You can back up another cell by including the cell name as an argument to the **cell backup** operation. Note that you need the necessary permissions in the remote cell. (Refer to the **cell(8dce)** reference page for the required privileges.)

5.4 Modifying or Extending the Cell Object

The **cell** task object is implemented as a script so that administrators can modify or extend it on a per-site basis. Here are a few examples of possible modifications or extensions you can make:

- Add a way to show GDS or DFS server information.

- Add options to the **cell show** operation to omit listing all the hosts in a cell or to show only certain DCE servers.

- Add a command to configure a new cell. Such a command could perform the lower-level operations currently performed by the **CONFIGURE** selection in the DCE Installation and Configuration main menu of the **dce_config** program.

Part 1 of this guide discusses ways to create new **dcecp** objects or modify existing objects written with the **dcecp** language.

Chapter 6

Managing Your Cell Name

Although cell names tend to be stable, there are times when you want to change them. Imagine that, shortly after you install and configure a new cell, a corporate reorganization makes your cell name inaccurate. Your old cell name **/.../sales.goodco.com** doesn't reflect your new divisional organization in which the cell name **/.../polyline.goodco.com** would be more appropriate. What's more, the Goodco company has just acquired new, international affiliations. However, their cells are registered in an X.500 directory service which, unfortunately, does not interconnect with DNS, the Domain Name System in which your cell is registered.

As the cell administrator, you can solve either or both of these problems by using a cell alias name. Cell alias names offer the flexibility you need to manage your cell name, letting you change the name of your cell or just add a second cell name as an alias that can be registered in another global directory service.

You can use the **cellalias** task object to create and manage cell alias names, updating all of the DCE services that store the name of your cell.

Cells must have two (or more) cell names to be registered in more than one global directory service. If you are changing your cell name (instead of simply adding an alias), you must also set the new name to be the *primary cell name*. In this case, the **cellalias** object updates CDS, the DCE Security Service, and DCE hosts with the new primary cell name.

Note that a previously existing cell name is not eliminated from the cell's services. CDS and the DCE Security Service must retain the old name so that they can respond appropriately to any client requests bearing the old name.

This chapter discusses various aspects of global names and CDS names. If you are not already familiar with the structure of global names and CDS names, you should read more about them now in Part 4 of this guide.

6.1 Registering in Multiple Global Directory Services

You can make your cell resources available to users or applications in other DCE cells by registering your cell in a global directory service such as DNS (Domain Name System) or GDS (an X.500 global directory service). Once your cell is registered, users in remote cells can access your cell's resources (provided they have the necessary permissions) by using global names. The following example shows a global DNS name identifying an ASCII line printer in a cell managed by the fictitious Goodco company:

/.../sales.goodco.com/subsys/bldg6/resources/floor2/printer_ascii

But let's say you also want to register your cell in GDS so that foreign cells that have access to only an X.500 global directory service can access your cell's resources. Now, your cell needs a second X.500-style name and, for this, you must establish an alias like the following:

/.../C=us/O=goodco/OU=sales

Use a **cellalias create** operation to create a second name for your cell. This operation creates a new cell principal in the registry service and performs a **registry verify** operation to ensure that all the replicas are up-to-date. Next, it creates a cell alias name in CDS by using the **cdsalias** object. Finally, it performs a **hostdata** operation on each host in the cell, updating each *dcelocal*/**dce_cf.db** file and *dcelocal*/**etc/security/pe_site** file with the cell alias name. This last step can take a long time to complete in a cell with many hosts.

The following creates the cell alias name **/.../C=us/O=goodco/OU=sales**:

dcecp> **cellalias create /.../C=us/O=goodco/OU=sales**

Once you have completed this operation, you can register your cell name with the authority responsible for the particular global service.

6.2 Changing Your Cell Name

Although cell names tend to be relatively stable, there might be a situation where you want to change your cell name. For instance, your company name has changed and you want that name reflected in your cell name. Whatever the reason, changing your cell name is a two-step process.

The first step is using a **cellalias create** operation to create a new alias name for your cell. The second step is using a **cellalias set** operation to set the new alias name to be the *primary cell name*. The following example illustrates the necessary steps and assumes you want to change your old cell name **/.../sales.goodco.com** to **/.../polyline.goodco.com**:

1. Use a **cellalias create** operation to create a second name for your cell. This operation creates a new cell principal in the registry service and synchronizes the registry. Next, it creates a cell alias name in CDS by using the **cdsalias** object. Finally, it uses the **hostdata** object to update the *dcelocal*/**dce_cf.db** and *dcelocal*/**etc/security/pe_site** files on each host in the cell with the new cell alias.

    The following creates the cell alias name **/.../polyline.goodco.com**:

    dcecp> **cellalias create /.../polyline.goodco.com**

2. Use a **cellalias set** operation to set the new name to be the *primary cell name*. This operation modifies the new cell principal name so that it's not an alias and performs a **registry verify** operation to ensure that all the replicas are up-to-date. Next, it uses the **cdsalias** object to set the alias name in CDS to be the primary cell name and synchronizes the CDS replicas. Finally, it performs a **hostdata** operation on each host in the cell, interchanging the values stored in the **cell_name** and **cell_aliases** data items respectively.

The following example sets the new alias name, **/.../polyline.goodco.com**, to be the primary cell name. The old cell name (**/.../sales.goodco.com**) becomes a cell alias name.

dcecp> **cellalias set /.../polyline.goodco.com**

6.3 Modifying or Extending the cellalias Object

The **cellalias** task object is implemented as a script so that administrators can modify or extend it on a per-site basis. Here are a few examples of possible modifications or extensions you can make:

- Extend the script to create hierarchical cells. Chapter 21 describes the procedure to create a hierarchy of cells.

- Add a **-verbose** option to display the results of each step as it completes.

Part 1 of this guide discusses ways to create new **dcecp** objects or modify existing objects written with the **dcecp** language.

## Chapter 7

Managing DCE Hosts

Larger DCE cells can contain many host computers, with some running both DCE servers and application servers while others act only as client systems. Still other hosts might run application servers but also act as clients to their resident users. Such flexibility in DCE host configurations can make it difficult to control or track what's running or available on each host in a cell. The **host** task object represents DCE and application processes associated with hosts, letting administrators more easily manage DCE server and application processes on machines.

You can use the **host** task object to show information about processes on local and remote hosts in a cell, and start and stop DCE processes on hosts throughout a cell. You can also configure local DCE hosts in a cell and remove (unconfigure) remote DCE hosts from a cell. Online help for this object is available using the **host help** and **host operations** commands in **dcecp**.

All of the **host** object operations performed on a remote host except **host catalog** require **dced** to be running on the remote host.

7.1 Listing the DCE Hosts in a Cell

You can determine the number and names of DCE hosts configured in your DCE cell by using the **host catalog** operation. This operation might be useful for determining whether a specific host has already been configured into your cell. The host does not have to be running for this operation to work because the **host catalog** operation actually performs a **directory list /.:/hosts** operation and doesn't interact with the host. This method relies on the convention that hosts register their names in the **/.:/hosts** directory. If your hosts register in some other directory, you need to modify the **host catalog** operation in the **host** task object. You can read more about the purpose and use of CDS directories in Chapter 18.

The **host catalog** operation resembles the **cell show** operation except that it doesn't separately list DCE servers. The following example operation lists all DCE hosts that have been configured in the cell:

```
dcecp> host catalog
/.../my_cell.goodco.com/hosts/bigbox
/.../my_cell.goodco.com/hosts/drifter
/.../my_cell.goodco.com/hosts/duh
/.../my_cell.goodco.com/hosts/heater
/.../my_cell.goodco.com/hosts/pc1
/.../my_cell.goodco.com/hosts/pc2
/.../my_cell.goodco.com/hosts/pc3
/.../my_cell.goodco.com/hosts/peewee
/.../my_cell.goodco.com/hosts/xoltar
/.../my_cell.goodco.com/hosts/xray
/.../my_cell.goodco.com/hosts/zoof
```

You can omit the cell name by using the **-simplename** option as in the following example:

```
dcecp> host catalog -simplename
hosts/bigbox
hosts/drifter
hosts/duh
hosts/heater
hosts/pc1
hosts/pc2
hosts/pc3
hosts/peewee
hosts/xoltar
hosts/xray
hosts/zoof
```

7.2 Showing All Servers Configured for a DCE Host

In larger cells, in which DCE servers and application servers reside on multiple hosts, you'll likely want to see what servers are configured to run on particular hosts from time to time. The DCE control program's **host show** operation reads a DCE host's server configuration and execution information and returns a list of configured servers on that host. The list contains each server's simple name and indicates whether it is running. The list also indicates whether a security server is a master or replica and whether a DTS entity is a clerk or server.

This operation relies on the **server** object (and consequently on the DCE host daemon) to show information about configured servers. You can read more about controlling server operation in Chapter 10.

The following example shows the servers configured to run on DCE host **xoltar**:

```
dcecp> host show /.:/hosts/xoltar
video_clip running
dts-entity running clerk
```

9.1 DCE Host Services

Some DCE host services such as the runtime libraries are inert and require no administration once DCE has been configured on a host. But other services are active programs. One such active service is the *endpoint mapper* which acts as a lookup service on a host. The endpoint mapper lists server communication ports (called *endpoints*) in the host's *endpoint map*. Remote clients looking for particular servers query the endpoint mapper which returns information contained in the endpoint map. The endpoint mapper, along with other active services, are contained in a single program called the *DCE host daemon* or **dced**. Typically, once a host has been configured with DCE Version 1.1 software, the host booting process starts the **dced** process along with other daemons or processes. Occasionally however, you may need to manually start or restart this daemon.

The **dced** program comprises a set of DCE host services that satisfies many needs of DCE client and server applications on a host system:

- The endpoint mapper service acts as a directory of servers running on a host. Clients can acquire a registered server's communication endpoint by looking in the host endpoint map.

- A security validation service manages DCE security on the local host.

- A server configuration and execution service lets adminitrators remotely set servers' starting and stopping conditions, explicitly start and stop individual servers, and monitor running servers' states.

- A key management service lets administrators manage server passwords remotely.

- A hostdata service lets administrators remotely manage data stored in files on a host. Administrators will find this most useful for remotely managing a host's cell name and cell alias information.

- An attribute schema capability lets administrators add new attributes to server configuration information.

Normally, any system that hosts a DCE server (such as a DCE cell directory server) or that runs a DCE-based application server or client that uses authentication, must also run the **dced** process.

You can omit the cell name by using the **-simplename** option as in the following example:

```
dcecp> host catalog -simplename
hosts/bigbox
hosts/drifter
hosts/duh
hosts/heater
hosts/pc1
hosts/pc2
hosts/pc3
hosts/peewee
hosts/xoltar
hosts/xray
hosts/zoof
```

7.2 Showing All Servers Configured for a DCE Host

In larger cells, in which DCE servers and application servers reside on multiple hosts, you'll likely want to see what servers are configured to run on particular hosts from time to time. The DCE control program's **host show** operation reads a DCE host's server configuration and execution information and returns a list of configured servers on that host. The list contains each server's simple name and indicates whether it is running. The list also indicates whether a security server is a master or replica and whether a DTS entity is a clerk or server.

This operation relies on the **server** object (and consequently on the DCE host daemon) to show information about configured servers. You can read more about controlling server operation in Chapter 10.

The following example shows the servers configured to run on DCE host **xoltar**:

```
dcecp> host show /.:/hosts/xoltar
video_clip running
dts-entity running clerk
```

7.3 Testing Whether a DCE Host is Running

Because DCE communications often involve several steps before clients communicate with their servers, communication failures can be difficult to diagnose. For instance, a server may not be running on a host or the DCE services may not be currently running, even though the host has been configured into the cell. You can use a **server ping** operation to test whether a server process is running but, if this fails, you might need a way to see if the DCE host is even accessible through the network. The DCE control program's **host ping** operation tests whether a host's DCE services are accessible on the network, returning a **1** if it is and a **0** if it isn't accessible.

The **host ping** operation tests for the presence of the remote host's DCE daemon (**dced**). You can read more about the purpose and use of **dced** in Chapter 9.

The following example tests whether **dced** on host **duh** is accessible on the network:

```
dcecp>  host ping /.:/hosts/duh
1
```

7.4 Starting Configured DCE Processes on a Host

Each host's DCE daemon (**dced**) can maintain configuration information for servers set to run on that particular host. This information is established using an application's installation script or by using the **server** object directly. While the **server** object provides its own **start** operation that can start individual servers on a host, you must explicitly name each server. The **host start** operation lets you start all configured DCE servers and clients and all configured application servers on a host with a single command.

To operate on a remote host, its DCE daemon must be running. Remote **host start** operations also require at least one CDS server and one security server to be running in the cell. The **host start** operation operates on DCE servers and clients and on application servers that are configured by using the **server** object.

Application servers must be configured with the **starton** attribute set to **boot** or **explicit**. You can read more about configuring application servers in Chapter 10.

The following example starts all configured servers on host **bigbox**:

dcecp> **host start /.:/hosts/bigbox**

7.5 Stopping DCE Processes Running on a Host

Like the **host start** operation discussed in the previous section, the **host stop** operation is more encompassing than a **server stop** operation. It lets you stop all DCE processes on a host with a single command rather than issue a separate **server stop** operation for each server. This operation stops application servers, then DCE processes and finally, when stopping DCE processes on the local machine, stops **dced**. You can read more about controlling servers in Chapter 10.

To operate on a remote host, its DCE daemon must be running. Remote **host stop** operations also require at least one CDS server and one security server to be running in the cell. The **host stop** operation operates on DCE servers and clients and on application servers that have been configured by using the **server** object.

The following example stops all DCE processes and application servers on host **bigbox**:

dcecp> **host stop /.:/hosts/bigbox**

7.6 Configuring a DCE Host in a Cell

Once DCE Version 1.1 software has been installed on a host, you can configure the local host as a DCE client machine by using a **host configure** operation. You must have root or system administrator privileges on the local host to execute a **host configure** operation.

You can read more about requirements for DCE server and client systems in the *OSF DCE Administration Guide—Introduction*.

Note that you cannot configure DCE servers such as a DCE Security Service registry or a CDS server by using a **host configure** operation. Instead, use the DCE Installation and Configuration program to configure DCE servers in your cell.

Before configuring a DCE client system, be sure the DCE software has been installed on the host. For information about installing DCE, refer to your DCE installation instructions or the *OSF DCE Administration Guide—Introduction*.

To configure a DCE client system, perform the following steps:

1. Log into a privileged account (**root** or system administrator) on the host to be configured.

2. Start the DCE control program and perform a **host configure -client** operation. Include an argument specifying the cell-relative name of the local host being configured. The operation adds this name to CDS. Use required options to specify the host names where the master security server and a CDS server are running. Other required options are **-administrator**, which specifies the principal name of the person configuring the host (usually the cell administrator), and **-password** followed by the administrator's password.

   The following example shows configuring host **ptarmigan** as a DCE client system. The cell's security server is on host **eagle** and the CDS server is on host **owl**. The administrator's principal name is **cell_admin** and the administrator's password is **-dce-**.

   ```
   dcecp> host configure /.:/hosts/ptarmigan -client -secmaster eagle \
             -cds owl -administrator cell_admin -password -dce-
   ```

7.7 Removing a DCE Host from a Cell

Occasionally, you might want to remove a DCE host from a cell. For instance, your organization is replacing some older systems that are being sold to another organization.

Removing or unconfiguring a DCE host is more than just erasing DCE information from the host's disk because CDS and the DCE Security Service both maintain host-specific information that needs to be removed as well. The **host unconfigure** operation deletes all objects, directories, and links from the **/.:/hosts/**_hostname_ CDS directory including the directory itself. It also deletes all principal names beginning with **hosts/**_hostname_**/** which, in turn, removes all accounts with the same name. Finally, it removes all local configuration files and stops all running DCE processes ending with the DCE daemon (**dced**).

The **host unconfigure** operation operates only on remote hosts. You cannot perform this operation on a local host because it removes the DCE Security Service registry information needed to complete the operation. Also note that you need cell administrator privileges to perform a **host unconfigure** operation.

To remove a remote DCE host from a cell, use a **host unconfigure** operation providing the host name of the host to be unconfigured. The following example removes host **calypso** from the cell:

```
dcecp>  host unconfigure /.:/hosts/calypso
```

You can remove multiple DCE hosts from a cell by providing a **dcecp** list of names of the hosts to be unconfigured. The following example removes hosts **calypso**, **hydra**, and **nova** from the cell:

```
dcecp>  host unconfigure {/.:/hosts/calypso /.:/hosts/hydra /.:/hosts/nova}
```

If you have cell administrator privileges in a foreign cell, you can remove a remote DCE host from that cell by supplying a global DCE name of the host to be unconfigured. The following example removes host **gobo** from foreign cell **/.../their_cell.goodco.com**:

```
dcecp>  host unconfigure /.../their_cell.goodco.com/hosts/gobo
```

7.8 Modifying or Extending the Host Object

The **host** task object is implemented as a script so that administrators can modify or extend it on a per-site basis. For example, administrators might want to add GDS and DFS information to the object. You could also add calls to specialized commands to start or stop application servers. For instance a **printer stop** operation could be useful.

Part 1 of this guide discusses ways to create new **dcecp** objects or modify existing objects written with the **dcecp** language.

Chapter 8

Managing DCE Users

One of the most frequent DCE administration tasks is likely to be managing users in your DCE environment. Corporate reorganizations, changing business needs, and fluctuating economics all exert pressures causing users to come and go or to move between various groups or organizations.

DCE users represent a big part of what DCE is designed to support; the DCE services authenticate and admit some while denying access to those who are unauthorized. Indeed, users have complex management requirements; their information is spread among multiple services that help validate and control their activities. User information includes principal names, group and organization information, account information, and information in CDS.

The DCE control program includes separate administration objects for managing each piece of user information in a DCE cell. While these separate objects might be very useful for making minor adjustments to certain user information, their constant use for repetitive tasks such as adding and removing users from a cell would prove quite tedious. A simpler method relies on the **user** task object that you can use to more easily create, delete, and show user information in a DCE cell. Online help for this object is available using the **user help** and **user operations** commands in **dcecp**.

8.1 Creating a New User

Each **user** in a DCE environment is a person with a unique identity (principal name). Each principal is a member of at least one security group and organization and has an account in the DCE Security Service registry database. Although it's not required, each principal can also have a directory in CDS.

When you create a user with the **user** task object, you perform several lower-level operations:

1. The **user create** operation creates a new principal name and adds the principal to a security group and organization. If the security group or organization does not exist when you invoke the operation, you can force their creation by using the **-force** option. The principal attributes assume default values, but you can specify other attributes if necessary. All of the attributes are listed in the **user(8dce)** reference page.

    Typically, a security group's name is included in access control lists (ACLs) that regulate user access to various server and data objects in the DCE environment. A security organization maintains policies that are applied to all the principals that are members of that organization. Policies control things like the lifespan of accounts, whether or when account passwords expire, or whether passwords can contain nonalphanumeric characters. You can read more about administering principals, groups, and organizations in Chapter 30.

2. The **user create** operation creates an account for the principal and creates the user's password. The account attributes assume default values but you can specify other attributes if necessary. All of the attributes are listed in the **user(8dce)** reference page.

    A principal's account contains information about the principal such as group and organization names, account creation and expiration information, and information about tickets (which identify principals to resources in a DCE environment). You can read more about administering accounts in Chapter 31.

3. Finally, the **user create** operation adds a directory called
   /.:/users/_principalname_ to CDS. This directory can store user-specific
   application location information. The operation also adds an ACL
   entry to the default ACL which gives the user **rwtci** permissions on
   the directory. These permissions allow users to insert objects and
   links, but they cannot delete the directory or administer replication on
   the directory. Furthermore, users cannot create additional directories
   unless you give them **w** (write) access to the clearinghouse. You can
   read more about the purpose and use of CDS directories in Chapter 18.
   You can read more about ACLs and CDS directories in Chapter 16.

You generally need numerous permissions to create new users in your DCE
cell, so you should log into the cell administrator's account (or a similar
privileged account). The **user(8dce)** reference page lists the required
permissions.

To create a new user in a DCE cell, invoke a **user create** operation. The
following example creates a principal name **P_Pestana** and an account with
the same name. The **create** operation requires your password to prevent
someone else from using an unattended session to create an unauthorized
account. You must also provide the **-password** option to specify a password
for the user. The required **-group** and **-organization** options add principal
P_Pestana to the named group and organization. The optional **-fullname**
option creates a fullname to help other human users recognize the principal.

```
dcecp> user create P_Pestana -fullname {Patricia Pestana} \
          -mypwd mxyzptlk -password change.me -group users \
          -organization managers
```

You can create multiple users by specifying a list of user names as an
argument to the **user create** operation. This method poses some limitations,
however. All created users will have the same initial password, group
name, and organization name. Furthermore, you cannot specify the
fullname and **uid** attributes since these are unique for each user. The
following example creates several users with a password **change.me**, a
group name of **users**, and an organization named **staff**:

```
dcecp> user create {R_Lee B_Joy N_Lynn D_Dee} -mypwd mxyzptlk \
          -password change.me -group users -organization staff
```

8.2 Showing User Information

Sometimes you might want to view the attributes for a user. For instance, you might want to see the expiration date for one or more accounts or view the fullname of a principal.

The **user show** command returns the attributes associated with users that are included as arguments to the command. The attributes include principal attributes and ERAs, and account attributes and policies. The information is returned as if the following commands were run in the following order:

- **principal show**

- **account show -all**

The following command displays the principal and account attributes associated with user **P_Pestana**:

```
dcecp>  user show P_Pestana
{fullname {Pat Pestana}}
{uid 5139}
{uuid 00001413-ad4f-21cd-8c00-0000c08adf56}
{alias no}
{quota unlimited}
{groups users}
{acctvalid yes}
{client yes}
{created /.../my_cell.goodco.com/cell_admin \
    1994-08-01-16:41:32.000+00:00I-----}
{description {}}
{dupkey no}
{expdate none}
{forwardabletkt yes}
{goodsince 1994-08-01-16:41:32.000+00:00I-----}
{group users}
{home /}
{lastchange /.../my_cell.goodco.com/cell_admin \
    1994-08-01-16:41:32.000+00:00I-----}
{organization managers}
{postdatedtkt no}
{proxiabletkt no}
{pwdvalid yes}
{renewabletkt yes}
{server yes}
{shell {}}
{stdtgtauth yes}
nopolicy
```

You can show information about multiple users by specifying a list of user names as an argument to the **user create** operation.

8.3 Deleting a User

When users leave your organization, you might need to delete the user from the cell. Use the **user delete** command to do this. This operation removes the principal name from the registry which, in turn, deletes the account and removes the principal from any groups and organizations. The operation also deletes the **/.:/users/***principalname* directory and any contents from CDS.

You need numerous permissions, such as those generally associated with cell administrator, to delete a user. See the **user(8dce)** reference page.

The following example operation removes user **P_Pestana** from the cell:

```
dcecp>  user delete P_Pestana
```

You can remove multiple users from your cell by specifying a list of user names as an argument to the **user delete** operation, as follows:

```
dcecp>  user delete {W_Rosenberry J_Hunter P_Pestana}
```

If you have permissions in a foreign cell, you can remove one or more users from that cell by specifying the global principal name of the users to be deleted. For example:

```
dcecp>  user delete /.../their_cell.goodco.com/J_Jones
```

8.4 Modifying or Extending the User Object

The **user** task object is implemented as a script so that administrators can modify or extend it on a per-site basis. For example, administrators might want to add GDS and DFS information to the object. Other possible modifications include the following:

- Changing the location of the CDS directory created for users, or removing it completely.

- Changing the default ACLs placed on the various objects.

- Adding an option to give users write access to the clearinghouse where the master replica of the **/.:/users/**_username_ directory resides. This allows users to create their own subdirectories. The option could add individual principal names to the clearinghouse ACL. An easier method could add principals to a group that has write access to the clearinghouse.

- Setting certain attributes or policies on all newly created principals and accounts to match the site's policies. For example, you could set principals to have a **pwd_val_type** ERA and set accounts to generate random passwords.

- Setting up site-specific defaults for passwords (to be changed by the user later), groups, organizations, principal directories, and so on.

- Supporting a **user modify** command. Such a command could change group or organization information or some other attributes associated with users.

Part 1 of this guide discusses ways to create new **dcecp** objects or modify existing objects written with the **dcecp** language.

## Part 3

DCE Host and Application Administration

## Chapter 9

Managing DCE Host Services and Host Data

Some services like DTS, CDS, and the DCE Security Service registry, which produce or maintain cell-wide information, are centralized. Although the services they provide are available throughout a cell, the servers themselves typically reside on just a few selected hosts in a cell.

Other DCE services are pervasive; that is, they reside on every host in a DCE cell. The DCE software that runs on every DCE host provides essential services that enable local client and server programs to interact with remote client and server programs in a reliable and secure way. Consequently, each host in a DCE cell has administrative aspects which are discussed in the first part of this chapter.

Each DCE host maintains local data that is essential to host operation in a DCE environment. Occasionally, you may find it necessary to modify parts of this data as your cell configuration changes, or as you add DCE capabilities or DCE applications. The second part of this chapter discusses how to use the DCE control program to gain remote, authenticated access to this data.

When DCE operations do not succeed for some reason, you want to inform the right people about what happened. DCE's serviceability messaging facility lets you route error messages based on the severity level of the message. The last part of this chapter explains how to manage this facility.

9.1 DCE Host Services

Some DCE host services such as the runtime libraries are inert and require no administration once DCE has been configured on a host. But other services are active programs. One such active service is the *endpoint mapper* which acts as a lookup service on a host. The endpoint mapper lists server communication ports (called *endpoints*) in the host's *endpoint map*. Remote clients looking for particular servers query the endpoint mapper which returns information contained in the endpoint map. The endpoint mapper, along with other active services, are contained in a single program called the *DCE host daemon* or **dced**. Typically, once a host has been configured with DCE Version 1.1 software, the host booting process starts the **dced** process along with other daemons or processes. Occasionally however, you may need to manually start or restart this daemon.

The **dced** program comprises a set of DCE host services that satisfies many needs of DCE client and server applications on a host system:

- The endpoint mapper service acts as a directory of servers running on a host. Clients can acquire a registered server's communication endpoint by looking in the host endpoint map.

- A security validation service manages DCE security on the local host.

- A server configuration and execution service lets adminitrators remotely set servers' starting and stopping conditions, explicitly start and stop individual servers, and monitor running servers' states.

- A key management service lets administrators manage server passwords remotely.

- A hostdata service lets administrators remotely manage data stored in files on a host. Administrators will find this most useful for remotely managing a host's cell name and cell alias information.

- An attribute schema capability lets administrators add new attributes to server configuration information.

Normally, any system that hosts a DCE server (such as a DCE cell directory server) or that runs a DCE-based application server or client that uses authentication, must also run the **dced** process.

It is clear that if the **dced** process failed for some reason, it would take all of its component services down along with it, leaving the host unable to respond to client requests. Similarly, a failure of one of the component services (for example the key management service) might be caused by the **dced** process unexpectedly exiting for some reason. This relationship between **dced** and its component services is worth remembering if problems occur.

9.2 Starting and Stopping DCE Host Services

Although the **dced** process generally starts as part of the host booting process, sometimes you may need to start the process manually.

Before starting **dced**, any underlying network services on which client/server communication depends must be available; on most UNIX systems, for example, network interfaces and routing services must be enabled. Once these transport-layer services are established, you can start **dced**. After **dced** starts, RPC-based servers can start.

The endpoint mapper listens on privileged or reserved communication ports (well-known endpoints) for client requests for service. Consequently, **dced** must be started as a privileged user.

Part of **dced** (the endpoint map) contains information that clients use to locate servers on a host system. The **dced** process maintains a copy of this information in a database file named *dcelocal***/var/dced/Ep.db** so it won't be lost if you stop and then restart **dced** for some reason. Another database file called *dcelocal***/var/dced/Srvrexec.db** maintains information about servers (such as each server's process ID) that are currently running on the host. The information in both of these databases becomes obsolete when a system reboots because most servers get different endpoints and different process IDs each time they start.

You can configure **dced** to start each time a host boots. In some cases, the *dcelocal***/etc/rc.dce** file is linked to or copied to **/etc/rc.dce**. This way, **dced** is invoked when other daemons are started. The *dcelocal***/etc/rc.dce** file is also responsible for deleting the **Srvrexec.db** and **Ep.db** database files before starting **dced**. If your system does not automatically delete these files, you'll have to manually delete them before starting **dced**.

While you normally do not need to start **dced** in a shell, if you ever need to do so, log in as **root** and enter the following command:

dcelocal/**bin/dced**

By default, **dced** listens on one endpoint for each transport that is supported by the host on which it is running. That is, if a host supports both TCP/IP and UDP/IP transports, **dced** will listen on one TCP and one UDP socket for client requests. An optional *protseq* argument lets you limit the transports that **dced** uses to the ones you specify. Intended as a debugging capability, this feature should be used with care; if you limit transports, clients will not be able to locate servers over the excluded transports, and servers will not be able to register themselves in the endpoint map by using the excluded transports. For information about the optional *protseq* argument, see the **dced(8dce)** reference page.

If the DCE daemon stops or exits unexpectedly, you can restart it. The restarted **dced** process does *not* lose any previously registered server bindings. It simply loads the information from the **Ep.db** and **Srvrexec.db** files. As a rule, stopping and restarting **dced** is not recommended because it also stops the security validation service.

Although you should run the host services on all hosts where DCE client or server applications run, there are some situations where you can avoid running them:

- DCE clients that don't perform authentication

- DCE servers that don't perform authentication and that don't use the endpoint mapper or other active DCE host services

Once you've started the DCE host services, you can perform all DCE host and server administration tasks by using the DCE control program, **dcecp**. The control program offers secure, remote access to host and server administrative functions, which means you can manage all of your DCE Version 1.1 hosts without having to log into each host. Part 1 of this book explained how to use **dcecp** in interactive mode as well as how to write **dcecp** scripts to manage DCE activities. You should be acquainted with those basics before performing administrative tasks explained in this chapter or elsewhere in this document.

9.3 Managing Host Data

Each host in a DCE cell maintains local data that is essential for operating in a DCE environment. For instance, each host's DCE identity relies on certain data items that specify the host's host name, cell name, and any cell aliases. Currently, these data items are stored in a local file called *dcelocal*/**dce_cf.db**. These and other data items can be modified remotely using the DCE control program's **hostdata** object.

The **hostdata** object has a much broader application, too; administrators will find it extremely useful for accessing general data and files on remote hosts using secure and platform-independent methods. The last part of this chapter examines this powerful access method.

9.3.1 Permissions for Accessing Host Data

Access control lists (ACLs) prevent unauthorized principals from creating, changing, or deleting hostdata information. Two types of ACLs protect hostdata information. One type of ACL protects the container in which the hostdata items reside. A second type protects each individual hostdata item.

This section shows how to manage ACLs that protect hostdata information. For detailed information about setting and using ACL protections, see Chapter 28.

9.3.1.1 Permissions for the Hostdata Container

In DCE Version 1.1, the hostdata items reside in a *container* which is really a backing storage mechanism maintained by **dced**. On UNIX systems this is usually a file called *dcelocal*/**var/dced/Hostdata.db**. The file is owned by root and its access via **dced** is protected by an ACL. These ACL permissions control who can access the data in the container. Each DCE host has one hostdata Container ACL with the following name:

/.../*cellname*/**hosts**/*hostname*/**config/hostdata**

The hostdata Container ACL has the following permissions:

c (control) Modify the Container ACL

r (read) Read the list of hostdata items in the container

i (insert) Create new hostdata items

I (Insert) Although the **I** permission is present, it does not apply to host-data items. The permission applies to server control facilities, which are explained in Chapter 10.

Use the **dcecp acl** object to view or modify ACLs. For example, use the following operation to view the ACL for the hostdata container object on host **silver**:

```
dcecp> acl show /.:/hosts/silver/config/hostdata
{user hosts/silver/self criI}
{unauthenticated r}
{any_other r}
```

9.3.1.2 Permissions for the Hostdata Items

Each of the following host identity data items is protected by an ACL:

*/.../cellname/***hosts/***hostname/***config/hostdata/host_name**

*/.../cellname/***hosts/***hostname/***config/hostdata/cell_name**

*/.../cellname/***hosts/***hostname/***config/hostdata/cell_aliases**

*/.../cellname/***hosts/***hostname/***config/hostdata/post_processors**

Each ACL has the following permissions:

c (control) Modify the ACL

d (delete) Delete the item

p (purge) Delete the backing storage for an item

r (read)   Read an item's data

w (write)   Modify an item's data

Use the **acl** object to view or modify ACLs. For example, use the following operation to view the ACL for the **cell_aliases** hostdata item on host **silver**:

```
dcecp> acl show /.:/hosts/silver/config/hostdata/cell_aliases
{user hosts/silver/self cdprw}
{unauthenticated r}
{any_other r}
```

9.3.2 Modifying Host Cell Name Information

Using the **hostdata** object, you can add, change, and remove data items on DCE hosts. While administrators will find this useful for modifying a host's cell name or cell alias information, they can also operate on other data that is accessible on a host.

Each DCE host maintains a protected local copy of the cell name and cell aliases of the cell in which the host is registered. Hosts keep this information in a local file called *dcelocal/dce_cf.db* which is owned by **root**. A hust uses this information for authentication purposes—as part of its host identity information.

Although host cell name information tends to be fairly stable, there are circumstances where it is necessary to change this information:

- When a host moves to a different cell

- When a host's cell name changes or the cell name acquires an alias

When either of these situations occurs, however, it's usually not enough to just update the cell name information on the host. Cell name information must also be updated in CDS and in the DCE Security Service registry as well. For these purposes, **dcecp** provides the **host** and **cellalias** task objects which update cell name information wherever it needs to be changed.

When a host moves to a different cell, you should usually perform a **host unconfigure** operation to remove the host from one cell. Then run a **host configure** operation to establish the host in the new cell. For details on using the **host** task object, refer to Chapter 7.

- The **log list** operation returns a list of the components registered by the server. The **-comp** option allows you to also return a list of the subcomponents for one or more named components.

- The **log show** operation returns a list describing the current serviceability routing specifications for a server.

- The **log modify** operation sets message routing specifications for one or more specified servers.

For a complete description of the **dcecp log** object and the syntax for its supported operations, refer to the **log(8dce)** reference page.

The remainder of this section describes only the **log modify** operation and how to use it to establish routings for serviceability messages. Remember that routing is always set on a per-server basis and is recorded in the **log** object for each server.

The syntax for the **log modify** operation is

log modify {*string_binding_to_server* | *RPC_server_namespace_entry* } \
  {**-change** *serviceability_routing_specifications*}

You can specify multiple target servers as a space-separated list. Specify each server by supplying either the RPC string binding that describes the server's network location (*string_binding_to_server*) or a namespace entry of the server (*RPC_server_namespace_entry*). When specifying multiple servers, you can mix the forms in the same list.

A *serviceability_routing_specification* is a space-separated list of serviceability routing elements. No spaces are allowed within the specification of an individual routing element. Each routing element is a substring consisting of four fields containing Portable Character Set (PCS) data, as follows (shown in string syntax form):

severity:*output_form*:*destination*[:*application-defined*]

where:

severity	A message severity level: **FATAL**, **ERROR**, **WARNING**, **NOTICE**, or **NOTICE_VERBOSE**.
output_form	Specifies how messages of the associated severity level should be processed, and must be one of the following:

BINFILE	Write these messages as binary log entries
TEXTFILE	Write these messages as human-readable text
FILE	Equivalent to **TEXTFILE**
DISCARD	Do not record these messages
STDOUT	Write these messages as human-readable text to standard output
STDERR	Write these messages as human-readable text to standard error

Files written as **BINFILE**s can be read and manipulated with a set of log file APIs, which are described in the *OSF DCE Application Development Guide—Directory Services*.

The **BINFILE**, **TEXTFILE**, and **FILE** *output_form* specifiers may be followed by a 2-number specifier of the form

.gens.count

where:

gens	Is an integer that specifies the number of files (that is, generations) that should be kept
count	Is an integer specifying how many entries (that is, messages) should be written to each file

The multiple files are named by appending a **.** (dot) to the simple specified name, followed by the current generation number. When the number of entries in a file reaches the maximum specified by *count*, the file is closed, the generation number is incremented, and the next file is opened.

When the maximum number of files have been created and filled, the generation number is reset to **1**, and a new file with that number is created and written to (thus overwriting the already-existing file with the same name), and so on. Thus the files wrap around to their beginning, and the total number of log files never exceeds *gens*, although messages continue to be written as long as the program continues writing them.

destination   Specifies where the message should be sent, and is a pathname. You can leave this field blank if the *output_form* specified is **DISCARD**, **STDOUT**, or **STDERR**. The field can also contain a **%ld** string in the filename which, when the file is written, will be replaced by the process ID of the program that wrote the message(s). Filenames may *not* contain : (colon), ; (semicolons), % (percent sign), or the space character.

application-defined   Is used for application-specific information. Standard DCE programs ignore it.

9.4.2.1.1 String Syntax

The string syntax for a serviceability routing specification is

*severity***:***output_form***:***destination*[**:***application-defined*][**;** ...]

Note that you can define multiple routing specifications as a semi-colon separated list.

For example, this specification

FATAL:TEXTFILE:/dev/console;STDOUT:
ERROR:TEXTFILE.5.100:/tmp/errors
EXIT:DISCARD:
***:FILE:/tmp/svc-log**
NOTICE:BINFILE:/tmp/log%ld
WARNING:STDOUT:

instructs the serviceability mechanism to do the following:

- Send fatal error messages to the console and to standard output
- Send other error messages to a log-rolled file
- Discard normal exit reports
- Write all messages to a log file
- Send informational messages to a temporary binary log
- Send warnings to standard output

9.4.2.1.2 Tcl Syntax

The Tcl syntax for a serviceability routing specification is

{*severity output_form destination application-defined*}

where *severity*, *output_form*, *destination*, and *application-defined* are specified as previously described. In Tcl syntax, multiple routing specifications take the following form:

{ {*specification*} {*specification*} {*specification*} }

For example, the sample specification shown previously for string format would be expressed in Tcl syntax as follows:

```
{FATAL { {TEXTFILE /dev/console} STDOUT} }
{ERROR TEXTFILE.5.100 /tmp/errors}
{EXIT DISCARD}
{* FILE /tmp/svc-log}
{NOTICE BINFILE /tmp/log%ld }
{WARNING STDOUT {} }
```

9.4.2.2 Using a Routing File

If a file called *dce-local-path*/**var**/**svc**/**routing** exists, the contents of the file (if in the proper format) will be used to determine the routing of messages written by the serviceability mechanism.

The default location of the serviceability routing file is normally /opt/dcelocal/var/svc/routing. However, you can specify a different location for the file by setting the value of the environment variable **DCE_SVC_ROUTING_FILE** to the complete desired pathname.

The routing file contains lines that specify the routing desired for the various kinds of messages (based on message severity level). Each line consists of three fields as follows:

severity:*output_form*:*destination*[:*application-defined*][; ...]

You can supply multiple routings by specifying additional *output_form*:*destination* pairs as a semicolon-separated list.

In the routing file, blank lines beginning with the # character are treated as comments.

9.4.2.3 Using Environment Variables

Serviceability message routing can also be specified by the contents of certain environment variables. If you use environment variables, the routings you specify will override any conflicting routings specified by a routing file.

The routings are specified (on the basis of severity level) by putting the desired routing instructions in the following environment variables:

- **SVC_FATAL**
- **SVC_ERROR**
- **SVC_WARNING**
- **SVC_NOTICE**
- **SVC_NOTICE_VERBOSE**
- **SVC_BRIEF**

Each variable should contain a single string in the following format:

severity:*output_form*:*destination*[:*application-defined*][; ...]

You can supply multiple routings by specifying additional *output_form*:*destination* pairs as a semicolon-separated list.

Chapter 10

DCE Application Administration

As DCE evolves, commonly needed functions are being included in the DCE infrastructure. As an example, DCE Version 1.1 includes server control capabilities that can manage server operation and help servers exit in a controlled and efficient manner. Application developers can rely on these capabilities rather than implement special mechanisms to handle them independently in every server.

Moving commonly needed functions out of applications and into the DCE infrastructure provides important benefits. Applications can be smaller and easier to develop and maintain. Even more important, because applications are not encumbered with lots of special code, they are easier to reconfigure and reconnect with different kinds of clients. This adaptability is critical as organizations strive to keep up with changing business needs.

DCE applications have always had administrative aspects. Often, programs include the necessary functions to manage their own administrative needs, but this approach can be awkward and somewhat inflexible for administrators. Now, virtually all administrative functions are available to programmers and administrators alike through **dcecp**. This does not mean programmers no longer need to deal with these issues. We expect some programmers to provide scripts written with **dcecp** that configure client and server programs to start and stop under specified conditions.

Although this approach offers a convenient and consistent way to administer applications, it also creates an area where programming and administrative concerns overlap. Our discussions in this chapter will include this area of overlap, noting circumstances where administrative action might be needed.

10.1 Controlling Server Operation

The conventional notion of a DCE application server assumes that a server is running, waiting for client requests to service. While this is an effective model for some general server operations, it does not offer the flexibility needed by DCE applications. Commercial environments will likely have many kinds of servers. Some may need to be constantly available, while others may be needed only at certain times of the day. Still others may be needed on an infrequent or unpredictable basis.

An application programmer or administrator could solve these kinds of problems by writing a script or application that monitors server operation, automatically starting or restarting servers when necessary. Such solutions frequently rely on host utilities like startup and shutdown programs or schedulers like **cron**. However, this often requires administrators to log into separate system administration accounts on each host. Moreover, this approach places more burden on developers and administrators to devise independent server control mechanisms which may not be portable, especially in heterogeneous environments.

DCE solves some of these problems by providing a server control facility that offers a variety of ways to control DCE application servers. The server control facility is part of the DCE daemon (**dced**) so servers can rely on it wherever **dced** runs. Additionally, the facility's administration functions are accessible via **dcecp**, so administrators can use consistent (portable) methods to manage servers from any host where **dcecp** is available. Furthermore, access to the server control facility is authenticated, preventing unauthorized or accidental tampering of server control information.

The following sections show some common configuration needs and describe ways to configure and unconfigure servers, how to start and stop servers, and how to view server information.

10.1.1 Common Server Configuration Needs

Before you configure a server, you might need to perform some preliminary steps. If a server uses DCE authentication and authorization, its principal name must be registered with the DCE Security Service or run under the DCE identity of the parent process. For details on creating server accounts, see Chapter 31.

10.1.1.1 Naming Server Configuration Information

Server configuration information is accessible using a name of the form: */.../cellname/**hosts**/hostname/**config/srvrconf**/servername*. If you have the necessary permissions, you can use the global name to access the configuration database on a remote host (even a host in another cell). The following example shows configuration information for the **video_clip** server on host **krypton** in remote cell **/.../their_cell.goodco.com**:

```
dcecp> server show \
          /.../their_cell.goodco.com/hosts/krypton/config/srvrconf/video_clip
{uuid 2fa417e8-bb4c-11cd-831b-0000c08adf56}
{program {vclip}}
{arguments {-catalog}}
    .
    . (Output Omitted)
    .
```

The next example shows configuration information for the **video_clip** server on host **silver** in the local cell:

```
dcecp> server show /.:/hosts/silver/config/srvrconf/video_clip
{uuid 2fa417e8-bb4c-11cd-831b-0000c08adf56}
{program {vclip}}
{arguments {-catalog}}
    .
    . (Output Omitted)
    .
```

Each ACL is named for the server execution information it protects and has a name like the following:

*/.../cellname/***hosts***/hostname/***config/srvrexec***/server_name*

This ACL has the following permissions:

c (control)   Modify the ACL

r (read)   Read the server execution information

w (write)   Modify the server execution information

s (stop)   Stop the server

As an example, use the following operation to view the ACL for the server execution information for the **video_clip** server on host **silver**:

```
dcecp> acl show /.:/hosts/silver/config/srvrexec/video_clip
{user appl_admin crws}
{unauthenticated r}
{any_other r}
```

This ACL takes its default values from the container's Initial Object ACL. You can operate on the Initial Object ACL by using the **-io** option to **acl** operations. The following example shows the Initial Object ACL for the **video_clip** server:

```
dcecp> acl show /.:/hosts/silver/config/srvrexec -io
{unauthenticated r}
{any_other r}
```

10.1.2 Configuring Servers

Use the **server create** operation to make an application server accessible to the server control facility. Configuring a server means creating the information needed to start and control the server. Typically this includes a server's starting command line and arguments, along with other information needed to start DCE applications.

Some servers need to be available whenever a host system is running. For instance, you might want a server that provides information on host activity to start at the host boot time and run until the host shuts down. Other kinds of services might be needed or only for brief periods. The server control facility has an administrative interface that lets you specify some conditions for starting and stopping servers:

- **Explicit**: You can set a server so that you can explicitly start it whenever you want.

- **Boot**: You can set a server to start at boot time.

- **Automatic**: You can set a server to start on demand; that is, it starts whenever a client request for its services is received at the host system.

- **Failure**: You can set a server to start automatically if it exits unexpectedly.

The following example creates an entry for a fictitious video clip server named **video_clip** on the local host. For a remote host or a host in another cell, use the cell-relative or the global name. The program name **vclip** invokes the server that is located in the **/usr/local/bin** working directory. The server has a catalog mode that was set by specifying **-catalog** as the argument. The server uses the DCE Security Service, so the server has a principal name **Vclip_Srv_1**. The **-entryname** option specifies the entry name in the Cell Directory Service (CDS) where the server stores its binding information. The **-starton** option sets the server to start when **dced** receives an explicit **server start** operation that names the **video_clip** server. The **failure** attribute further specifies to restart the server if it exits with a status that is not successful. The **-services** option has annotation information to help administrators identify servers when this information is returned with **server show** operations. The **interface** attribute is needed because the DCE daemon copies this information into the host endpoint map when the server starts.

```
dcecp> server create /.:/hosts/silver/config/srvrconf/video_clip \
          -program {/usr/local/bin/vclip} \
          -directory {/tmp} -arguments {-catalog} \
          -principal {Vclip_Srv_1} \
          -entryname {/.:/subsys/applications/video_clip_1} \
          -starton {explicit failure} \
          -services {{annotation {Video Clip Catalog and Server}} \
          {interface {d860322b-d499-11cd-9dfb-0000c08adf56 1.0}}}
```

The next example configures the same server to start whenever the host system boots. The only difference from the preceding example is that the **-starton** option has a value of **boot**.

```
dcecp> server create /.:/hosts/silver/config/srvrconf/video_clip \
          -program {/usr/local/bin/vclip} \
          -directory {/tmp} -arguments {-catalog} \
          -principal {Vclip_Srv_1} \
          -entryname {/.:/subsys/applications/video_clip_1} \
          -starton {boot failure} \
          -services {{annotation {Video Clip Catalog and Server}} \
          {interface {d860322b-d499-11cd-9dfb-0000c08adf56 1.0}}}
```

The final configuration example sets the **video_clip** server to start whenever a client request for its services is received at the host system. The **-starton** option value is **auto**. Section 10.1.4 discusses the steps for disabling and enabling services.

```
dcecp> server create /.:/hosts/silver/config/srvrconf/video_clip \
          -program {/usr/local/bin/vclip} \
          -directory {/tmp} -arguments {-catalog} \
          -principal {Vclip_Srv_1} \
          -entryname {/.:/subsys/applications/video_clip_1} \
          -starton {boot failure} \
          -services {{annotation {Video Clip Catalog and Server}} \
          {interface {d860322b-d499-11cd-9dfb-0000c08adf56 1.0}}}
```

10.1.3 Listing and Retrieving Server Configuration Information

When you want to see a list of the names of servers configured on a particular host, use a **server catalog** operation, as shown. This operation doesn't show every server available on a host, just those that have configuration information stored in the server configuration database.

```
dcecp> server catalog /.:/hosts/silver
/.../my_cell.goodco.com/hosts/silver/config/srvrconf/video_clip
```

List the names of all the configured servers in a DCE cell by using a **foreach** command to repeat the **server catalog** operation for each host in a cell:

```
foreach h [directory list /.:/hosts]{
    echo [server catalog $h]
}
```

If you're unsure of the configuration information established for a server, you can view it using a **server show** operation, as shown. Use the **-executing** option to view information about a running server.

```
dcecp> server show /.:/hosts/silver/config/srvrconf/video_clip
{uuid d860322b-d499-11cd-9dfb-0000c08adf56 1.0}
{program {/usr/local/bin/vclip}}
{arguments {-catalog}}
{prerequisites {}}
{keytabs {683cf29a-e456-11cd-8f04-0000c08adf56}}
{services {{annotation "Video Clip Catalog and Server"}}}
{principals {Vclip_Srv_1}}
{starton {explicit failure}}
{uid 1441}
{gid 1000}
{dir {/tmp}}
```

10.1.4 Unconfiguring Servers

You can remove server configuration information from a host's configuration database by using a **server delete** operation. You would perform this operation, for instance, when a server moves to a different host. A **server delete** operation does not stop a server that is currently running.

The following example removes the **video_clip** server's configuration information from the configuration database on host **silver**:

dcecp> server delete /.:/hosts/silver/config/srvrconf/video_clip

10.1.5 Starting and Stopping Servers

Once a server has been appropriately configured, you can use a **server start** or **server stop** operation to start or stop the server remotely. For example, the following **server start** operation starts the explicit server **video_clip** on host **silver** in the local cell:

dcecp> **server start /.:/hosts/silver/config/srvrconf/video_clip**

The next example stops the explicit server **video_clip** on the local host **silver** in the local cell:

dcecp> **server stop video_clip**

10.1.6 Disabling and Enabling Services

You can prevent clients from using a service offered by a server—even when the server is running—by setting its services to disabled. When set to disabled, server endpoint information is not returned to requesting clients, thereby preventing clients from finding servers. Instead, clients receive a server status of **EPT not registered.** Clients that previously acquired the server endpoint can still communicate with the server, however.

When a server provides multiple interfaces, you can disable any one or more of its interfaces by specifying their interface identifiers. The following example disables one service of the **video_clip** server:

dcecp> **server disable /.:/hosts/silver/config/srvrexec/video_clip \
       -interface {d860322b-d499-11cd-9dfb-0000c08adf56 1.0}**

The next example enables the **vidsrv** service of the **video_clip** server after it has been disabled. This operation allows clients to acquire a server's endpoint.

dcecp> **server enable /.:/hosts/silver/config/srvrexec/video_clip \
       -interface {d860322b-d499-11cd-9dfb-0000c08adf56 1.0}**

You can disable or enable all services offered by a server by using a **server disable** or **server enable** command with no options. The following example disables all services offered by **bbs_server** on host **krypton**:

dcecp> **server disable /.:/hosts/krypton/config/srvrexec/bbs_server**

10.1.7 Extending Server Configurations

Some servers may require configuration information that is not supported by the set of attributes provided with your DCE software. You can add arbitrary information to your server configuration information by creating additional *extended registry attributes* ERAs with the **xattrschema** object.

For example, say you have a server that needs an attribute that specifies an object family. You create such an attribute by using the **xattrschema** object. The following example creates an ERA called **objfamily**. The operation specifies the permissions needed to query, update, test, and delete the ERA, and it specifies the ACL manager that supports the permissions.

dcecp> **xattrschema create **
      **/.:/hosts/silver/config/xattrschema/srvrconf/objfamily **
      **-attribute {{annotation {object family}} {encoding uuid} **
      {aclmgr {srvrconf r w r d}

Once you have created a new attribute, use a **server modify** operation, as explained Section 10.1.8, to insert the necessary data. More information about ERAs is provided in Chapter 32.

You can review the attributes associated with an ERA by using an **xattrschema show** operation as shown in the following example:

```
dcecp> xattrschema show
          /.:/hosts/silver/config/xattrschema/srvrconf/objfamily
{aclmgr {srvrconf {{query r} {update w} {test r} {delete d}}}}
{annotation {object family}}
{applydefs no}
{encoding uuid}
{intercell reject}
{multivalued yes}
{reserved no}
{scope {}}
{trigbind {}}
{trigtype none}
{unique no}
{uuid 1bef2222-e687-11cd-b74a-0000c08adf56}
```

ERAs in server configuration information are protected by two levels of ACLs. One ACL type protects the container in which the ERA resides. The second ACL type protects the individual ERA.

The ERA Container ACL is named as follows:

/.../*cellname*/**hosts**/*hostname*/**config/xattrschema**

The ERA Container ACL has the following permissions:

c (control)   Modify the Container ACL

r (read)   Read the ERA in the container

i (insert)   Create new ERA information

I (Insert)   Although the **I** permission is present, it does not apply to ERA items. The permission applies to server control facilities, which are explained in Section 10.1.1.3.

Use the **dcecp acl** object to view or modify the Container ACL. For example, the following operation views the ERA Container ACL on host **silver**:

```
dcecp> acl show /.:/hosts/silver/config/xattrschema
{user appl_admin criI}
{unauthenticated r}
{any_other r}
```

The ACL for an individual ERA is named as follows:

/.../*cellname*/**hosts**/*hostname*/**config/xattrschema/srvrconf**/*ERA_name*

ACLs on individual ERAs can prevent unauthorized principals from creating, reading, changing, or deleting ERA information. The following example shows permissions established for the **objfamily** ERA. In this example, the **c** permission has no effect because it was not assigned when the ERA was created with the **xattrschema create** operation. All users can query and test the ERA. Only the user named **appl_admin** can also update and delete the ERA.

```
dcecp> acl show /.:/hosts/silver/config/xattrschema/srvrconf/objfamily
{user appl_admin crwd}
{unauthenticated cr}
{any_other cr}
```

This ACL takes its default values from the container's Initial Object ACL. You can operate on the Initial Object ACL by using the **-io** option to **acl** operations. The following example shows the Initial Object ACL for the **xattrschema** container on host **silver**:

```
dcecp> acl show /.:/hosts/silver/config/xattrschema -io
{unauthenticated cr}
{any_other cr}
```

10.1.8 Changing Server Configurations

Sometimes you might want to change a server's configuration information. For instance, you want to change the **-starton** attribute from **boot** to **explicit** so that you can control the server manually.

To change the normal server configuration attributes, you must first delete all of the existing attributes and then create new ones. Avoid losing the current information by first using a **server show** operation to display it on your screen.

The steps are illustrated in the following example which uses a **server show** operation to capture the current server configuration information. The **server delete** operation removes the configuration information, and a **server create** operation inserts the new **-starton** attribute along with the remaining server configuration information.

```
dcecp> server show /.:/hosts/silver/config/srvrconf/video_clip
{uuid d860322b-d499-11cd-9dfb-0000c08adf56 1.0}
{program {/usr/local/bin/vclip}}
{arguments {-catalog}}
{prerequisites {}}
{keytabs {683cf29a-e456-11cd-8f04-0000c08adf56}}
{services {{annotation "Video Clip Catalog and Server"}}}
{principals {Vclip_Srv_1}}
{starton {explicit failure}}
{uid 1441}
{gid 1000}
{dir {/tmp}}
dcecp> server delete /.:/hosts/silver/config/srvrconf/video_clip
dcecp> server create /.:/hosts/silver/config/srvrconf/video_clip \
          -program /usr/local/bin/vclip \
          -directory /tmp -arguments {-catalog} \
          -principal Vclip_Srv_1 \
          -entryname /.:/subsys/applications/video_clip_1 \
          -starton {explicit failure} \
          -services {{annotation "Video Clip Catalog and Server"}}
```

You can directly change ERA information by using a **server modify** operation. The following example changes a server's ERA called **objfamily** to contain new values. This operation assumes the ERA has already been created using an **xattrschema create** operation described in Section 10.1.17.

```
dcecp> server modify /.:/hosts/silver/config/srvrconf/video_clip \
          -change {objfamily {c09dcc40-e4f4-11cd-bd59-0000c08adf56}}
```

10.1.9 Checking Whether Servers Are Running

You can check whether a particular server is running by performing a **server ping** operation. This might be a convenient test when some client users report they can't commmunicate with a server. The **server ping** operation communicates with the named server to test its presence, returning a **1** is a server is listening and a **0** if it is not listening. The following example tests whether the **video_clip** server is running:

```
dcecp> server ping /.:/hosts/silver/config/srvrconf/video_clip
1
```

10.2 Managing Client/Server Binding Information

In a DCE environment, clients and their servers frequently reside on different hosts in a network, so clients need a way to find servers.

Clients need three pieces of information to communicate with a server:

- The host name (or network address) of the host where the server is running

- The name of the network transport the server is using

- The communication port (endpoint) the server is using for client communications

Of course, an application programmer could simply hardcode a server's location information (also called *binding information*) into the client side of the application where it is immediately available for use. However, this approach requires that a programmer have advance knowledge of precise network details such as host names and available port numbers. Furthermore, servers with hardcoded binding information do not easily adapt to configuration changes. If you move a server to a different host, you need to recompile all of the clients with the server's new host name. So DCE provides more flexible ways for clients to obtain server bindings.

The standard way for clients to find servers is by using CDS and the server host's endpoint map. Figure 10-1 provides a high-level example of this method, showing how a fictitious dictionary client application on host **larry** finds a dictionary server on host **curly**.

Figure 10–1. Server Binding Information

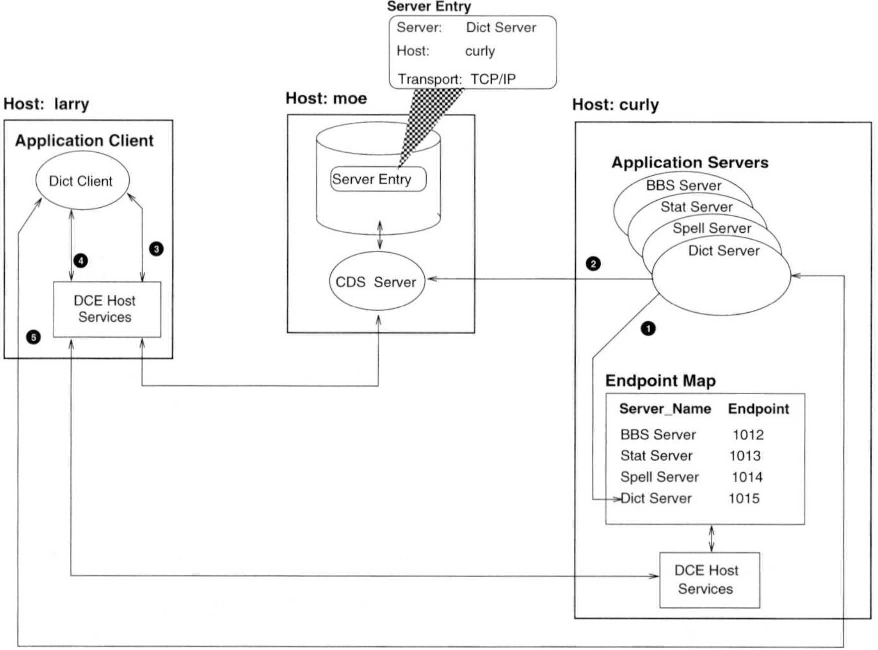

1. When the dictionary server starts up, DCE host software assigns the server a communications port (endpoint), which clients will use to communicate with this server. Here, the endpoint is TCP/IP port 1015. The DCE host software also places the server identification information along with the current endpoint in the host's endpoint map.

2. The dictionary server then advertises its availability to clients by placing (*exporting*) its host name (usually it's the host address) and the transport it uses to a server entry in CDS.

3. When the dictionary client makes a call to a remote procedure provided by the server, the DCE software on the client queries the CDS server to find the dictionary server's host name and the transport.

4. The client system's host software then queries the endpoint map on host **curly** to find the dictionary server's endpoint (port 1015).

5. Equipped with all the necessary binding information, the host services on host **larry** transmit the remote procedure call directly to port 1015 on host **curly**.

Although we've omitted some details in this high-level example, the figure still shows the major binding activities performed by clients and servers. That is, servers place their binding information in CDS and in the host endpoint map where clients look for it. There are other ways for clients to find servers and there are variations on the mechanism we've described. But these alternatives are generally controlled by the applications themselves rather than through conventional DCE administration facilities like **dcecp**.

This section discussed one basic client/server binding mechanism. The following sections examine the roles played by the endpoint map and by CDS. We'll also discuss specific administration tasks for managing binding information in endpoint maps and in CDS.

10.3 Using the Endpoint Map for Easy Application Development and Administration

Remote clients can find a server by using the server host's endpoint map to determine the server's communication endpoint. But how do remote clients know where to find the endpoint map itself? They know because the endpoint map is always accessible at a *well-known* endpoint (that is, it is always the same endpoint) on each host so clients can easily find it.

When hosts support multiple transports, the endpoint map *listens* on one port for each transport. In the IP address family (both TCP and UDP), the endpoint map process listens on port 135. In the Domain Domain Sockets (DDS) address family, it listens on port 12. In the DECnet NSP address family, it listens on port 69. A complete list of the protocol sequences and well-known endpoints used by the endpoint mapper service can be found in the header file **/opt/dcelocal/share/include/dce/ep.idl**.

Note that not all hosts support all transports. DCE software tries to ensure that at least one transport is shared between a client and a server.

While well-known endpoints provide convenient access to some critical servers, for most servers they are impractical. That's because some address families have a limited number of endpoints and well-known endpoints can be assigned only by a central administrative authority. So most servers use *dynamic endpoints*. When a server starts up, the RPC runtime library gets an available endpoint from the operating system and registers it in the host endpoint map.

Because a server can be assigned a different endpoint each time it starts, the endpoint information is stored in the endpoint map rather than CDS, which is a repository for more stable information; namely, the server's host address and the transports it uses. As long as the server stays on the same machine, host and transport information need not be updated, which tends to reduce bottlenecks at CDS.

This scheme makes application development and administration easier because it reduces the need to manage endpoints. Servers needn't worry about passing dynamic endpoints to clients. Furthermore, unless a server moves to a new host, or removes or adds a transport, it doesn't even have to update the information in CDS.

10.3.1 Automatic Endpoint Map Administration

Each server that uses the endpoint map stores a set of information in the endpoint map when it starts up. The information includes Universal Unique Identifiers (UUIDs) for objects and interfaces offered by the server, an annotation string, and other fields.

The endpoint map resides on disk in *dcelocal***/var/dced/Ep.db** and *dcelocal***/var/dced/Srvrexec.db**. After a system reboot, DCE-based servers restart and reregister with the endpoint mapper service, so the database files need to be deleted before the DCE daemon starts. This happens automatically on most systems.

DCE-based servers normally need to register with the endpoint mapper service on startup and unregister on termination. If any servers exit without unregistering, the endpoint map may contain stale entries.

DCE Version 1.1 provides server control facilities that help servers unregister and avoid leaving stale entries in the endpoint map. Servers that don't use these facilities (older servers, for example) are more likely to leave stale entries if they exit unexpectedly. So periodically, the DCE daemon (**dced**) purges stale entries by scanning the endpoint map, ''pinging'' each server that is registered, and deleting entries for servers that do not respond.

The background process of removing stale entries is not intended to be highly responsive. It is not intended to replace the need for servers to unregister themselves from the endpoint map when they no longer service RPCs. Rather, this processing is intended only to clean up after a server failure.

While the behavior of the pinging/purging mechanism is implementation dependent, in a typical implementation the database is scanned (that is, servers are pinged and stale entries removed) only infrequently; for example, a few times an hour. Once a ping to a server fails, the server is pinged several times over a shorter interval; for example, every 5 minutes. If the server continues to not respond, the **dced** process determines that its entry is ''stale'' and removes it from the database. Ultimately, the rate at which stale server entries are detected and purged depends on the number of stale entries in the database; the more stale entries, the longer it takes to detect and purge the stale entries.

10.3.2 Restricting Endpoints

You can restrict the assignment of endpoints (ports) for DCE servers and clients to a specific set. This is useful if your environment has applications other than DCE that are designed to use certain endpoints, and you do not want to be concerned about DCE servers or clients monopolizing them.

The facility is activated by setting the **RPC_RESTRICTED_PORTS** environment variable with the list of endpoints to which dynamic assignment should be restricted before starting a client or server application. **RPC_RESTRICTED_PORTS** governs only the dynamic assignment of server ports by the RPC runtime. It does not affect well-known endpoints.

The following example restricts servers to using TCP/IP endpoints ranging from 5000 to 5110, and 5500 to 5521. It restricts UDP/IP endpoints to the range of 6500 to 7000.

```
% set RPC_RESTRICTED_PORTS \
    ncacn_ip_tcp[5000-5110,5500-5521]:ncadg_ip_udp[6500-7000]
```

To use **RPC_RESTRICTED_PORTS** for DCE servers such as CDS, set the environment variable each time before starting your cell.

Note that this facility does not add any security to RPC and is not intended as a security feature. It merely facilitates configuring a network ''firewall'' to allow incoming calls to DCE servers.

10.3.3 Viewing Information in the Endpoint Map

For the most part, the endpoint map on each host takes care of itself, purging stale entries when necessary and removing the endpoint information each time the host reboots. So there's really no administration needed for the endpoint map.

However, when client/server communication problems arise, the information stored in the endpoint map might be useful to administrators, particularly for determining whether servers are supplying the correct endpoint information to clients. In this case, you can use the **endpoint** object to view endpoint map information. Besides its use in troubleshooting, you can also use the **endpoint** object for other specialized server operations such as adding new object UUIDs to existing mappings.

Endpoints are not protected by ACLs. This means anyone who can run **dcecp** can use an **endpoint show** operation on their host to view endpoint information on any other host in the cell. Other endpoint operations, such as creating or deleting endpoints, can be performed only by users who are logged into the local host. No other special privileges, such as system administrator or root privileges, are needed for local access to endpoint information.

You can view information stored in a host's endpoint map database by using an **endpoint show** operation. The following example shows the endpoint map information for the **video_clip** server on a remote host **megazoid**. Omit the *hostname* argument to operate on the local endpoint map.

```
dcecp>  endpoint show /.:/hosts/megazoid \
            -interface {2fa417e8-bb4c-11cd-831b-0000c08adf56 1.0} \
            {{object 99ff4fb8-c042-11cd-91cd-0000c08adf56} \
            {interface {2fa417e8-bb4c-11cd-831b-0000c08adf56 1.0}} \
            {binding {ncacn_ip_tcp 130.105.1.227 1028}} \
            {annotation {Text Development Utilities}}} \
```

You can view all of the endpoints in an endpoint map by not using any options with the **endpoint show** operation.

10.4 Managing Server Entries, Groups, and Profiles in CDS

An endpoint map acts as a directory of servers on a host. Similarly, CDS acts as a directory of servers in the cell. In the first part of this chapter, we gave a high-level look at how applications can use CDS to store relatively stable binding information such as a server's name, its host address, and the transports over which the server is available. In this section, we'll show how to use CDS facilities for organizing your servers and other distributed objects in meaningful ways.

Many of the operations discussed in the following sections operate on CDS directories that are protected by ACLs against unauthorized access. For detailed information about ACLs and CDS see Chapter 16.

10.4.1 Using Unique Server Entry Names to Identify Individual Servers and Objects

We know that servers store their binding information in CDS where clients can find it. But so far, we've been treating CDS like a black box. If a DCE cell consisted of just a few servers or objects and a handful of users, CDS could be as simple as a data file assessible to both servers and clients. Finding unique names for objects would probably not pose a big problem. And you could probably even devise some effective scheme for protecting objects from unauthorized use. But DCE cells can include many hundreds or even thousands of objects. Large cells will likely contain many similar or even identical servers that need convenient and effective ways to offer their services to clients.

DCE CDS answers this need by providing a hierarchical (tree-structured) name system that servers use to store binding information. CDS acts much like a hierarchical file system of directories that stores names and other information instead of files. You can build on its hierarchical structure, imposing directory names that can correspond to your company's organizational structure.

Servers have CDS names like **/.:/admin/finance/payroll/check_writer**. When this **check_writer** server exports its server entry name to CDS, CDS stores it in a directory named **/.:/admin/finance/payroll**. Consequently, clients won't confuse this **check_writer** with another **check_writer** named **/.:/admin/finance/accts_payable/check_writer**. Thus, unique server entry names fill a critical administration need, providing a way to access and control individual servers.

Part 4 of this book provides more information about CDS and the structure and uses of CDS names. For our current purposes, it's enough to know how and why CDS directory names help make potentially identical server entries unique.

While servers themselves often manage exporting and removing their names and binding information from CDS, sometimes administrators need to manually add, change, or remove binding information. For instance, when a server host machine crashes unexpectedly and stays offline for a long time, its resident servers cannot remove their entry names and binding information from CDS. Clients can waste time looking for these phantom servers. The DCE control program provides the **rpcentry** object that you can use to manage server entry names and their binding information in CDS.

Before we get to the actual management tasks, let's examine a server entry to see exactly what it is we'll be managing. Figure 10-2 shows possible information in a server entry.

Figure 10–2. Possible Information in a Server Entry

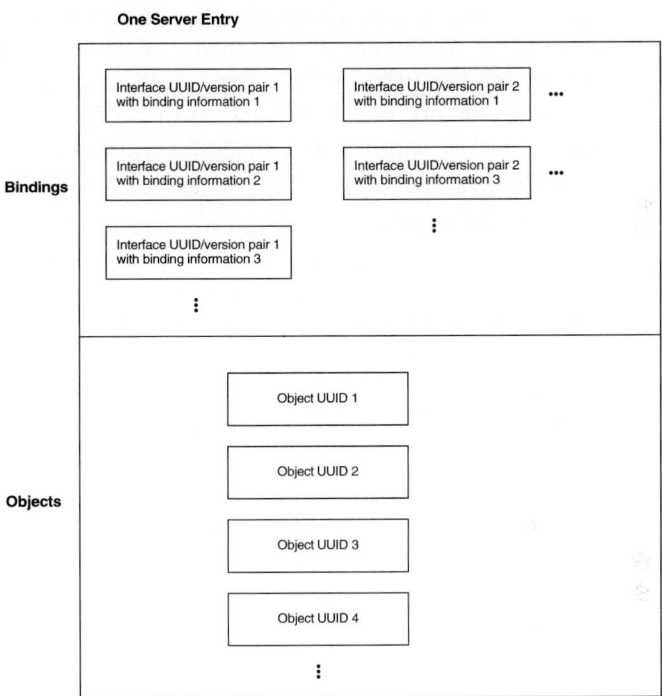

The top part of Figure 10-2 contains bindings. Each binding consists of an interface identifier and a binding. The interface identifier identifies an interface offered by the server, and its binding information indicates the host address and network transport to use to access that interface. The following example of a binding (shown in **dcecp** syntax) indicates the server is on the host with internet address 120.101.13.157 and is available using the User Datagram Protocol (UDP):

```
{nacdg_ip_udg 120.101.13.157}
```

When an interface identifier is available over several transports, the server entry contains bindings (one binding for each transport). Servers can offer more than one interface. Multiple interfaces can be available through a single endpoint. That is, different interfaces can have the same bindings.

The lower part of the figure contains object UUIDs. Object UUIDs offer additional information to clients; they identify specific objects or resources managed by the server. For instance, one print server offers printers on floor 2 while another print server offers printers on floor 1. In this case, object UUIDs let clients select printers on the appropriate floor. In other words, object UUIDs help clients distinguish from among otherwise identical services.

Although application servers can manage their own server entries in CDS, you may find it more convenient (and more straightforward) to manually add, remove, or change information in a server entry. There are four methods for managing server entries in CDS:

- Server entry names can be hardcoded into an application. You can change server entry information in the source code, but you need to recompile and rerun the application before the entry names take effect.

- Server entry names can be stored as the **entryname** attribute of the server's configuration information (using the **server** object) where it's accessible to the application. This is more convenient than recompiling but, more importantly, this method places the server's entry name in a standard (platform independent) place where administrators can see it too. You might need to restart an application to use this method, however.

- Server entry names can be passed to an application through environment variables or arguments. While these are effective methods and they are more convenient than recompiling, they are not platform-independent. This means you might need different approaches on different operating systems.

- Server entry names can be directly managed in CDS by using the DCE control program's **rpcserver** object. This manual method does not require recompiling or restarting applications.

The next sections discuss how to use the **rpcserver** object to manually manage server entries in CDS.

10.4.1.1 Creating a Server Entry in CDS

Often, servers will create their own entries in CDS either when they initialize or when they are configured after installation. But sometimes, you might want to create a server entry manually. When you create a server entry, it is empty; it doesn't contain any interface or binding information.

One reason to create an empty server entry is to establish ownership of the entry. Server entries are owned by the creator. If a server creates an entry, the server can also delete the entry later. You can preempt such a circumstance by creating the entry yourself. Later, the server exports its bindings to the existing server entry (provided that the ACL allows this).

Use an **rpcentry create** operation to create an empty server entry as in the following, which creates one named **/.:/subsys/applications/bbs_server**. The CDS directory **/.:/subsys/applications** must already exist for this operation to succeed.

```
dcecp>  rpcentry create /.:/subsys/applications/bbs_server
```

10.4.1.2 Deleting a Server Entry from CDS

Because server entries generally contain stable server binding information, they tend to stay around rather than be deleted. Even when a server goes away for a short time, say, overnight, it might not be practical to remove its entry. But when a server goes away for a long time, you can avoid the client expense of trying to use the phantom server by removing the server's entry from CDS.

Use an **rpcentry delete** operation to remove a server entry from CDS as shown in the following example:

```
dcecp>  rpcentry delete /.:/subsys/applications/bbs_server
```

10.4.1.3 Exporting Binding Information to a Server Entry in CDS

Servers usually export their own binding information to CDS when they initialize or when they are configured after installation. But sometimes, binding information may have been removed for some reason or by accident and you want to restore it. Or another transport has been added and you want to export the binding for the new transport.

You can manually export server binding information to a server entry by using an **rpcentry export** operation. If the entry does not already exist, the **rpcentry export** operation creates it provided the directory already exists and you have the necessary permissions.

The following example illustrates exporting a server's binding information to a server entry named **/.:/subsys/applications/bbs_server**. The object UUID identifies the data file resource used by **bbs_server**.

```
dcecp> rpcentry export /.:/subsys/applications/bbs_server \
          -interface {458ffcbe-98c1-11cd-bd93-0000c08adf56 1.0} \
          -binding {ncacn_ip_tcp 130.105.1.227} \
          -object {76030c42-98d5-11cd-88bc-0000c08adf56}
```

10.4.1.4 Importing Binding Information from a Server Entry in CDS

Application client programs can automatically import server binding information from CDS and use it in their quest to find and communicate with a server. But occasionally, an administrator might want to import a binding. For instance, a client might lack access to CDS but it could still communicate with the server if you supplied it with a valid binding.

Use an **rpcentry import** operation to return a server's binding information, as follows:

```
dcecp> rpcentry import /.:/subsys/applications/bbs_server \
          -interface {458ffcbe-98c1-11cd-bd93-0000c08adf56 1.0}
{ncacn_ip_tcp 130.105.1.227}
```

10.4.1.5 Viewing Information in a Server Entry

When clients are having difficulty communicating with servers, you might want to see what binding information is contained in a server entry as a troubleshooting step. Or say you are adding object UUIDs to server entries and you wonder whether a server entry has been overlooked. You can use an **rpcentry show** operation to view the information in a server entry as illustrated in the following example. The returned information includes the interface identifier, two bindings over which the server can be reached, and an object UUID of a resource maintained by the server.

```
dcecp> rpcentry show /.:/subsys/applications/bbs_server
{458ffcbe-98c1-11cd-bd93-0000c08adf56 1.0
   {ncadg_ip_udp 130.105.1.227}
   {ncacn_ip_tcp 130.105.1.227}}
{76030c42-98d5-11cd-88bc-0000c08adf56}
```

10.4.1.6 Removing Binding Information from a Server Entry in CDS

Occasionally, you might want to remove binding information from a server entry. If a server host crashes, its servers cannot remove their server entries from CDS. To prevent clients from trying to communicate with these phantom servers, you should unexport the bindings from CDS manually. Unlike the **endpoint delete** operation, this operation does not remove the entry name from CDS.

Use an **rpcentry unexport** operation to remove server binding information as shown in the following example. Notice that the object UUID is not removed from the server entry unless you specify it as an option to the **unexport** operation.

```
dcecp> rpcentry unexport /.:/subsys/applications/bbs_server \
         -interface {458ffcbe-98c1-11cd-bd93-0000c08adf56 1.0}
dcecp> rpcentry show /.:/subsys/applications/bbs_server
{76030c42-98d5-11cd-88bc-0000c08adf56}
```

10.4.2 Using Group Entries to Help Balance Server Workloads

When a client queries CDS for a server binding, the request includes the name of the entry to look in for the binding. When only one server offers the client's requested service, CDS will return the same binding for every client request for this service. While this model works fine for limited client requests, it can cause service bottlenecks when many client requests converge on one server. Applications can avoid bottlenecks by providing multiple servers to service large numbers of client requests. Server entry names alone don't provide a convenient way to distribute client requests evenly among multiple servers because you'd have to explicitly direct each client to a particular server. So CDS provides *group entries* as a convenient mechanism for distributing the client load across multiple servers.

A CDS group entry gathers related servers together under a common group name. Group entries contain members that are generally pointers to server entries, but members can point to other group entries, too. When a client requests a binding from a group entry, CDS returns, at random, one of the pointers contained in the group entry. If the entry picked at random is another group entry, CDS doesn't return that. Instead CDS goes to that group and picks another random member, continuing until a server entry is returned. This model requires that any group member can service the client request. Figure 10-3 shows how a group entry contains members that point to other groups and to server entries.

Figure 10–3. Possible Mappings of a Group

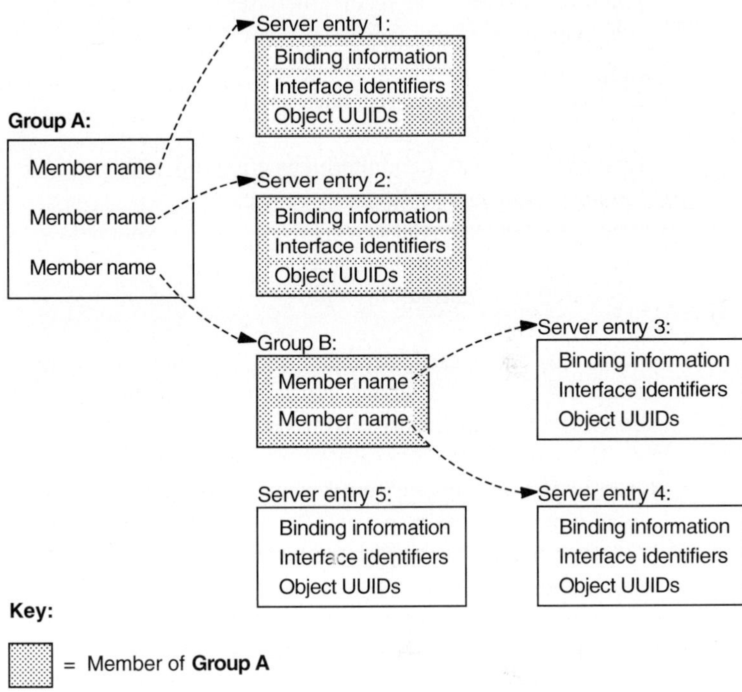

Now, let's see how group entries help balance a workload. Consider an organization with 12 identical laser printers equally spread among three departments. The following group entry examples show how each group entry name returns any one of the four printers assigned to its own department:

Group entry name: /.:/admin/finance/accts_payable_printers
/.:/admin/finance/accts_payable/laser_10
/.:/admin/finance/accts_payable/laser_11
/.:/admin/finance/accts_payable/laser_12
/.:/admin/finance/accts_payable/laser_13

Group entry name: /.:/admin/finance/accts_receivable_printers
/.:/admin/finance/accts_receivable/laser_10
/.:/admin/finance/accts_receivable/laser_11
/.:/admin/finance/accts_receivable/laser_12
/.:/admin/finance/accts_receivable/laser_13

Group entry name: /.:/admin/finance/payroll_printers
/.:/admin/finance/payroll/laser_10
/.:/admin/finance/payroll/laser_11
/.:/admin/finance/payroll/laser_12
/.:/admin/finance/payroll/laser_13

You could temporarily make one department's printers available to another group by adding its group name to the group entry of the other group as shown in the next group entry example:

Group entry name: /.:/admin/finance/accts_payable_printers
/.:/admin/finance/accts_payable/laser_10
/.:/admin/finance/accts_payable/laser_11
/.:/admin/finance/accts_payable/laser_12
/.:/admin/finance/accts_payable/laser_13
/.:/admin/finance/accts_receivable_printers

The configuration in the preceding example means the clients in accounts payable can use the printers in accounts receivable 20% of the time. You could offer a higher percentage of use by adding server entry names rather than the group name. The next group entry example shows a situation where the clients in accounts payable can use the printers in accounts receivable 50% of the time. However, don't try to increase the percentage of use by including a group name multiple times because you'll get an error.

Group entry name: /.:/admin/finance/accts_payable_printers
/.:/admin/finance/accts_payable/laser_10
/.:/admin/finance/accts_payable/laser_11
/.:/admin/finance/accts_payable/laser_12
/.:/admin/finance/accts_payable/laser_13
/.:/admin/finance/accts_receivable/laser_10
/.:/admin/finance/accts_receivable/laser_11
/.:/admin/finance/accts_receivable/laser_12
/.:/admin/finance/accts_receivable/laser_13

Although application servers can manage their own group entries in CDS, you may find it more convenient (and more straightforward) to manually add, remove, or change server information in a group entry. Like managing server entries, there are several methods for managing group entries in CDS:

- Group entry names can be hardcoded into an application. You can change group entry information in the source code, but you need to recompile and rerun the application before the entry names take effect.

- Group entry names can be passed to an application through environment variables or arguments. These are more convenient methods than recompiling, but you might need to restart an application to use either method.

- Group entry names can be directly managed in CDS by using the DCE control program's **rpcgroup** object. This manual method does not require recompiling or restarting applications.

The next sections discuss how to use the **rpcgroup** object to manually manage group entries in CDS.

10.4.2.1 Creating a New Group Entry in CDS

You can create an empty group entry in CDS by using an **rpcgroup create** operation. While group creation is frequently performed by applications that first use a group entry, creating an entry yourself establishes you as the owner of the entry. As the owner, you have ultimate control over who can export and manage information in the entry.

To create an empty group entry in CDS, use an **rpcgroup create** operation as in the following example:

dcecp> **rpcgroup create /.:/subsys/applications/admin_bbs_servers**

10.4.2.2 Adding a Member to a Group Entry in CDS

You can use an **rpcgroup add** operation to add a member to a group entry. If the group entry does not exist, the operation creates the group entry and adds the member. The member can be a server entry or another group entry. Note that no operations check whether the members you add actually exist. This lets you configure the namespace even before servers are up and running.

To add a member to the **/.:/subsys/applications/admin_bbs_servers** group entry in CDS, use an **rpcgroup add** operation as in the following example:

dcecp> **rpcgroup add /.:/subsys/applications/admin_bbs_servers \\
      -member /.:/subsys/applications/bbs_server4**

10.4.2.3 Viewing the Members of a Group Entry

You can list the members of a group entry by using an **rpcgroup list** operation. This is useful for troubleshooting or for just seeing how servers are distributed in group entries.

To list the members of a group entry in CDS, use an **rpcgroup list** operation, as shown in the following example, which lists the members of the group **/.:/subsys/applications/admin_bbs_servers**:

```
dcecp> rpcgroup list /.:/subsys/applications/admin_bbs_servers
/.../my_cell.goodco.com/subsys/applications/bbs_server3
/.../my_cell.goodco.com/subsys/applications/bbs_server4
```

10.4.2.4 Importing Binding Information from a Group Entry in CDS

Application client programs can automatically import server binding information from CDS and use it in their quest to find and communicate with a server. But occasionally, an administrator might want to import a binding. In the case where a client lacks access to CDS, it could still communicate with the server if you supplied the client with a valid binding.

You can use an **rpcgroup import** operation to return a server's binding information. You must specify an interface by using the **-interface** option as shown in the following example:

```
dcebcp>  rpcgroup import /.:/subsys/applications/admin_bbs_servers \
              -interface {458ffcbe-98c1-11cd-88bc-0000c08adf56 1.0}
{ncacn_ip_tcp 130.105.1.227}
```

You can use other options such as **-version** and **-object** to further specify a binding. Use the **-max** option to limit the number of bindings returned.

10.4.2.5 Removing Members from a Group Entry in CDS

Over time, organizational changes can require you to redeploy servers in your DCE cell. You might, for instance, want to move server entries from one group entry into another.

Use an **rpcgroup remove** operation to remove one or more members from a group. The following example removes **bbs_server3** from the group **/.:/subsys/applications/admin_bbs_servers**:

```
dcecp>  rpcgroup remove /.:/subsys/applications/admin_bbs_servers \
              -member /.../my_cell.goodco.com/subsys/applications/bbs_server3
dcecp>  rpcgroup list /.:/subsys/applications/admin_bbs_servers
/.../my_cell.goodco.com/subsys/applications/bbs_server4
/.../my_cell.goodco.com/subsys/applications/bbs_server5
/.../my_cell.goodco.com/subsys/applications/bbs_server6
```

10.4.2.6 Deleting a Group Entry from CDS

Organization changes or server redeployments can make some groups obsolete. When you want to remove a group entry from CDS, use an **rpcgroup delete** operation. The following example illustrates removing an obsolete group entry called **/.:/subsys/admin/temporaries/wp_services** from CDS:

dcecp> **rpcgroup delete /.:/subsys/admin/temporaries/wp_services**

10.4.3 Using Profiles to Direct Client Searches for Servers

Group entries offer clients a random choice from among multiple available services. Although a group entry can help in load balancing and resource allocation, its random nature resists fine tuning. Furthermore, it doesn't offer a way to prioritize servers for use by particular clients.

Profiles offer a complimentary way to organize servers because you can prioritize the search order of the profile members. (These were called *elements* in previous DCE versions.) Members identify servers by providing the following information:

- Interface identifier

  This field is the key to the profile. The interface identifier consists of the interface UUID and the interface version numbers.

- Member name

  The entry name of one of the following kinds of directory service entries:

  — A server entry for a server offering the requested RPC interface

  — A group corresponding to the requested RPC interface

  — A profile

- Priority value

  The priority value (0 is the highest priority; 7 is the lowest priority) is designated by the creator of a profile member to help determine the search order to select among like-priority members at random.

- Annotation string

  The annotation string enables you to identify the purpose of the profile member. The annotation can be any textual information; for example, an interface name associated with the interface identifier or a description of a service or resource associated with a group.

  Unlike the interface identifier field, the annotation string is not a search key.

Profiles are flexible; they contain members that can point to server entries, groups, and to other profiles. Profiles can also contain a special member called a *default profile member*. This optional member should point to a default profile, usually a comprehensive backup profile that can serve the needs of most users in an organization. Figure 10-4 shows some possible mappings of a profile.

You can use an **rpcprofile import** operation to return a server's binding information. You must specify an interface by using the **-interface** option as shown in the following example:

```
dcecp> rpcprofile import /.:/subsys/applications/wards_profile \
         -interface {458ffcbe-98c1-11cd-88bc-0000c08adf56 1.0}
{ncacn_ip_tcp 130.105.1.202}
{ncacn_ip_tcp 130.105.1.227}
```

You can use other options such as **-version** and **-object** to further specify a binding. Use the **-max** option to limit the number of bindings returned, as shown in the following example:

```
dcecp> rpcprofile import /.:/subsys/applications/wards_profile \
         -interface {458ffcbe-98c1-11cd-88bc-0000c08adf56 1.0} \
         -max 1
{ncacn_ip_tcp 130.105.1.202}
```

10.4.3.5 Removing Members from a Profile Entry in CDS

Over time, organizational changes can require you to redeploy servers in your DCE cell. You might, for instance, want to move server entries from one profile entry into another.

Use an **rpcprofile remove** operation to remove one or more members from a profile. In the following example, the **rpcprofile remove** operation removes member **/.:/subsys/applications/admin_bbs_servers** from the profile **/.:/subsys/applications/wards_profile**:

```
dcecp> rpcprofile remove /.:/subsys/applications/wards_profile \
         -member /.:/subsys/applications/admin_bbs_servers \
         -interface {458ffcbe-98c1-11cd-88bc-0000c08adf56 1.0}
```

10.4.3.6 Deleting a Profile Entry from CDS

Organization changes or server redeployments can make some profiles obsolete. When you want to remove a profile entry from CDS, use an **rpcprofile delete** operation. The following example illustrates removing an obsolete profile entry called **/.:/subsys/admin/temporaries/74232_profile** from CDS:

dcecp> **rpcprofile delete /.:/subsys/admin/temporaries/74232_profile**

10.5 Client Administration

So far, this chapter has focused on server administration issues. We've seen how to control some server operations, and how to store server binding information in CDS and in the host endpoint map where clients can find it. This section discussses the administration needs of application clients. Although client administration is very simple— there are just two related operations—it's an essential step in getting clients and servers working together.

We know that CDS is a hierarchical system of directories that stores server binding information in the form of server entries. We also know that CDS offers group entries and profile entries as a way to direct clients to appropriate servers. But how do clients know where to begin looking for a server?

As we discussed earlier in this chapter, servers register interfaces and their bindings in CDS. Each interface-binding combination is registered under a server entry name. When a client makes a remote procedure call, it passes a server entry name (or a group or profile entry name) to CDS along with the UUID of an interface that offers the remote procedure. CDS uses the server entry name (or group or profile entry name) as a starting point in the search for a binding that contains an interface UUID and version matching that passed by the client. This method presumes the client has previously acquired the server entry name (or group or profile name) used by the server.

Getting clients to use an appropriate server entry name is a 2-step process:

1. Determine what entry name a client should use.

2. Pass the name to the client program.

Note that a client uses whatever name you supply. The client program cannot distinguish whether the name is a server entry name or group entry name or profile entry name. To the client, all of these names look and behave the same.

10.5.1 Determining the Entry Name

You need to know the entry name exported by a server so you can provide it to client programs when you configure them. Here, we're just calling this name an entry name, but it can be a server entry name or group entry name or profile entry name. Your application documentation should help you decide which kind of entry to use.

If you are installing and configuring the server and client parts of an application, make a note of the server's entry name when you configure the server.

If you are not installing or configuring the server (for instance, the server was previously installed), you might need to do some detective work to determine the name to use. There are several places you can look.

If a server uses the server control facility described earlier in this chapter, you can probably use a **dcecp server show** operation to reveal its entry name. Of course, this means you need to know the server's object name on the host where the server resides. You can see all of the server object names on a host by using a **server catalog** operation. The following example lists all the server objects configured on host **silver**. The **server show** operation reveals the entry name used by the **info_server** program.

```
dcecp> server catalog /.:/hosts/silver
/.../my_cell.goodco.com/hosts/silver/config/srvrconf/video_clip
/.../my_cell.goodco.com/hosts/silver/config/srvrconf/info_server
dcecp> server show /.:/hosts/silver/config/info_server
{uuid 6d5e7184-71b7-11cd-a205-08000925634b}
{program {/usr/local/bin/infosrv}}
{arguments {-brief}}
{prerequisites {}}
{keytabs {}}
{entryname {/.:/subsys/applications/info_server_1}}
{services {}}
{principals {}}
{starton {explicit failure}}
{uid 1423}
{gid 1000}
{dir {/tmp}}
```

If a server starts from a boot program or script of some kind, look in the
program or script for the name or names (sometimes servers use multiple
names when they export multiple interfaces). The name might be supplied
as an argument to the command that starts the server, as in the following
example:

```
infosrv /.:/finance/operations/infoserv
```

When the server side does not easily reveal its entry name, try to determine
what entry other client programs are using. Client programs frequently start
from a boot program or script of some kind, and entry names are generally
provided as arguments to the command to start the client. These commands
often follow the same model shown in the previous example of the server
startup command.

10.5.2 Providing the Entry Name to Clients

Sometimes, very simple clients can have the server entry name encoded
within them so you don't have to pass any entry name. But more often, you
need to supply an entry name to a client program when it starts. This
approach is more flexible than hardcoding an entry name because it offers
an easy way to use a different entry name should the need arise.

The client configuration documentation should include instructions on how to pass the name to the client. One method uses a script or batch file that contains the command to start the client along with arguments that include the appropriate server entry name. The following example shows a server entry name passed as a command argument in a shell script that starts the client:

```
# Shell Script to start the InfoClient application
infoclient /.:/finance/operations/InfoServ_profile
```

Alternatively, the server entry name can be stored in an environment variable (called **RPC_DEFAULT_ENTRY** on UNIX systems). The following example shows a shell script that defines this variable and then invokes the client:

```
#! /bin/sh
# Shell Script to start the InfoClient application
export RPC_DEFAULT_ENTRY=/.:/finance/operations/InfoServ_profile
infoclient
```

Part 4

Cell Directory Service

Chapter 11

Introduction to the DCE Directory Service

Distributed processing involves the interaction of multiple systems to do work that is done on one system in a traditional computing environment. One challenge resulting from this network-wide working environment is the need for a universally consistent way to identify and locate people and resources anywhere in the network.

The DCE Directory Service makes it possible to contact people and to use resources such as disks, print queues, and servers anywhere in the network without knowing their physical location. The directory service is much like a telephone directory assistance service that provides a phone number when given a person's name. Given the unique name of a person, server, or resource, it can return the network address and other information associated with that name.

The DCE Directory Service stores addresses and other relevant information as *attributes* of the name. For example, attributes can contain the name of an organizational unit, such as European Sales; a location, such as the first floor of Building A; or a telephone number. Users can search for a name by supplying one or more of its attributes. For example, given the search criteria of **John Smith** and **Chicago**, the directory service could produce a list of telephone numbers for users in Chicago named John Smith.

Note: Search capabilities are currently limited to the global part of the DCE Directory Service environment.

- A user enters a report in a problem-tracking database. Although the database was recently moved to a new node, the user is not aware of the change because the database is always referred to by its name only. The directory service stores the current network address and provides it to the problem-tracking application and any other application that requests it.

The remainder of this chapter explains how the DCE Directory Service environment works with regard to cells. It introduces the main directory service components: the Cell Directory Service (CDS), the Global Directory Service (GDS), and the Global Directory Agent (GDA), which is a gateway between the local and global naming environments. The chapter also discusses DCE support for the Domain Name System (DNS), which is a global name service that is not a part of the DCE technology offering.

11.3 Directory Services and the Cell Environment

This section introduces the following main components of the DCE naming environment and explains their relationship to the cell:

- CDS

- GDS

- DNS

- GDA

CDS is a high-performance distributed service that provides a consistent, location-independent method for naming and using resources inside a cell (intracell). CDS can also be used for communication between cells (intercell) when cells are connected into a hierarchy.

GDS supports the global naming environment inside cells (intracell) and outside of cells (intercell). GDS is an implementation of a directory service standard known as X.500. This standard is specified by the International Organization for Standardization (ISO) 9594 and the International Telegraph and Telephone Consultative Committee (CCITT) X.500 series. Because it is based on a worldwide standard, GDS offers the opportunity for a universally interoperable global directory.

Figure 11-1 represents a hypothetical configuration of two cells that each use GDS to access names in the other cell. Names that are stored directly in GDS also are accessible from each cell. CDS is the directory service within each cell. The same organization administers both cells, which are configured based on geographic location and network topology.

Figure 11–1. Cell and Global Naming Environments

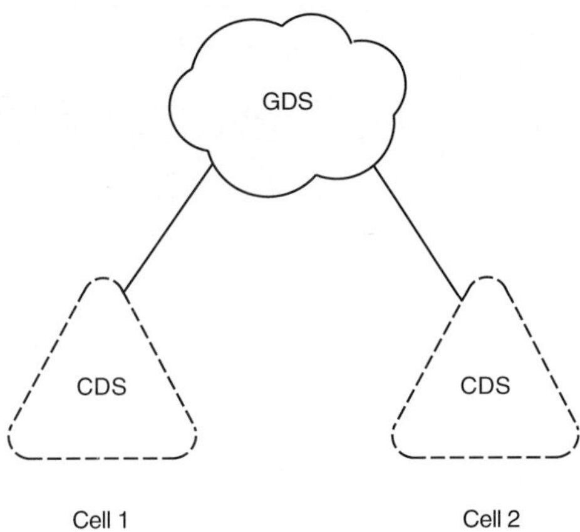

DNS is a widely used existing global name service for which DCE offers support. Many networks currently use DNS primarily as a name service for Internet host names. Although DNS is not a part of the DCE technology offering, the directory service contains support for cells to interoperate through DNS.

The GDA is the DCE component that makes cell interoperation possible. The GDA enables CDS to access a name in another cell through one of the global naming environments (GDS or DNS), or through the CDS of the parent cell, if the cell is part of a hierarchical cell configuration. The GDA is an independent process that can exist on a system separate from a CDS server, although by default the DCE configuration script configures the GDA on the same machine as a CDS server. CDS needs to be able to contact at least one GDA to participate in the global naming environment.

Figure 11-2 shows how the GDA helps CDS access names outside of a cell. When CDS determines that a name is not in its own cell, it passes the name to a GDA, which searches the appropriate naming environment (CDS, GDS, or DNS) for more information about the name. The GDA returns information that enables the original CDS server to contact the CDS server in whose cell the name resides. The GDA can help CDS find names in a cell that is registered in DNS (Scenario A), a cell that is registered in GDS (Scenario B), or a cell that is registered in the originating cell's parent cell (not shown). The GDA decides which name service to use based on the syntax of the name. Section 11.5 describes name syntaxes in detail.

Figure 11–2. Interaction of CDSs, GDAs, and Global Directory Services

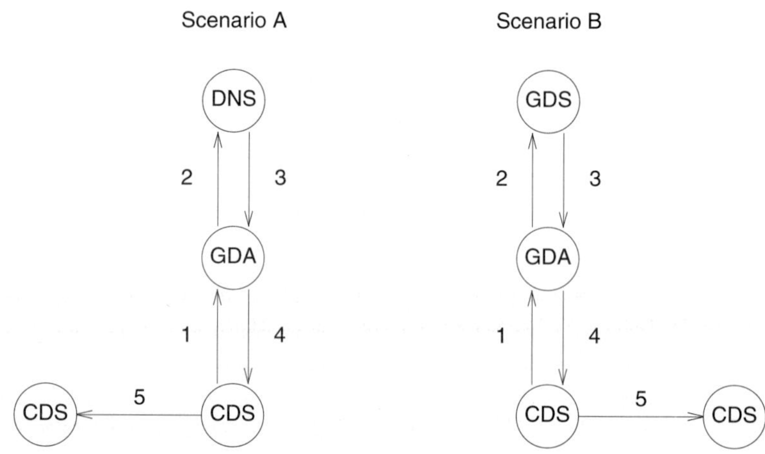

11.4 How Cells Determine Naming Environments

In addition to delineating security and administrative boundaries for users and resources, cells determine the boundaries for sets of names. Because different naming components operate in a cell and outside of a cell, naming conventions in the cell and global environments differ as well. The DCE naming environment supports two kinds of names: *global* names and *cell-relative*, or *local*, names. The following subsections introduce the concept of global and local names. Section 11.5 describes CDS, GDS, and DNS names in detail.

11.4.1 Global Names

All entries in the DCE Directory Service have a global name that is universally meaningful and usable from anywhere in the DCE naming environment. The prefix **/...** indicates that a name is global. A global name can refer to an object within a cell (named in CDS) or an object outside of a cell (named in GDS).

The following example shows the global name for an entry created in GDS. The name represents user Ellie Bloggs, who works in the administrative organization unit of the Widget organization, a British corporation.

```
/.../C=GB/O=Widget/OU=Admin/CN=Ellie Bloggs
```

The GDS name syntax consists of a global prefix **/...** and a set of elements, called Relative Distinguished Names (RDNs). Each RDN consists of one or more pairs of parts separated by an = (equal sign) character. The items that are separated by an equal sign are multiple AVAs (Attribute Value Assertions). See the *OSF DCE GDS Administration Guide and Reference* for more information about AVAs. The first part of a pair is an abbreviation that indicates a type of information. Some common abbreviations are Country (**C**), Organization (**O**), Organization Unit (**OU**), and Common Name (**CN**). The second part of the pair is a value. (See Section 11.5.2 for more information on GDS names.)

The following example shows a global name for a price database server named in CDS. The server is used by the Portland sales branch of XYZ Company, an organization in the United States.

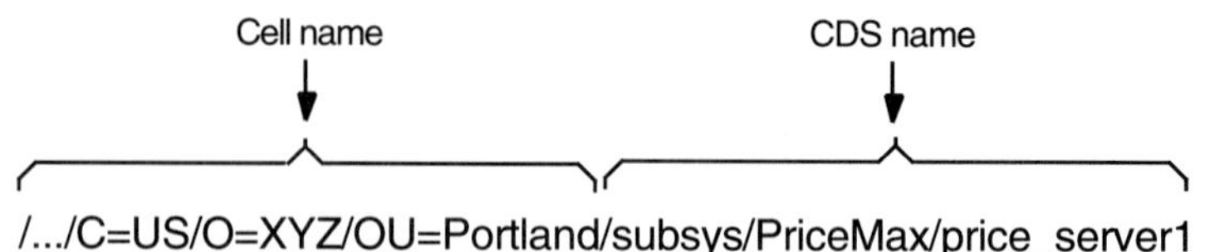

As the example illustrates, global names for entries that are created in CDS look slightly different from pure GDS-style names. The first portion of the name, **/.../C=US/O=XYZ/OU=Portland**, is a global cell name that exists in GDS. The remaining portion, **/subsys/PriceMax/price_server1**, is a CDS name.

The cell name exists because cells must have names to be accessible in the global naming environment. The GDA looks up the cell name in the process of helping CDS in one cell find a name in another cell. Cell names are established during initial configuration of the DCE components. Before configuring a cell that will participate in standard intercell communication (that is, via the DNS or GDS global directory services), the DCE administrator must obtain a unique cell name from either of the global naming environments, depending on whether the cell needs to be accessed through GDS or DNS.

The next example shows the global name of a host at ABC Corporation. The global name of the company's cell, **/.../abc.com**, exists in DNS.

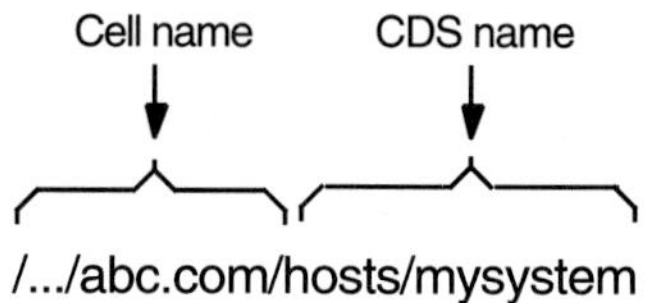

11.4.2 Hierarchical Cell Names

In a hierarchy of cells, the names of one or more cells, called *child cells*, are registered in a cell's CDS; this cell is called the *parent cell*. The cell at the top of the hierarchy must be registered in a global directory service (GDS or DNS), but the cells underneath do not need to be since they use CDS to communicate. A child has one and only one parent at any given time, while a parent can have more than one child.

The GDA is the communications gateway between the CDS namespaces of cells in a hierarchy, as it is between CDS and the global directory services. When the GDA receives a request for information about a cell, and the cell is a child cell, the GDA returns information about the CDS in the parent cell. The CDS of the parent cell provides the pointers to the child cell.

A child cell's name begins with the parent's global cell name; that is, the name of the cell beginning at the global root /... prefix. (This name is also known as the parent cell's *fully-qualified* name.) It ends with the specific child cell name. The parent's global name can contain CDS syntax as well as GDS or DNS syntax, depending on where the parent cell is located in the hierarchy.

The following example shows the global cell names of two child cells:

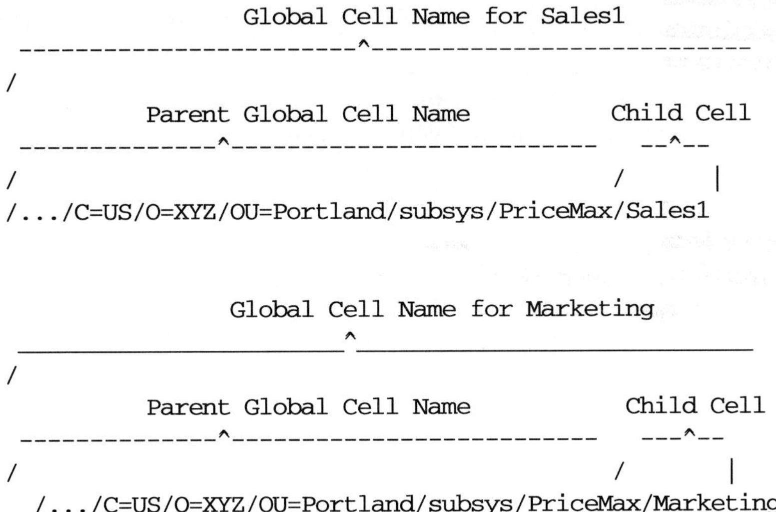

```
                  Global Cell Name for Sales1
       -----------------------------^---------------------------
      /
          Parent Global Cell Name            Child Cell
       ----------------^----------------------    --^--
      /                                       /     |
      /.../C=US/O=XYZ/OU=Portland/subsys/PriceMax/Sales1


                  Global Cell Name for Marketing
       ___________________________^___________________________
      /
          Parent Global Cell Name            Child Cell
       ---------------^----------------------    ---^--
      /                                       /     |
        /.../C=US/O=XYZ/OU=Portland/subsys/PriceMax/Marketing
```

The global cell name for each child includes

- The parent's global name, **/.../C=US/O=XYZ/OU=Portland**

- The child's unique CDS name, **/Sales1** or **/Marketing**

If a DCE administrator is establishing a hierarchy of cells during initial cell configuration, he or she must obtain a unique GDS or DNS cell name for the cell at the top of the hierarchy from the GDS or DNS global directory service authorities. All of the cells beneath this cell share this name. The *OSF DCE Administration Guide—Introduction* provides details on how to obtain GDS and DNS cell names.

If a DCE administrator establishes a hierarchy of cells after the cells have been configured, the global names of the child cells change to point to the parent's cell name. Chapter 21 of this guide provides details on how to establish a hierarchy of cells.

11.4.3 Alias Cell Names

You can give a cell more than one global name by creating an *alias* name for the cell. In this case, the cell has a *primary name*, which is the name that DCE services return for the cell when queried, and one or more cell aliases that the DCE services recognize in addition to the primary name. For example, if your cell is registered in the DNS global directory service, and you want to register it in GDS as well, you obtain a GDS name for the cell and set it up as a cell alias. The DNS name remains the primary name.

You can also change between primary and alias names for a cell; to return to the previous example, you can make the newly created GDS cell alias the primary name for the cell, and change the DNS name to a cell alias. Another case in which you may need to make a cell's alias name its primary name is when creating a cell hierarchy from existing independent cells. Chapter 6 of this guide explains how to use the **dcecp cellalias** task object to manage your cell names. Chapter 21 of this guide explains how to create a hierarchical cell.

11.4.4 Cell-Relative Naming in a Standalone Cell

In addition to their global names, all CDS entries have a cell-relative, or local, name that is meaningful and usable only from within the local cell where that entry exists. The local name is a shortened form of a global name, and thus is a more convenient way to refer to resources within a user's own cell. Local names have the following characteristics:

- They do not include a global cell name.

- They begin with the **/.:** prefix.

Local names do not include a global cell name because the **/.:** prefix indicates that the name being referred to is within the local cell. When CDS encounters a **/.:** prefix on a name, it automatically replaces the prefix with the local cell's name, forming the global name. CDS can handle both global and local names, but it is more convenient to use the local name when referring to a name in the local cell. For example, these names are equally valid when used within the cell named **/.../C=US/O=XYZ/OU=Portland**:

/.../C=US/O=XYZ/OU=Portland/subsys/PriceMax/price_server1

/.:/subsys/PriceMax/price_server1

The naming conventions required for the interaction of local and global directory services may at first seem confusing. In an environment where references to names outside of the local cell are necessary, the following simple guidelines can help make the conventions easy to remember and use:

- Know your cell name.

- Know whether a name that you are referring to is in your cell.

- When using a name that is within your cell, you can omit the cell name and include the **/.:** prefix.

- When using a name that is outside of your cell, enter its global syntax, including the **/...** prefix and the cell name.

- When someone asks for the name of a resource in your cell, give its global name, including the **/...** prefix.

- When storing a name in persistent storage (for example, in a shell script), use its global name, including the **/...** prefix. Local names (that is, names with a **/.:** prefix) are intended only for interactive use and should not be stored. (If a local name is referenced from within a foreign cell, the **/.:** prefix is resolved to the name of the foreign cell and the resulting name lookup either fails or produces the wrong name.)

11.4.5 Cell-Relative Naming in a Hierarchy of Cells

In a hierarchy of cells, cell-relative names and local names may not be the same. A parent cell can reference a name in a child cell by using cell-relative naming (**/.:**). Consequently, you can no longer determine whether a cell is in your local cell by merely looking at its name. In the following example, the child cell (**eng**) is named relative to its parent cell:

/.:/eng

This type of naming allows you to access names in a child cell (for example, **/.:/eng/hosts/admin**) from the parent cell, without having to specify the global name of the cell.

Note: When referencing names in a child cell from a parent cell, you should be mindful that your status is that of a foreign user. Therefore, the child cell may have access controls imposed on it that will deny you access to its namespace.

11.4.6 Local Filenames

When referring to pathnames of files in the local cell, you can shorten a local name even further by using the **/:** prefix. This prefix translates to the root of the cell file system. The default name of the file system root is **/.:/fs**, which is one level down from the root of the cell namespace. So, for example, the following are all valid ways to refer to the same file from within the **/.../widget.com** cell:

/.../widget.com/fs/smith/myfile

/.:/fs/smith/myfile

/:/smith/myfile

(See the *OSF DCE DFS Administration Guide and Reference* for more information on local file system abbreviations.)

11.5 An In-Depth Analysis of DCE Names

The rest of this chapter describes in depth the different kinds of names that make up the DCE namespace. Appendix A and the *OSF DCE GDS Administration Guide and Reference* contain further details about valid characters and naming conventions in CDS, GDS, and DNS names.

11.5.1 CDS Names

Every cell contains at least one server that is running a CDS server. A CDS server stores and maintains names and handles requests to create, modify, and look up data. The total collection of names shared by CDS servers in a cell is called a *cell namespace*. The cell namespace administrator can organize CDS names into a hierarchical structure of directories. CDS directories, which are conceptually similar to the directories in your operating system's file system, are a logical way to group names for ease of management and use.

In a cell namespace, any directory that has a directory beneath it is considered the *parent* of the directory beneath it. Any directory that has a directory above it is considered a *child* of the directory above it. The top level of the cell namespace is called the *cell root*. You can refer to the cell root either by the global name of the cell or by the short-form **/.:** prefix.

Figure 11-3 shows a simple cell namespace hierarchy, starting at the cell root. The cell root (**/.:**) is the parent of the directories named **/.:/hosts** and **/.:/subsys**. The **/.:/subsys** directory is a child of the cell root directory and the parent of the **/.:/subsys/dce** directory.

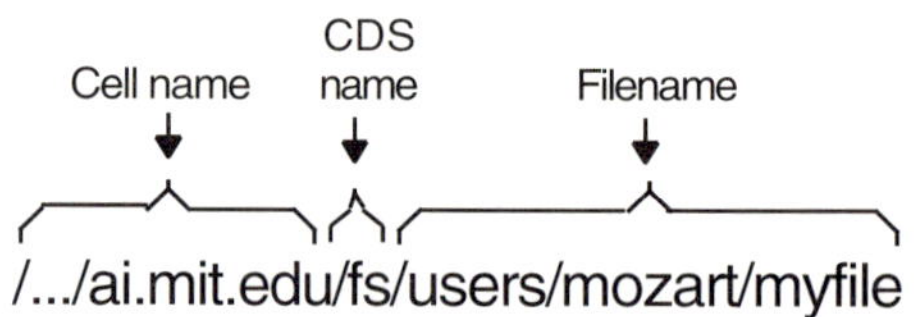

The global name contains a DNS cell name, **/.../ai.mit.edu**. The **fs** portion is the file system junction entry in CDS, and **/users/mozart/myfile** is the name of a file.

Thus, the DCE namespace is a connected tree of many kinds of names from many different sources. The GDA component of the directory service provides connections out of the cell and to other cells through a global namespace, such as GDS or DNS. In a similar manner, junctions enable connections downward from the cell namespace to other services.

Chapter 12

CDS Concepts

The Cell Directory Service (CDS) is a high-performance distributed service that provides a consistent, location-independent method for naming and using resources inside a cell. CDS offers the ability to replicate CDS names; that is, to store copies of them on more than one node. CDS automatically keeps multiple copies consistent. Names also can be distributed among several nodes so that no one node has to store all of them. This feature is particularly valuable in large cells.

The ability to replicate and distribute information has many benefits, including the following:

- Availability—Because you can store the same name in more than one place, data is likely to be available even in the event of a system or network failure.

- Efficiency—CDS finds names efficiently because you can store them close to where they are used most often. Furthermore, once CDS finds a name, it can connect to the same name immediately on all subsequent lookups.

- Load Sharing—Because names are in more than one place, several systems can share the load of looking them up.

- Expandability—New names are easily accommodated as the network grows and more applications use CDS.

12.1 How CDS Works

Operation of the CDS involves several major participants:

- client applications

- servers

- clerks

- clearinghouses

CDS uses a client/server model. An application that depends on CDS to store and retrieve information for it is a client of CDS. Client applications create names for resources on behalf of their users. Through a client application, a user can supply other information for CDS to store as attributes of a name. Then, when a client application user refers to the resource by its CDS name, CDS retrieves data from the attributes for use by the client application.

A system running CDS server software is a CDS server. A CDS server stores and maintains CDS names and handles requests to create, modify, or look up data.

A component called the *clerk* is the interface between client applications and CDS servers. Every DCE node must run a CDS clerk. The clerk receives a request from a client application, sends the request to a server, and returns the resulting information to the client. This process is called a *lookup*. The clerk is also the interface through which client applications create and modify names. One clerk can work on behalf of many client applications.

The clerk caches, or saves, the results of lookups so that it does not have to repeatedly go to a server for the same information. The cache is written to disk periodically so that the information can survive a system reboot or the restart of an application. When you stop the CDS advertiser, the cache is written to disk. Caching improves performance and reduces network traffic.

Figure 12-1 shows a sample configuration of CDS clerks and servers on a 9-node local area network (LAN). Every node is a clerk, and CDS servers run on two selected nodes.

Figure 12–1. CDS Clerks and Servers on a LAN

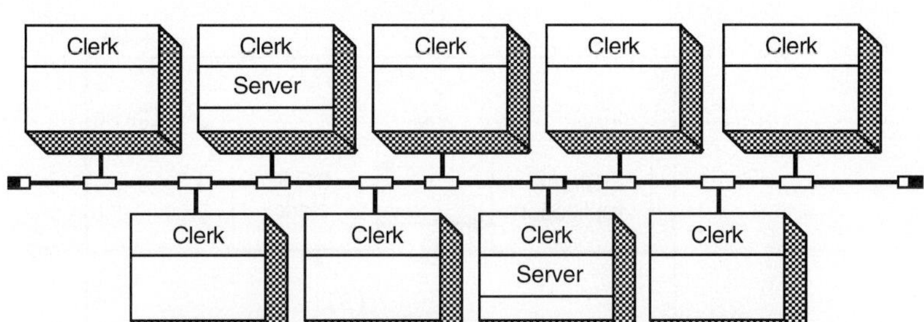

Every CDS server has a database called a *clearinghouse* in which it stores names and other CDS data. The clearinghouse is where a CDS server adds, modifies, deletes, and retrieves data on behalf of client applications. Although more than one clearinghouse can exist at a server node, it is not recommended as a normal configuration.

Figure 12-2 shows the interaction between a CDS client, clerk, server, and clearinghouse during a simple lookup. It illustrates the following CDS lookup steps:

1. The client application on Node 1 sends a lookup request to the local clerk.

2. The clerk checks its cache and, not finding the name there, contacts the server on Node 2.

3. The server checks to see if the name is in its clearinghouse.

4. The name exists in the clearinghouse, so the server gets the requested information.

5. The server returns the information to the clerk on Node 1.

6. The clerk passes the requested data to the client application. The clerk also caches the information so that it does not have to contact a server the next time a client requests a lookup of that same name.

Figure 12–2. A Sample CDS Lookup

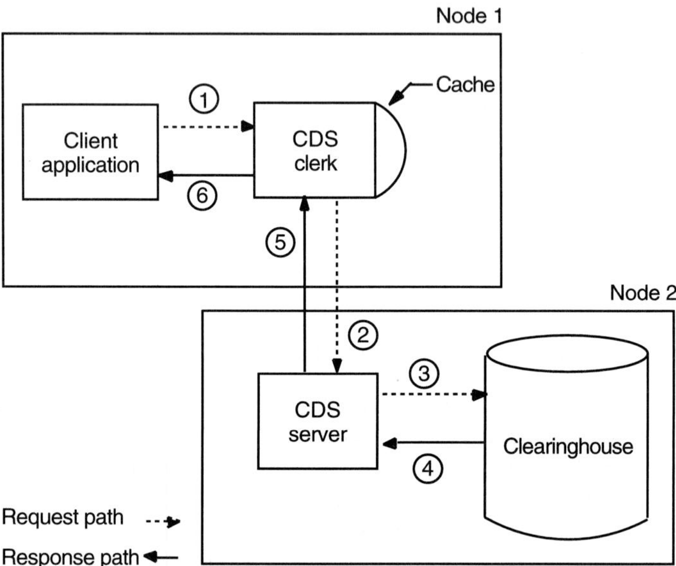

12.2 Replicas and Their Contents

Directories are the units by which you distribute and replicate names throughout the cell's namespace. Each physical copy of a directory, including the original, is called a *replica*. When you create a replica of a directory, you replicate all of the entries in it as well.

Replicas are stored in clearinghouses. You can think of a clearinghouse as the collection of directory replicas at a particular server. After you create a directory in one clearinghouse, you can create replicas of it in other clearinghouses to increase availability for looking up information. CDS periodically ensures that the contents of all replicas of a directory remain consistent.

Two types of replicas can exist:

- Master

- Read-only

A replica's type affects the processing that can be done on it and the way CDS updates it. The type of replica that CDS uses when it looks up or changes data is invisible to users. However, it helps to understand how the two types differ.

The master replica is the first instance of a specific directory in the cell's namespace. After you make copies of the directory, you can designate a different replica as the master, if necessary. However, only one master replica of each directory can exist at a time. (See Chapter 21 for complete information on how to redesignate the master replica of a directory.)

The master replica is the only directly modifiable replica of a directory. CDS can create, change, and delete information in a master replica. Because it is modifiable, the master replica incurs more overhead than read-only replicas, which CDS keeps up-to-date periodically with changes made to the master replica.

A read-only replica is a copy of a directory that is available only for looking up information. CDS does not create, modify, or delete names in read-only replicas; it simply updates them with changes made to the master replica.

Replicas can contain three kinds of entries:

- object entries

- soft links

- child pointers

12.2.1 Object Entries

An object is any real resource—like a disk, application, or node—that is given a CDS name. When an object name is created, client applications and the CDS software supply attributes to be stored with the name. An attribute, consisting of an attribute name and value(s), describes a particular operational property of an object. The name and its attributes make up the *object entry*. When a client application requests a lookup of the name, CDS returns the value of the relevant attribute or attributes.

Object entries are typically created and managed through a client application interface. For example, the DCE control program and the Name Service Interface (NSI) of the RPC runtime let users create entries that represent RPC servers, groups, and profiles. These are special kinds of entries that enable an RPC application to locate and select servers. (See the *OSF DCE Application Development Guide* for details on how RPC uses CDS for this purpose.)

You can also create object entries through the DCE control program (**dcecp**). (See Part 1 of this document and the *OSF DCE Command Reference* for information on the commands that allow you to create and manage object entries by using **dcecp**.)

Every object can have a defined class, which is an optional attribute of the object entry. DCE components that use the directory service can define their own object classes and supply class-specific attributes for the directory service to store on their behalf. Class-specific attributes have meaning only to the particular class of objects with which they are associated.

The clearinghouse object entry represents a special class of object that is predefined by CDS. A clearinghouse object entry serves as a pointer to the location of a clearinghouse in the network. CDS needs this pointer so that it can look up and update data in a clearinghouse.

When you create a clearinghouse, CDS creates its clearinghouse object entry automatically. The clearinghouse object entry acquires the same name as the clearinghouse. The clearinghouse object entry is like any other object entry in that it describes an actual resource, but it is different because it is solely for internal use by CDS. Clearinghouses can only be created in the cell root directory. Therefore, all clearinghouse object entries are stored in the cell root directory. CDS itself updates and manages clearinghouse object entries when necessary. They do not require any external management except in rare problem-solving situations. (See your vendor for help in these situations.)

12.2.2 Soft Links

A *soft link* is a pointer that provides an alternate name for an object entry, directory, or other soft link in the cell's namespace. You can do minor restructuring of a cell's namespace by creating soft links that point from an existing name to a new name. Soft links also can be a way to give something multiple names so that different kinds of users can refer to a name in a way that makes the most sense to them.

Soft links can be permanent, or they can expire after a period of time that you specify. If the name that a soft link points to is deleted, CDS deletes the soft link automatically when it expires.

CDS managers should use soft links carefully. They should not use soft links to completely redesign the cell's namespace or to provide shortcuts for users who do not want to use the full name of an object entry. Overuse of soft links makes CDS names more difficult to keep track of and manage.

12.2.3 Child Pointers

A *child pointer* provides the following kinds of connections for cells:

- Between a directory to another directory immediately beneath it in a cell's namespace

- Between a parent and its child cell

Users and applications do not create child pointers; CDS creates a child pointer automatically when someone creates a new directory. The child pointer is created in the directory that is the parent of (one level above) the directory to which it points. CDS uses child pointers to locate directory replicas when it is trying to find a name. Child pointers do not require management except in rare problem-solving situations.

12.2.4 Summary

To summarize, a cell consists of a complete set of names that are shared and managed by one or more CDS servers in a cell. A name can designate a directory, object entry, soft link, or child pointer. The logical representation of a cell's namespace is a hierarchical structure of directories and the names they contain. Every physical instance of a directory is called a *replica*. Names are physically stored in replicas, and replicas are stored in clearinghouses. Any node that contains a clearinghouse and runs CDS server software is a *CDS server*.

Figure 12-3 shows the components of a CDS server node. Every server manages at least one clearinghouse containing directory replicas. A replica can contain object entries, soft links, and child pointers. The figure shows only one replica and one of each type of entry that is possible in a replica. Normally, a clearinghouse contains many replicas, and a replica contains many entries.

Figure 12–3. Components of a CDS Server Node

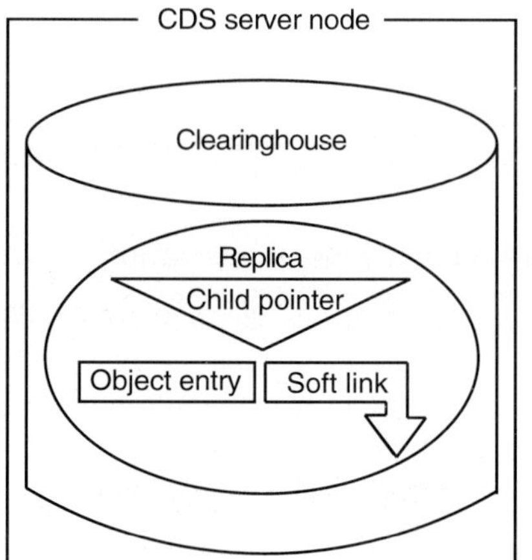

12.3 Security in the Cell Directory Environment

In a secure DCE cell operation, a server does not complete a user's request unless the user's identity has been verified through the DCE Authentication Service. So, for example, a CDS server allows a user to create a new directory only if that user's identity has been verified. The process of verifying that users are who they say they are is called *authentication*. The proof is in the form of a user name, or principal name, coupled with a special kind of password.

CDS servers themselves must be authenticated principals for two reasons:

- To prove to clients that they are trustworthy

- To prove to each other that they have the permission to modify and manage the data that they share

The principal name of a CDS server is automatically selected by the configuration program and is placed in a group that contains the names of all CDS servers in the cell. The group is stored as an entry in the DCE Security Service database. After initial contact with a CDS server, the clerk confirms through the DCE Security Service that the server is a valid member of the server group.

Authentication is not an end in itself, but is instead a step in the process of authorization. Once the identity of a principal has been verified, the software must next determine whether that principal has the permissions that are required to perform a requested action. This is called *authorization*. Therefore, to create a new directory, the user in the previous example must not only be authenticated, but have the appropriate permissions as well.

Servers need to be authenticated to each other because they share and modify replicated data. For example, suppose server A and server B both store a replica of the same directory. Associated with each directory is a list of all the servers authorized to maintain that directory. When a user modifies an entry in the replica at server B, server B must notify server A of the change. Server A does not accept the update unless server B is an authenticated principal and is one of the principals authorized to modify that directory.

The CDS permissions are read, write, insert, delete, test, control, and administer. Each has a slightly different meaning depending on the kind of name it is associated with, but, in general, their meanings are as follows:

- Read permission lets users view data.

- Write permission lets users add or change data.

- Insert permission lets users create entries in a directory.

- Delete permission lets users delete entries.

- Test permission lets users test whether an attribute of a name has a specific value without being able to see any values—that is, without having read permission to the name. The main advantage of this permission is that it gives application programmers a more efficient way to check for a value: rather than reading a whole set of values, the application can test for a particular value.

- Control permission lets users manage the access control list (ACL) of an entry.

- Administer permission lets users manage directory replication.

Note that it is possible to define a special ACL for users who cannot be authenticated or who deliberately request unauthenticated operations. In such a case, the user's identity is not verified, and the ACL entry for unauthenticated users determines whether the user has the permissions to perform the requested action. (See Part 6 of this guide for details on creating ACLs for unauthenticated users.)

12.4 CDS User Interfaces

CDS has several *entities* that can be managed via user interfaces that are provided in DCE. A CDS entity is any individually manageable piece of the CDS software. CDS directories, soft links, and object entries are the most common entities that you manage with the DCE user interfaces. Some object entries, though, are normally managed through the client application that creates them.

The DCE control program provides many commands for managing CDS entities. Chapter 15 of this guide contains information about these commands.

CDS also comes with two other user interfaces:

- The CDS control program (**cdscp**)

- The browser

The CDS control program, which is available on all clerks and servers, is an interface that accepts commands targeted for these entities and directory replicas. However, most of **cdscp** commands have equivalents in **dcecp**, and you are encouraged to use the **dcecp** commands instead. The small number of **cdscp** commands that must use for operations on CDS servers, clerks, and replicas are described in Chapter 15.

The browser is a tool for viewing the content and structure of a namespace. It runs on workstations with windowing software that is based on the OSF/Motif® graphical user interface. Using a mouse to manipulate pull-down menus, you can view the directory structure of a namespace, view child directories of a particular directory, view the object entries and soft links in a directory, and set a filter to display only object entries of a particular class. (For users who do not have windowing software, similar functions are available with both **dcecp** and **cdscp**.)

In addition to **dcecp**, **cdscp**, and the browser, other DCE user interfaces allow access to and management of CDS names. For example, users can control access to CDS directories and their contents by using an ACL editor such as the **dcecp acl** object or the **acl_edit** program which is supplied with the DCE Security Service. RPC application programmers can create server entries, groups, and configuration profiles in the cell's namespace with the **dcecp** or **rpccp** programs. (See Part 3 (RPC) and Part 6 (Security) of this guide for details on how to use these interfaces.)

How CDS Looks Up Names

This chapter illustrates the relationship between a name and the physical resource that it describes, and explains how CDS handles requests to look up names. Understanding these concepts can help you to plan for the location of clearinghouses and directories in your cell namespace. It can also help you to isolate the source of a problem if you encounter lookup errors or failures. Note that the figures in this chapter do not reflect the actual structure of a typical DCE cell namespace. For simplicity, the figures show fewer directories and directory levels.

13.1 Translating from Names to Resources

Just as directory names in a logical namespace hierarchy translate to physical replicas in clearinghouses, CDS names translate to physical resources that are used either internally by CDS or by client applications. The attributes of a name are what make the translation possible. This section describes the relationship between CDS names and the physical resources that they describe.

Figure 13-1 shows three directories and their contents in a logical namespace, and how replicas of those directories are physically implemented in two clearinghouses. The clearinghouses themselves have CDS names: **/.:/Paris_CH** on Node 1 and **/.:/NY_CH** on Node 2. The **_CH** suffix is a recommended convention for naming clearinghouses. The **/.:/Paris_CH** clearinghouse contains replicas of the root directory and the **/.:/subsys/PrintQ** directory. The **/.:/NY_CH** clearinghouse contains replicas of the root directory and the **/.:/subsys** directory. Recommended practice is to create at least two replicas of every directory. Therefore, the **/.:/subsys** and **/.:/subsys/PrintQ** directories each need to be replicated in at least one other clearinghouse somewhere in the cell.

Figure 13–1. Logical and Physical Views of a Namespace

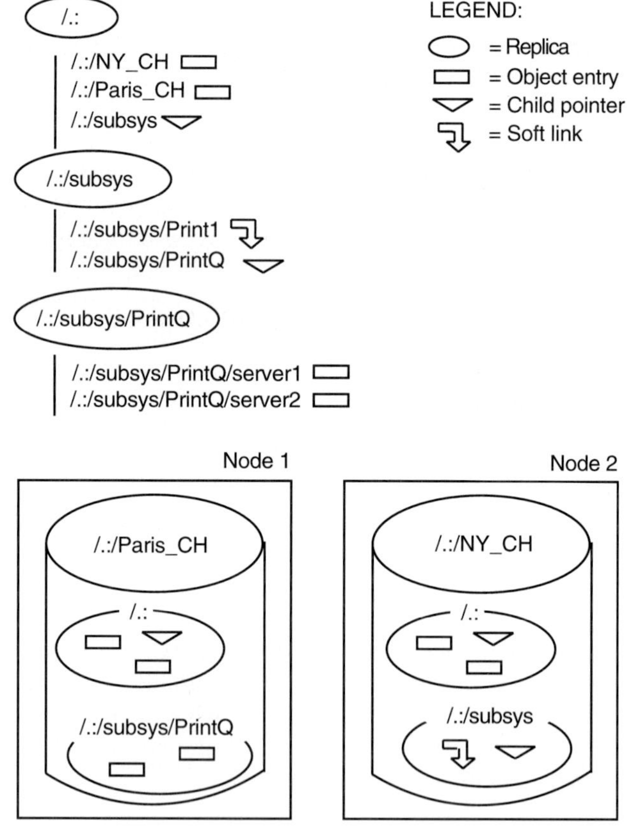

To discover the physical location of a resource, CDS looks up an attribute that is associated with its name. Figures 13-2 through 13-4 illustrate the connection between the various kinds of CDS names and the resources that they describe. The figures are based on the namespace in Figure 13-1. All of the names in Figures 13-2 through 13-4 are in the same cell namespace, as evidenced by the use of the **/.:** prefix to represent the cell root. (See Chapter 22 for information about name resolution across multiple cells.)

Figure 13-2 shows the relationship between two clearinghouse object entries and the clearinghouses that they describe. A clearinghouse object entry differs from other kinds of object entries in that it is created, used, and maintained by the CDS software instead of by a client application. However, it is like any other object entry in that it describes a physical resource in the network: the clearinghouse. CDS creates the object entry automatically when you create and name the clearinghouse.

Figure 13-2 shows two clearinghouse object entries: **/.:/Paris_CH**, which points to the clearinghouse that is named **/.:/Paris_CH** on Node 1, and **/.:/NY_CH**, which points to the clearinghouse that is named **/.:/NY_CH** on Node 2. Each clearinghouse object entry has an attribute called **CDS_CHLastAddress** attribute, whose **Tower** subattribute contains RPC binding information that CDS uses to contact the node where the clearinghouse resides. (See Appendix B for a list of CDS attributes and their descriptions.)

Figure 13–2. Clearinghouse Object Entries and Clearinghouses

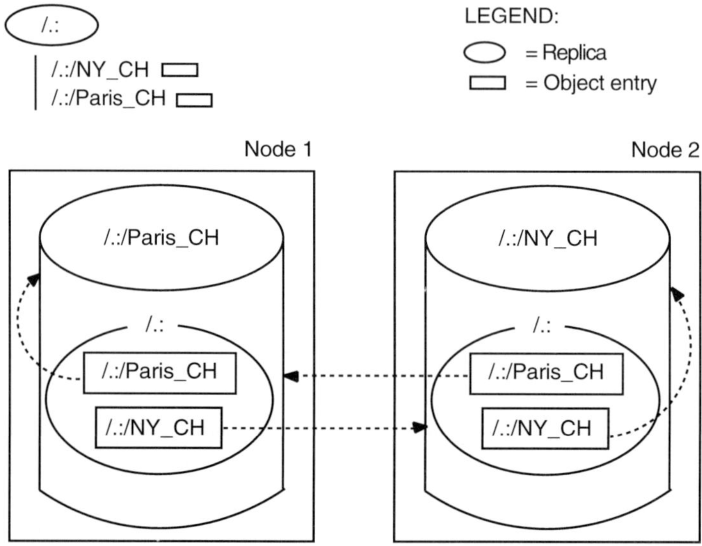

Figure 13-3 shows the relationship between a soft link, the object entry it points to, and the resource that the object entry describes. The soft link, **/.:/subsys/Print1**, has an attribute called **CDS_LinkTarget**, which contains the name that the link points to: an object entry that is named **/.:/subsys/PrintQ/server1**. The object entry describes a print server machine that is used by an application called **PrintQ**. The replica containing the **/.:/subsys/PrintQ/server1** object entry exists in the **/.:/Paris_CH** clearinghouse. The object entry has an attribute called **CDS_CHLastAddress** attribute, whose **Tower** subattribute contains RPC binding information that enables the **PrintQ** application to contact the print server machine.

Figure 13–3. A Soft Link and Its Resolution

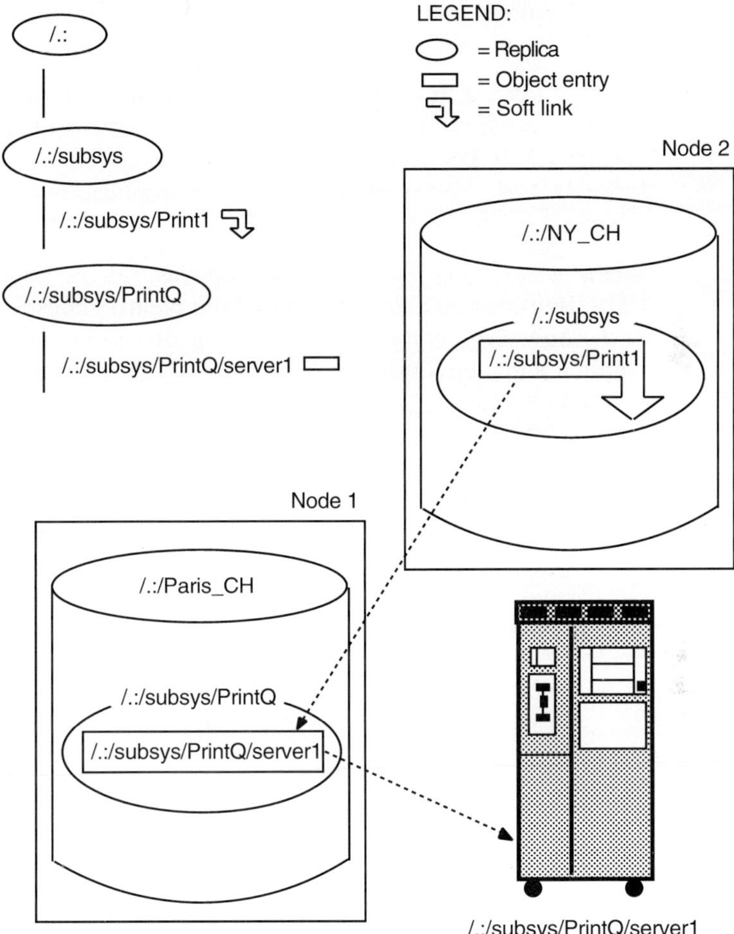

Figure 13-4 shows the relationship between directories and their associated child pointers. It illustrates that, although a child pointer has the same name as its associated directory, the child pointer is a separate entry in the namespace and resides in the parent of the directory to which it refers.

In the case of hierarchical cells, the directory resides in the child cell and the child pointer, which has the same name as the associated directory and resides in the parent cell.

The root replicas in both clearinghouses contain a child pointer for the **/.:/subsys(:)** directory. The **/.:/subsys** child pointer has an attribute called **CDS_Replicas** which contains the name and address of the **/.:/NY_CH** clearinghouse, where a replica of the **/.:/subsys** directory exists.

In the **/.:/NY_CH** clearinghouse, the replica of the **/.:/subsys** directory contains a child pointer for the **/.:/subsys/PrintQ** directory. The child pointer's **XSCDS_Replicas** attribute contains the name and address of the **/.:/Paris_CH** clearinghouse, where a replica of the **/.:/subsys/PrintQ** directory exists.

When a directory has multiple replicas, as is normally the case, the **CDS_Replicas** attribute lists all of the clearinghouses containing a replica of the directory. You can use the **dcecp directory show** command with the **-replica** and **clearinghouse** options to display this attribute.

Figure 13–4. Child Pointers and Directories

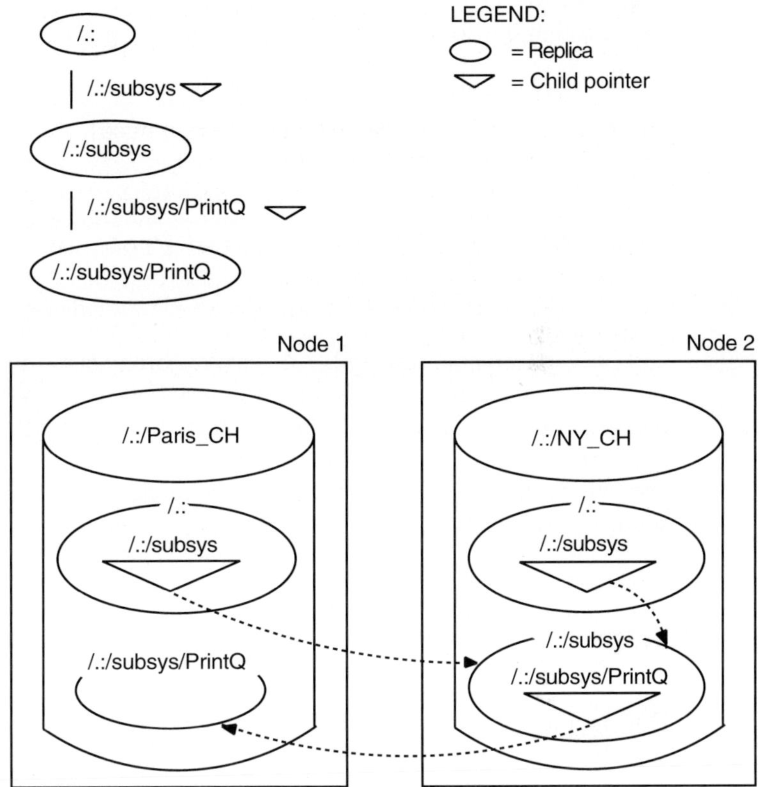

13.2 How CDS Finds Names

As Figures 13-1 through 13-4 illustrate, CDS finds information about the physical location of a resource by looking up one or more attributes that are associated with its name. First, though, the clerk must know how to find the name. If a name does not yet exist in the clerk's cache, the clerk must know of at least one CDS server to contact in search of the name.

The clerk can learn about CDS servers and their locations in any of three ways:

- Through the solicitation and advertisement protocol

- During a regular lookup

- By response to the **cdscache create** command

13.2.1 The Solicitation and Advertisement Protocol

Clerks and servers on the same LAN communicate by using the solicitation and advertisement protocol. A server broadcasts messages at regular intervals to advertise its existence to clerks on its LAN. The advertisement message contains data about the cell that the server belongs to, the server's network address, and the clearinghouse it manages. Clerks learn about servers by listening for these advertisements on the LAN. A clerk also sends out solicitation messages that request advertisements at startup.

13.2.2 Lookups

During a lookup, if a clearinghouse does not contain a name that the clerk is searching for, the server managing that clearinghouse gives the clerk as much data as it can about where else to search for the name. If a clearinghouse contains replicas that are part of the full name being looked up, but not the replica containing the target simple name, it returns data from a relevant child pointer in the replica it does have. The data helps the clerk find the next child directory in the path toward the target simple name. The child pointer's **CDS_Replicas** attribute contains this data, in the form of clearinghouse names and binding information.

13.2.3 The cdscache create Command

A DCE administrator can run the **dcecp cdscache create** command to create knowledge in the clerk's cache about a server. This command is useful when the server and clerk are separated by a wide area network (WAN), and the clerk therefore cannot learn about the server from advertisements on a LAN.

Figure 13-5 is an example of how the clerk works downward from the root of the cell namespace to locate an object entry. The object entry, **/.:/Sales/Spell**, describes a spell-checking server at a company's London sales headquarters.

Figure 13–5. How the Clerk Finds a Name

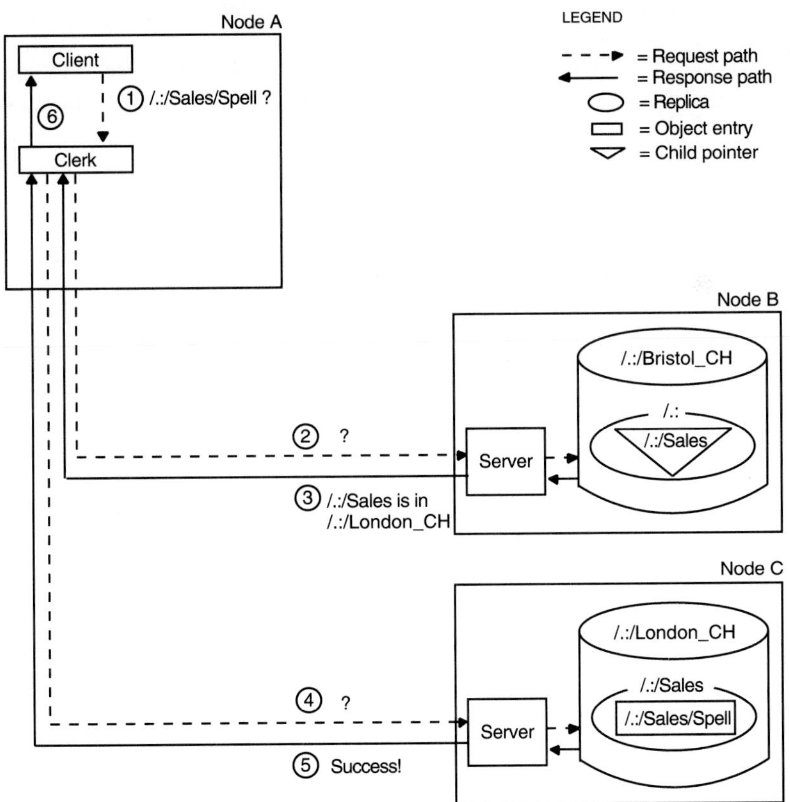

As shown in Figure 13-5, the clerk locates the desired object entry by performing the following steps:

1. On Node A, a spell-checking application requests the network address of the **/.:/Sales/Spell** server. The clerk does not have that name in its cache, and the only clearinghouse it knows about so far is the **/.:/Bristol_CH** clearinghouse on Node B.

2. The clerk contacts the server on Node B with the lookup request.

3. The **/.:/Bristol_CH** clearinghouse does not contain the target object entry, but it does contain a replica of the root directory. From the **/.:/Sales** child pointer in the root, the clerk can learn how to contact clearinghouses that have a replica of the **/.:/Sales** directory. The server on Node B returns this data to the clerk, informing it that a replica of **/.:/Sales** is in the **/.:/London_CH** clearinghouse on Node C.

4. The clerk contacts the server on Node C with the lookup request.

5. The **/.:/Sales** replica in the clearinghouse on Node C contains the **/.:/Sales/Spell** object entry, so the server passes the address of the spell-checking server to the clerk.

6. The clerk returns the information to the client application, which can now make a remote call to the spell-checking server.

Long lookups, as illustrated in Figure 13-5, do not normally happen often after a clerk establishes its cache and becomes more knowledgeable about clearinghouses and their contents. However, the figure illustrates the resources and connections that could be involved in an initial lookup. The figure also illustrates the importance of maintaining connectivity between parent and child directories in the namespace. If somewhere the directory path is broken or a clearinghouse is unreachable, a clerk may not be able to find a name.

Chapter 14

How CDS Updates Data

Once names exist in the namespace, users who have the appropriate access can make changes to the data associated with the names. Any addition, modification, or deletion of CDS data initially happens in only one replica: the master replica. This chapter introduces the main methods by which CDS keeps other replicas consistent: *update propagation* and the *skulk* operation. It also describes two timestamps that help to ensure consistency in CDS data. By understanding the concepts in this chapter, you can more effectively plan the content and replication of directories and the organization of hierarchical cells in your namespace.

14.1 Update Propagation

An update propagation is an immediate attempt to apply one change to all replicas of the directory in which the change was just made. Its main benefit is that it delivers each change in an efficient and timely way.

Unlike a skulk operation, however, update propagation does not guarantee that the change gets made in all replicas. If a particular replica is not available, the update propagation does not fail; the change simply does not get made in that replica. The skulk operation ensures that, when the replica is available again, it becomes consistent with the other replicas in its set.

You can tune the degree of persistence that CDS uses in attempting an update propagation—or prevent propagation altogether—by adjusting a directory attribute called **CDS_Convergence**. Convergence also affects the frequency of skulks on a directory. (See Chapter 18 for details on viewing and changing a directory's convergence.)

14.2 Skulk Operation

The skulk operation is a periodic distribution of a collection of updates. Its main functions are to ensure that replicas receive changes that may not have reached them during an update propagation and to remove outdated information from the namespace.

For hierarchical cells, the skulk updates the child pointers in the parent cell and the *up pointers* in the child cell (which point to the parent) so they reflect the updated information.

Skulk maintenance functions include the following:

- Removing soft links that have expired. You can specify an expiration time when you create a soft link.

- Maintaining child pointers, which includes removing pointers to directories that were deleted.

- Removing information about deleted replicas.

CDS skulks each directory individually. During a skulk, CDS collects all changes that were made to the master replica since the last successful skulk and then disseminates the changes to all read-only replicas of the directory. All replicas must be available for a skulk to be considered successful. If CDS cannot contact a replica, it continues making changes in the replicas that it can contact, while generating an event to notify you of the replica or replicas it could not update. CDS then periodically reattempts the skulk until it completes successfully.

A skulk can begin in one of three ways:

- A CDS manager can enter a command to start an immediate skulk on a directory.

- CDS starts a skulk as an indirect result of other namespace management activities, which include the following:

  — Adding or removing a replica

  — Creating or deleting a directory

  — Redesigning replica types

  — Adding or deleting a child cell name in a parent cell

  All of these activities produce changes in the structure of the namespace, so an immediate skulk ensures that the new structure is reflected throughout the namespace as quickly as possible.

- The CDS server initiates skulks automatically at a routine interval called the *background skulk time*.

  The background skulk time interval guarantees a maximum lapse of time between skulks of a directory, regardless of other factors, such as namespace management activities and user-initiated skulks. A CDS server periodically checks each master replica in its clearinghouse and initiates a skulk if changes were made in a directory since the last successful skulk of that directory.

14.3 How Timestamps Help Keep Data Consistent

CDS uses several timestamps to help ensure the consistency and accuracy of data. The following two timestamps exist for every entry:

- Creation Timestamp (CTS)
- Update Timestamp (UTS)

CDS assigns a CTS to everything that is in a cell namespace: clearinghouses, directories, object entries, soft links, and child pointers. The CTS is a unique value reflecting the date, time, and location where a clearinghouse, directory, or entry in a directory was created. It consists of two parts: a time portion and the system identifier of the node on which the name was created. The two parts guarantee uniqueness among timestamps that are generated on different nodes.

During propagation of a new name or a changed name to each replica of the directory where it was created, every CDS server checks the validity of the CTS before accepting the new name.

The UTS reflects the most recent change that was made to any of the attributes of a clearinghouse, directory, object entry, soft link, or child pointer. When a CDS server receives an update to an existing entry in a directory, it checks the validity of the UTS before accepting the update.

Directories and replicas have several other timestamps that CDS uses when determining whether to skulk a directory or make a change in a directory. (See the **directory(8dce)** reference page for information about other timestamp attributes used by CDS.)

Chapter 15

Managing the DCE Directory Service

The DCE control program (**dcecp**) provides most of the commands you need to manage CDS. This chapter describes the CDS entities that the DCE control program permits you to manage and summarizes the available commands for managing these entities.

A few CDS management tasks cannot be performed using **dcecp**. To perform these tasks, you need to use the CDS control program (**cdscp**). This chapter provides some information that you need to run **cdscp** and notes the operations for which the program's commands are required.

For detailed descriptions of **dcecp** and **cdscp** commands discussed in this chapter, see the **dcecp(8dce)** and **cdscp(8cds)** reference pages.

15.1 Using the DCE Control Program

Chapter 1 of this guide introduced you to **dcecp** and its command syntax, so this chapter does not repeat this information. This chapter describes the commands that **dcecp** supplies specifically for managing CDS.

15.1.1 CDS Managed Objects

DCE control program commands operate on the following objects representing CDS entities:

directory
: This object represents a CDS directory. The directory can be a parent or child directory, or a master or read-only replica of the parent or child directory. In addition to child directories, a CDS directory can contain soft links and object entries for other CDS resources.

link
: This object represents a soft link in a CDS directory. A soft link is a pointer to (alternate name for) a child directory, object entry, or other soft link.

object
: This object represents a object entry, which is the name of a CDS resource that appears in the cell namespace. Some object entries name resources that CDS clients can access (for example, a disk, machine, or application). Others name resources solely for internal use by CDS (for example, servers and clearinghouses).

clearinghouse
: This object represents a CDS clearinghouse. A clearinghouse is a database that is located on a CDS server machine for use by servers.

cdscache
: This object represents a CDS cache. A CDS cache is a collection of information about servers, clearinghouses, and other CDS resources that a CDS clerk establishes on the local system for its reference.

cdsalias
: This object represents an alias name of a DCE cell as known to CDS. This object can be used to establish a hierarchical relationship between two DCE cells.

15.1.2 DCE Control Program Operations for CDS

Table 15-1 lits the operations that **dcecp** performs on CDS objects.

Table 15–1. DCE Control Program Operations for CDS

Operation	Definition
add	Adds a child directory to a parent in the cell namespace.
catalog	Displays a list of a DCE cell's alias names.
create	Creates an object in the cell namespace. The object type can be a directory, object entry, soft link, clearinghouse, CDS cache, or CDS cell alias.
delete	Deletes an object in the cell namespace. The object type can be a directory, object entry, soft link, clearinghouse, or CDS cell alias.
disable	Removes the knowledge of a clearinghouse from the server running on the local machine.
dump	Displays an in-core dump of a CDS cache.
help	Displays a help message for a CDS object type, describing the operations that it performs or operations that can be performed on it. The object type can be a directory, object entry, soft link, clearinghouse, or CDS cache.
list	Displays the names of all of the CDS objects contained in a directory.
merge	Copies the contents of a directory into another directory.
modify	Modifies the attribute information for a CDS object type. The object type can be a directory, object entry, or soft link.
operations	Displays the operations that a CDS object type can perform or can have performed on it. The object type can be a directory, object entry, soft link, or clearinghouse.

Operation	Definition
ping	Checks if all or selected servers are running in a DCE cell.
remove	Removes a child directory from a parent in the cell namespace.
set	Sets the primary name of a cell to a different alias, or creates a hierarchical relationship between two cells through an alias.
show	Displays the attribute information for a CDS object type. The object type can be a directory, object entry, soft link, or clearinghouse.
synchronize	Tells a child or parent directory to synchronize with its replicas (perform a skulk).

15.1.3 CDS Object Attributes

Every CDS object has attributes, which are pieces or sets of data associated with the object. Attributes can reflect or affect the operational behavior of the object. Some attributes are created and modified only by CDS; you can modify others as needed for your environment. For a complete list of the attributes of a particular CDS object, refer to the appropriate reference page. Also, you can use the **dcecp show** operation for most objects to display the names and values of all attributes or specific attributes of the objects.

15.2 Using the CDS Control Program

At the current time, you must use **cdscp**, rather than **dcecp**, for certain CDS maintenance tasks. For example, only **cdscp** allows you to stop a CDS clerk (**disable clerk**) or to reconstruct a directory's replica set by changing the version number (**set directory to new epoch**).

In addition to describing the **cdscp** commands that **dcecp** does not currently implement, this section provides basic instructions for using **cdscp**.

15.2.1 Starting and Exiting

To start **cdscp**, enter the following command:

$ cdscp

To exit from **cdscp**, enter the following command:

cdscp> **quit**

To read a file of the **cdscp** commands while inside the control program, enter the following command:

cdscp> **do** *filename*

15.2.2 DCS Control Program Commands

Table 15-2 lists the **cdscp** commands that you use to manage CDS clerks, servers, directory replicas, and cells.

Table 15–2. CDS Control Program Commands

Commands	Definitions
disable clerk	Stops the execution of a CDS clerk.
disable server	Stops the execution of a CDS server.
set cdscp confidence	Permits you to set the confidence level of CDS clerk calls.
set directory to new epoch	Reconstructs a directory's replica set by designating a new master replica.
show cdscp confidence	Permits you to see the current confidence level of CDS clerk calls.
show cell	Displays the information needed for creating a cell entry in DNS or GDS.
show clerk	Displays the attributes of a CDS clerk.
show server	Displays the attributes of a CDS server.

Chapter 16

Controlling Access to CDS Names

This chapter presents information on the following CDS authorization topics:

- Overview of DCE authorization for CDS

- DCE authorization components supported by CDS

- DCE permissions supported by CDS

- Controlling access to CDS clerk and server management operations

- Control program commands and required permissions

- Editing ACLs on CDS names

- How CDS servers gain access to the namespace

- Setting up access control in a new namespace

16.1 Overview of DCE Authorization for CDS

CDS authorization allows you to control user access to the following CDS components:

- Names that are stored in the namespace, including clearinghouses, directories, object entries, soft links, and child pointers

- Execution of privileged CDS clerk and server commands

You control access to a name in the namespace by creating an ACL. An ACL contains individual ACL entries that specify the permissions you grant a user (principal) to the name with which the ACL is associated. The ACL entries that you create determine collectively which principals can use the name and what management operations they are allowed to perform on it.

CDS ACL management software, incorporated into all CDS clerks and servers, performs access checking for incoming CDS requests. When a principal requests an operation on a CDS name, ACL management software on a server that stores the name examines the ACL entries associated with the name. The software then grants or denies the operation, based on the permissions granted to the requesting principal in the ACL entries. Similarly, when a principal requests a privileged operation on a CDS clerk or server, ACL management software on that system examines the ACL entries that are associated with the principal name that represents the clerk or server. The software then grants or denies the operation, based on the permissions granted to the requesting principal in the ACL entries.

The DCE control program (**dcecp**) provides commands that add, modify, copy, delete, and display ACLs that are associated with CDS names, clerks, and servers. See the *OSF DCE Command Reference* for detailed information on the commands. The remainder of this chapter describes DCE authorization as it applies specifically to CDS. Before you try to create or modify permissions to CDS names, clerks, or servers, read Part 6 of this guide for complete information on the DCE authorization mechanism.

16.2 ACL Types Supported by CDS

CDS supports the following DCE ACL types:

- Object ACL—You can use the Object ACL type to grant permissions to any CDS name (that is, object entries, soft links, child pointers, clearinghouses, and directories), as well as to CDS clerks and servers. When associated with a CDS directory, the permissions you grant with the Object ACL type apply only to the directory itself, not to the directory's contents or to any child directories.

- Initial Object Creation ACL—The Initial Object Creation ACL type applies only to CDS directory names. Use this ACL type to grant permissions specifically to a directory's future contents, including soft links, application-defined object entries, child pointers, and clearinghouse object entries. The permissions you grant by using the Initial Object Creation ACL type apply only to the future contents of the directory, not to the directory itself. The permissions are inherited only by names that are created in the directory *after* you create the ACL entry; permissions are not propagated to names that already exist in the directory.

  To edit an Initial Object Creation ACL, you use the **-io** option of the **dcecp acl modify** command.

- Initial Container Creation ACL—The Initial Container Creation ACL type applies only to CDS directory names. Use this ACL type to grant permissions to a directory that automatically propagate (the default) to all child directories that you may later create under that directory. The permissions you grant by using the Initial Container Creation ACL type are inherited only by the child directories that you create *after* you create the ACL entry; permissions are not propagated to child directories that already exist.

  To edit an Initial Container Creation ACL, you use the **-ic** option of the **dcecp acl modify** command.

16.3 How Permissions Propagate to CDS Directories and Their Contents

By creating all three ACL types (Object ACL, Initial Object Creation ACL, and Initial Container Creation ACL) for a directory, you can grant access not only to the directory itself but also to the directory's future contents and all child directories (and their contents) that may later be created.

Note: Permissions do not propagate from parent cells to child cells. You must set permissions for each child cell individually.

For example, suppose you just created a new directory named **/.:/sales**. If you create an ACL entry of the Object ACL type that grants user **Smith** read permission to the **/.:/sales** directory, **Smith** can do the following:

- Read the attributes associated with the **/.:/sales** directory

- Display the names stored in the **/.:/sales** directory

If you create a second ACL entry of the Initial Object Creation ACL type that grants user **Smith** read permission to the **/.:/sales** directory, **Smith** can do the following:

- Read the attributes associated with the **/.:/sales** directory

- Display the names stored in the **/.:/sales** directory

- Read the attributes associated with all the names that you may later create in the **/.:/sales** directory, unless prohibited by explicit ACL modification after their creation

If you create a third ACL entry of the Initial Container Creation ACL type that also grants user **Smith** read permission to the **/.:/sales** directory, **Smith** can do the following:

- Read the attributes associated with the **/.:/sales** directory

- Display the names stored in the **/.:/sales** directory

- Read the attributes associated with all the names that you may later create in the **/.:/sales** directory

- Perform all of the three preceding operations on all child directories that may later be created under the **/.:/sales** directory

(See Part 6 of this guide for complete information on default ACLs.)

16.4 ACL Entry Types Used for Principals

You use ACL entry types to specify the category of principal for which the ACL entry is created. These ACL entry types are described in Table 16-1.

Table 16–1. ACL Entry Types Used for CDS Principals

Entry Type	Purpose
user	Specifies an ACL entry for an individual principal whose credentials were authenticated within the local cell.
group	Specifies an ACL entry for an authorization group whose members have been authenticated within the local cell.
other_obj	Specifies an ACL entry for authenticated principals in the local cell who are not individual users named by an ACL entry of the type **user** or members of a group named by an ACL entry of the type or **group**.
foreign_user	Specifies an ACL entry for an authenticated principal in a foreign cell.
foreign_group	Specifies an ACL entry for an authorization group whose members were authenticated in a foreign cell.
foreign_other	Specifies an ACL entry for authenticated principals in a foreign cell who are not individual users named by an ACL entry of the type **foreign_user** or members of a group named by an ACL entry of the type **foreign_group**.
any_other	Specifies an ACL entry for an authenticated principal who is not otherwise covered by any of the preceding ACL entry types.

Entry Type	Purpose
mask_obj	Specifies an ACL entry containing a mask that is substituted for the permissions of any principals, whose credentials are either authenticated or unauthenticated.
unauthenticated	Specifies an ACL entry for principals who cannot pass authentication procedures.
user_delegate	Specifies an ACL entry for an intermediary that acts for an authenticated principal in the local cell.
group_delegate	Specifies an ACL entry for an intermediary that acts for the authenticated principals who are members of an authorization group in the local cell.
other_delegate	Specifies an ACL entry for an intermediary that acts for authenticated principals in the local cell who are not individual users named by an ACL entry of the type **user_delegate** or who are not members of a group named by an ACL entry of the type **group_delegate**.
foreign_user_delegate	Specifies an ACL entry for an intermediary that acts for an authenticated principal in a foreign cell.
foreign_group_delegate	Specifies an ACL entry for an intermediary that acts for the members of an authorization group in a foreign cell.
foreign_other_delegate	Specifies an ACL entry for an intermediary that acts for authenticated principals in a foreign cell who are not individual users named by an ACL entry of the type **foreign_user_delegate** or members of a group named by an ACL entry of the type **foreign_group_delegate**.

Entry Type	Purpose
any_other_delegate	Specifies an ACL entry for an intermediary that acts for authenticated principals in the local cell or in a foreign cell who are not named by an ACL entry of any other type for intermediaries of authenticated principals or groups.

16.5 DCE Permissions Supported by CDS

CDS supports the following DCE permissions: read (**r**), write (**w**), insert (**i**), delete (**d**), test (**t**), control (**c**), and administer (**a**). Each permission has a slightly different meaning, depending on the kind of CDS name with which it is associated. In general, the permissions are defined as follows:

- Read Permission—Allows a principal to look up a name and view the attribute values that are associated with it.

- Write Permission—Allows a principal to change the modifiable attributes that are associated with a name, except its ACLs.

- Insert Permission—Allows a principal to create new names in a directory (for use with directory entries only).

- Delete Permission—Allows a principal to delete a name from the namespace.

- Test Permission—Allows a principal to test whether an attribute of a name has a particular value without being able to actually see any of the values; that is, without having read permission to the name.

  Test permission provides application programs with a more efficient way to verify a CDS attribute value. Rather than reading an entire set of values, an application can test for the presence of a particular value.

- Control Permission—Allows a principal to modify the ACL entries that are associated with a name. (Note that read permission is also necessary for modifying a CDS entry's ACLs; otherwise, **dcecp** and **acl_edit** will not be able to bind to the entry.) Control permission is automatically granted to the creator of a CDS entry.

- Administer Permission—Allows a principal to issue CDS commands that control the replication of directories. Administer permission is for use with directory entries only.

A principal needs some permission to a name before it can try to perform management operations on the name. Otherwise, CDS does not recognize the name when the principal tries the management operation and returns an error stating that the name does not exist. If the principal has some permissions, but not those required to perform the operation, CDS returns an error explaining that the principal had insufficient rights to perform the operation.

The creator of a name is automatically granted all permissions that are appropriate for the type of name that is created. For example, a principal that is creating an object entry is granted read, write, delete, test, and control permissions to the object entry. A principal that is creating a directory is granted read, write, insert, delete, test, control, and administer permissions to the directory.

Note: Unlike the security mechanisms that are enforced by most other file systems, CDS does not require a principal to have access to all intermediate elements in the pathname (full name) of a name in order to perform an operation on the name. For example, consider an object entry **object1** stored in the **/.:/sales** directory. In CDS, you can grant a principal access to the object entry **/.:/sales/object1** without necessarily granting the principal access to either the **/.:/sales** directory or the cell root directory (**/.:**).

16.6 Controlling Access to CDS Clerk and Server Management Operations

CDS authorization allows you to control the use of CDS commands that involve local management operations on CDS clerks and servers. Principal names for each clerk and server are stored in the security namespace. An object entry that contains the binding information for each clerk and server is stored in the CDS namespace in the **/.:/hosts** subdirectory. Servers are represented as **/.:/hosts/***hostname***/cds-server**. Clerks are represented as **/.:/hosts/***hostname***/cds-clerk**.

Each clerk and server maintains a separate ACL that contains entries specifying the principals allowed to perform these operations. Unlike the ACLs that are associated with names in the namespace, the ACLs that are associated with clerks and servers exist exclusively to provide local control of the use of these commands.

Whenever a new clerk or server is initialized, an ACL is created on the clerk or server system. An initial ACL entry is also created, granting the machine principal and the namespace authorization group (**subsys/dce/cds-admin**) read, write, and control permissions to the clerk or server process on that system. All other principals, both authenticated and unauthenticated, are granted read permission. The creation of this ACL entry ensures that, immediately after its creation, any user logged into the system as the machine principal is permitted to execute privileged clerk or server CDS commands.

Note: Use of the machine principal for this purpose is provided as a convenience and assumes that the account itself (user name and password) is already moderately secure. Namespace administrators may prefer to modify this scheme and grant permission to particular clerks and servers on behalf of other individual principals or authorization groups.

To edit an ACL that is associated with a CDS clerk or server, you use the **dcecp acl modify** command with the **-change** option. For example, to change the permissions for the user **michaels** in the ACL that is associated with the CDS clerk on node **orion**, enter the following command:

dcecp> **acl modify /.:/hosts/orion/cds-clerk -change {user michaels rw}**

Keep in mind that clerks and servers are also represented by entries in the namespace. To edit an ACL that is associated with the namespace entry for a CDS clerk or server, you must include the **-entry** option, as well as the **-change** option, in the **acl modify** command line. For detailed instructions on how to modify an ACL on the CDS entry for a DCE resource, see Section 16.8.

16.7 Control Program Commands and Required Permissions

Table 16-2 lists all the **dcecp** commands that operate on CDS objects with the permissions that a principal must have to execute the commands.

Table 16–2. DCE Control Program Commands and Required Permissions

Commands	Required Permissions
cdsalias catalog	Read permission to the cell's root directory whose alias you want to list.
cdsalias connect	Administer permission to the root directory of the child cell and insert permission to the root directory of the parent directory.
cdsalias create	Administer permission to the cell root directory.
cdsalias delete	Administer permission to the cell root directory.
cdsalias connect	Administer permission to the cell root directory. The server principal requires insert permission to the parent cell's root directory when you want to establish a hierarchial cell relationship (**-child** option).
directory add	Insert permission to the parent directory where the child pointer (**-member** option) is to be placed.
directory create	For a new directory—Insert and read permissions to the parent directory, and write permission to the clearinghouse that stores the master replica of the new directory. Also, the server principal needs read and insert permissions to the parent directory of the new directory.

Commands	Required Permissions
directory create (continued)	For a replica of an existing directory (the **-replica** option)—Administer permission to the directory that you intend to replicate, and write permission to the clearinghouse (**-clearinghouse** option) that stores the new replica. Also, the server principal needs read, write, and administer permissions to the directory that you intend to replicate.
directory delete	For a directory—Delete permission to the directory, and write permission to the clearinghouse that stores the master replica of the directory. Also, the server principal needs administer permission to the parent directory, or delete permission to the child pointer that points to the directory you intend to delete. For a replica of an existing directory—Administer permission to the directory whose replica (**-replica** option) you want to delete, and write permission to the clearinghouse (**-clearinghouse** option) from which you are deleting the replica.
directory list	Read permission to the directory whose contents you want to list.
directory modify	Write permission to the directory for which you want to add (**-add** option) or change (**-change** option) the attribute or attribute value. Delete permission to the directory for which you want to remove the attribute or attribute value (**-remove** option).
directory remove	Write permission to the parent directory of the child pointer (**-member** option) you want to remove.

Commands	Required Permissions
directory synchronize	Administer, write, insert, and delete permission to the directory. Also, the server principal needs administer, read, and write permissions to the directory.
directory show	Read permission to the directory whose attributes you want to list. If you specify a wildcard directory name, you also need read permission to the directory's parent directory. For a replica of a directory (**-replica** option)—Read permission to the directory of which the replica is a member. For a child directory (**-member**)—Read permission to the child.
object create	Insert permission to the parent directory that is to store the object entry.
object delete	Delete permission to the object entry, or administer permission to the parent directory that stores the object entry.
object modify	Write permission to the object entry for which you want to add (**-add** option) or change (**-change** option) the attribute or attribute value. Delete permission to the object entry, or administer permission to the parent directory of the object for which you want to remove (**-remove** option) the attribute or attribute value.
object show	Read permission to the object entry whose attributes you want to list.
cdscache create	Write permission to the clerk that is to create the server entry in the local CDS cache.

Commands	Required Permissions
cdscache delete	Write permission to the clerk that is to delete the server entry in the local CDS cache.
cdscache dump	Superuser (root) privileges on the clerk system where the CDS cache resides. No CDS permissions are required.
cdscache show	Read permission to the clerk that is to retrieve the server (**-server** option) or clearinghouse (**-clearinghouse** option) information from the CDS cache.
clearinghouse create	Write permission to the server on which you intend to create the clearinghouse, and administer permission to the cell root directory. Also, the server principal needs read, write, and administer permissions to the cell root directory.
clearinghouse delete	Write and delete permissions to the clearinghouse to be deleted, and administer permission to all directories that store replicas in the clearinghouse. Also, the server principal needs delete permission to the associated clearinghouse object entry, and administer permission to all directories that store replicas in the clearinghouse.
clearinghouse disable	Write permission to the server that is to lose knowledge of the clearinghouse.
clearinghouse show	Read permission to the clearinghouse whose attributes you want to list. If you specify a wildcard clearinghouse name, you also need read permission to the cell root directory.
link create	Insert permission to the directory in which you intend to create the soft link.

16.10.3 Establishing Maximum Permissions for Unauthenticated Principals

If you want to apply a namespace-wide set of maximum permissions for all unauthenticated principals, you should do so immediately *after* you configure your first CDS server and *before* you create and populate any directories below the cell root. By creating an unauthenticated ACL entry and an **any_other** entry for the cell root by using the Object ACL and Initial Container Creation ACL types, you can take advantage of automatic propagation of the unauthenticated entry to the entire namespace as it evolves.

Managing Clerks, Servers, and Clearinghouses

CDS clerks, servers, and clearinghouses are initially created and started as part of the CDS clerk and server configuration. Thereafter, clerk and server processes are created and started with a series of commands that are executed either manually or by the startup scripts on the systems where they are running. These CDS entities are largely self-regulating and, apart from routine monitoring, require only minor management intervention.

This chapter explains how to monitor CDS clerks, servers, and clearinghouses and perform other management tasks, such as backing up namespace information.

17.1 Monitoring Clerk, Server, and Clearinghouse Counters

Every clerk, server, and clearinghouse maintains a set of attributes called *counters* to keep track of the read, write, and other operations that it performed, or that were performed on it, since it was last started up. You can monitor these counters to determine the type and volume of the CDS traffic that is being generated on your network.

Clerk, server, and clearinghouse counters are fully described in the *OSF DCE Command Reference*.

17.1.1 Displaying Clerk Counters

Use the CDS control program (**cdscp**) **show clerk** command to display the current counter values for a clerk. For example, to display the current values of all attributes that are associated with a clerk, you enter the following command:

cdscp> **show clerk**

17.1.2 Displaying Server Counters

Use the **cdscp show server** command to display the current counter values for a server. For example, to display the current values of all the attributes that are associated with a server, you enter the following command:

cdscp> **show server**

17.1.3 Displaying Clearinghouse Counters

Use the DCE control program's (**dcecp**) **clearinghouse show** command with the **-counters** option to display the current counter values for a specified clearinghouse. For example, the following command displays the current values of all attributes that are associated with the remote clearinghouse **/.:/Paris1_CH**:

dcecp> **clearinghouse show /.:/Paris1_CH -counters**

17.2 Monitoring Clerk Communications with Specific Clearinghouses

Every CDS clerk maintains a separate set of clearinghouse counters to keep track of read, write, and other operations that it directs to each of the clearinghouses with which it communicates. These records collectively represent the cached clearinghouse entity for a particular clerk.

You can monitor a clerk's cached clearinghouse counters so that you can look at the distribution of the clerk's transactions to each of the clearinghouses that it uses and find out where a clerk's requests are most often directed. To do this, you use the **dcecp cdscache show** command with the **-clear** option. For example, to display the cached clearinghouse counters that are maintained by the local clerk for the **/.:/NY1_CH** clearinghouse, you enter the following command:

dcecp> **cdscache show /.:/NY1_CH -clear**

The following command displays the cached clearinghouse counters for all the clearinghouses that are used by the local clerk:

dcecp> **cdscache show /.:/* -clear**

17.3 Displaying the Contents of a Clearinghouse

Use the **dcecp clearinghouse show** command with the **-clear** option and specify the **CDS_CHDirectories** attribute to display the directory names of all the directories that are stored in a particular clearinghouse. For example, to display the names of the directories that are stored in the clearinghouse **/.:/Chicago2_CH**, you enter the following command:

dcecp> **clearinghouse show /.:/Chicago2_CH CDS_CHDirectories -clear**

(See Chapter 19 for more examples of displaying clearinghouse information.)

17.4 Forcing the Clearinghouse to Checkpoint to Disk

Under normal operations, the server will periodically checkpoint the clearinghouse from memory to disk. However, you can perform this task immediately by having write permission to the server and entering the **dcecp clearinghouse initiate** command with the **checkpoint** option. For example, to checkpoint the clearinghouse **/.:/Boston3_CH** from memory to disk, you enter the following command:

dcecp> **clearinghouse initiate /.:/Boston3_CH -checkpoint**

17.5 Disabling Clerks and Servers

You may occasionally have to disable the clerk or server that is running on a particular system when you need to perform diagnostic or troubleshooting work that requires active clerk or server processes to be suspended. Usually, you can use the **dce_config** procedure to start and stop DCE daemons. You can disable CDS clerks and servers by using the **disable clerk** and **disable server** commands of **cdscp**.

17.5.1 Disabling a Clerk

To disable the clerk that is on the local node, enter the following command:

cdscp> **disable clerk**

17.5.2 Disabling a Server

To disable the server that is on the local node, enter the following command:

cdscp> **disable server**

17.6 Restarting Clerks and Servers

CDS clerk and server processes are created and started automatically by startup scripts that execute whenever the host system is rebooted. Sometimes, however, you may need to run these scripts yourself if a clerk or server fails to start automatically upon reboot, or if you want to restart a clerk or server that you disabled to perform a backup or do diagnostic work on the host system.

17.6.1 Restarting a Clerk

To restart a clerk, follow these steps:

1. Log into the clerk system as superuser (**root**).

2. Enter the following command to see if the **dced** process is already running:

    # **ps -e**

3. If the **dced** process appears on the list of active processes, proceed to step 4. If the **dced** process does not appear on the list of active processes, enter the following command to start the process:

    # **dced**

4. Enter the following command to start the **cdsadv** process:

    # **cdsadv**

17.6.2 Restarting a Server

To restart a server, follow these steps:

1. Log into the server system as superuser (**root**).

2. Enter the following command to see if the **dced** process is already running:

   # **ps -e**

3. If the **dced** process appears on the list of active processes, proceed to step 4. If the **dced** process does not appear on the list of active processes, enter the following command to start the process:

   # **dced**

4. Enter the following command to see if the **cdsadv** process is already running:

   # **ps -e**

5. If the **cdsadv** process appears on the list of active processes, proceed to step 6. If the **cdsadv** process does not appear on the list of active processes, enter the following command to start the process:

   # **cdsadv**

6. Enter the following command to restart the server:

   # **cdsd**

When the server process starts, it starts all clearinghouses on the system.

17.7 Preserving a Clearinghouse Across a Server System Upgrade

If you plan to upgrade the operating system software on a CDS server system, and you want to preserve the clearinghouse (or clearinghouses) on the system, follow this procedure:

1. Make sure that you disable the clerk and server.

2. Before you perform the system upgrade, back up the following CDS files:

    cds_attributes
    cds_files
    _ch.checkpointnnnnnnnn*
    _ch.tlognnnnnnnn*
    ***_ch.version**
    cds_cache.*nnnnnnnn*
    cds_cache.version
    cds_cache.wan

    (See the *OSF DCE Administration Guide—Introduction* and the *OSF DCE Porting and Testing Guide* for the full pathnames of all CDS files.)

3. Perform the system upgrade.

4. Restore all the files that you backed up in step 2.

5. Follow the procedure described in Section 17.6 for restarting a server. When the server process starts, it automatically locates the appropriate restored files and starts all clearinghouses on the system.

17.8 Backing Up Namespace Information

Because updates and skulks of directories can occur asynchronously, and because of the distributed nature of a namespace, you cannot always depend on traditional backup methods to preserve CDS data.

The rest of this chapter tells when to use the following backup mechanisms:

- Directory replication

- Operating system backups

17.8.1 Using Replication to Back Up Namespace Information

Directory replication is always the most reliable way to back up the information that is in your namespace. When you create a new replica of a directory at a clearinghouse, you are not only distributing the information but also creating an up-to-date, real-time backup of the information. If a replica in one clearinghouse becomes unavailable, users can look up the information they need in another replica of the directory in some other clearinghouse. The more replicas of a directory you create, the more likely users will always be able to find the information that is contained in the directory somewhere in the namespace.

If an entire clearinghouse is corrupted, you can restore it by creating a new clearinghouse and then creating new replicas of the directories that were stored there. (See Chapter 18 for complete information on how to create a replica.)

17.8.2 Using Operating System Backups

Because a namespace is a distributed database to which modifications are synchronized at variable intervals, any traditional backup of a particular server system always contains old and incomplete information. If you frequently create, modify, or delete names, restoring an out-of-date backup can cause recently created names to disappear, recent modifications to be reversed, or recently deleted names to reappear in the namespace. The degree to which a traditional backup reflects the current condition of a clearinghouse depends entirely on the following conditions:

- How recently the backup was created

- What modifications were made since that time

- Whether the backup included the clearinghouse files in the directory *dcelocal*/**var/directory/cds**

If you decide to use operating system backups, you only need to back up the server systems whose clearinghouses store master replicas of directories. To ensure that you back up your namespace completely, check for the following:

- The servers on these systems are disabled by using the **cdscp disable server** command.

- The files in the root directory *dcelocal*/**var/directory/cds** are included in the backup.

If your namespace is small enough to be maintained in one clearinghouse, you can reliably use traditional operating system backups to save and restore the clearinghouse data. If only one clearinghouse exists, only one replica (the master replica) of each directory exists. This eliminates the need to account for the discrepancies that may exist among multiple directory replicas. Remember that the more frequently you back up clearinghouse data, the more up-to-date that information will be if you need to restore it.

Chapter 18

Managing CDS Directories

If you manage a namespace in a small, slow-growth network of 25 nodes or less, you can maintain all your names in the root directory and may not need to create additional directories. However, if you manage a namespace in a network of more than 25 nodes, you should consider creating at least one additional level of directories under the root.

This chapter explains how to create directory hierarchies in the cell namespace and describes tasks related to managing directories, such as

- Creating and deleting directory replicas

- Skulking a directory

- Modifying a directory's convergence

18.1 Creating Directories

By creating directories, you make it possible to replicate and manage groups of object entries according to where, how often, or by whom they are used. Grouping related object entries into separate directories also makes it easier to control access because it allows you to take advantage of default ACL entry propagation.

CDS cell configuration creates an initial hierarchy of directories under the root so that DCE components can fix locations within the namespace where they can create and catalog their object entries. Among the directories created by cell configuration is the **subsys** directory, beneath which Independent Software Vendors (ISVs) can create their own directories to store the object entries that are used by their distributed applications.

Alternatively, ISVs and other users of the namespace may prefer to create a hierarchy of directories of their own design under the root to store their information.

(See the *OSF DCE Administration Guide—Introduction* for more information on the initial hierarchy that is established by cell configuration.)

18.1.1 Permissions for Creating a Directory

To create a directory, you need the following permissions:

- Insert permission to the parent of the new directory.

- Write permission to the clearinghouse that stores the master replica of the new directory.

- The server principal for the server system where you enter the DCE control program's (**dcecp**) **directory create** command must have read and insert permissions to the parent directory of the new directory.

  If the server is included in the server authorization group **subsys/dce/cds-servers**, these permissions should already be in place. If in doubt, use the **dcecp acl show** command on the parent directory to verify that the server principal has the appropriate permissions. (See the **acl(8dce)** reference page for more information on arguments to the **acl show** command.)

18.1.2 Entering the directory create Command

Use the **directory create** command to create a new directory (master replica) with the name that you specify. When you use this command, CDS, by default, stores the master replica of the new directory in the same clearinghouse that stores the master replica of the new directory's parent directory.

For example, to create a directory named **/.:/sales** and store the master replica of the new directory in the root directory's initial clearinghouse, you enter the following command:

dcecp> **directory create /.:/sales**

Note: For the directory creation to succeed, the master replica of the new directory's parent directory must be available when you enter the command.

You can use the **directory create** command's **-clearinghouse** option to store the master replica of a new directory in a different clearinghouse than the parent directory's clearinghouse. For example, to place the new directory created in the previous example into another clearinghouse (**/.:/Chicago1_CH**), you would enter the following command:

dcecp> **directory create /.:/sales -clearinghouse /.:/Chicago1_CH**

(See the **directory(8dce)** reference page for complete information on arguments and options to the **directory create** command.)

18.1.3 Checking the ACL Entries for a New Directory

After you create a directory, you want to verify that the users and applications for whom the directory was created have the appropriate permissions. To do this, use the **acl show** command on the directory to see the associated ACL entries. For example:

```
dcecp>   acl show  /.:/sales
{unauthenticated r--t-}
{group subsys/dce/cds-admin rwdtc}
{group subsys/dce/cds-server rwdtc}
{any_other r--t-}
```

(See the **acl(8dce)** reference page for complete information on the **acl show** command.)

If the required permissions were not inherited from the new directory's parent directory, use the **acl modify** command to create the necessary ACL entries. For example:

```
dcecp>   acl modify /.:/sales -add {user cell_admin rwdtcia}
```

(See the **acl(8dce)** reference page for complete information on the arguments and options for the **acl modify** command.)

18.1.4 Upgrading the Directory Version on the Cell Root Directory

Upgrading the directory version on the cell root directory has special significance. This procedure implies that all CDS servers in the cell have been upgraded to the latest version, given that a cell root directory is replicated in all CDS servers in the cell. After you have set the **CDS_UpgradeTo** attribute on the cell root directory, the server software soon recognizes this and sets the **CDS_UpgradeTo** attribute on all directories in the cell. Eventually, the **CDS_DirectoryVersion** attribute on all the affected directories in the cell will be upgraded to the new value.

18.1.5 Upgrading the Directory Version on a Directory

To use new features in a given release of CDS, you may need to explicitly update the directory version of a directory. This typically occurs when the servers replicating the directory all have been upgraded to the latest version of software, as older versions will not recognize the new features.

To upgrade the directory version, you need write permission to the directory and you must use the following commands:

dcecp> **directory modify** *directory-name* **-add** {**CDS_UpgradeTo** *<v.n>*} **-single**
dcecp> **directory synchronize** *directory-name*

Eventually, all clearinghouses that contain a replica of this directory will detect the presence of the **CDS_UpgradeTo** attribute and upgrade the **CDS_ReplicaVersion** attribute on the appropriate replica. You can also use the following command on all clearinghouses that are replicating the directory:

dcecp> **clearinghouse verify** *clearinghouse-name*

This command forces the server background thread to run, thereby freeing you to perform other tasks until the job finishes. After you have verified all affected clearinghouses, you will need to perform another skulk of the directory to finally set the **CSA_DirectoryVersion** attribute to the appropriate value. The **CDS_DirectoryVersion** attribute is not upgraded until all of the **CDS_ReplicaVersion** attribute values of all replicas contain the new value.

18.2 Creating a Read-Only Replica

From time to time, you will want to create read-only replicas of directories. You create read-only replicas of a directory for the following purposes:

- To distribute the information that is contained in the directory throughout your network, and to make the information more accessible to users and applications at other locations.

- To improve response time, especially in a namespace where users are dispersed over long distances. You should create read-only replicas in clearinghouses that are located near the user groups and applications that most frequently use the information that is contained in the directory.

- To preserve a backup of the information that is contained in the master replica of the directory. Maintaining multiple replicas ensures that the temporary loss of an individual replica does not cause an interruption in service and that the loss of a replica can be easily recovered. Even directories that store information used at only one particular site should be replicated in at least one other clearinghouse, preferably on a server at another location, so that a local failure at one site does not cause both replicas to be unreachable at the same time. (See Chapter 17 for more information on using directory replication as a means of backing up CDS information.)

Read-only replicas of directories are safe from alteration by users. Users can look up information in a read-only replica, but they are not permitted to create new information or modify existing information.

You create read-only replicas with the **-replica** option of the **directory create** command. You should create the replicas in clearinghouses whose users need to access the directory but do not need, or are not permitted, to update its contents.

18.2.1 Before You Create a Replica

Before you try to create a replica, verify that the clearinghouse containing the master replica of the directory you intend to replicate is running and reachable. To verify that this condition is satisfied, follow these steps:

1. For the directory that you intend to replicate, use the **directory show** command to display the directories attribute values and look at the **CDS_Replicas** attribute. The value of this attribute shows the names of the clearinghouses that currently store a replica of the directory. For example:

```
dcecp> directory show /.:/sales
{RPC_ClassVersion {01 00}}
{CDS_CTS 1994-08-12-09:52:30.396-04:00I0.000/00-00-c0-f7-de-56}
{CDS_UTS 1994-08-12-09:52:31.506-04:00I0.000/00-00-c0-f7-de-56}
{CDS_ObjectUUID a37d84d0-b5dc-11cd-8ffe-0000c0f7de56}
{CDS_Replicas
 {{CH_UUID ce7ed810-b5db-11cd-8ffe-0000c0f7de56}
  {CH_Name /.../Chicago1/Chicago1_CH}
  {Replica_Type Master}
  {Tower {ncacn_ip_tcp 130.105.5.16}}
  {Tower {ncadg_ip_udp 130.105.5.16}}}}
{CDS_AllUpTo 1994-08-12-09:52:31.566-04:00I0.000/00-00-c0-f7-de-56}
{CDS_Convergence medium}
{CDS_ParentPointer
 {{Parent_UUID d034bc25-b5db-11cd-8ffe-0000c0f7de56}
  {Timeout
   {expiration 1994-08-12-09:52:30.396}
   {extension +1-00:00:00.000I0.000}}
  {myname /.../Chicago1/sales}}}
{CDS_DirectoryVersion 3.0}
{CDS_ReplicaState on}
{CDS_ReplicaType Master}
{CDS_LastSkulk 1994-08-12-09:52:31.566-04:00I0.000/00-00-c0-f7-de-56}
{CDS_LastUpdate 1994-08-12-09:52:31.506-04:00I0.000/00-00-c0-f7-de-56}
{CDS_RingPointer ce7ed810-b5db-11cd-8ffe-0000c0f7de56}
{CDS_Epoch a3df2a50-b5dc-11cd-8ffe-0000c0f7de56}
{CDS_ReplicaVersion 3.0}
```

2. With this information, use the **directory show** command with the
   -clearinghouse and **-replica** options to verify that you can get a
   response from the clearinghouse that stores the master replica. For
   example:

18.3.1 Permissions for Deleting a Replica

To delete a replica, you must have the following permissions:

- Administer permission to the directory whose replica you want to delete

- Write permission to the clearinghouse from which you are deleting the replica

18.3.2 Entering the directory delete Command

Use the **directory delete** command with the **-replica** and **-clearinghouse** options to delete a replica from the clearinghouse that you specify. For example, the following command deletes a replica of the **/.:/eng** directory from the **/.:/Chicago2_CH** clearinghouse:

dcecp> **directory delete /.:/eng -replica -clearinghouse /.:/Chicago2_CH**

Note: You can delete a directory's master replica only by deleting the directory itself (by using the **directory delete** command). (See Chapter 21 for complete information on how to delete a master replica.)

18.4 Skulking a Directory

The skulk operation is a periodic distribution of recent modifications that were made to the namespace. CDS skulks every directory at regular intervals according to the value assigned to the directory's **CDS_Convergence** attribute. To ensure that updates are distributed to all replicas of a directory as soon as possible, you can initiate a skulk of the directory by using the **directory synchronize** command rather than waiting for the next scheduled skulk to distribute the new information. You can use this command to perform the following tasks:

- Distribute crucial updates that were made to a directory's contents or replica set when you do not want to wait for the next skulk

- Skulk directories that store replicas on servers that were inoperative for an extended period and were just brought back online

18.4.1 Permissions for Skulking a Directory

To skulk a directory, you must have the following permissions:

- Administer, write, insert, or delete permission to the directory.

- The server principal for the server system where you enter the **directory synchronize** command needs read, write, and administer permissions to the directory that you intend to skulk.

  If the server is included in the server authorization group **subsys/dce/cds-servers**, these permissions should already be in place. If in doubt, use the **acl show** command to verify that the server principal has the appropriate permissions. (See the **acl(8dce)** reference page for complete information on the **acl show** command arguments.)

18.4.2 Entering the directory synchronize Command

Use the **directory synchronize** command to initiate an immediate skulk on a directory.

After you enter the command, **dcecp** temporarily suspends the **dcecp>** prompt while the skulk is in progress. Skulks of directories with large replica sets may take some time to execute. If the prompt returns with no error messages, the skulk is successful. If error messages are displayed before the prompt returns, the skulk failed.

For a skulk to succeed, every replica in the directory's replica set must be reachable. Skulks may sometimes fail, especially on directories with large replica sets, or when the servers that store replicas of the directory are located over great distances where network connectivity is not always reliable.

Skulk failure does not make CDS unusable. Although the skulking process is unable to update information in a replica that it cannot contact, it always updates information in the replicas that it can reach. Temporarily, some replicas contain the latest information and some do not. When a skulk fails,

CDS automatically repeats the skulking process, at an interval based on the directory's convergence value, until all replicas in the set are updated with the latest changes. When all replicas contain identical information, CDS considers the skulk successful.

If skulks of a particular directory continue to fail, you can determine the cause by reviewing the log of CDS events on the server that stores the master replica of the directory. For example, the following command initiates a skulk on the **/.:/admin** directory:

dcecp> **directory synchronize /.:/admin**

18.4.3 Synchronizing CDS Server Clocks

After performing a skulk operation on a directory, you may receive the message

```
Server clocks are not synchronized
```

indicating that the server clocks are not synchronized. If so, you should first check to see whether the system clocks on the server systems are indeed synchronized. If they are and you still receive the message, then perhaps the system clock on an individual server was mistakenly set to a future time and subsequently restored. This causes a problem for CDS because there may be timestamps stored in a clearinghouse that are invalid (any timestamp greater than 5 minutes in the future from the current time).

If this is the case, you should adjust the system clock to the current time and then enter the following command:

dcecp> **clearinghouse repair** *<clearinghouse-name>* **-timestamps**

This command will disable the clearinghouse, analyze and repair bad timestamps, checkpoint the clearinghouse to disk, and reenable the clearinghouse. To use the command, you need write permission to the server on which the clearinghouse resides. Also, you should execute this command on all clearinghouses that replicate the directory (and its objects) that needs to be repaired.

After executing the **clearinghouse repair** command, you should be able to skulk the directory successfully.

18.5 Modifying a Directory's Convergence

The value assigned to a directory's **CDS_Convergence** attribute determines how frequently the server that stores the master replica of the directory initiates a skulk of the directory's replica set. A directory's convergence can be set to a value of **high**, **medium**, or **low**.

A directory that is set to a convergence value of **high** is skulked at least once every 12 hours. If an update is made to the directory, the server that stores the master replica immediately attempts to propagate the new information to the entire replica set. If this update propagation fails, the server schedules a skulk of the directory to begin within the hour. If this initial skulk fails, additional skulks are initiated at 1-hour intervals until the skulk succeeds.

A directory that is set to a convergence value of **medium** is skulked at least once every 12 hours. If an update is made to the directory, the server that stores the master replica immediately attempts to propagate the new information to the entire replica set. If the propagation fails, the server waits for the next skulk to synchronize the replica set.

A directory that is set to a convergence value of **low** is skulked at least once every 24 hours. The server on which a low-convergence directory resides makes no immediate attempt to propagate updates and waits for the next skulk to synchronize the replica set.

Every newly created directory inherits the convergence value of its parent directory. When you create a namespace, the root directory is automatically assigned a convergence value of **medium**. Unless you change this value, or the convergence values of any lower-level directories after you create them, all directories that you create under the root also have a convergence value of **medium**. For most directories, you never need to modify this value. However, you may occasionally find it useful to set a directory's convergence to **high** or **low**.

18.5.1 Before You Modify a Directory's Convergence

Before you modify a directory's convergence, you want to verify the current convergence value of the directory. To do this, use the **directory show** command to display the directory's attribute values and look at the **CDS_Convergence** attribute value.

18.5.2 Permissions for Modifying a Directory's Convergence

To modify a directory's convergence, you must have write permission to the directory.

18.5.3 Entering the directory modify Command

Use the **directory modify** command with the **-change** option to assign a value of **high**, **medium**, or **low** to a directory's **CDS_Convergence** attribute. For example, the following command sets the convergence value of the **/.:/sales/us** directory to **high**:

dcecp> **directory modify /.:/sales/us -change {CDS_Convergence high}**

Chapter 19

Viewing the Structure and Contents of a Namespace

When you need to view the structure and contents of the cell namespace, you can use one or more programs provided by CDS. The CDS browser (**cdsbrowser**) allows you to display namespace information in a windowing environment, while the DCE control program (**dcecp**) and CDS control program (**cdscp**) display the information through their command line interfaces. This chapter explains how to use the CDS browser, **dcecp**, and **cdscp** to display namespace information.

19.1 Viewing the Namespace with the CDS Browser

The CDS browser is a tool for viewing the content and structure of a namespace, which runs on workstations with the OSF/Motif graphical user interface or compatible software. The program can display an overall directory structure as well as show the contents of directories, enabling you to monitor growth in the size and number of directories in a namespace. You also can customize the CDS browser so that it displays only a specific class of object names.

To start the CDS browser, enter the following at your system prompt:

$ cdsbrowser

To end a CDS browser session and return to your system prompt, choose Quit from the File pull-down menu. (See the **cdsbrowser(8cds)** reference page for a complete description of the **cdsbrowser** command.)

19.1.1 Displaying the Default Namespace

The CDS browser lets you view the default namespace for your system. You can see only the entries in the namespace to which you have read permission. Directories to which you do not have read permission do not appear. When you use the CDS browser, it sets the confidence level of clerk calls to low.

When you start the CDS browser, an icon representing the root directory is the first item to be displayed in the window. Directories, soft links, and object entries all have distinct icons associated with them. Table 19-1 shows the CDS browser icons and what they represent.

Table 19–1. CDS Browser Icons and Their Meaning

Icon	Entry Type	Icon	Entry Type
	Directory		Object entry
	Clearinghouse object entry		Soft link

To expand (open) the root directory, double-click on it. Double-click on the expanded directory to collapse (close) it. When you expand a directory, you see all of the soft links and object entries that it contains. Object entries can represent clearinghouses or any resource for which a client application creates entries in the namespace. Note that object entries representing clearinghouses are shown with a different icon than are ordinary object entries. All entries, such as object entries, soft links, and directories, are shown indented from their parent directories.

19.1.2 Expanding and Collapsing Selected Directories

By double-clicking on single directories, you can continue expanding a particular directory pathname one level at a time. Other methods are available to expand all directories at once or to expand selected groups of directories.

To expand or collapse a group of directories, select them and double-click on them. Note that, because double-clicking has a toggle effect, you can expand or collapse groups of directories only one level at a time. If you double-click multiple directory levels at one time, the result may be the opposite of what you expect.

To expand or collapse selected directories level by level, click on the first directory that you want to select, then continue selecting directories by shift-clicking (pressing **<Shift>** and clicking) on them. When you select the last directory, press **<Shift>** and double-click, instead of single-clicking, on it. This selects the last directory and expands or collapses all of the directories that you selected.

19.1.3 Expanding and Collapsing the Entire Cell Namespace

To expand all directories on all levels at once, choose the Expand All option from the File menu. Likewise, choose Collapse All from the File menu to close an expanded namespace.

Note: Use Expand All with care if you have a large namespace. The larger a namespace, the longer it takes to display its entire contents.

19.1.4 Filtering the Namespace Display

Using the Filters menu, you can selectively display object entries of a particular class. For example, if you are interested in seeing the entries for clearinghouse objects only, choose the class **CDS_Clearinghouse** from the Filters menu. For any directory that you expand after choosing a filter, you see only names of objects whose class matches the filter.

Note that soft links are still displayed because they are not object entries and only object entries can be filtered out. To reset the filter so that you can again view all object entries, choose the * (asterisk) from the Filters menu.

19.1.5 Navigating the Namespace

Once you begin expanding the namespace, it can exceed the boundaries of your CDS browser window, even if you enlarge the window. You can use the horizontal and vertical scroll bars and stepping arrows to scroll through the namespace.

Dragging the slider up and down the vertical scroll bar on the right side of the display window produces an index window. The index window shows the name where the slider is currently positioned in the namespace. When the index window contains the name that you want to view, release the mouse button to position that name at the top of the CDS browser window.

In displays that are larger than the length of the window, scrolling through directory levels can produce a reference line toward the top of the window. The line orients you by showing the full directory pathname from the current name to the root. It also indicates that you have scrolled past other parts of the namespace that are no longer displayed.

19.2 Listing the Contents of Directories

The DCE control program provides a **directory list** command that allows you to display a list of the descendants of a directory within the cell namespace. A directory's descendants are all the child pointers, clearinghouses, object entries, and soft links existing in it.

To use the **directory list** command, you must have read permission to the CDS names that you want to display.

For a complete listing of a directory's contents, you enter the **directory list** command with the name of the directory or directories whose contents you wish to view. For example:

```
dcecp> directory list /.:/eng
/.../eng_cell.osf.org/hosts/eng/aud-acl \
/.../eng_cell.osf.org/hosts/eng/aud-svc \
/.../eng_cell.osf.org/hosts/eng/cds-clerk \
/.../eng_cell.osf.org/hosts/eng/cds-server \
/.../eng_cell.osf.org/hosts/eng/dts-entity \
/.../eng_cell.osf.org/hosts/eng/profile \
/.../eng_cell.osf.org/hosts/eng/self \
/.../eng_cell.osf.org/hosts/eng/CDS_CTS \
/.../eng_cell.osf.org/hosts/eng/CDS_UTS \
```

By default, the **directory list** command displays the full names of the objects (the object names preceeded by */...*/*pathname*) contained in the directory. To list only the RDNs of the objects, enter the **directory list** command with the **-simplename** option.

To display the names of a particular kind of directory descendant only, you include the appropriate option of the **directory list** command. For example, you enter the following command to display the names of all the soft links that are stored in the **/.:/eng** directory:

```
dcecp> directory list /.:/eng/ -links
/.../eng_cell.osf.org/hosts/eng/CDS_CTS \
/.../eng_cell.osf.org/hosts/eng/CDS_UTS
```

19.2.1 Displaying the Attribute Values of CDS Names

To display any or all of the current values of the attributes associated with the names in a namespace (except for clerks or servers), use the **dcecp show** command.

The basic syntax of the **show** command is as follows:

object-type **show** *object-name*

where *object-type* is the type of CDS object about which you want to display information, and *object-name* is a complete directory specification terminating with a simple name (that is, the full CDS name) of the object you are inquiring about.

To use the **show** command, you must have read permission to the name that you want to display.

In the following example, the **show** command is used to display the current values of the **CDS_CHDirectories** attribute associated with the **/.:/Chicago2_CH** clearinghouse. The display returned by the command shows two values for the attribute, each value having two parts. The parts of the attribute value are UUID of Directory and Name of Directory. The **show** command displays the values separately. For each value, it first lists the attribute name on a line ending with a colon, then the parts of the value.

```
dcecp> clearinghouse show /.:/Chicago2_CH
{RPC_ClassVersion
 {01 00}}
{CDS_CTS 1994-01-24-07:12:51.966-05:00I0.000/00-00-c0-f7-de-56}
{CDS_UTS 1994-02-03-07:17:35.794-05:00I0.000/00-00-c0-f7-de-56}
{CDS_ObjectUUID 0094e40e-bb43-1d43-9e0a-0000c0f7de56}
{CDS_AllUpTo 1994-02-03-09:17:06.393-05:00I0.000/00-00-c0-f7-de-56}
{CDS_DirectoryVersion 3.0}
{CDS_CHName /.../Chicago2/Chicago2_CH}
{CDS_CHLastAddress
 {Tower ncacn_ip_tcp:130.105.5.16[]}}
{CDS_CHLastAddress
 {Tower ncadg_ip_udp:130.105.5.16[]}}
{CDS_CHState on}
{CDS_CHDirectories
 {dir_uuid 00595ca5-bb46-1d43-9e0a-0000c0f7de56}
 {directory /.../Chicago2}}
{CDS_CHDirectories
 {dir_uuid 00888574-bb53-1d43-9e0a-0000c0f7de56}
 {directory /.../Chicago2/subsys}}
{CDS_CHDirectories
 {dir_uuid 0069ff14-bb55-1d43-9e0a-0000c0f7de56}
 {directory /.../Chicago2/subsys/dce}}
{CDS_CHDirectories
 {dir_uuid 0023cc38-bb56-1d43-9e0a-0000c0f7de56}
 {directory /.../Chicago2/subsys/dce/sec}}
{CDS_CHDirectories
 {dir_uuid 0026d57c-bb57-1d43-9e0a-0000c0f7de56}
 {directory /.../Chicago2/hosts}}
{CDS_ReplicaVersion 3.0}
{CDS_NSCellname /.../Chicago2}
```

In the following example, the **show** command displays all of the object entries that are stored in the **/.:/sales** directory:

```
dcecp> object show /.:/sales
{CDS_CTS 1994-06-23-15:56:44.734+00:00I0.000/08-00-2b-0f-59-bf}
{CDS_UTS 1994-08-08-22:23:54.226+00:00I0.000/08-00-2b-0f-59-bf}
{CDS_ClassVersion 1.0}
```

The following command displays all of the soft links stored in the **/.:/mfg** directory:

```
dcecp> link show /.:/mfg
{CDS_CTS 1994-06-23-15:56:44.734+00:00I0.000/08-00-2b-0f-59-bf}
{CDS_UTS 1994-08-08-22:23:54.226+00:00I0.000/08-00-2b-0f-59-bf}
{CDS_LinkTarget = /.../abc/mfg/robotics_controller1}
```

19.2.2 Displaying Clerk and Server Attribute Information

To show the values of the attributes associated with clerk and server entries in the cell namespace, you must use **cdscp**. The basic syntax of the **cdscp** **show** command is as follows:

show *entity-type entity-name*

where *entity-type* is the type of CDS object about which you want to display information, and *entity-name* is a complete directory specification terminating with a simple name (that is, the full CDS name) of the object about which you are inquiring.

To use the **show** command, you must have read permission to the CDS name that you want to display.

You are not permitted to use wildcard characters in the simple names of clerks and servers on the **show** command line.

In the following example, the **show** command displays the current values of all attributes that are associated with the local clerk:

```
cdscp> show clerk
```

The returned display is as follows:

```
                    SHOW
                   CLERK
                      AT    1991-10-15-15:56:50
            Creation Time = 1991-10-09-17:03:32.32
  Authentication failures = 0
          Read Operations = 1068
              Cache Hits = 137
          Cache bypasses = 433
          Write operations = 1250
  Miscellaneous operations = 590
```

Chapter 20

Using the CDS Subtree Commands to Restructure CDS Directories

Sometimes, because of corporate restructuring or for other reasons, you need to combine or rearrange various directories or subtrees of directories in your CDS namespace.

For example, suppose the engineering group in your organization, **/.:/eng**, is combined with the research and development group, **/.:/rnd**, and that the two groups begin to share a common set of applications and other network resources. You can reflect this organizational change in your namespace hierarchy by merging the contents of these directories.

Similarly, if the engineering group becomes subordinate to the research and development group, you can reflect this change by creating an empty directory named **/.:/rnd/eng** and then merging the contents of the **/.:/eng** directory into **/.:/rnd/eng**, effectively appending **/.:/eng** below **/.:/rnd**.

20.1 Overview of the Merge and Append Procedures

To merge or append CDS directories, you use the DCE control program
(**dcecp**) **directory merge** command. The basic steps for both procedures
are as follows:

1. At your system prompt, enter **dcecp** to invoke the DCE control
   program.

2. Merge or append one existing directory with another existing
   directory. To do this, use the **directory merge** command to combine
   the directory's information about its descendants (object entries, soft
   links, and child directories) with another directory's information or to
   append the information below an existing bottom-level directory.

3. Delete the source directory or subtree (and its contents) that you
   merged in step 2 from its old location in the hierarchy by using the
   directory delete command. Replace the deleted directory
   information with a single soft link of the same name to redirect
   lookups of the information at the new location by using the **link
   create** command.

Note: The presence of clearinghouses, duplicate names, or
     unreachable names in a merged directory requires special
     handling. The **merge** and **append** operations described in the
     following sections assume that no duplicate names exist in the
     source and target directory or subtree, and that the
     clearinghouses that store the master replicas of affected
     directories are enabled and reachable at the time the
     operations are initiated.

The example **merge** and **append** operations described in this section are
based on an example namespace, shown in the following figure.

Figure 20–1. Example Namespace Hierarchy

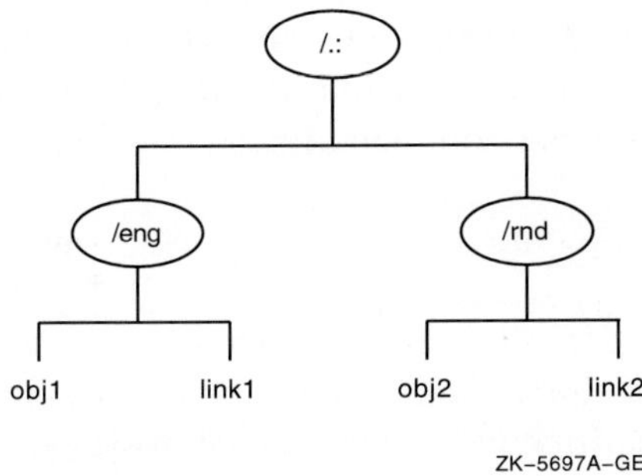

The example namespace consists of two directories under the root: **/.:/eng** and **/.:/rnd**. The source directory (**/.:/eng**) contains two entries: **/.:/eng/obj1** and **/.:/eng/link1**. The target directory (**/.:/rnd**) also contains two entries: **/.:/rnd/obj2** and **/.:/rnd/link2**.

20.2 Merging CDS Directories

The following procedure merges the source directory **/.:/eng** into the target directory **/.:/rnd**:

1. Perform a skulk on the **/.:/eng** directory before merging it with the **/.:/rnd** directory. This synchronization of the source directory's replicas can prevent errors that cause the merge operation to fail.

    dcecp> **directory synchronize /.:/eng**

2. Run the **directory merge** command to merge the **/.:/eng** and **/.:/rnd** directories:

    dcecp> **directory merge /.:/eng -into /.:/rnd**

    Note that the **directory merge** command merges only the immediate contents of the source directory named in the command-line argument (that is, the object entries, soft links, and child directories in these directories).

To copy the descendants of any child directories of a directory to a target location, you must use the **-tree** option of the command. For example, if the **/.:/eng** directory in the previous example included the child directories **dev** and **qa**, and you wanted to merge the contents of these directories into the target directory **/.:/rnd**, you would enter the following command line:

dcecp> **directory merge /.:/eng -into /.:/rnd -tree**

By default, the **directory merge** command places all object entries, soft links, and child directories in the target directory's master clearinghouse. You can, however, place child directories in another clearinghouse. To do this, you use the **-clearinghouse** option of the command to specify the name of the other clearinghouse.

Note that you are allowed to specify only one alternate clearinghouse in the **-clearinghouse** option. If you wish to place child directories in different alternate clearinghouses, you must issue separate **directory merge** commands for each clearinghouse, or you must issue a single **directory merge** command to place all the child directories in one clearinghouse, then relocate the directories after the merge operation.

Note: The CDS objects created by the **directory merge** command retain all of the writable attribute values and some of the read-only attribute values of the source objects. However, these objects do not inherit the ACLs of the source objects. If the merged object is a directory, the **directory merge** command gives it the default ACLs of the initial container. If the merged object is any other CDS object type, the **directory merge** command gives it the default ACLs of the initial object.

If the **directory merge** command encounters problems with the merge operation, it behaves in one of two ways. If you include the **-nocheck** option, the command does not check for errors before performing the operation. It proceeds immediately to perform the operation, and, if it encounters an error, stops. If you omit the **-nocheck** option, the command checks for certain error conditions before starting the merge. If it finds errors, it displays messages for the errors and stops; otherwise, it proceeds with the merge.

Error messages returned by the **directory merge** command identify the CDS entity causing the problem and provide a brief description of the problem. You should fix any problems that the command encounters, before running it again. (See Section 20.3 for more information on the types of errors that can occur during a merge operation.)

3. After the merge operation, the **/.:/eng** directory (and its contents) still exists at the source location. Run the following commands to delete the **/.:/eng** directory from its original location and create a soft link named **/.:/eng** in place of the deleted directory. The soft link will redirect lookups of the **obj1** and **link1** object entries to their new locations in the **/.:/rnd** directory.

   It is recommended that you perform a skulk on a source directory before deleting it. This synchronization of the directory's replicas can prevent errors that cause the delete operation to fail.

   The sequence of commands to synchronize and delete the **/.:/eng** directory and then create soft links for the former contents are as follows:

   ```
   dcecp> directory synchronize /.:/eng
   dcecp> directory delete /.:/eng -tree
   dcecp> link create /.:/eng -to /.:/rnd
   ```

   The **directory delete** command invoked with the **-tree** option deletes a directory and all the object entries, soft links, and child directories beneath that directory. If you use the the **directory delete** command without the **-tree** option, all of the directories to be deleted must be empty, or errors will occur.

   Figure 20-2 shows the structure of the example namespace before and after the merge operation in our example.

Figure 20–2. Example Namespace Before and After the Merge Operation

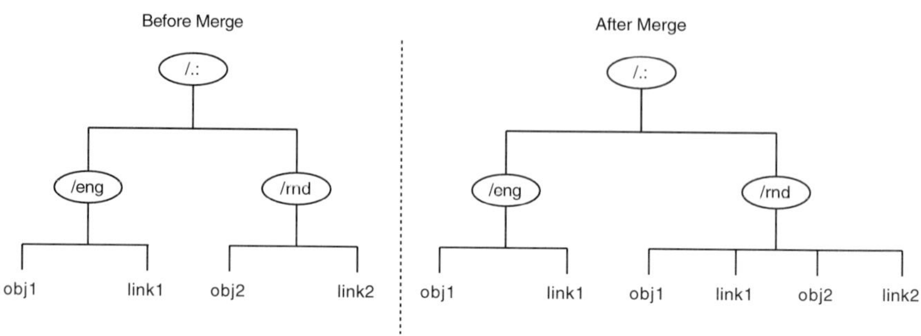

20.2.1 Appending CDS Directories

The following procedure appends the source directory **/.:/eng** to the **/.:/rnd** directory (that is, copies the **/.:/eng** directory into the empty target directory **/eng** under the **/.:/rnd** directory):

1. Run the **directory create** command to create a new empty directory named **/.:/rnd/eng** into which the contents of the source directory **/.:/eng** can be placed:

    dcecp> **directory create /.:/rnd/eng**

    By default, the **directory create** command creates new directories in the same clearinghouse as the parent directory. If you wish to create a directory in another clearinghouse, you must use the **-clearinghouse** option of the command to specify the other clearinghouse.

2. Perform a skulk on the **/.:/eng** directory before appending it to the **/.:/rnd** directory. This synchronization of the source directory's replicas can prevent errors that cause the append operation to fail:

    dcecp> **directory synchronize /.:/eng**

3. Run the **directory merge** command to append the source directory **/.:/eng** to the **/.:/rnd** directory (or merge it into the new **/.:/rnd/eng** directory):

    dcecp> **directory merge /.:/eng -into /.:/rnd/eng**

If the source directory contains any child directories whose contents you want to copy over, you must specify the **-tree** option in the **directory merge** command line. Additionally, you need to specify the **-clearinghouse** option if you wish to place the child directory and its contents in a different clearinghouse from the **/.:/rnd/eng** directory.

If the merge operation is not successful, you can delete any partially merged information at the target location and run the command again. Be sure, though, to delete any duplicate names and to make certain that connectivity to the affected clearinghouses can be maintained.

Note: The CDS objects created by the **directory merge** command retain all of the writable attribute values and some of the read-only attribute values of the source objects. However, these objects do not inherit the ACLs of the source objects. The ACLs on the target objects are either those that are inherited from the initial container (the parent directory into which the objects are merged) or the initial object.

4. After the append operation, the **/.:/eng** directory (and its contents) still exists at the source location. You need to delete the **/.:/eng** directory from its original location and create a soft link named **/.:/eng** in place of the deleted directory. The soft link will redirect lookups of the **obj1** and **link1** object entries to their new locations in the **/.:/rnd/eng** directory.

It is recommended that you perform a skulk on a source directory before deleting it. This synchronization of the directory's replicas can prevent errors that cause the delete operation to fail.

The sequence of **dcecp** commands for removing the **/.:/eng** directory from the source location is the following:

```
dcecp> directory synchronize /.:/eng
dcecp> directory delete /.:/eng
dcecp> link create /.:/eng -to /.:/rnd/eng
```

Figure 20-3 shows the structure of our example namespace before and after the append operation.

21.2 Modifying a Directory's Replica Set

A directory's replica set always contains a master replica; it can also contain other read-only replicas. The values that are stored in the **CDS_Replicas** attribute that is associated with a directory contain information that describes the directory's replica set, including how many replicas exist, their replica types, and the name of the clearinghouse where each of the replicas is stored. You can use the CDS control program (**cdscp**) **set directory to new epoch** command to overwrite the current values that are stored in the directory's **CDS_Replicas** attribute and to perform either or both of the following tasks in a single command:

- Designate a new master replica in a directory's replica set.

- Exclude a replica from a directory's replica set.

Note: As part of the **set directory to new epoch** command, CDS initiates an immediate skulk on the directory to distribute modifications to all members of the replica set as soon as possible.

21.2.1 Before You Modify a Replica Set

Before you modify a directory's replica set, you need to know how many replicas exist, their replica types, and the name of the clearinghouse where each of the replicas is stored. The command that you use to modify a directory's replica set does not allow you to accidentally leave a replica out of the new set. You must explicitly list all existing replicas that are in the set. You can include or exclude any replica from the new set, but you must account for all replicas. Only one of the replicas that you include in the new set can be designated as the master replica.

To display the names of all of a directory's replicas, use the **dcecp directory show** command. This command queries the directory's **CDS_Replicas** attribute to gather this information. (See Chapter 18 for information on how to use the **dcecp directory show** command.)

21.2.2 Permissions Required for Modifying a Replica Set

The permissions for modifying a directory's replica set are as follows:

- You must have administer permission to the directory. Also, the server principal needs administer, read, and write permissions to the directory.

- When designating a new master replica, you also need write permission to the clearinghouse that stores the current master replica. The server principal needs write permission to the clearinghouse that stores the read-only replica that you intend to designate as the new master replica.

  The server principal on the server where the new master replica will be located needs administer, read, and write permissions to the directory.

When you know which replicas to include and exclude and have changed permissions that need to be changed, issue the **set directory to new epoch** command to modify a directory's replica set. Instructions for your two options—designating a new master replica, and excluding an existing read-only replica—are given in the sections that follow.

21.2.3 Designating a New Master Replica

Sometimes, for configuration management reasons, you may want to designate a different replica as a directory's master replica.

For example, you can specify a new master replica when

- A server system whose clearinghouse contains one or more master replicas will be down for an extended period of time or removed permanently from the network.

- A clearinghouse that stores one or more master replicas will be deleted from the namespace.

- You want to locate a master replica closer to where the majority of updates to the directory originate.

To designate a new master replica, you use the **cdscp set directory to new epoch** command.

Figure 21-1 illustrates an example replica set. This replica set of the **/.:/eng** directory consists of three replicas: the master replica, which is stored in clearinghouse **/.:/NY1_CH**, a read-only replica stored in clearinghouse **/.:/NY2_CH**, and a read-only replica stored in clearinghouse **/.:/Chicago1_CH**.

Figure 21–1. Example Replica Set

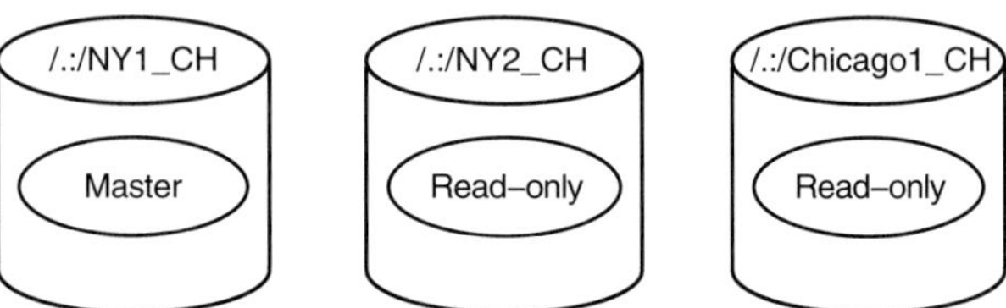

The following command designates the read-only replica that is stored in clearinghouse **/.:/Chicago1_CH** as the directory's new master replica, designates the former master replica (stored in clearinghouse **/.:/NY1_CH**) as a read-only replica, and leaves the read-only replica stored in clearinghouse **/.:/NY2_CH** as it is:

cdscp> **set directory /.:/eng to new epoch master **
> **/.:/Chicago1_CH readonly /.:/NY1_CH /.:/NY2_CH**

Figure 21-2 shows the result of the preceding command.

Figure 21–2. Example Replica Set After Master Redesignation

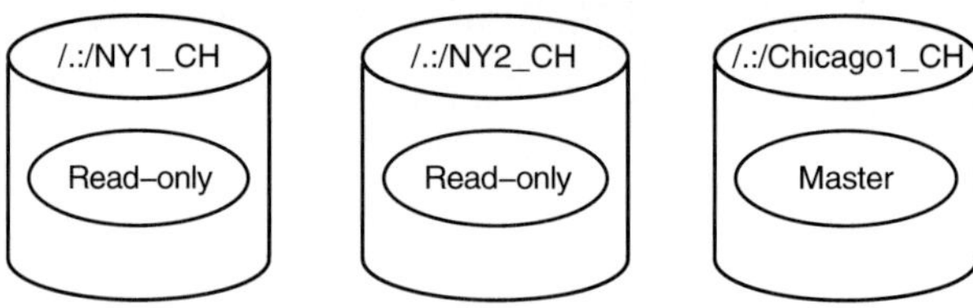

21.2.4 Excluding a Replica from a Replica Set

You can temporarily exclude a replica from its replica set when the clearinghouse in which the replica is stored unexpectedly becomes unavailable. This makes it possible for CDS to complete skulks of the directory during the time the excluded replica is unavailable.

To exclude a replica from a replica set, you use the **cdscp set directory to new epoch** command with the **exclude** argument to rebuild a directory's replica set, excluding the replica that you specify. Remember that you must account for all existing replicas in the command.

In the following example, the replica set of the **/.:/eng** directory consists of three replicas: the master replica, which is stored in clearinghouse **/.:/Chicago1_CH**, and the read-only replicas that are stored in clearinghouses **/.:/NY1_CH** and **/.:/NY2_CH**.

In this case, the **/.:/NY1_CH** clearinghouse is cut off from the network because of accidental damage to the network transmission lines. Connectivity to the clearinghouse will not be restored for several days. During this period, skulks of the **/.:/eng** directory will fail unless you temporarily exclude the read-only replica that is stored in clearinghouse **/.:/NY1_CH**.

To make it possible for skulks of the **/.:/eng** directory to succeed during the repair period, enter the following command to overwrite the current values of the **/.:/eng** directory's **CDS_Replicas** attribute with new values that include only the replicas that are stored in the **/.:/NY2_CH** and **/.:/Chicago1_CH** clearinghouses:

```
cdscp> set directory /.:/eng to new epoch master /.:/Chicago1_CH readonly \
> /.:/NY2_CH exclude /.:/NY1_CH
```

Figure 21-3 shows the result of the preceding command.

Figure 21–3. Example Replica Set After Replica Exclusion

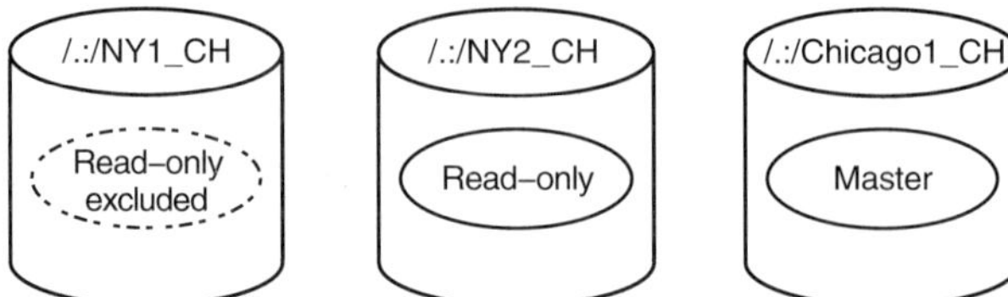

When connectivity with the **/.:/NY1_CH** clearinghouse is reestablished, enter the following command to reintroduce the read-only replica that is stored in clearinghouse **/.:/NY1_CH** to the replica set:

cdscp> **set directory /.:/eng to new epoch master /.:/Chicago1_CH readonly \ > /.:/NY1_CH /.:/NY2_CH**

Note: Always reintroduce excluded replicas to their replica sets as soon as possible after the clearinghouse in which they reside again becomes available.

21.3 Deleting Directories

You may sometimes want to delete a directory from your namespace when the information that it contains is no longer needed by users. You must take two considerations into account when deleting a directory:

- Does the directory contain child directories or the entries for any other CDS object? Before a directory can be deleted, it must be empty.

- Are there any replicas of the directory? They must each be deleted separately.

Both of these considerations are discussed in following sections.

To delete a directory, you must have the following permissions:

- Delete permission to the directory.

- Write permission to the clearinghouse that stores the master replica of the directory.

- The server principal for the server from which you enter the **directory delete** command needs administer permission to the parent directory or delete permission to the child pointer that points to the directory you intend to delete.

  If the server is included in the server authorization group **subsys/dce/cds-servers**, these permissions should already be in place. If in doubt, use the **acl show** of the **dcecp** utility and verify that the server principal has the appropriate permissions. (See the **acl(8dce)** reference page for complete information on the **acl show** command.)

21.3.1 Deleting a Nonreplicated Directory

To delete a directory that has no replicas, use the **dcecp** utility's **directory delete** command. For example, to delete the directory **/.:/sales**, all of its immediate contents, and the contents of any of its child directories, you would enter the following:

dcecp> **directory delete /.:/sales -tree**

Note: Be careful when using the **-tree** option of the **directory delete** command. The command does not ask you to confirm that you want to delete the directory that you specify in the command line; it proceeds immediately with the delete operation. This can result in the loss of directories that you want to keep.

Remember that you can change the behavior of **dcecp** commands through scripts. In the case of the **directory delete** command, you could write a script that prompted for a confirmation of the delete operation whenever the command was run with its **-tree** option. See Part 1 of this guide for a discussion of writing scripts.

A way to guard against the inadvertent deletion of directories and their entries is to view the contents before you run the **directory delete** command. To display the contents of a CDS directory by entry type, use the **directory list** command with the **-object**, **-link**, and **-directory** options.

The following is an example in which a directory named **/.:/sales** is deleted. The directory has one object entry and one soft link:

```
dcecp>    directory list /.:/sales -simplename
work_disk link1
dcecp>  directory list /.:/sales -simplename -object
work_disk
dcecp>  directory list /.:/sales -simplename -link
link1
dcecp>  directory delete /.:/sales -tree
dcecp>  directory show /.:/sales
Error: Requested entry does not exist
```

If a directory to be deleted is not empty, the **directory delete** command will fail. To recover from this kind of failure, you must remove all the entries in the directory and its child directories, then run the **directory delete** command again. Use the **link delete** and **object delete** commands to delete the soft links and object entries in any directories. Then run the **directory delete** command to delete the directories.

21.3.2 Deleting a Directory Replica

If a directory is replicated, all the replicas have to be deleted individually. Then the directory can be deleted using the commands described in the previous section.

To display a list of all replicas of a directory, use the **dcecp** utility's **directory show** command. Look at the **CDS_Replicas** attribute of the directory in the list. Each replica's **CDS_Replicas** attribute has several subattributes. Look at the **CH_Name** subattribute for each replica to get the name of the clearinghouse where it is located. For example:

```
dcecp> directory show /.:/sales
{RPC_ClassVersion {01 00}}
{CDS_CTS 1994-05-06-11:41:05.314-05:00I0.000/08-00-09-25-13-52}
{CDS_UTS 1994-06-21-03:06:08.842-05:00I0.000/08-00-09-25-13-52}
{CDS_ObjectUUID 5f97a584-bf9b-11cd-9362-080009251352}
{CDS_Replicas
  {{CH_UUID de3401e6-bb98-11cd-aac5-080009251352}
   {CH_Name /.../absolut_cell/absolut_ch}
   {Replica_Type Master}
   {Tower {ncacn_ip_tcp 130.105.5.93}}
   {Tower {ncadg_ip_udp 130.105.5.93}}}}
{CDS_AllUpTo 23854-01-29-19:45:44.841-05:00I0.000/08-00-09-25-13-52}
{CDS_Convergence medium}
{CDS_ParentPointer
  {{Parent_UUID df13b228-bb98-11cd-aac5-080009251352}
   {Timeout
    {expiration 1994-08-24-19:30:30.827}
    {extension +1-00:00:00.000I0.000}}
   {myname /.../absolut_cell/sales}}}
{CDS_DirectoryVersion 3.0}
{CDS_ReplicaState on}
{CDS_ReplicaType Master}
{CDS_LastSkulk 1994-01-29-19:45:44.841-05:00I0.000/08-00-09-25-13-52}
{CDS_LastUpdate 1994-06-21-03:06:08.842-05:00I0.000/08-00-09-25-13-52}
{CDS_Epoch 60ac0730-bf9b-11cd-9362-080009251352}
{CDS_ReplicaVersion 3.0}
```

The name of the directory and the name of the clearinghouse can be used to uniquely identify each replica. Use these names in a series of **directory delete** commands to remove the replicas. The name of each replica is the argument to the command, and the name of the clearinghouse should be used as the value of the **-clearinghouse** option. The **-replica** option should also appear in the command line to indicate that the directory to be deleted is a replica. A sample command line is the following:

dcecp> **directory delete /.:/sales -replica -clearinghouse /.:/NY1_CH**

Note: The **directory delete** command does not require that directory replicas are empty in order to operate on them. It will delete the replicas, all their contents, and their child directories immediately, without prompting for confirmation of the operation.

You may want to write a **dcecp** script that looks at the **CDS_Replicas** attribute, finds all the replicas and deletes them with one command. See Part 1 of this guide for a discussion of writing scripts.

21.4 Relocating a Clearinghouse

> **Note:** This section describes the procedure that you use to temporarily relocate a clearinghouse from one CDS server system to another. Note that the procedure cannot be used to configure additional CDS server systems. (See the *OSF DCE Administration Guide—Introduction* for information on how to configure CDS servers and CDS clerks.)

Occasionally, you may need to relocate a clearinghouse from the server system where it currently resides to another server system. For example, you may want to move a clearinghouse when

- You need to temporarily disconnect the host server system from the network for repair or for other reasons.

- You no longer want the current host system to function as a CDS server.

- You want to move the clearinghouse to a server system that is physically closer on the network to the user groups and applications that use the information contained in the clearinghouse.

To relocate a clearinghouse, follow these steps:

1. Disassociate the clearinghouse from the server where it is currently running.

2. Copy the clearinghouse database files from their current location (source server system) to their new location (target server system).

3. Create a new clearinghouse on the target server system by using the same name that was used on the source server system from which you copied the database files.

21.4.1 Dissociating a Clearinghouse from Its Host Server System

Whenever a CDS server starts, one of the tasks the server software performs is to start its clearinghouse (or clearinghouses). The server performs this task automatically by examining a list of the clearinghouses that are resident on the system. Before you relocate a clearinghouse, use the **dcecp clearinghouse disable** command to update the clearinghouse files and ensure that the files are consistent before you copy them to the target server.

The **clearinghouse disable** command also removes, from the source server's internal memory, knowledge of the clearinghouse that you specify. This ensures that the relocated clearinghouse is not automatically started at the source server during server restarts.

To use the **clearinghouse disable** command, you must have write permission to the server on which the clearinghouse resides.

The following example command removes knowledge of clearinghouse **/.:/Chicago2_CH** from the memory of its host server:

```
dcecp>  clearinghouse disable  /.:/Chicago2_CH
```

21.4.2 Copying the Clearinghouse Database Files to the Target Server System

After you disable the clearinghouse and remove knowledge of the clearinghouse from the host server, you must copy the clearinghouse database files to a specific location on the new host server system.

A clearinghouse database consists of the following three files:

- *clearinghouse-name*.**checkpoint***nnnnnnnn*

- *clearinghouse-name*.**tlog***nnnnnnnn*

- *clearinghouse-name*.**version**

where *nnnnnnnn* represents an 8-digit number.

You should verify the existence of these files before you attempt to copy them to the new host system. (See the *OSF DCE Administration Guide— Introduction* and the *OSF DCE Porting and Testing Guide* for the full pathnames of all CDS files.)

Note: You may sometimes find two **.checkpoint***nnnnnnnn* files in the directory. This can happen as a result of a system crash or other interruption during the clearinghouse's most recent checkpoint operation. If you do find two files, copy both of them to the target server system. The server software that is on that system automatically reconciles any problem that may exist as soon as the clearinghouse is enabled at the target server.

To move the dabase files to the new CDS server, use the **ftp** utility or a similar network file transfer utility. Copy the three database files from the existing server host to the new CDS server host. The directory where the files reside on the old and new CDS server is *dcelocal*/**var/directory/cds**.

21.4.3 Starting the Clearinghouse on the Target Server

After copying the clearinghouse database files to the appropriate location on the target server system, use the **create clearinghouse** command to start the clearinghouse at the new location. Make sure that you specify the same clearinghouse name that was used at its original (source) location. After you enter the command, the server detects the clearinghouse files, adds knowledge of them to its memory, then starts the clearinghouse.

To use the **clearinghouse create** command for the purpose of relocating a clearinghouse, you must have write permission to the server on which you intend to relocate the clearinghouse.

In the preceding example, the database files for clearinghouse **/.:/Chicago2_CH** were successfully copied to a server system named **orion**. The following command, which is issued on **orion**, relocates the clearinghouse named **/.:/Chicago2_CH** on that server:

dcecp> **clearinghouse create /.:/Chicago2_CH**

21.5 Deleting a Clearinghouse

You may need to delete a clearinghouse from the server system on which it resides when

- The system is scheduled for reallocation or removal from your network.

- You no longer want the system to function as a CDS server.

21.6.1 Creating a Cell Hierarchy

The top-level cell in a hierarchical
global directory service, either
hierarchical cell configuration, y
global namespace and use it as th
underneath this cell in the hiera
name.

To register a cell in a global direct

1. Establish a GDS or DNS n
   DCE Administration Guide–

2. Run the DCE configuration
   in the *OSF DCE Administra*

3. Define the cell in the GI
   Chapter 22 of this guide.

Once you have established one ce
or more child cells to the CDS na
cells to those children's CDS nan
many levels you plan for your hi
how to add an existing (already co

21.6.2 Adding a Cell to a Cell Hierar

To add a cell as a child in a hierar
it is the top cell in the hierar
placeholder GDS or DNS name fo
process of adding the cell to the
cell name of the child, which is a
the child, and then set it to the pri
connect the parent and child ce
follow the initial cell configuratio

1. Determine which cell in the
   A child cell has one and onl

21.5.1 Before You Delete a Clearinghouse

Before you attempt to delete a clearinghouse, make sure of the following:

- The clearinghouse is known to the server.

- The clearinghouse does not store a master replica.

When you clear a clearinghouse, the server on which the clearinghouse was
running no longer has information about the clearinghouse in its internal
memory. If you subsequently try to delete the clearinghouse, CDS will not
find it and will return a message that it does not exist. Before you can delete
a cleared clearinghouse, you must recreate it using the **clearinghouse
create** command.

CDS does not allow you to delete a clearinghouse that contains a directory's
master replica. Before you delete such a clearinghouse, you must designate
another replica in that directory's replica set as the master replica. If no
other replicas of the directory exist, create a read-only replica at another
clearinghouse and then designate it as the directory's new master replica
before you delete the original master replica from the clearinghouse. (See
Section 21.2 for instructions on modifying a directory's replica set.)

21.5.2 Permissions for Deleting a Clearinghouse

The following permissions are required for deleting a clearinghouse:

- You need write and delete permissions to the clearinghouse, and
  administer permission to all of the directories that store replicas in the
  clearinghouse.

- The server principal needs delete permission to the associated
  clearinghouse object entry, and administer permission to all directories
  that store replicas in the clearinghouse.

21.5.3 Deleting a Clearinghouse

Use the **clearinghouse dele**
command also deletes the c
entry, and all read-only replic

Clearinghouse deletion can
clearinghouse only after suc
that stored read-only replicas

The following example comn

dcecp> **clearinghouse delete**

21.6 Creating and Managi

You can use CDS to conne
configuration. In this config
directory service to connect
acts as the higher-level direc
cells connected through the p
at the top of the hierarchy n
such as GDS or DNS, but the
to communicate with each ot

The next sections describe h
to an existing hierarchy, anc
name when it is part of a hier

Note: In order to create hiei
need to use CDS 4.0 d

---

2. A child cell's primary name must always be composed of the primary name of its parent. Therefore, you must run the **getcellname** command on the parent cell you have selected to obtain the "fully qualified" primary name of the cell; that is, its primary name beginning with the global root prefix **/...**. For example:

```
dcecp> getcellname
/.../coolco.com/northeast/marketing
```

See the **getcellname(8dce)** reference page for details about the **getcellname** command.

3. The other component of a child cell name is its CDS name. Select a CDS name that will represent the child cell. Note that, because both cell names and principal names can be hierarchical, problems can occur when a child cell name matches a principal name in the parent cell. Consider, for example, a principal named **me** in a child cell named **/.../coolco.com/northeast/marketing/inbound**. The principal object name is

/.../coolco.com/northeast/marketing/inbound/sec/principal/me

A principal named **inbound/me** exists in the parent cell **/.../coolco.com/northeast/marketing**. The principal object name is

/.../coolco.com/northeast/marketing/sec/principal/inbound/me

The fully qualified name of either of these principals is:

/.../coolco.com/northeast/marketing/inbound/me

In this case, it is impossible to determine in which cell, child or parent, the principal exists. Is it the principal named **inbound/me** in the cell named **/.../coolco.com/northeast/marketing**, or the principal **me** in the child cell **/.../coolco.com/northeast/marketing/inbound**?

Consequently, you must ensure that the name you select does not conflict with any principal names on the parent cell. To test whether or not the CDS name you select is the same as a principal name on the parent, use the **dcecp principal show** command and specify the CDS name you want to use for the child cell.

If the program returns the error message

```
Error: Registry object not found
```

it means there is no principal named **northeast/marketing/inbound** and it is safe to use it as a child cell name.

4. Use the **dcecp cellalias create** to create a cell name alias that represents the intended new primary name for the cell. Specify the child cell's fully qualified name, which is of the form *parent-fully-qualified-name/child-CDS-name*. For example:

    /.../C=US/O=BIGCO/OU=LEGAL/contracts/fineprint

    This command returns the names of any hosts in the cell that it cannot contact. You must modify the files *dcelocal*/**dce_cf.db** and *dcelocal*/**etc/security/pe_site** on any hosts that the command is unable to contact, before proceeding to the next step.

5. After **dcecp cellalias create** has completed (and you have fixed any hosts that the command was unable to contact), use the **dcecp host stop** and **dcecp host start** commands to stop and restart all of the servers in the cell.

6. Use the **dcecp cellalias set** command to set the newly created cell name alias to be the child cell's primary name. This step changes the cell's name from the placeholder GDS or DNS name you established during initial cell configuration to the new child cell name.

    This command returns the names of any hosts in the cell that it cannot contact. You must modify the files *dcelocal*/**dce_cf.db** and */dcelocal*/**etc/security/pe_site** on any hosts that the command is unable to contact before proceeding to the next step.

7. After **dcecp cellalias set** has completed (and you have fixed any hosts that the command was unable to contact), use the **dcecp host stop** and **dcecp host start** commands to stop and restart all of the servers in the cell.

8. Establish cross-cell authentication between the child cell and its parent. To do this, you run the **dcecp registry connect** command on the child cell, as described in Chapter 33.

9. Define the new child cell in the CDS namespace of the parent. You do this by running the **dcecp cdsalias connect** command in the child cell. For example:

dcecp> **cdsalias connect**

See the **cdsalias(8dce)** reference page for a complete description of the **cdsalias** object.

In order to be able to run the **cdsalias connect** command successfully, you need administrative permission to the child cell's root (**/.:**) directory, and the **cds-server** principal on the machine that contains the master replica of the child cell's root directory needs insert permission to the parent cell's root directory.

The DCE administrator of the parent cell will need to modify the root directory's ACL to give the **cds-server** principal on the **/.:** master replica machine in the child cell the proper permissions. There are several ways to accomplish this task. One way is to modify the ACL so that the **cds-server** principal on the machine in the child cell where you plan to run the **dcecp cdsalias connect** command has **i** permission to the parent cell's root. For example, the DCE administrator on the parent cell can use the **dcecp acl modify** command as follows:

dcecp> **acl modify /.: {foreign_user**
```
/.../coolco.com/northeast/marketing/inbound/hosts\
  /mr/cds-server -i}
```

If you choose this method of granting permission to the parent cell's root directory, the DCE administrator of the parent cell will also need to edit the *dcelocal***/etc/security/pe_site** file on the machine within the parent cell that he or she is using to modify the parent cell's **/.:** ACL to include the child cell's name. This step is necessary to permit **dcecp** to contact the child cell's registry during the ACL modification process (**dcecp** needs to contact the registry in the child cell to verify the foreign user). Once the **cdsalias connect** process is complete, the parent cell's DCE administrator can remove the child cell name from the *dcelocal***/etc/security/pe_site** file.

Another way to ensure the appropriate permission to the parent cell's
/.: directory is to modify its ACL to include the **any_other** type entry
and the **unauthenticated** mask entry. This method grants
unauthenticated insert permission to the cell's root directory, so you
should modify the ACL again to remove the possibility for this kind of
access after you have finished adding the child cell to the hierarchy.
See Section 28.2.5 for more details about these entries. If you choose
this method of granting permission, no modification to a parent cell
pe_site file is necessary.

Once the **cdsalias connect** command successfully completes, the cell is
established as a member of the hierarchy.

Note that the old name for the cell continues to exist as a cell name alias so
that cells outside the hierarchy that previously communicated with the cell
by using its old name, and which do not know its new primary name, can
still reach it by using the old name. For example, the old cell name

/.../fineprint.com

continues to exist as a cell name alias for the newly created child cell

/.../C=US/O=BIGCO/OU=LEGAL/contracts/fineprint

See Chapter 6 for more information on creating cell name aliases and
changing cell names with the **dcecp cellalias** command. See the
cellalias(8dce) reference page for a complete description of **cellalias**
command syntax.

21.6.3 Changing Primary Cell Names in a Cell Hierarchy

In a hierarchical cell configuration, a cell's fully qualified primary name
defines who its parent cell is; that is, if you take the cell's fully qualified
primary name and remove the last simple name component, you now have
the parent cell's fully qualified primary name. For example, if a child cell's
fully qualified primary name is

/.../coolco.com/northeast/sales/boston

then its parent's fully qualified primary name is

/.../coolco.com/northeast/sales

Parent and child primary names must always be synchronized; that is, they must always be identical with the exception of the last simple name for the hierarchical relationship to exist between them. Thus, in a hierarchical cell, you cannot change a cell's primary name without affecting its relationship to the hierarchy.

If you change a child cell's primary name, you orphan it from its parent. At this point, the child is no longer in the hierarchy. If you want it to remain in the hierarchy, you must make it a child of the cell whose primary name it (the child cell) is now using. For example, if a child cell's primary name is

/.../goodco.com/northeast/sales/boston

and you change its primary name to

/.../goodco.com/northeast/marketing/boston

then you must add the cell as a child of the **/.../goodco.com/northeast/marketing** cell by running the **dcecp** commands **registry connect** and **cdsalias connect** as described in the previous section.

Similarly, if you change the primary name of a parent, you orphan all of its children unless you change each child cell's primary name to be the parent's new primary name plus the child cell's simple name. If the parent's new primary name is a former cell name alias that its children recognize, you must run the **dcecp cellalias set** command on each of the children to establish the parent's new primary name plus the child's simple name as the child's new primary name.

Then, on each child, list the cell principal's primary name and all of its aliases. The cell principal's primary name must match the cell's primary name, so you must change the cell principal's primary name to be the same as the new primary cell name. To do this, use the **dcecp principal modify** command with the **-alias no** option and specify the new primary name. For example:

dcecp> **principal modify northeast/marketing/inbound/newname -alias no**

If the parent's new primary name is not a name that the children recognize as an alias for their parent, you must take the following steps:

1. Create the new parent primary name/child simple name combination as a cell name alias for the child. Do this in the child cell with the **dcecp cellalias create** for each child.

2. On each child, use the **dcecp cellalias set** command to establish this name as the child's new primary name.

3. On each child, change the cell principal's primary name to the new primary cell name (as described earlier in this section).

See Chapter 6 for more information on creating cell name aliases and changing cell names with the **dcecp cellalias** command. See the **cellalias(8dce)** and **principal(8dce)** reference pages for a complete description of **cellalias** and **principal** command syntax.

Chapter 22

Managing Intercell Naming

To find names outside of the local cell, CDS clerks must have a way to locate directory servers in other cells. The Global Directory Agent (GDA) enables intercell communications by serving as a connection to other cells through the global naming environment. This chapter describes how the GDA works and how to manage it. The chapter also describes how to define the local cell in either of the global naming environments (GDS or DNS), which is a step that is necessary to make the local cell accessible to other cells.

22.1 How the Global Directory Agent Works

The GDA is an intermediary between CDS clerks in the local cell and CDS servers in other cells. A CDS clerk treats the GDA like any other name server, passing it name lookup requests. However, the GDA provides the clerk with only one specific service; it looks up a cell name in the GDS or DNS namespace and returns the results to the clerk. The clerk then uses those results to contact a CDS server in the foreign cell.

A GDA must exist inside any cell that wants to communicate with other cells. It can be on the same system as a CDS server, or it can exist independently on another system. You can configure more than one GDA in a cell for increased availability and reliability. Like a CDS server, a GDA is a principal and must authenticate itself to clerks.

CDS finds a GDA by reading address information that is stored in the **CDS_GDAPointers** attribute associated with the cell root directory. Whenever a GDA process starts, it creates a new entry or updates an existing entry in the **CDS_GDAPointers** attribute. The entry contains the address of the host on which the GDA is currently running. If multiple GDAs exist in a cell, they each create and maintain their own address information in the **CDS_GDAPointers** attribute.

When a CDS server receives a request for a name that is not in the local cell, the server examines the **CDS_GDAPointers** attribute of the cell root directory to find the location of one or more GDAs. Figure 22-1 shows how a CDS clerk and CDS server interact to find a GDA.

Figure 22–1. How the CDS Clerk Finds a GDA

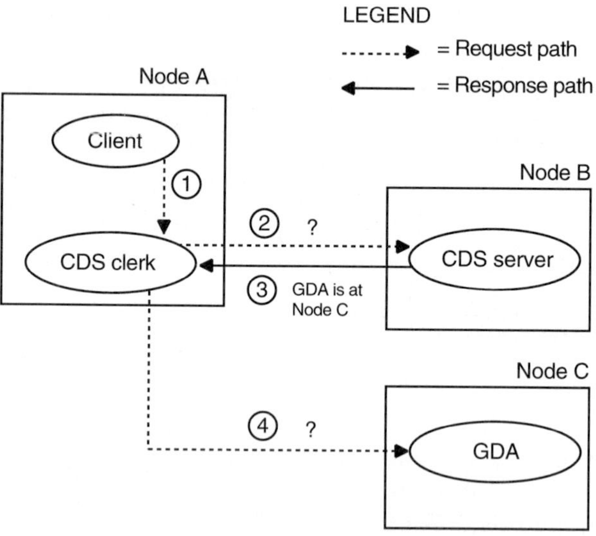

The following steps summarize the GDA search that is illustrated in the preceding figure:

1. On Node A, a client application passes a global name, beginning with the **/...** prefix, to the CDS clerk.

2. The clerk passes the lookup request to a CDS server that it knows about on Node B.

3. The server's clearinghouse contains a replica of the cell root directory, so the server reads the **CDS_GDAPointers** attribute and returns the address of Node C, where a GDA is running.

4. The clerk passes the lookup request to the GDA.

Figure 22-2 shows how CDS and a GDA interact to find a name in a foreign cell that is defined in DNS. Suppose the name is **/.../widget.com/printsrv1**, which represents a print server in the foreign cell.

Figure 22–2. How the GDA Helps CDS Find a Name

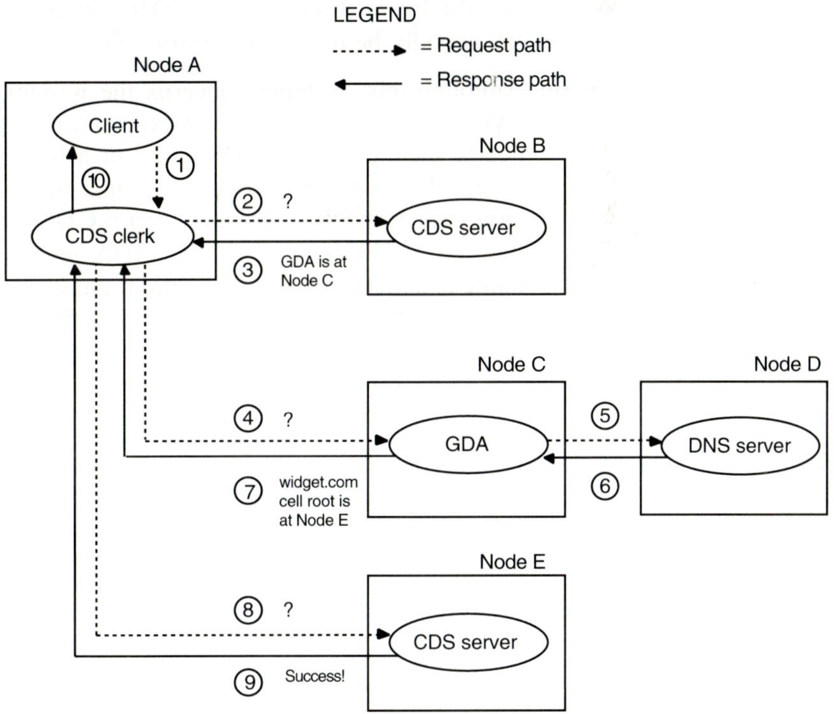

23.1.1 Applications Support

Operating systems and distributed applications require synchronized time measurements to coordinate their processes. DTS synchronizes the system clocks in a network with each other and, in the presence of an external time-provider, to the UTC time standard. Any distributed application that reads the system clock, which is the majority of applications, needs DTS. As the number of distributed applications and systems in a network increases, DTS becomes increasingly vital to process coordination.

There are several types of existing applications that use the synchronized time DTS provides to system clocks. These applications must reference synchronized system clocks in order to coordinate the events that occur throughout the network. Applications use synchronized clocks for the following functions:

- Event Measurement—Applications can read the system clock to start and stop timers and to measure the elapsed time between events.

- Event Reporting—Applications can read the clock when an event occurs and append a timestamp to the event report.

- Event Scheduling—Applications can read the system clock and add a relative time to determine the occurrence of a future event.

- Event Sequencing—Applications can determine the order of events by reading the event report timestamps that are derived from the synchronized system clock.

For new applications, DTS provides an API. This API provides routines that new applications can use to obtain and manipulate binary timestamps. The DTS API supports ANSI C language constructs. (See the *OSF DCE Application Development Guide—Core Components* for further information on the DTS API.)

23.1.2 External Time-Provider Support

For most networks, it is desirable to synchronize the system clocks with the UTC time standard. Many commercial devices are available for obtaining the UTC time that is provided by standards organizations; these devices receive signals by short-wave radio, satellite, and telephone. If your network or cell is larger than a single LAN, it is recommended that you use at least one external time-provider in combination with the DTS software. (See Appendix C for a list of suppliers of time-provider hardware. Sample time-provider programs are available online in *dcelocal*/**usr/examples/dts**.)

DTS servers can synchronize with time-providers by means of the TPI, which is described in the *OSF DCE Application Development Guide—Core Components*. The TPI specifies the communications between the DTS server process and the time-provider process.

When a DTS server attempts to synchronize, it uses the TPI to check for a time-provider process. If one is available, the server synchronizes only with the time-provider. If no time-provider is present, the server synchronizes with other servers in the network.

By using a time-provider with a DTS server, you can ensure that the server is closely synchronized with UTC. When other servers request a time from the server with the time-provider (the TP server), the TP server's precise time is propagated throughout the network. (See Section 23.2 for further information about time-providers and the server synchronization process.)

23.1.3 Manageability

The DTS synchronization functions run as background processes; little or no input is required from system managers to synchronize system clocks after DTS is initially configured. DTS is also fault tolerant. It prevents malfunctioning clocks from providing the wrong time to other clocks in the network. Occasionally, however, system managers may need to perform the following functions:

- Identify system clock problems

- Adjust system clocks

- Change DTS attributes due to varying network conditions

- Modify system configurations when the network topology changes

DTS provides a full-featured management interface that allows system managers to adjust system clocks, change the values of the DTS management parameters, and add or subtract servers from the network.

To aid in solving problems with system clocks, DTS provides event reporting that notifies system operators and managers in the rare event that a system clock is inaccurate or fails to synchronize.

23.1.4 Quantitative Inaccuracy Measurement

Unlike other network time services, DTS uses manufacturers' specifications and direct observation to determine the inaccuracy of system clocks relative to UTC. DTS appends an inaccuracy measurement to each time value that it uses internally. This measurement takes into account cumulative clock error, communications delays, and processing delays. DTS uses combined time and inaccuracy measurements from one or several sources to calculate the most accurate new clock settings for client systems. (See Section 23.2.3 for further information about the DTS synchronization process.)

23.2 Basic DTS Concepts

The following subsections describe system clock and network characteristics, DTS synchronization concepts, DTS clock adjustment, and DTS time representations. System managers need to read these subsections to gain a basic understanding of DTS concepts before progressing to Chapter 25.

23.2.1 Time Measurement Factors

The following subsections describe the factors that affect time measurement and explain how DTS handles them.

23.2.1.1 Clock Error

All system clocks have common properties that contribute to clock error and interfere with the synchronization process. System clock error tends to increase over time; the rate of change of error is known as *drift*. If each system clock in a network started at the same time and ran at the same rate, the clocks would remain synchronized. Because each system clock drifts at a different rate, however, the system clocks throughout a network become desynchronized.

The difference between any two clock readings is known as the *skew* between the clocks. The clocks that are used in many computer systems have a specified maximum drift of a few seconds per day. If uncorrected for several days, the skew between networked system clocks can inhibit the performance of distributed applications.

The DTS server or clerk on each node tracks the drift of its client's system clock and periodically synchronizes with other DTS nodes to reduce the skew between its client's time value and those of the other DTS nodes. The DTS server or clerk adjusts the system clock on its client node as the final step in this repeating synchronization process.

23.2.1.2 Communications and Processing Uncertainties

Communications delays also inhibit the synchronization process, especially when two systems communicate over a WAN or low-speed link. DTS can adjust for the known processing delays that are required to send and receive messages between systems. Due to the varying quality of communications links, however, the time that is required to send, receive, and acknowledge messages varies from one message to the next. These delays cannot be known exactly because transit over the network and the time required to read an incoming timestamp both vary.

Rather than using estimates of communications and processing delays, DTS records all known error factors that accompany a time measurement sent over the network. This measurement enables DTS to determine the relative quality of a time source regardless of its geographic location or changing conditions on communications links.

23.2.2 Inaccuracy Values

In order to synchronize system clocks to the most accurate settings, DTS needs a way to determine the accuracy of time sources relative to each other and to UTC. This section describes how DTS determines the relative accuracy of any time source that is available in the network.

DTS uses an inaccuracy value, or tolerance, to determine the relative precision of time values that it obtains from system clocks and external time-providers. This DTS feature effectively transforms each time value into an interval, or range, rather than a point on a continuum.

Inaccuracy values are determined by the following three factors:

- Drift—When reading a clock, DTS calculates the amount of time that the clock may have drifted since DTS previously read the clock. Drift is the largest component of most inaccuracy values.

- Communications Delay—The inaccuracy also contains the uncertain portions of the communications delays between systems. Although DTS compensates for processing delays, it cannot predict or directly measure the varying delays that occur on network links. The inaccuracy values that a clerk or server obtains from co-located systems on a LAN tend to be much lower than those obtained from servers outside the LAN.

- Leap Seconds—UTC time is measured by atomic clocks, which are extremely stable. The standard, however, keeps time based on the earth's position. Due to the slowing of the earth's rotation, it occasionally becomes necessary to advance UTC time by 1 second. These events are known as *leap seconds*. Leap seconds may occur in the final second of any month, and normally occur about once every 18 months. At the end of each month, DTS accounts for leap seconds by increasing all inaccuracy measurements by 1 second. DTS later adjusts the clocks to remove the extra second of inaccuracy if an external time-provider determines that a leap second did not actually occur.

Without DTS to correct it, a system clock's inaccuracy is always increasing. For example, suppose that a clock starts with a UTC time of 0:00:00.00 (midnight) and zero inaccuracy. Due to drift, when the clock next shows a time of 0:00:00.00, the inaccuracy is 8 seconds. UTC time may be 23:59:52.00 or 0:00:08.00, but is probably somewhere in between. Therefore, the system time is an interval that contains UTC time and is bounded by the inaccuracy, as shown in Figure 23-1. Using the DTS format for displaying time, the combined time and inaccuracy interval is expressed as follows:

```
1993-08-03-00:00:00.000I08.000.
```

Figure 23–1. Time and Inaccuracy

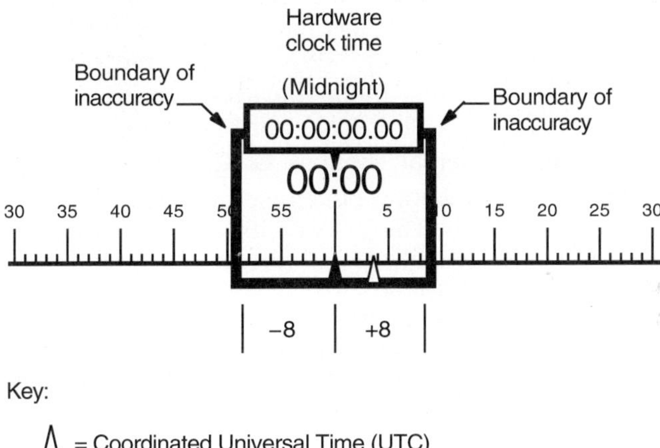

23.2.3 Synchronizing System Clocks

To maintain uniform system times, DTS servers and clerks periodically synchronize the clocks in all network systems. The DTS entity that is on each system performs these synchronizations by requesting that servers send their combined clock and inaccuracy values (time intervals) to the originating system. The entity then uses the values that are sent by the servers to compute a new system time.

DTS servers and clerks have slightly different synchronization procedures. Before attempting to synchronize with other systems, DTS servers always check that an external time-provider is present on the server system. A given server requests times from other servers if no time-provider is available. When no time-provider is available and a server synchronizes with its peer servers, the server uses its own system time as one of the input values when it computes a new system time.

Most network systems run the DTS clerk process. Clerks cannot have time-providers, and they do not use the system time of their client systems to compute new times. When a clerk is synchronizing its client system's clock, the clerk uses only the time values that it obtains from servers to compute a new system time.

When a DTS clerk requests time intervals from several servers, it uses them to calculate a new time that is correct (that is, contains UTC) and that minimizes inaccuracy. When the servers respond and the DTS clerk calculates network communications uncertainties and drift for each of the time values, the clerk has a set of intervals (**t1** through **t4** in Figure 23-2). Since each interval contains UTC, the intersection is the smallest interval the clerk can choose that also contains UTC. This intersection is the computed time. The DTS entity uses the computed time interval to adjust the clock on the system that receives the server values.

In addition to eliminating large inaccuracy values during synchronization, DTS also discards intervals that are received from faulty clocks (**t2** in the figure). DTS detects and rejects clock intervals that do not intersect with the majority of the intervals. When DTS detects a faulty interval, it notifies the system manager by displaying an event message, identifying the server that sent the faulty value.

A server that has a high-drift clock or is far away in the network submits its time to the DTS entity (**t1** in the figure), but the large time interval is ignored since more accurate times are available. Note that, in Figure 23-2, the endpoints of correct time (**t1**) are further from the computed time midpoint than those of the interval that is declared faulty (**t2**).

Figure 23–2. Computed Time

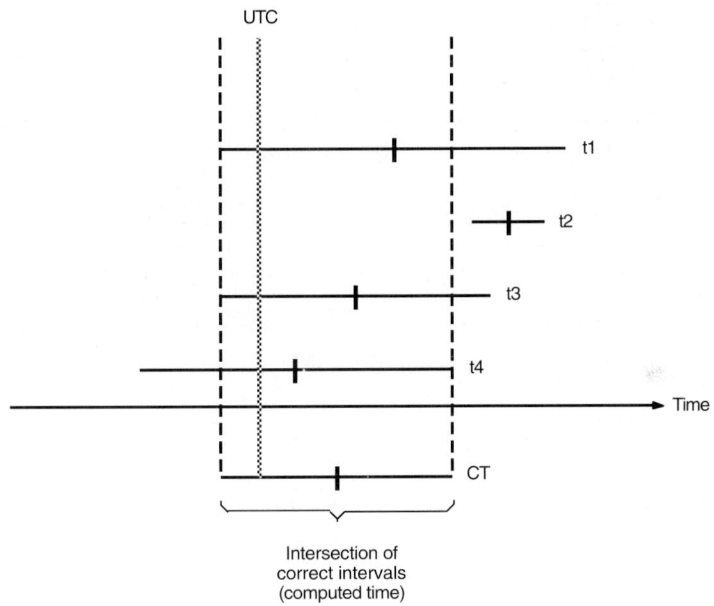

During the synchronization process, servers with the greatest accuracy have the most influence in determining new system times throughout the network. In the previous figure, the server that submitted time value **t3** has the smallest correct interval and is therefore the closest to the computed time. Server systems with external time-providers are usually the servers with the most accurate times. Beyond TP servers, those servers with the highest quality clocks and best communications links tend to influence the time on other systems to the greatest degree.

The synchronization process also reduces the skew between systems. The computed time interval is often smaller than the interval that is supplied by any single clock. Note that the computed time in the previous figure is a smaller interval than any of the source intervals. As the synchronization procedure is constantly repeated on each network system, the skew between systems is reduced and they are more closely synchronized. However, if a time-provider is absent from the network, the clocks may collectively drift away from UTC.

23.2.4 How DTS Adjusts System Clocks

Many system clocks are based on an oscillator and operate with a combination of hardware and software. The hardware for each clock contains a timer that sends interrupts to the operating system at fixed intervals; each interrupt is a single ''tick.'' A software register that contains the current value of the time is incremented by a fixed amount (for example, 10 milliseconds) at each tick. DTS adjusts the rate of the clock by changing only the incremental value that is added to the software register. It does not directly affect the ticks of the hardware clock.

DTS adjusts system clocks at the rate of 100 to 1; that is, it requires 100 time units to adjust 1 time unit of error. For example, it takes 1 minute and 40 seconds to correct a 1-second error. This rate of adjustment exceeds the normal rate of drift so that synchronization is carried out without further significant interference from the clock.

Figure 23-3 illustrates how DTS changes the increment to the software register. The top line represents a 10-millisecond increment to the normal clock at every 10-millisecond tick. The middle line illustrates the adjustment to a fast clock; DTS slows the clock by incrementing the register by 9.9 milliseconds instead of 10 milliseconds at each tick. The bottom line illustrates the adjustment to a slow clock; DTS speeds it up by incrementing the register by 10.1 milliseconds instead of the usual 10 milliseconds at each tick.

Figure 23–3. Adjustment of the Clock

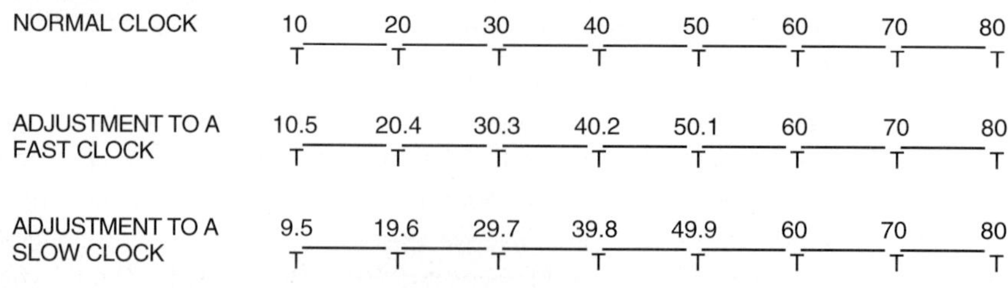

It is occasionally preferable to set the system clock immediately, rather than adjusting it gradually. DTS provides this option for the following situations:

- During system startup when you want to set the initial system time

- If it has been a long time since the last synchronization, and you decide that the skews between system clocks are too large to wait for a gradual adjustment

- When a network has had catastrophic hardware problems, causing a large number of the clocks to become faulty

- When the time interval for a given clock does not intersect with the intervals of other clocks, and the error exceeds a predetermined tolerance

23.2.5 DTS Time Representation

UTC is the international time standard that has largely replaced GMT. The standard is administrated by the International Time Bureau (BIH) and is in widespread use. For all its internal processes, DTS uses opaque binary timestamps that represent UTC. You cannot read or disassemble a DTS binary timestamp. The DTS API allows other applications to convert or manipulate the timestamps, but they cannot be displayed. DTS also translates the binary timestamps into ASCII text for display on a client system.

23.2.5.1 Absolute Time

An absolute time is a point on a time scale. For DTS, absolute times reference the UTC time scale. Absolute time measurements are derived from system clocks or external time-providers. When DTS reads a system clock time, the time is recorded in an opaque binary timestamp that also includes the inaccuracy and other information. When you use the DCE control program (**dcecp**) **clock show** command to display an absolute time, it is converted to ASCII text, as shown in the following display:

```
1993-11-21-13:30:25.78523-04:00I010.0825
```

DTS displays all times in an ISO-compliant format. The International Organization for Standardization (ISO) format that generated the previous display example is detailed as shown in Figure 23-4.

Figure 23–4. ISO-Compliant Time Format

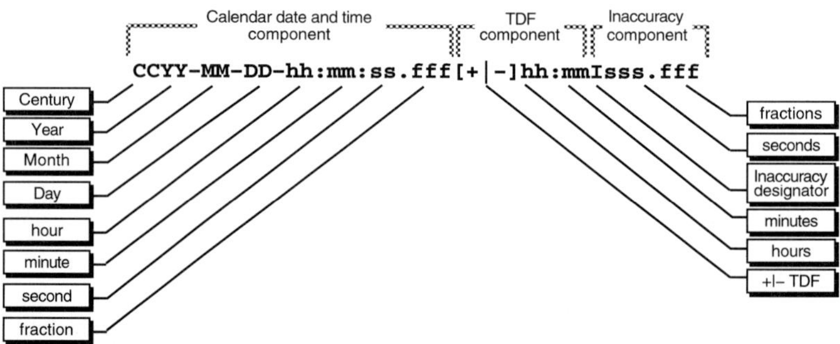

In the format example shown in the preceding figure, the relative time preceded by the + (plus sign) or - (minus sign) indicates the hours and minutes that the calendar date and inaccuracy are offset from UTC. The presence of one of these characters in the string also indicates that the calendar date and time are the local time of the system, not UTC. The delineator I indicates the beginning of the inaccuracy component that is associated with the time. You can express the DTS time that you want to display in several ways. The DTS time BNF format is defined in Appendix D.

Although the **dcecp clock show** command displays all times in the previous format (see Figure 23-4), the interface also accepts the following variations to the ISO format on input, as shown in Figure 23-5.

Figure 23–5. ISO-Compliant Time Format Variation

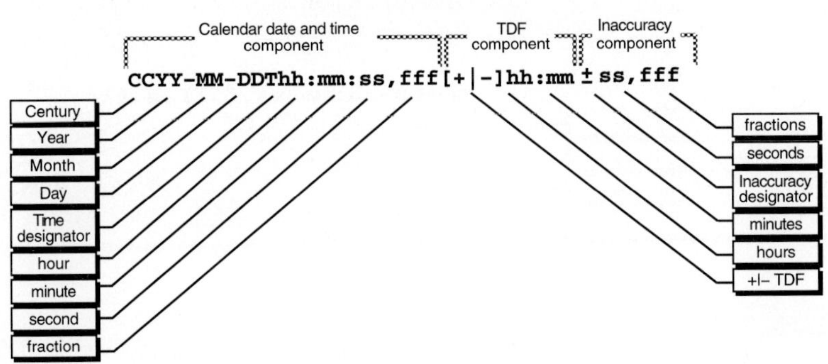

In the preceding example, the delineator T separates the calendar date from the time, a **,** (comma) separates seconds from fractional seconds, and the ± (plus-or-minus sign) indicates the beginning of the inaccuracy component.

DTS offers a translation feature that changes UTC-based absolute times to your local time whenever the time is displayed. The local time displayed is derived from UTC plus a Time Differential Factor (TDF), which can have a positive or negative value. In the previous example, the string **[+/-]** *hh:mm* denotes the TDF. When installing a system, you select a time-zone rule for the system, which determines the TDF and any seasonal changes to the TDF. After the initial startup, all subsequent output times reflect the local time. If an absolute time is displayed by your system, and it does not contain TDF information, it is a UTC time.

The following section describes relative time, which is derived from absolute time.

23.2.5.2 Relative Time

A relative time is a discrete time interval that is usually added to or subtracted from another time. The TDF that is associated with absolute times is an example of a relative time. Relative times are normally used as input for commands or system routines.

Figure 23-6 shows the format for relative time.

Figure 23–6. Relative Time Format

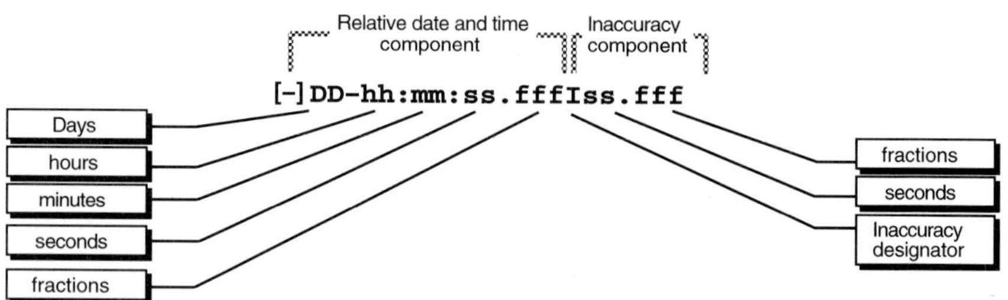

The simple relative times that you specify with DTS-related **dcecp** commands do not use the calendar date nor inaccuracy fields because these fields are associated with absolute times. Positive relative times are not signed, but negative relative times are preceded with a **-** (minus sign).

The following example shows a relative time used in a typical DTS-related **dcecp** command:

```
21-08:30:25.000
```

Simple relative times are often subtracted from or added to other relative or absolute times. For example, if you say, ''I will meet you in an hour,'' you add a relative time of +01:00 to the present absolute time. In the case where you add or subtract a relative time and an absolute time, note that the inaccuracy of the input absolute time is carried over to the resulting absolute time. For example, 1993-11-30-00:30:25.000I00.030 minus 00-00:15:25.000 equals 1993-11-30-00:15:00.000I00.030.

23.3 How DTS Works

DTS has two major software components:

- Clerks

- Servers

The following subsections describe each of these components and tell you how they interact to provide time to client applications and to synchronize system clocks.

23.3.1 Clerks

Any system that is not a DTS server is a DTS clerk. Most network systems run clerk software. Clerks maintain server lists and perform the synchronization functions for DTS client systems.

In order to build server lists and synchronize with the servers on the list, clerks need to be able to locate servers automatically. They discover servers by using remote procedure call (RPC) profiles. Recall that profiles are search tables that contain the following types of entries:

- Server Entries—The CDS names of individual resource providers.

- Service Group Entries—A group of resource providers identified by a single CDS name.

- Profile Entries—The names of other configuration profiles. These entries allow hierarchical nesting of profiles.

Each DTS clerk node contains up to three profiles. When it attempts to locate servers, a clerk first performs an RPC lookup of the entries in a base profile called the *node initial profile*. The clerk then looks for the LAN profile entry. If the LAN profile entry is not found, the clerk searches for the default profile entry; the default profile may contain the LAN profile entry. When the clerk locates the LAN profile, it reads the server entries to build a list of local servers. This process is repeated at set intervals.

If a clerk does not obtain enough server entries as dictated by the DTS management attribute **minservers**, it attempts to locate additional servers, usually those outside the LAN. To locate these servers, a clerk locates the cell profile, which has a well-known CDS name. The cell profile contains global server entries; that is, servers that are normally found outside the LAN. (See Section 23.3.2 for further information on servers.)

After building a server list with enough entries, a clerk can directly request time values from several of the servers on the list. The clerk then receives these time values and uses them to compute a new system time for its client system.

23.3.2 Servers

Servers provide many of the communications and synchronization functions
for DTS. Like clerks, they import information about other servers from
LAN and cell profiles. Servers, however, also export bindings to their own
CDS namespace entries and export their names to the LAN and cell profiles.
(See the following subsections on the server subtypes for further information
on how servers are configured and located.)

External time-providers can be connected to servers, which propagate the
precise time intervals they obtain from the time-providers throughout the
network.

Before one server can obtain time values from another, the servers must
have the same epoch number. Epochs divide the DTS implementation into
logically separate areas. Servers only synchronize with other servers that
have the same epoch number. All servers have the same epoch number
when they are created. Infrequently, you may wish to change a server's
epoch number, using the management interface, to isolate it from the
network in order to correct a problem.

23.3.2.1 The Local Server Set

Local servers reside on the same LAN and maintain their clocks by
synchronizing with each other. Due to the high throughput on this type of
network, the skews between the local servers on a LAN are normally
maintained at under 200 milliseconds. If at least one of the servers in the
local set synchronizes with an accurate time-provider, inaccuracies at each
server may be less.

When a server is first initialized, it exports its binding to its entry in the
namespace and adds its name entry to the LAN profile. Every server is
automatically entered in the LAN profile for the related portion of the
network. Local servers also import bindings from the LAN profile to build
lists of servers with which they can synchronize.

Local servers perform time interval computations, adjust their clocks, and provide time values to each other for synchronization purposes. Each server attempts to synchronize with every other server in the local set at periodic intervals. At longer intervals, clerks request time values from the local servers. Clerks, however, need only to request intervals from the number of servers determined by the **minservers** attribute, which is usually a subset of all the local servers.

23.3.2.2 The Global Server Set

Local servers are available only to the servers and clerks that are in a single LAN, but global servers are available throughout a cell. Any server can be configured as either a local or a global server (See the DCE control program **dts configure** command). The number of global servers is usually small, but global servers have several important functions that enable DTS to synchronize every node in the network. Global servers are necessary in the following situations:

- When a network has multiple LANs or an extended LAN

- When systems that are not on LANs have access to LANs through point-to-point links

- When clerks or local servers cannot access the required number of local servers determined by the **minservers** attribute

You can reconfigure a local server as a global server by using the **dcecp dts configure** command with the **-global** option. Configuring a server as a global server causes the server to export its binding to its entry in the namespace and its name to the cell profile.

Local servers and clerks request time values from global servers when they cannot obtain the number of local server responses that are mandated by the **minservers** attribute. Certain local servers also regularly request the time from global servers. See the following subsection.

23.3.2.3 Couriers

Local servers called *couriers* request time values from one randomly selected global server at every synchronization. When DTS starts up, it automatically sets the server's **courierrole** attribute value to **backup**. You can change the server's courier role by manually changing this attribute value. To do this, you use the **dcecp dts modify** command with the **-change** option. If a server is connected to an external time-provider, you want to reconfigure it as a courier.

Couriers maintain lists of global servers whose bindings they import from the cell profile. At every synchronization, couriers use the responses of all local servers and one global server when synchronizing their own clocks. Couriers provide network-wide synchronization through the following procedure:

1. Couriers request time values from at least one global server in a remote area and request the balance of values from local servers up to the number determined by the **minservers** attribute.

2. Couriers use the global server times and local server times to synchronize the clocks that are in their respective systems.

3. Couriers relay newly computed clock times to other servers and clerks on the LAN during future synchronizations.

For a network containing multiple LANs or point-to-point links, one server on each LAN or segment needs to be configured as a courier. This configuration ensures that various portions of the network remain synchronized and are not isolated from each other.

Using the management interface, you can also designate one or more servers to be backup couriers. These local servers temporarily assume courier functions in the event that no courier servers are available on the LAN. In such a case, the backup courier with the lowest ordered Universal Unique Identifier (UUID) regularly synchronizes with global servers until a courier is again available.

If a courier cannot find any global server, then it uses local servers and increments its **no global server detected** count.

Chapter 24

Planning Your DTS Implementation

This chapter describes how to plan your DCE DTS implementation, including personnel selection for the planning process and planning for DTS on a LAN, an extended LAN, or a WAN. DTS installation is described in the *OSF DCE Administration Guide—Introduction*, so installation considerations are only included in this chapter by reference. It is important to note, however, that many of the planning considerations for DTS are tied to the overall planning of DCE, especially the CDS and Security components. (See the *OSF DCE Administration Guide—Introduction* for background information on the interdependencies among the DCE components.)

24.1 The DTS Planning Team

Two main categories of personnel interact with the DTS software: system managers and applications programmers. Programmers do not usually need to be involved in the planning stages of the DTS implementation. If you are writing a program to import a source of UTC time into the service, however, you may wish to locate the time-provider at the server that is closest to the programmer. Close proximity to the time-provider helps the programmer when testing the software application with the time-provider hardware.

System managers or network architects usually plan the DTS implementation. They decide which nodes are servers and which are clerks, and they decide how the DTS implementation grows with the network. DTS is scalable for large networks so that expanding an implementation to include new nodes is relatively simple.

System managers also install the software and maintain DTS. As the network grows, system managers ensure that the service is running with acceptable accuracy and install new servers, time-providers, and clerks.

24.2 General Planning Guidelines

Consider the following questions as you plan your DTS implementation:

- Is your cell a single LAN, an extended LAN, a WAN, or a combination of LANs and WANs?

- What is the current or proposed network topology (component placement)?

- How many servers will be required? Where will they be located?

- Will global servers be required? Where will they be located?

- Will you need to configure any couriers if you are using global servers?

- Will you use an external time-provider to obtain UTC?

The following sections will help you answer these questions.

Although there are many network configurations that affect DTS planning, several general rules apply regardless of your network configuration or the number of nodes in the network. These guidelines are summarized as follows:

- DTS must be installed with the other DCE components.

- Locate DTS servers on the same nodes as the servers for the other DCE components wherever possible.

- Each cell should have a minimum of three DTS servers; preferably four servers to provide redundancy.

- Each LAN should have at least one server.

- Locate the servers at the sites with the greatest number of nodes.

Although other factors must be considered when you plan your network, these factors depend on network topology and configuration. The following sections present some typical cell arrangements to aid you in implementing DTS on your own network.

24.3 Configuring DTS for a LAN

If your nodes are in a single LAN, regardless of the number of nodes, planning your DTS implementation is relatively simple. To detect faulty time servers, configure at least three systems as servers. If you want to provide redundancy for your DTS implementation, plan to install four or more servers in the network. That way, if one of the servers fails, DTS can still synchronize with reliable results.

To ensure the reliability of your DTS implementation, make sure that the network connections between server nodes are stable. If you plan to add WAN links to your LAN, do not move the servers to the remote nodes, since WAN links are usually less reliable than the LAN.

If you have a single LAN, the location of the servers on the LAN is not critical. You can locate one of the servers on a readily accessible node to aid in troubleshooting, but there are no other recommended server locations. Neither global servers nor couriers are required.

Managing the DCE DST

This chapter describes management tasks that you perform for the DCE DTS. The DCE control program (**dcecp**) has commands that you can use for performing these tasks. The chapter contains brief descriptions of these commands. Detailed descriptions of the commands appear in the *OSF DCE Command Reference*.

Prior to the creation of **dcecp**, the DTS control program (**dtscp**) was used to manage DTS. You can still use this control program, but all of its operations have been incorporated into **dcecp**. Again, you can refer to the *OSF DCE Command Reference* for detailed descriptions of **dtscp** commands for manging DTS.

25.1 Using the DCE Control Program

Since detailed information about **dcecp** and its command syntax appears in Chapter 1 of this guide, this chapter does not repeat the information. It describes only the commands that **dcecp** provides specifically for managing DTS.

The **dcecp** commands for DTS perform various operations on objects representing components of the service. For example, the **dts stop** command stops the server or clerk on the local node. The following subsections describe the DTS objects that **dcecp** operates on and the types of operations that the control program can perform on these objects.

25.1.1 DTS Objects

The DCE control program has functions that operate on the following DTS objects:

- **dts**

  This object represents either of the following:

  — A local or global server that supplies the time to client applications and systems in a distributed computing environment.

  — An intermediary program that plays the role of a clerk on a client system. DTS clerks obtain the time from a DTS server and adjust the clock.

- **clock**

  This object represents the local system's clock and the time that the clock tells.

25.1.2 dcecp Operations for DTS

Table 25-1 summarizes the operations performed by **dcecp** commands on DTS objects.

Table 25–1. dcecp Operations for DTS

Operation	Description
activate	Changes the state of the clerk or server process from inactive to active and causes the object to synchronize its time.
configure	Configures a server as a global or local server.
deactivate	Changes the state of a clerk or server process from active to inactive and causes the object to stop synchronizing its time.
help	Displays a list of operations that can be performed on the clerk, server, or clock, or a verbose description of the specified object.
modify	Modifies the attribute information for a clerk or server.
operations	Displays a short list of the operations that can be performed on the clerk, server, or clock.
set	Sets the clock gradually or immediately to the time specified by the argument (in DTS-style timestamp format).
show	For a clerk or server, displays information about attributes or counters. For a clock, displays the clock's time in the DTS-style timestamp format.
stop	Stops the clerk or server process.
synchronize	Tells **dtsd** to gradually or immediately synchronize (the **-abruptly** option) with the DTS servers.

25.1.3 DTS Object Attributes and Counters

DTS clerk and server objects have attributes and counters, which are pieces or sets of data that reflect or affect their operational behavior. Some DTS clerk and server attributes are used internally by the DTS daemon and you are allowed only to view the values (with the **dcecp dts show** command). Others contain values that you can reset according to the needs of your environment (with the **dcecp dts modify** command). Counters are used internally by the DTS daemon and contain values that you can only view.

Table 25-2 lists the server and clerk attributes that you can set. Table 25-3 lists the server and clerk attributes that you cannot set.

For detailed descriptions of both the DTS server and clerk attributes and counters, see the **dts_intro(8dts)** reference page.

Table 25–2. Settable DTS Object Attributes

Servers	Clerks
checkinterval	—
courierrole	—
epoch	—
globaltimeout	globaltimeout
localtimeout	localtimeout
maxinaccuracy	maxinaccuracy
minservers	minservers
queryattempts	queryattempts
serverentry	—
servergroup	—
serverprincipal	—
syncinterval	syncinterval
tolerance	tolerance

Table 25–3. Unsettable DTS Object Attributes

Servers	Clerks
actcourierrole	—
autotdfchange	autotdfchange
clockadjrate	clockadjrate
clockresolution	clockresolution
globalservers	globalservers
lastsync	—
localservers	localservers
maxdriftrate	maxdriftrate
nexttdfchange	nexttdfchange
provider	—
status	—
tdf	tdf
timerep	timerep
type	type
uuid	uuid
version	version

25.2 DTS Timestamp Format

All responses to **dcecp** and **dtscp** commands contain a timestamp that conforms to the input and output format shown in Figure 25-1.

Figure 25–1. DTS Timestamp Format

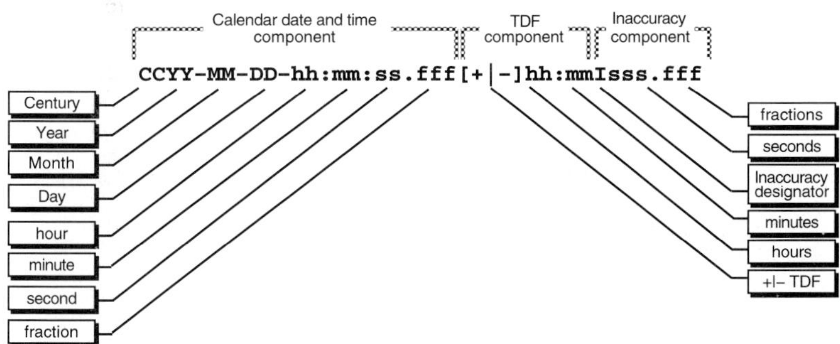

The following example shows a typical DTS time display:

```
1994-03-16-14:29:47.52000-05:00I000.003
```

The timestamp uses the DTS format that is explained in Chapter 23. In this example, the year is 1994, the day is March 16, and the time is 14 hours, 29 minutes, and 47.52 seconds. A negative TDF of 5 hours and an inaccuracy of 3 milliseconds are included in the timestamp.

25.3 Reconfiguring DTS on Nodes

DTS is initially configured during the overall DCE configuration procedure for a node (see the *OSF DCE Administration Guide—Introduction*). The DCE configuration procedure automatically creates and activates DTS servers and DTS clerks on designated nodes. You can, however, reconfigure DTS on a node at any time. If you choose to do this, you must perform the following steps:

1. Stop the clerk or server process (DTS daemon) that is currently executing on the node.

2. Run the **dce_config** script to restart the DTS daemon on the node as a clerk or server.

3. Set any clerk or server attribute values as needed.

The following subsections provide detailed instructions for performing each of the reconfiguration steps just listed.

25.3.1 Stopping an Existing Clerk or Server

To stop the existing DTS clerk or DTS server on a node, use the **dcecp dts stop** command. Execution of this command first deactivates the clerk or server (that is, disables the function by which the clerk or server synchronizes the system clock), then stops the process. You enter the **dts stop** command as follows:

```
dcecp> dts stop
```

The **dts stop** command calls the **dcecp dts deactivate** command to deactivate the clerk or server process. This is the command that you should use whenever you want to deactivate a clerk or server process, but not stop it. You enter the **dts deactivate** command as follows:

dcecp> **dts deactivate**

25.3.2 Creating a New Clerk or Server

To create a new clerk or server on the node, use the functions of the **dce_config** script that configure additional DTS clerks and servers (see the *OSF DCE Administration Guide—Introduction*). The **dce_config** functions for configuring additional clerks and servers restart the DCE daemon (**dtsd**) as either a clerk or server.

Just as during initial DTS configuration, if you are creating a server, you must tell the **dce_config** script the type of server that it is to create: global or local. Before you choose the server type, you should consider the role that the server will play in propagating the network time.

Local servers can have a noncourier role (the value of the **courierrole** attribute is set to **noncourier**). A noncourier server does not participate in time propagation. Local servers can also have a courier role (the value of the **courierrole** attribute is set to **courier**) or a backup courier role (the value of the **courierrole** attribute is set to **backup**). Courier servers have primary responsibility for synchronizing the clocks between the nodes in a segment of the network. Backup couriers are secondary links, which propagate the time when no courier server is available. When you create a local server, the courier role is automatically set to **backup**.

Global servers must play the **noncourier** role. They cannot be designated as couriers or backup couriers.

Section 25.6.1 provides more information about server courier roles and instructions for changing the courier role after you create a server.

25.3.3 Setting Clerk and Server Attribute Values

Once you have created a new clerk or server on a node, you will want to set certain of the entity's attribute values.

If you reconfigure a node to be a server, you need to match the epoch (the **epoch** attribute value) of the newly created server to the epoch that is shared by the preexisting servers in the network segment. You want to do this so that the new server can synchronize immediately with these servers. Instructions for changing server epoch numbers are given in Section 25.6.2.

You may also want to check the rest of the attributes that apply only to servers to see that they complement the value settings of the attributes for preexisting servers. For instance, if the server has an external time-provider, you may want to check the **checkinterval** attribute. This attribute specifies the amount of time that the server waits before synchronizing with the other servers on the LAN.

If you have changed your mind about a server's courier role since you created the server, you can modify the **courierrole** attribute value.

If you created a clerk, you may want to check the new clerk's attribute values against those of the preexisting clerks and servers in the network.

General instructions for modifying the attributes of DTS clerks and DTS servers are covered in Section 25.5.

25.4 Temporarily Reconfiguring DTS

From time to time, a situation or problem may arise in your network that requires you to temporarily reconfigure DTS on one or more nodes. Perhaps a node in the LAN is having problems and you need to have another node take over the clerk or server role of the problem node. Rather than adding an unnecessary server or clerk to the network, you can *convert* the clerk or server so that it plays the needed role.

If you convert a clerk or server, the change is only temporary. When DCE is stopped and restarted on a node, the node will revert to its initial DTS configuration. A node that was initially configured as a DTS server will become a server; a node that was initially configured as a DTS clerk will become a clerk. In order to permanently change the DTS configuration on a node, you must run the **dce_config** script as discussed in Section 25.3.

To temporarily convert a clerk to a server, or visa versa, perform these steps:

1. Stop the clerk or server process that is currently executing on the node by using the **dcecp dts stop** command:

    dcecp> **dts stop**

    After you stop the clerk or server, quit **dcecp**.

2. Restart the DTS daemon on the node as a clerk or server by executing the **dtsd** command with the appropriate option (the **-c** option for a clerk or the **-s** option for a server). For example, to create a local server, enter the following command:

    dtsd -s

    The example command creates a local server that is a backup courier (the server's **courierrole** attribute value is set to **backup** by default). If desired, you can designate another courier role for the server in the **dtsd** command line by using the command's **-k** option. Other than a backup courier, the local server created in the example can be a courier (**courier**) or cannot have any courier role (**noncourier**).

    In the following example, the local server is given the role of a courier:

    dtsd -s -k courier

    To create a global server, you enter the **dtsd** command with the **-g** option:

    dtsd -s -g

Note: If you are reconfiguring a node that previously ran a DTS clerk so that it runs a DTS server, you need to perform extra steps. You must create a principal account for the new server in the DCE Security Service registry, and you must add the server's name to the existing DTS server group (**dts-entity**). Otherwise, DTS clerks will not be able to find the newly created server. For instructions on creating a principal account, see Chapter 31 of this guide. For instructions on adding a principal name to a group, refer to Chapter 30.

3. Set any clerk or server attribute values as needed by using the DCE control program's **dts modify** command. The following section provides instructions for modifying DTS clerk and server attributes.

25.5 Modifying Clerk and Server Attributes

Many management tasks involve modifying the attributes of DTS clerks and DTS servers. The DCE control program has several commands for displaying and changing the attributes of these entities.

To display the attribute values of a DTS clerk or DTS server, you use the **dts show** command. (The **dts show** command can also be used to view the values of DTS entity counters; however, you cannot modify counter values.

For example, to display the attributes values for all the clients and servers on the local node, enter the following command:

```
dcecp> dts show
{checkinterval +0-01:30:00.000I-----}
{epoch 0}
{tolerance +0-00:10:00.000I-----}
{tdf -0-05:00:00.000I-----}
{maxinaccuracy +0-00:00:00.100I-----}
{minservers 3}
{queryattempts 3}
{localtimeout +0-00:00:05.000I-----}
{globaltimeout +0-00:00:15.000I-----}
{syncinterval +0-00:02:00.000I-----}
{type server}
{courierrole backup}
{actcourierrole courier}
{clockadjrate 10000000 nsec/sec}
{maxdriftrate 1000000 nsec/sec}
{clockresolution 10000000 nsec}
{version V1.0.1}
{timerep V1.0.0}
{provider no}
{autotdfchange no}
{nexttdfchange 1994-10-30-06:00:00.000+00:00I0.000}
{serverprincipal hosts/gumby/self}
{serverentry hosts/gumby/dts-entity}
{servergroup subsys/dce/dts-servers}
{status enabled}
{uuid 000013ed-000b-0000-b8ef-03a4fcdf00a4}
```

The example display shows the attribute values for the single server located
on the local node. The attributes that the **dts show** command displays for a
clerk are different. Also, there will be more attributes displayed for a server
(see Tables 25-2 and 25-3).

If you wish to modify the attributes for a DTS clerk or server, you can use
the **dcecp dts modify** command. Several examples of this command appear
in the following subsections, which describe the settable attributes for clerks
and servers. These subsections also offer suggestions for various attribute
settings, depending on your network configuration.

25.5.1 The minservers Attribute

The **minservers** attribute specifies how many servers must supply time values to the system before DTS can synchronize the local clock.

The default and minimum recommended value for the **minservers** attribute is **3**; your system requires values from three servers in order to compute a reliable new time. Depending on whether it is a server or clerk, the system has different requirements of the other systems in the network:

- A clerk requires values from three servers.

- A server requires values from two other servers. Each server uses its own clock value when computing a new time.

To reset the **minservers** attribute value, enter the **dts modify** command with the **-change** option to set the desired value. The command accepts values from **1** to **10**. For example, to increase the required number of servers to **4**, issue the following command:

dcecp> **dts modify -change {minservers 4}**

Although there is no direct relationship between the **localservers** attribute, which specifies the number of local servers in a LAN, and the **minservers** attribute, the **minservers** attribute value is usually a subset of all the local servers. To see the current values of both or either of these attributes, you can use the **dts show** command. Wait until the DTS nodes on your LAN are running for at least 10 minutes before you issue the command. That way, the **dts show** command is sure to show all of the local servers in your node's synchronization list. The **dts show** command can be entered with options (**-attributes** or **-all**) or without any options, as follows:

```
dcecp> dts show
{checkinterval +0-01:30:00.000I-----}
{epoch 0}
{tolerance +0-00:10:00.000I-----}
{tdf -0-05:00:00.000I-----}
{maxinaccuracy +0-00:00:00.100I-----}
{minservers 4}
{queryattempts 3}
{localtimeout +0-00:00:05.000I-----}
{globaltimeout +0-00:00:15.000I-----}
{syncinterval +0-00:02:00.000I-----}
{type server}
{courierrole backup}
{actcourierrole courier}
{clockadjrate 10000000 nsec/sec}
{maxdriftrate 1000000 nsec/sec}
{clockresolution 10000000 nsec}
{version V1.0.1}
{timerep V1.0.0}
{provider no}
{autotdfchange no}
{nexttdfchange 1994-10-30-06:00:00.000+00:00I0.000}
{serverprincipal hosts/gumby/self}
{serverentry hosts/gumby/dts-entity}
{servergroup subsys/dce/dts-servers}
{status enabled}
{uuid 000013ed-000b-0000-b8ef-03a4fcdf00a4}
```

In the previous example, the **minservers** attribute value is set to **4**. This setting provides redundancy; in the case where there are no global servers in the network, the system synchronizes even if a local server becomes unavailable.

Whenever the system cannot contact the number of servers specified by the **minservers** attribute setting, the system increments the **toofewservers** counter, logs the event, and displays the event message **Too Few Servers Detected**. Information included in the event message shows the number of servers that are currently available and the number required. If you see this event message displayed, check whether any of the servers have failed, test the communications links to ensure that the system has not been isolated from the servers, or add servers to the network.

You can use the **minservers** attribute in other ways, depending on your network configuration. Consider the following cases:

- If you have only a few systems in your network and you want to synchronize the nodes regardless of server drift, lower the **minservers** attribute value to **1** or **2**. Although the resulting synchronized time is a less reliable measure of UTC, you increase the likelihood that the systems will synchronize. If the setting is less than **3**, however, the system cannot identify faulty servers. Subsequent server clock drift causes divergence from UTC.

- To increase fault tolerance and ensure that the systems compute reliable times, set the **minservers** attribute value to **3** (the default setting) or higher. The systems can then identify faulty servers and compute the narrowest overlapping interval for the time values that they receive. Remember, however, that your system will not synchronize until there are at least three servers available.

The number of nodes in your network and the types of applications that you use determine whether guaranteed synchronization or reliable times and fault tolerance are more important.

25.5.2 Use of minservers Attribute with Global Servers

If your network consists of more than a single LAN, it should have a set of global servers. You can create global servers by advertising local servers to the cell profile. (See Section 25.6.1.1 for further information.)

The presence of global servers in your network can influence the value that you choose for the **minservers** attribute. If the number of local servers available to a clerk or server is less than the **minservers** attribute setting, the clerk or server automatically searches the cell profile for a global server name. The clerk or server then requests time values from the global and local servers.

You can check to see whether global servers exist by entering the **dts show** command and viewing the **globalservers** attribute value. The **dts show** command can be entered with options (**-attributes** or **-all**) or without any options, as follows:

```
dcecp> dts show
{checkinterval +0-01:30:00.000I-----}
{epoch 0}
{tolerance +0-00:10:00.000I-----}
{tdf -0-05:00:00.000I-----}
{maxinaccuracy +0-00:00:00.100I-----}
{minservers 3}
{queryattempts 3}
{localtimeout +0-00:00:05.000I-----}
{globaltimeout +0-00:00:15.000I-----}
{syncinterval +0-00:02:00.000I-----}
{type server}
{courierrole backup}
{actcourierrole courier}
{clockadjrate 10000000 nsec/sec}
{maxdriftrate 1000000 nsec/sec}
{clockresolution 10000000 nsec}
{version V1.0.1}
{timerep V1.0.0}
{provider no}
{autotdfchange no}
{nexttdfchange 1994-10-30-06:00:00.000+00:00I0.000}
{serverprincipal hosts/gumby/self}
{serverentry hosts/gumby/dts-entity}
{servergroup subsys/dce/dts-servers}
{status enabled}
{uuid 000013ed-000b-0000-b8ef-03a4fcdf00a4}
```

The **dts show** displays the name, node ID, and node name for all of the
global servers known by the local node.

25.5.3 Use of minservers Attribute with Systems on Point-to-Point Lines

If you are using DTS on a system that connects to a LAN through a point-to-point WAN link, the solitary system never has more than one local server available. The recommended **minservers** attribute setting for such a system is **3**. If the system is configured as a clerk, it does not have any local servers and must query three global servers to synchronize. If the system is configured as a server, it must query two global servers to synchronize.

25.5.4 The maxinaccuracy Attribute

The **maxinaccuracy** attribute specifies the greatest allowable bound on your system's inaccuracy before DTS causes the system to synchronize. When the system exceeds the bound determined by the **maxinaccuracy** attribute setting, DTS forces the system to synchronize until the inaccuracy is reduced to a level that is at or below the setting. Use the **maxinaccuracy** attribute setting as a trigger for synchronization. You can vary the setting to vary the tolerance of intersystem synchronizations, but be aware that, as the setting becomes lower, network overhead rises. The default setting is 0.10 seconds (100 milliseconds).

The effects of the **maxinaccuracy** attribute setting on the system's synchronization behavior are the following:

1. The system's clock value accumulates more inaccuracy than the **maxinaccuracy** attribute value and DTS initiates a synchronization.

2. DTS computes a new time value.

3. DTS adjusts the system clock.

4. If the new clock setting still exceeds the **maxinaccuracy** attribute value, or if clock drift later causes the inaccuracy to reach the value, the cycle is repeated.

Note that, if synchronization repeatedly fails to achieve an inaccuracy that is less than the **maxinaccuracy** attribute value, the system can be continuously synchronizing. (See Section 25.5.5 for information on how the **syncinterval** attribute prevents this loop.)

The default **maxinaccuracy** attribute value is designed to keep the system accurate enough for most applications without being intrusive to network communications or system processing. If your network includes one or more time-providers that ensure extremely low inaccuracy, you can lower the **maxinaccuracy** attribute value. Raise the value in the following cases:

- If a time-provider is not used in the network

- If a system is part of a WAN-only network configuration

- If the applications that call DTS do not require the level of precision achieved by the default setting

The following example shows how to change the **maxinaccuracy** attribute value to 0.2 seconds:

```
dcecp> dts modify -change {maxinaccuracy 00-00:00:00.200}
```

25.5.5 The syncinterval Attribute

The **syncinterval** attribute prevents your system from synchronizing more often than the specified interval. This attribute prevents the **maxinaccuracy** attribute from causing continuous synchronizations. As mentioned in Section 25.5.4, the **maxinaccuracy** attribute triggers system synchronization as long as the system's inaccuracy is above a specified value. The **syncinterval** attribute prevents synchronization from occurring more frequently than the specified interval value. (The **syncinterval** attribute value is randomized to prevent several systems from synchronizing simultaneously and is an average rather than an exact value.)

The **maxinaccuracy** and **syncinterval** attributes are interdependent; system synchronization occurs automatically when *both* of the following conditions are met:

- The inaccuracy of its clock equals or exceeds the **maxinaccuracy** attribute value.

- The time since the last synchronization equals or exceeds the **syncinterval** attribute value (slightly randomized).

Note that, if the system reaches the **syncinterval** attribute setting but has not yet reached the **maxinaccuracy** attribute setting, the system does not synchronize.

The default **syncinterval** attribute value is 2 minutes for servers and 10 minutes for clerks. If you are trying to minimize the skew between systems, you can lower the **syncinterval** attribute value. For example, if you want a clerk to synchronize every 5 minutes if its inaccuracy reaches 100 milliseconds, enter the following command:

dcecp> **dts modify -change {syncinterval 00-00:05:00.0000}**

The **syncinterval** attribute does not prevent the **clock synchronize** command from working. You can synchronize a system at any time by entering this command. The **syncinterval** attribute only affects automatic synchronizations triggered by the **maxinaccuracy** attribute. (See the **clock(8dce)** reference page for more information.)

25.5.6 The tolerance Attribute

The **tolerance** attribute determines how DTS reacts if the system clock becomes faulty. A faulty clock is a rare condition, but some causes of faulty clocks include the following:

- Defects in the clock hardware, including clock drift that is greater than the manufacturer's specifications.

- Malfunctioning time-providers.

- Hardware clock ticks are lost by the operating system.

- The system memory containing the clock value is corrupted.

During the synchronization process, DTS detects that a system's clock is faulty if the clock value and its inaccuracy fail to intersect with those of the servers used for synchronization. This process is shown in Figure 25-2, where value **t2** is faulty.

Figure 25–2. Local Fault

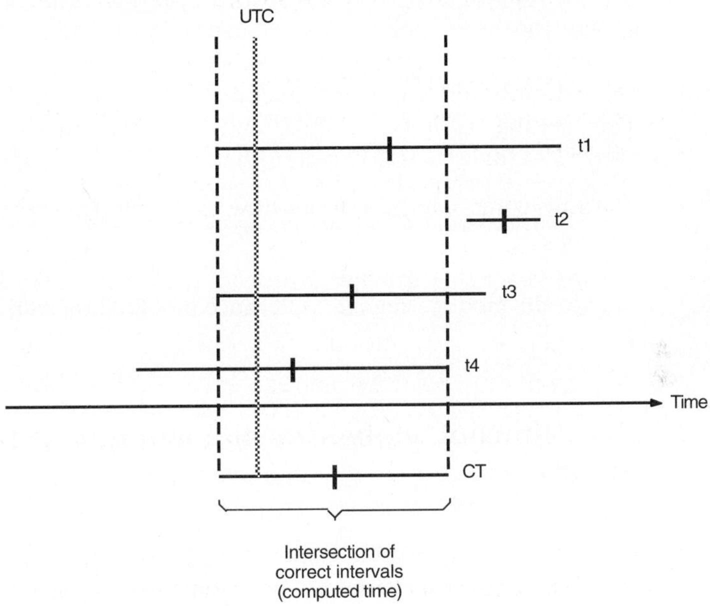

If DTS detects a faulty system clock during synchronization, the severity of the fault and the system's **tolerance** attribute setting determine how DTS reacts. When the fault is detected, DTS performs one of the following operations:

- If the faulty time interval that is supplied by the clock is within the bounds of the error tolerance, DTS increases the inaccuracy of the value supplied by the clock and adjusts the clock gradually.

- If the faulty time interval that is supplied by the clock is outside the bounds of the error tolerance, DTS immediately sets the clock to the new computed time.

Before you change the default **tolerance** setting (5 minutes), determine the requirements of the applications that use the system time. Some distributed applications, such as the CDS server, require that systems have no more than 5 minutes of inaccuracy. Larger error tolerances may prevent such applications from properly sequencing CDS namespace entries. For these applications, you will want to set the **tolerance** attribute value to 5 minutes or less.

Some applications may require DTS to adjust the system clock gradually and monotonically (forward). You can increase the **tolerance** attribute setting for these applications to ensure that the clock is abruptly set only in the event of a catastrophic error. If you could set the **tolerance** attribute value to infinity, you could guarantee that the clock is never set abruptly. This setting is not available, but you can enter any setting less than 10675199-00:00:00.000 (approximately 29,227.5 years).

The following example shows how to set the **tolerance** attribute value to 3 minutes:

```
dcecp> dts modify -change  {tolerance 00-00:03:00.000}
```

25.5.7 The localtimeout, globaltimeout, and queryattempts Attributes

When a system queries a server, it waits for a response for the period that is specified by the **localtimeout** or **globaltimeout** attribute. The **localtimeout** attribute setting applies when the system attempts to contact a local server; the **globaltimeout** attribute setting applies when the system attempts to contact a global server.

The **queryattempts** attribute determines how many times DTS resets the timeout timer before the system quits trying to contact a given server. Once the timeout setting has elapsed the number of times that is determined by the **queryattempts** attribute, the system quits querying the server. If the system is querying a global server, DTS then generates a **Server Not Responding** event report and removes the server from the system's list of global servers. If a response from the global or local server is required in order to meet the **minservers** attribute setting, DTS generates a **Too Few Servers** event report, and the system does not synchronize.

The default setting for the **queryattempts** attribute is **3**. The following example shows how to set the **queryattempts** attribute value to **4**:

```
dcecp> dts modify -change  {queryattempts 4}
```

The default setting for the **localtimeout** attribute is 5 seconds, and the default setting for the **globaltimeout** attribute is 15 seconds. The global setting is larger to account for the communications delay on WAN links that are often used to access the global set. It is unlikely that you will have to change the **localtimeout** attribute setting. The **globaltimeout** attribute setting, however, may need to be changed due to the variations in WAN topologies and transmission quality. In the following example, the **globaltimeout** setting is changed to 20 seconds:

```
dcecp> dts modify -change  {globaltimeout 00-00:00:20.000}
```

If you continually receive **Server Not Responding** event reports for a global server, increase the **globaltimeout** setting. If you increase the setting and the event reports continue, there may be a problem with the communications link to the server.

25.5.8 The serverentry and serverprincipal Attributes

During the initial configuration of DCE and DTS, one DTS entry name is created for use with CDS, and one DTS name is created for use with the registry service. If you subsequently wish to change the name of a server, you can do this by changing two of the server's attributes: the **serverentry** attribute and **serverprincipal** attribute. The default settings for these **dcecp** attributes are the same as the default settings for the names that are created during the initial DCE configuration; *they are the recommended settings*. This section describes additional considerations for the settings of these attributes. If you decide to change the settings of the **serverentry** and **serverprincipal** attribute values, be sure that the new values are appropriate. If not, you will experience trouble with DTS.

The **serverentry** attribute specifies the CDS entry name where bindings for the server are exported. If you change the setting of this attribute, the entry is also modified in the namespace. The following is an example command that sets the **serverentry** attribute value:

```
dcecp> dts modify  - change {serverentry /.:/hosts/cyclops/dts_ref_node}
```

The **serverprincipal** attribute specifies the principal name of the server that is used for authentication. If you change the name by using **dcecp**, you must create a matching principal name and account in the security service registry. When you do this, you must add the new principal name to the existing DTS server group (**dts-servers**). The machine principal must be a member of this authorization group. See Chapter 31 of this guide for further information on creating a new principal account and Chapter 30 for information on adding a principal name to an existing server group.

The following example command sets the **serverprincipal** attribute:

dcecp> **dts modify -change {serverprincipal /.:/hosts/ajax/dts_machine}**

25.6 Management Tasks Specific to Servers

Managing DTS servers involves some special tasks. These tasks include the following:

- Setting a server's epoch

- Assigning the courier role to a server

- Designating a server as a global server

- Setting the attributes for a connection to a time-provider

The following subsections describe these server-specific tasks.

25.6.1 Designating Global and Courier Servers

If your network has WAN links or is an extended LAN, you may need to use global and courier servers to synchronize the nodes in separate network segments. To synchronize nodes across a network, you assign global roles to some servers and courier roles to selected local servers. (See Chapter 23 for advice on planning the location of global and local courier servers.) To assign server roles, follow the instructions in the following subsections.

25.6.1.1 Advertising Global Servers

To assign a server to the global set of servers, you must advertise the server with the **dcecp dts configure** command. Advertising the server simultaneously adds binding information to the server's CDS name and also adds the server's entry to the cell profile. Since CDS and the cell profile are available to every node in your network, DTS can perform a lookup in the cell profile to obtain the locations of nodes that it cannot reach on the LAN.

The following command example shows how to advertise a server as a global server, thereby registering it with CDS and entering it in the cell profile:

dcecp> **dts configure -global**

The **-global** option designates that a server should be configured as a global server rather than as a local server.

To remove a server's designation as a global server, use the **dts configure** command, as follows:

dcecp> **dts configure -notglobal**

This command unadvertises the global server, removing its entry from the cell profile and its binding information from its CDS name.

25.6.1.2 Assigning the Courier Role to Servers

Courier servers play an important role in maintaining synchronization between the systems in separate parts of your network. A courier server requests a time value from at least one global server at every synchronization. This procedure enables a courier server to propagate times from remote systems to a LAN or local area, thereby keeping the LAN in synchronization with all the other parts of the network.

There are three courier roles that you can assign to a server (the **courierrole** attribute), as follows:

- **backup**

- **courier**

- **noncourier**

The default courier role for a global or local server at its creation is **backup**.

Use the **courier** setting for the **courierrole** attribute to designate a server as the primary link to other portions of your network. Use the **backup** setting to designate a server as a secondary link to other areas of the network. A backup courier is only effective if no other courier is available on the LAN.

Note that there are no significant processing or overhead penalties associated with the backup courier role; you can designate one of the servers on a LAN as a courier, and designate all the other servers on the LAN as backup couriers. If you have configured several servers as backup couriers and the courier becomes unavailable, the backup courier with the lowest-ordered UUID becomes the effective courier.

To assign the courier role to a server, enter the following **dcecp** command:

```
dcecp>   dts modify -change {courierrole courier}
```

To assign the backup courier role to a server, enter the following command:

```
dcecp>   dts modify -change {courierrole backup}
```

25.6.2 Matching Server Epochs

At startup, a server's epoch number must match those of the other servers with which it synchronizes. When synchronizing, a server disregards clock values that are from servers whose epoch numbers do not match its own.

When DTS servers are initially enabled, the epoch number for each server is 0, so you need not change the epoch numbers at initial installation. Later, if you add a server to an existing network, or change a clerk to a server, ensure that the new server and the preexisting servers have matching epoch numbers. Enter the DCE control program's **dts show** command to find out the epoch number of the server. For example:

```
dcecp> dts show /.:/hosts/orion/dts-server
```

Examine the attributes list that the command returns for the server's **epoch** attribute value. If the epoch of the server that you just created matches those of the other servers, the new server can synchronize immediately. If the epochs do not match, however, and you do not change the epoch of the new server, the new server ignores the preexisting servers. The following example shows how to change a server's epoch number after you enable the server:

dcecp> **clock set -abruptly -epoch 0**

Once you know that a server is starting up with the proper epoch number, *do not* change the epoch unless serious system or network problems corrupt all of the server clock values. In the unlikely event that the majority of the server clocks become faulty, use the **dts show** and **clock set** command to isolate problem servers so that you can perform troubleshooting and maintenance without affecting the rest of the DTS application.

25.6.3 Setting the checkinterval Attribute for Connection to a Time-Provider

If a server is connected to a time-provider, set its **checkinterval** attribute. DTS uses the **checkinterval** attribute to periodically check all the servers on a LAN to make sure that they remain synchronized with the time-provider. When the amount of time specified by the **checkinterval** attribute setting has elapsed, the server with the time-provider (the TP server) performs the following procedure:

1. The TP server requests time values from all the other servers on the LAN.

2. The TP server starts the synchronization process.

3. The TP server identifies the server time intervals that do not intersect with its own.

4. The TP server issues event messages for each faulty server it detects.

In the previous sequence, note that the TP server does not actually set the system clock after it starts the synchronization process. The TP server merely runs the process to detect faulty servers. The DTS software assumes that the time value at the TP server is the most accurate available, so the TP server does not use the values it collects from other servers to change its clock. Instead, the TP server functions as a reference timekeeper for the other servers.

You can set the check interval to a lower value for a more rapid notification of faulty servers, but be aware that lower settings can increase the load on network resources. The following example shows how to set the **checkinterval** attribute value:

dcecp> **dts modify /.:/hosts -change {checkinterval 00-00:00:30.0000]**

25.7 Changing the System Time

There are three ways you can change the system's time by using **dcecp** commands. The following subsections describe reasons for changing the system time, and then show examples of the commands that you can use to modify the time and change the system clock.

25.7.1 Updating the Time Monotonically

If your network does not use time-providers, and the network systems have been running for some time, you may want to update the time on several systems to match UTC or another external reference. When time-providers are absent from your network, the systems remain closely synchronized, but their clocks may drift away from accepted time standards such as UTC.

Use the **dcecp clock set** command when you want to modify the time on a server system to make it more accurate. The DTS synchronization process ensures that the new time you supply with the command is propagated to the other network systems. In order to update the system clock to a new time, the new time and inaccuracy you specify for a system must form a smaller interval than the current system interval.

In order to use the **clock set** command effectively, you must have temporary access to a trusted time reference. Such references can include the time signals that many standards organizations disseminate by radio or telephone. You can also use a clock that you have recently verified as accurate. (See Appendix C for suppliers of UTC time.)

Because it is a manually entered command that is used to modify an absolute time, the **clock set** command is not useful for small inaccuracy settings. The minimum reliable inaccuracy that you can achieve with the command is approximately 1 second. Human error and processing delays combine to make lower settings unreliable. For example, you enter the command and new time and then begin monitoring the reference. When you perceive that the reference has reached the desired time, you press **<Return>** to initiate the command. Your perception of the reference mark and your pressing of **<Return>** do not exactly coincide. Furthermore, once the command is initiated, DTS takes time to interpret and execute the command.

The following example shows how to monotonically update the time on a server system; that is, how to reset the clock and eventually propagate the adjustment throughout the network:

```
dcecp> clock set  1994-10-07-09:30:15.00I01.00
```

If your systems require synchronization that is closer than 1 second to a standard such as UTC, consider purchasing one of the time-providers listed in Appendix C. All of the time-providers that are described in the listing compensate for transmission and processing delays, and can provide time references that are accurate to the millisecond level.

25.7.2 Updating the Time Nonmonotonically

Use the **clock set** command with the **-abruptly** option when you want to abruptly set the time for a server system. The **clock set** command with the **-abruptly** option immediately (nonmonotonically) changes the system clock setting to the specified time, rather than gradually (monotonically) adjusting the time.

Note: Exercise caution when changing the system time abruptly. The abrupt adjustment of the time is appropriate at system startup or when the system clock is faulty and you identify and correct the problem. Changing the system time to a setting that falls outside the time intervals of the system's known servers causes DTS to declare the system faulty at the next synchronization.

Because the **clock set** command is usually used to correct gross clock errors, it is likely that the time you specify for a given system will appear faulty to the system's known servers if the system and servers have the same epoch number. You *can* prevent the systems whose times you are changing from being declared faulty. Use the **clock set** command's **-epoch** option along with the **-abruptly** option to set the new time to isolate it from the other systems. You can then change the time and epoch for the other systems until all the systems once again share the same epoch. This process is useful in the rare case when the majority of servers in the network are faulty.

In order to use the **clock set** command effectively, you must have temporary access to an accurate time reference. Such references can include the time signals that many standards organizations disseminate by radio or telephone. You can also use a clock that you have recently verified as accurate. (See Appendix C for a list of time reference sources.)

Because it is a manually entered command that is used to modify an absolute time, the **clock set** command is not useful for small inaccuracy settings. The minimum reliable inaccuracy that you can achieve with the command is approximately 1 second. Human error and processing delays combine to make lower settings unreliable. For example, you enter the command and new time and then begin monitoring the reference. When you perceive that the reference has reached the desired time, you press **<Return>** to initiate the command. Your perception of the reference mark and your pressing of **<Return>** do not exactly coincide. Furthermore, once the command is initiated, DTS takes time to interpret and execute the command.

The following example shows how to change both the time and epoch for a system:

```
dcecp> clock set 1993-10-07-09:30:15.0000I01.0000 -abruptly -epoch 1
```

25.7.3 Forcing System Synchronization

Once you create and enable DTS on all the systems that are in your network, they synchronize without any further intervention. There are situations, however, when you may want to force a system to synchronize immediately rather than waiting for the amount of time that is specified by the **syncinterval** and **maxinaccuracy** attributes. As an example, you may want to synchronize a system with a TP server that you have just added to the network.

To forcibly synchronize the clock on a system, you use the **dts synchronize** command. If you enter the **dts synchronize** command without the optional **-abruptly** option, the time is adjusted gradually. If you enter the **dts synchronize** command with the **-abruptly** option, the time is immediately adjusted. In the situation posed by our example, you might want to use the command with the **-abruptly** option to have the narrow time interval contributed by the time-provider quickly propagated throughout the network:

dcecp> **dts synchronize -abruptly**

25.8 Controlling Access to DTS

You can assign privileges that control access to DTS objects by using DCE Authorization Service access control lists (ACLs).

The DTS principal that represents the server on a given system is the primary access control object for DTS. This principal has controlled access by human users and clerk or server processes. The default name that you can use for the DTS object in any **dcecp** command is **/.:hosts/**_hostname_**/dts-entity**.

The ACL for the DTS server can contain any type of ACL entry that is valid for a principal (human or process) or authorization group to which this principal belongs. See Chapter 28 of this guide for a discussion of the DCE ACLs facility and descriptions of ACL types and their entries.

To display the ACL entries in the DTS server principal's ACL, you can use the **dcecp acl show** command. For example:

```
dcecp> acl show /.:/hosts/Detroit2/dts-entity
{unauthenticated r--}
{user hosts/Detroit2/self rwc}
{group subsys/dce/dts-admin rwc}
{any_other r--}
```

To modify any of the entries in the DTS server principal's ACL, you can use the **acl modify** command. Instructions for using this command appear in Chapter 28.

Chapter 26

Interoperation with Network Time Protocol

Network Time Protocol (NTP) is an Internet-recommended standard. The NTP synchronization subnetwork is represented by a tree-structured graph with nodes representing time servers and edges representing the transmission paths between them. The root nodes of the tree are designated primary servers that synchronize to a radio broadcast or calibrated atomic clock. Remaining nodes are designated secondary servers that synchronize to other servers (primary and secondary).

The number of subnetwork hops between a particular server and a primary server determines the stratum of that server; that is, the smaller the number of hops, the lower the stratum. A lower-stratum server always has a higher accuracy than a higher-stratum server. All servers have identical functionality and can operate simultaneously as clients of the next lower stratum and servers for the next higher stratum.

Servers, both primary and secondary, typically run NTP with several other servers at the same or lower stratum. A selection algorithm attempts to select the most accurate and reliable server or set of servers from which to actually synchronize the local clock.

NTP and DTS both can be used in large computer networks that have embedded local nets (that is, those connected by routers, gateways, and bridges) and use both broadcast and point-to-point transmission media. DTS and NTP can run simultaneously on the same LAN.

The following sections describe how to give time to and get time from local and remote NTP time sources, and how to prevent loops.

26.1 Getting the Time from NTP Time Sources

DTS provides two sample time-provider programs:

- **dts_ntp_provider.c**—Takes the time from an NTP server as it would from a radio receiver. The user specifies the name of the NTP server and the inaccuracy.

- **dts_null_provider.c**—Used on a DTS server whose clock is already synchronized by an external agent, such as NTP. It sets the inaccuracy, but it prevents DTS from setting the time. The user sets the inaccuracy based on local experience with NTP. The null provider may be useful for sites that already have a radio clock that is managed by NTP. Make the node with the radio clock a DTS server and use the null time-provider.

26.1.1 Getting the Time from Local NTP Time Sources

Run the DTS server on a node that is running an NTP clock driver with a clock and the null time-provider. Specify the inaccuracy in a manner that is consistent with the time source; for instance, a radio clock. Other DTS servers will take the time from this source. In this case, since the system is connected to a time source, it is an NTP Stratum 1 server.

Observe the rules and advisories that follow:

- Rule—If this is the only local time source (radio clock) in the subnetwork, ensure that no other DTS node gives the time to NTP. If, however, there are other local time sources, this restriction does not apply.

- Rule—Do not run the null time-provider if there is no local time source.

- Advisory—Use a very small poll rate, about 1 second.

- Advisory—Since NTP makes the **adjtime( )** system call, be aware that the local node will occasionally have an unspecified inaccuracy.

Figure 26-1 shows how a DTS server/client with a local time source takes time from an NTP Stratum 1 server.

Figure 26–1. Local Time Source

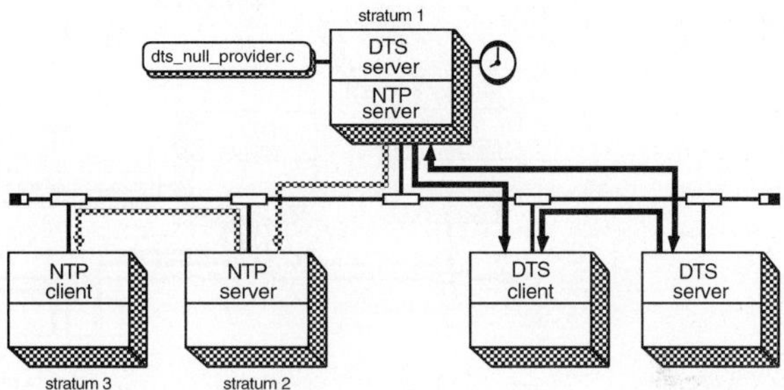

26.1.2 Getting the Time from Remote NTP Time Sources

Run the DTS server with the NTP time-provider (**dts_ntp_provider.c**) on a node with access to an NTP server. Specify the inaccuracy in a manner that is consistent with local NTP experience.

Observe the following advisories:

- Advisory—If links to remote sources are distant, consider having one of the subnetwork nodes run the NTP locally.

- Advisory—Note that the NTP time-provider does not accept time from an NTP node at Stratum 8 or higher.

- Advisory—The NTP node needs to be as close to Stratum 1 as possible.

Figures 26-2 and 26-3 both show a DTS server getting the time from a remote NTP time source, which is a Stratum 3 server. However, in Figure 26-2 (Scenario 1), all of the advisories in this section are followed; in Figure 26-3 (Scenario 2), the first advisory, running NTP locally on one of the subnetwork nodes if the link to a remote source is distant, is ignored.

Figure 26–2. Getting the Time from a Remote NTP Time Source (Scenario 1)

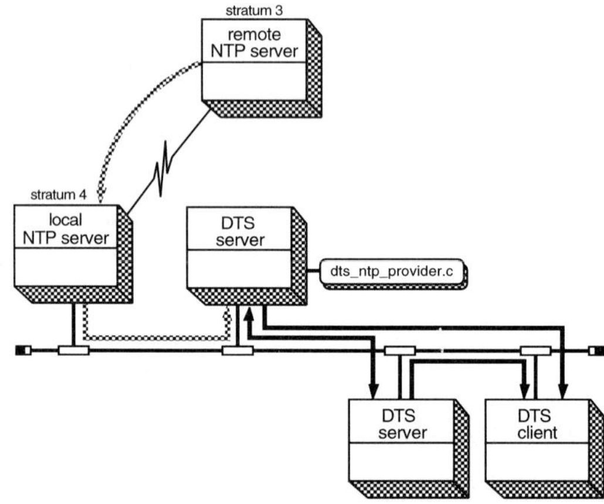

Figure 26–3. Getting the Time from a Remote NTP Time Source (Scenario 2)

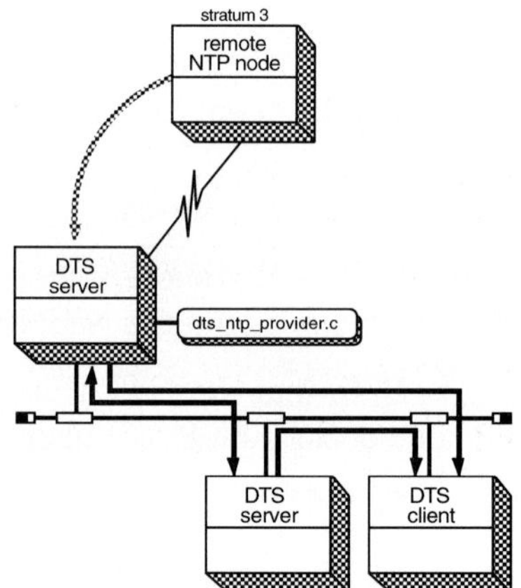

26.2 Giving the Time to NTP Nodes

Any DTS server or clerk that runs the **ntpd** daemon or the **xntpd** daemon with the **-s** option and a special configuration file (**ntp.conf**) can be configured as an NTP server.

For systems running the **ntpd** daemon, the **ntp.conf** configuration file must contain the following line:

```
peer /dev/null DTSS 8 -5 local
```

In addition, add **-s** to the **ntpd** entry in the file **/sbin/init.d/ntpd** or, for systems with **rc.local**, modify the line that starts **ntpd** accordingly.

For systems running the **xntpd** daemon, the **ntp.conf** configuration file must contain the following line:

```
peer 127.127.1.8
```

In addition, add **-s** to the **xntpd** entry in the file **/sbin/init.d/xntpd** or, for systems with **rc.local**, modify the line that starts **xntpd** accordingly.

In this configuration, NTP *never* sets the clock. NTP can, however, give the time to other NTP clients. Do *not* allow loops between DTS and NTP to form. If NTP gives the time to DTS, then DTS gives the time back to the *same* set of NTP servers, unexpected results can occur.

The NTP configuration file is set up to ensure that an NTP server that obtains the time from DTS is a Stratum 8 node. In addition, **dts_ntp_provider** is prohibited from accepting time from a node at Stratum 8 or higher.

A DTS (server) node can give time to an NTP node if the following rules and advisories are observed:

- Rule—The **ntp.conf** file must declare this node at Stratum 8.

- Advisory—Multiple nodes in the set can be running **ntpd -s** or **xntpd -s**.

- Advisory—If any DTS-managed system has a local time source, that system should be used as an NTP **-s** server.

- Advisory—Although this operation can occur on either a DTS server or a DTS client node, a DTS server is preferred.

Note: If null providers are used, the rules in Section 26.1.1 must also be followed, since null providers running on NTP nodes can bypass the stratum check.

Figure 26-4 shows two DTS server nodes running **ntpd -s** and providing time to an NTP subnetwork. The **ntp.conf** file defines these servers at Stratum 8.

Figure 26–4. Giving the Time to NTP

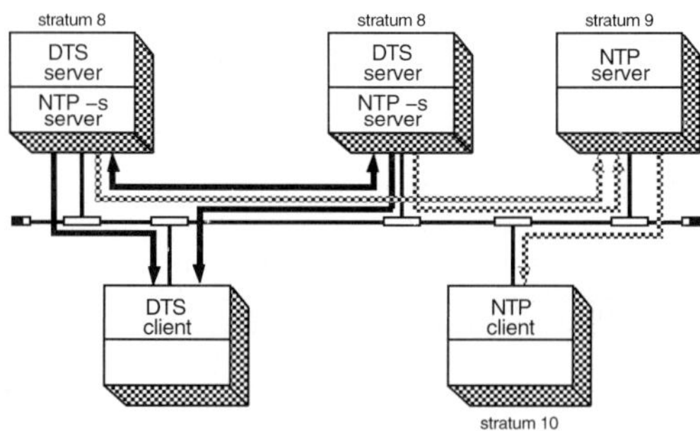

26.3 Preventing Loops

Do *not* allow loops, such as NTP → DTS → NTP, to form.

Run the null time-provider (**dts_null_provider.c**) only if you have a local time source. If you do not have a local time source, you can run the null time-provider, but do *not* disseminate NTP time anywhere in the local set.

Figure 26-5 shows a configuration that is *not* recommended. This configuration works only as long as the remote NTP Stratum 2 node does not fail.

Figure 26–5. Configuration Before Stratum 2 Node Fails

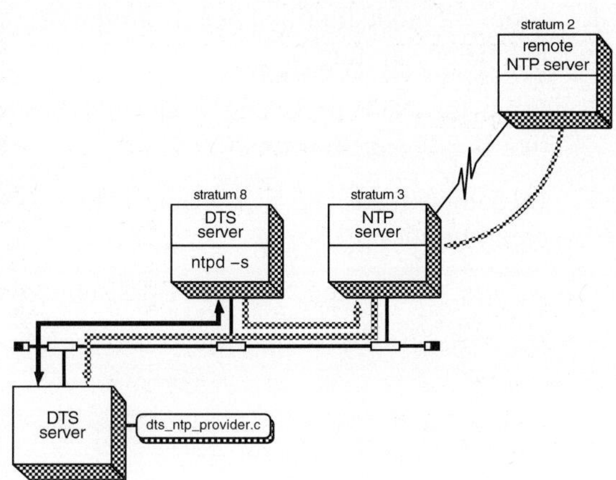

If the remote NTP Stratum 2 node fails, the Stratum 3 node starts accepting time from the Stratum 8 node. Once this occurs, the Stratum 3 node drops to Stratum 9 and the Stratum 4 node drops to Stratum 10, as shown in Figure 26-6.

Figure 26–6. Configuration After Stratum 2 Node Fails

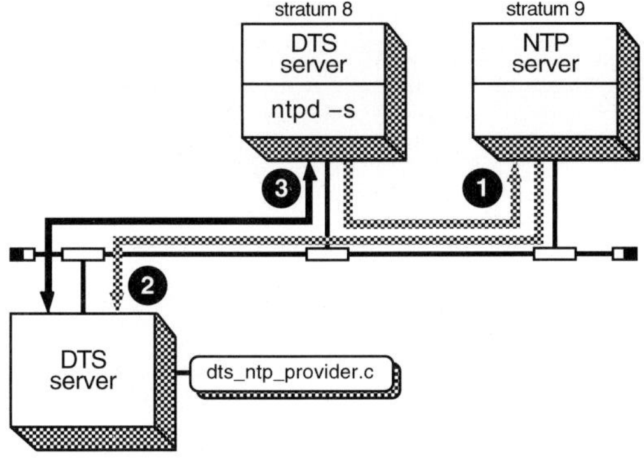

The scenario in Figure 26-6 shows the creation of a loop:

1. From the node that is labeled Stratum 8, proceed to the NTP node that is labeled Stratum 9.

2. From the NTP node that is labeled Stratum 9, continue to the node that is labeled Stratum 10.

3. DTS then feeds the time back to the node that is labeled Stratum 8, creating a loop.

If this occurs, time in the NTP and DTS subnetwork can drift from UTC.

Part 6

DCE Security Service

Chapter 27

Overview of DCE Security

This chapter provides a brief introduction to the DCE Security Service. The DCE Security Service consists of the following services:

- Registry service—Maintains the registry database, which is a replicated database of principals, groups, organizations, accounts, and administrative policies.

- Authentication service—Handles user authentication or the process of verifying that principals are correctly identified. The authentication service also issues tickets that a principal uses to access remote services. The ticket contains data that is presented by the principal requesting the service to the principal providing the service.

- Privilege service—Supplies the user's privilege attributes, which are used to ensure that a principal has the rights to perform requested operations.

In addition, the DCE Security Service provides the following:

- Access control list (ACL) facility—Establishes and grants access rights to an object based on the object's access permissions.

- Extended registry attribute (ERA) facility—Provides tools to extend the registry database schema to define additional attributes and tools to attach those attributes to registry objects.

The DCE host daemon (**dced**) acts as the security client.

The DCE Registry, Authentication, and Privilege Services are implemented as a single daemon: the security server (**secd**).

27.1 DCE Authentication Service Servers and Clients

The authentication service consists of the registry database, security servers, and security clients.   A security client communicates with a security server (*dcelocal*/**bin/secd**) to request information and operations. The security servers access the registry database to perform queries and updates and to validate user logins. To gain access to the registry database, the authentication service must talk to the registry service. Figure 27-1 is a simplified representation of the relationship between security clients, servers, and the registry database.

Figure 27–1. Machines, Servers, and the Database

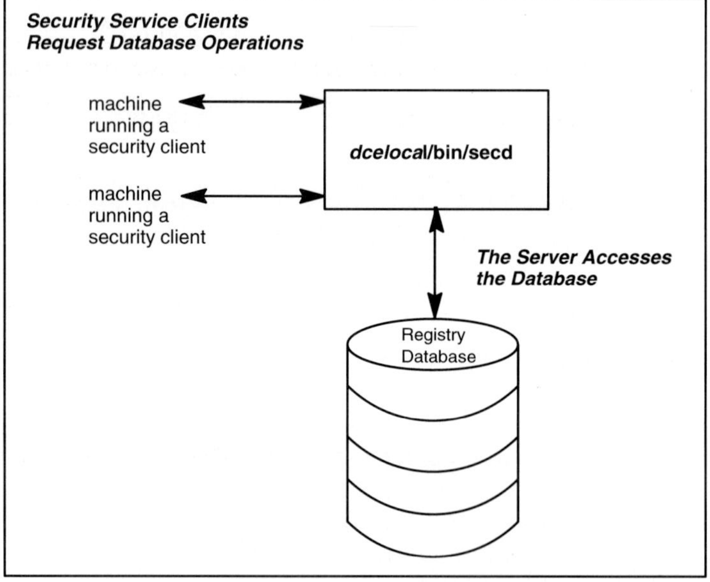

27.2 The Registry Database

The registry database contains the following information:

- Principals—Principals are the users of the system. Principals can be interactive principals (human users) or noninteractive (servers, machines, and cells). Principals can be associated with access permissions.

- Groups—Groups are collections of principals that are identified by a group name. Groups can be associated with access permissions.

- Organizations—Organizations are collections of principals; these principals are identified by an organization name. Organizations define the policies associated with the principals in the registry. Organizations cannot be associated with access permissions.

- Accounts—Accounts contain the passwords and accounting information that allow principals authenticated access to objects within the cell. (Authenticated access can also occur between principals in different cells, as described in the following text.)

- Policies and Properties—Policies and properties regulate such things as password length and format and certain authentication requirements.

- The **replist** object —This object is used to manage replicas of the registry database.

- The **xattrschema** object—This object is the extended registry schema created with the ERA facility.

(See Chapter 41 for a detailed description of the structure of the registry database and the types of information it contains.)

The collection of objects controlled by a registry database is an entity known as a *cell*. Authenticated communications are possible between cells only if those cells have special accounts in the registry database at the cell they wish to communicate with. These special accounts set up cross-cell authentication, which gives principals from one cell authenticated access to another cell. (See Chapter 33 for information about establishing accounts for cross-cell authentication.)

27.3 Physical Security of the Database

The DCE Security Service provides safeguards for network security, protecting information that is transmitted across the network by guaranteeing the identities of principals who engage in cross-machine communications. The security server and the database that it serves, however, reside on a local machine. The registry database is only as secure as the security provided by the machine on which it resides. In addition to ensuring that sensitive data can be accessed on the local machine only by root, you need to provide physical security for the machine on which the security server resides. This can include situating the machine in a locked room, keeping a log of when and by whom the machine is accessed, and any other methods that may be appropriate to your needs.

(See the *OSF DCE Application Development Guide—Core Components* for a more detailed discussion of authentication.)

27.4 How the Registry Database is Stored

Each security server maintains a working copy of the registry database in virtual memory and a permanent copy on disk. All reads and updates operate on the copy that is in virtual memory. The servers use the copy that is on disk to initialize the copy in virtual memory when they start up. An atomic update log is used to guarantee the database state in the event of server failure.

Figure 27-2 shows the server and the disk and virtual memory copies of the registry database.

Figure 27–2. Disk Memory and Virtual Memory Copies of the Registry Database

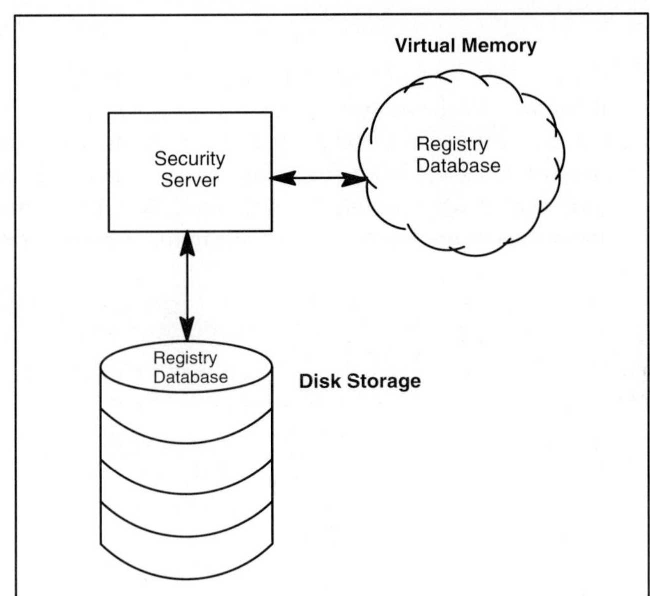

Each security server periodically saves its entire database from virtual memory to disk. The database is stored in *dcelocal*/**var/security/rgy_data**.

27.5 Replicated Databases

The registry database can be replicated within its cell. Each instance of a security server in a cell maintains a working copy of the database. Throughout this guide, the combination of a security server and its data (the registry database) is referred to as a *replica*. Typically, you create several replicas in a cell to enhance performance and reliability.

The task of keeping the cell's replicas consistent is handled automatically by the security servers. Any changes that you make are automatically reflected in all replicas, as described in the following section.

27.6 How Updates Are Handled

Updates are made to only one database, and the changes are propagated to all others. While propagations are pending, all replicas are accessible even if they are not completely up-to-date. In other words, even replicas to which the changes were not yet applied are available. This replication mechanism ensures that all replicas remain available for login validation and for read operations even when changes are in the process of being propagated.

27.6.1 Master and Slave Replicas

Only one replica in a cell, the *master replica*, accepts updates to its database from clients. Other replicas, called *slave replicas*, accept only reads from clients. The master replica propagates any updates to the slave replicas. For example, either a master or a slave replica can provide account information to a client program such as **/bin/login**. However, if you are adding an account or changing password information, those updates can be handled only by the master replica.

The process of updating the database differs slightly between the master replica and slave replicas. Figures 27-3 and 27-4 illustrate the master and slave update processes. The processes are described in the sections that follow the figures.

Figure 27–3. The Master Replica Update Process

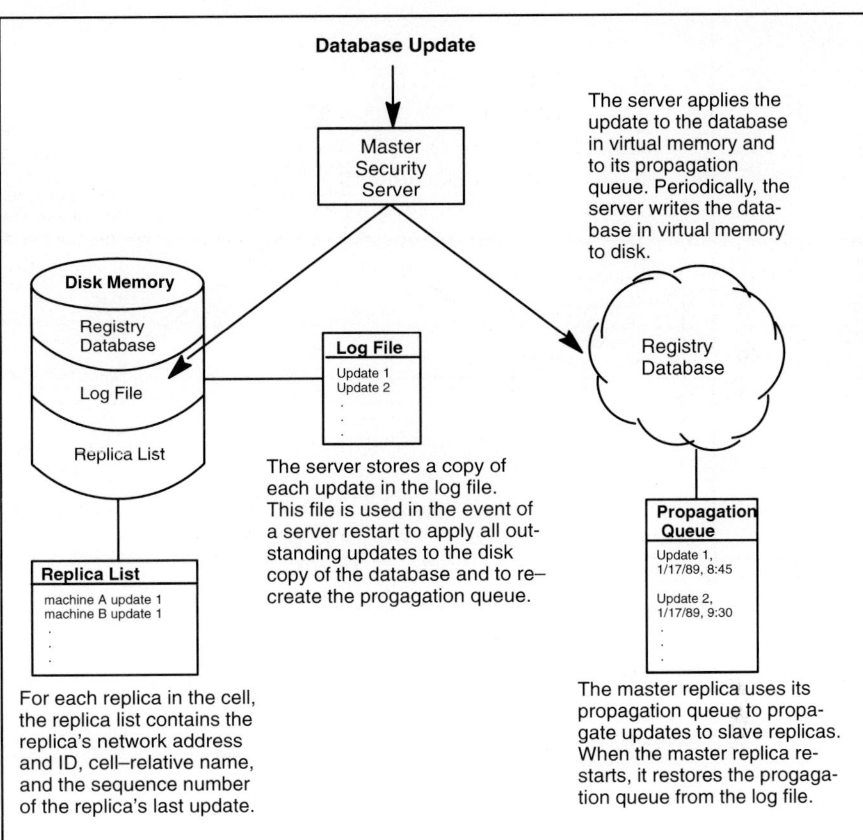

Figure 27–4. Slave Replica Update Process

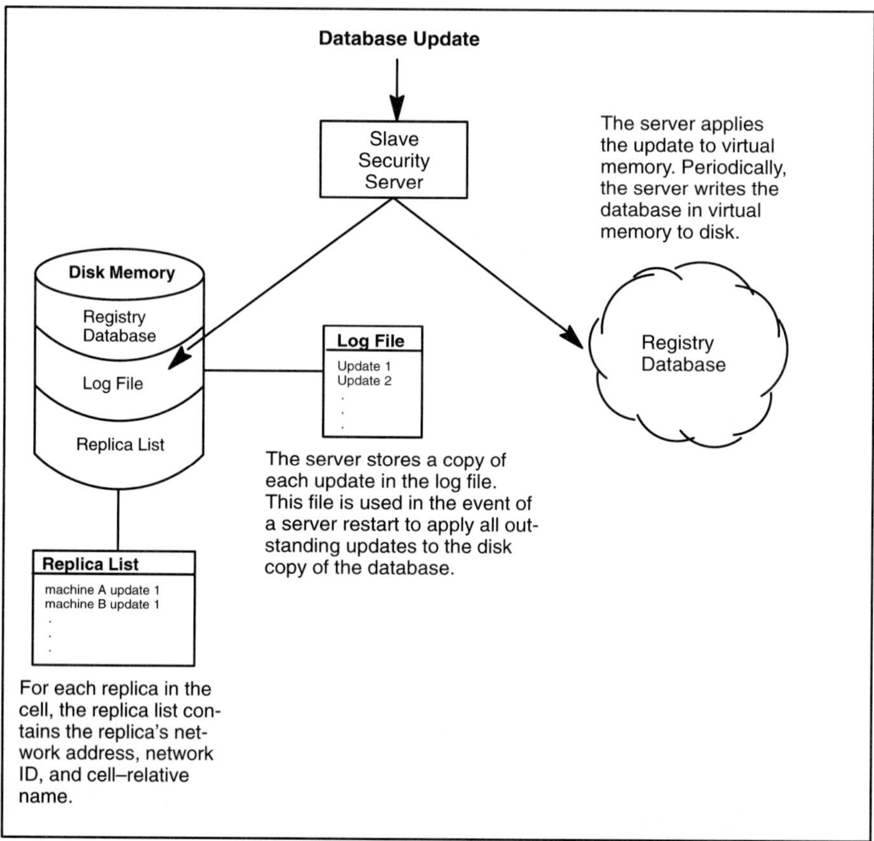

27.6.2 Handling Database Updates

When a master or slave replica receives updates, it applies the updates to its database in virtual memory, and saves a copy of each update in a log file that is stored on disk. Updates accumulate in the log file in sequenced numerical order. If a server restarts unexpectedly, the log file ensures that no updates are lost.

Periodically, the replica writes the database in virtual memory to disk, thus bringing the disk copy up-to-date. Then, if the replica is a slave, it clears the log file of all updates. If the replica is the master, it clears the log file of all updates that have been propagated to the slave replicas. Updates that have not been propagated to the slaves are retained and used to reconstruct the propagation queue, if necessary.

Only the master replica maintains a propagation queue, which is used to hold changes to be propagated to the slave replicas, as described in Section 27.6.3. When the master replica receives an update, it adds it to the propagation queue in addition to its virtual memory database and its log file. Each update in a propagation queue is identified by a sequence number and a timestamp. The sequence number is used internally to track the propagation of updates to slave replicas. The timestamp is provided to show users the date and time of updates.

When a master or slave replica restarts, it initializes its database in virtual memory and then applies any outstanding updates in the log file to its database. If the replica is the master replica, it also recreates the propagation queue from the log file so that any outstanding slave updates can be propagated. This mechanism ensures that no updates are lost when a server is shut down.

27.6.3 Propagating Database Changes

To propagate updates to the slave replicas, the master replica first updates its copy of the database by using the process described in Section 27.6.2. Then, the master replica attempts to propagate the update to each slave replica on its replica list. The replica list contains each slave replica's ID and network address. It also contains the sequence number of the last update that was made to the slave. The master replica always propagates in sequenced numerical order. By examining the sequence number that is associated with a replica in its replica list, and the sequence numbers of the updates that are in its propagation queue, the master can determine which of the updates on its propagation queue must be propagated to which slave. This mechanism helps ensure that the unavailability of a single slave replica does not interfere with updates to the rest of the slave replicas.

> **Note:** In the discussions of DCE authorization in this chapter and the
> chapters that follow, the term *user* is analogous to principal.
> A principal can be a human user, server, or a machine.

28.1 Authorization Overview

An ACL contains a list of entries that specify the principals who can access
an object and the operations that those principals can perform. The
principals can be named explicitly or be members of a group that is
identified in the ACL entry. The ACL is associated with the object it
protects. The operations a principal can perform are specified by
permissions.

DCE permissions can be set for the following:

- Owner, group, and other

- Specific individual principals in the local cell and in foreign cells

- Specific individual groups in the local cell and in foreign cells

- Any other principals in a specific foreign cell for whom individual
  permissions have not been set

- Any principals in any cell who have been authenticated by the DCE
  Authentication Service

- Delegate users, servers, or groups, in local or foreign cells

- Unauthorized users

ACLs also provide a masking capability and a method for integrating
protections from DCE versions that are different from the current version.

File systems are frequently designed to provide access permissions for file
system objects, such as files and directories. ACLs in DCE are more
extensive. In DCE, many objects can have ACLs and be assigned
permissions. DCE ACLs control access to objects managed by DCE
components, like the Distributed File Service, the DCE Security Service,
and the DCE Directory Service.

ACLs for the security service (the component that controls accounts) can, for example, authorize certain principals to change all of the information associated with an account, authorize other principals to change only a subset of the information associated with accounts, and restrict other principals from changing any of the information associated with accounts.

DCE can support particular sets of permissions that correspond to particular types of objects. For example, for containers there can be an "insert" permission that other objects, such as principals, do not need. This extensive usage of ACLs is in contrast to that of POSIX systems, for example, where only file system objects are protected by permission bits, with a standard set of permissions (read, write, and execute) being used. The DCE control program has a command, **acl permissions**, that shows the permissions specific to the ACL associated with the named object.

28.1.1 ACL Managers

An ACL manager is that portion of a server that handles ACLs. One ACL manager can support several different types of ACLs. From a more abstract point of view, each ACL type is supported by a corresponding ACL manager type. Informally, ACL manager types are sometimes called ACL managers. Figure 28-1 shows ACL managers in servers.

The client side allows you to connect to any server exporting the ACL interface so that one program can manipulate all ACLs. The DCE control program and the **acl_edit** command use the feature.

28.2 ACL Entries and Masks

ACL entries are of several different *ACL entry types*, each type being for a particular purpose. All ACL entries are represented in a uniform list syntax.

28.2.1 ACL Syntax

The DCE control program uses the command syntax that is supported by the Tcl language. Within Tcl, the list that represents an ACL entry contains either two or three elements, depending on the ACL entry type, and is in the following form:

{*type*[*key*] *permissions*}

The three sample ACL entries in Figure 28-2 are in the format that Tcl accepts for input.

Figure 28–2. Sample ACL Entries

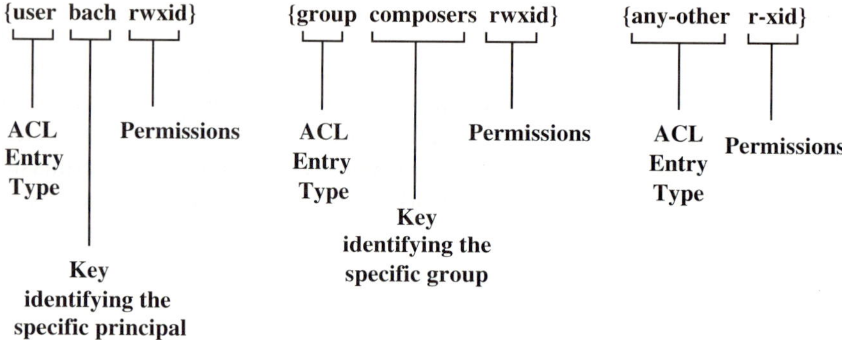

The first sample ACL entry sets permissions for a principal in the local cell, named **bach**. The ACL entry type is **user**, the key is **bach,** and the permissions are **rwxid**. The entry components are separated by the space character.

The second sample ACL entry sets permissions for a group in the local cell, named **composers**. The ACL entry type is **group**, the key is **composers,** and the permissions are **rwxid**.

The third sample ACL entry sets permissions for all other principals in the local cell or foreign cells (unless they match a more specific entry). The ACL entry type is **any-other**, there is no key, and the permissions are **r-xid**. Not all types of ACL entries require a key.

On output, the Tcl format for ACL permissions contains either a permission character or a - (dash) for each possible permission. Two examples are

```
{user mozart crwx---}
{user brahms -------}
```

For input, the output format is acceptable, or you can use a relaxed form that omits the dashes. For input, the same examples can be shortened to

```
{user mozart crwx}
{user brahms -}
```

The single dash is retained to show that user **brahms** is denied all permissions.

28.2.2 ACL Entry Types for Principals and Groups

ACL entry types let you define entries for the following:

- Principals and groups
  - Principals and groups in the local cell
  - Principals and groups in foreign cells
  - Delegate entries
  - All principals in the local cell for whom individual ACL entries have not been created.
  - All principals in the local and all foreign cells whose privilege attributes do not match any of the other ACL entries.
- Masks used for authenticated and unauthenticated users
- As-yet-undefined entry types that can be copied and displayed (if not interpreted) by dissimilar DCE releases.

If any principal or group is not authenticated, the permissions in the entry are further constrained by the **unauthenticated** mask (described later in this chapter). All entries for authenticated principals, except **user_obj** and **other_obj** entries, are further constrained by the **mask_obj** mask (also described later in this chapter).

The following list shows the entry types for principals and groups, their meaning, and their entry format. All ACLs have a default cell defined in them, as referred to in the table. It is changeable, and serves to define the cell for various data types.

This list uses the following syntax variables:

principal_name	The name of a principal in the registry database
group_name	The name of a group defined in the registry database
cell	The global pathname of a cell in the format */.../name*.
permissions	The permissions made available by the object's ACL manager.

The principal and group ACL entry types are as follows:

user_obj   Establishes permissions for the object's real or effective user. An example is the owner of a file. The entry format is

{**user_obj** *permissions*}

group_obj   Establishes permissions for members of the object's real or effective group. An example is the group of a file. The entry format is

{**group_obj** *permissions*}

other_obj   Establishes permissions for all other principals in the default cell, unless they are specifically named in ACLs of entry type **user**, are members of a group named in an ACL with an entry type of **group**, or match the principal indicated by the **user_obj** or **group_obj** entry. The entry format is

{**other_obj** *permissions*}

user

Establishes permissions for a specific principal in the default cell of the ACL. This ACL entry type requires a key that is a principal name. The entry format is

{**user** *principal_name permissions*}

group

Establishes permissions for members of a specific group in the default cell. This ACL entry type requires a key that is a group name. The entry format is

{**group** *group_name permissions*}

foreign_user

Establishes permissions for a specific principal in a foreign cell, one other than the default cell of the ACL. You must identify the principal by supplying a principal name and cell name as a key. The entry format is

{**foreign_user** *cell_name/principal_name* \
  permissions}

foreign_group

Establishes permissions for a specific group in a foreign cell, one other than the default cell of the ACL. You must identify the group by supplying a group name and a cell name as a key. The entry format is

{**foreign_group** *cell_name/group_name permissions*}

foreign_other

Establishes permissions for other principals in a specific foreign cell, one other than the default cell of the ACL, that are not specifically named in ACL entries of entry type **foreign_user** or are members of a group named in an ACL entry of type **foreign_group**. You must identify the foreign cell by supplying a cell name as a key. The entry format is

{**foreign_other** *cell_name permissions*}

any_other Establishes permissions for all other principals in local or foreign cells unless they match a more specific entry in the ACL. The entry format is

{**any_other** *permissions*}

user_obj_delegate Establishes permissions for an intermediary acting for the object's real or effective user. The entry format is

{**user_obj_delegate** *permissions*}

group_obj_delegate Establishes permissions for an intermediary acting for members of the object's real or effective group. The entry format is

{**group_obj_delegate** *permissions*}

other_obj_delegate Establishes permissions for an intermediary acting for all other principals in the default cell, unless they are specifically named in ACLs of entry type **user**, are members of a group named in an ACL with an entry type of **group**, or match the principal indicated by the **user_obj** or **group_obj** entry. The entry format is

{**other_obj_delegate** *permissions*}

user_delegate Establishes permissions for an intermediary acting for a specific principal in the default cell of the ACL. This ACL entry type requires a key that is a principal name. The entry format is

{**user_delegate** *principal_name permissions*}

group_delegate Establishes permissions for an intermediary acting for members of a specific group in the default cell. This ACL entry type requires a key that is a group name. The entry format is

{**group_delegate** *group_name permissions*}

foreign_user_delegate   Establishes permissions for an intermediary acting for a specific principal in a foreign cell, one other than the default cell of the ACL. You must identify the principal by supplying a principal name and cell name as a key. The entry format is

> {**foreign_user_delegate** *cell_name/principal_name* \
> *permissions*}

foreign_group_delegate   Establishes permissions for an intermediary acting for a specific group in a foreign cell, one other than the default cell of the ACL. You must identify the group by supplying a group name and a cell name as a key. The entry format is

> {**foreign_group_delegate** *cell_name/group_name* \
> *permissions*}

foreign_other_delegate   Establishes permissions for an intermediary acting for other principals in a specific foreign cell, one other than the default cell of the ACL, that are not specifically named in ACL entries of entry type **foreign_user** or are members of a group named in an ACL entry of type **foreign_group**. You must identify the foreign cell by supplying a cell name as a key. The entry format is

> {**foreign_other_delegate** *cell_name permissions*}

any_other_delegate   Establishes permissions for an intermediary acting for all other principals in local or foreign cells unless they match a more specific entry in the ACL. The entry format is

> {**any_other_delegate** *permissions*}

28.2.3 Group Permissions and Project Lists

Principals accrue group permissions from their project list, a list of all the groups of which a principal or alias is a member. When a principal tries to access an object, the principal has the access rights that accrue from the logical OR of permissions granted to every group with an entry in the ACL and in which the principal is a member. Note that the principal accrues rights only from the name or alias with which the principal logged in, not both names and aliases. (See Chapter 30 for more information on aliases and project lists.)

For example, suppose an ACL contains the following entries:

```
{user_obj crwxid-}
{group_obj crwx---}
{other_obj -r-----}
{group composers crwx---}
{user bach crwx---}
{user mozart crwx---}
{group performers --w-idt}
```

User **cole** is a member of the group **composers** and the group **performers**. Because **cole** accrues permissions from both groups, his access permissions are **crwxidt**. (The security service provides a method to prevent a group from being included in a project list, thus preventing the group's permissions from being accrued as part of the project list. See Chapter 30 for more information.)

28.2.4 Using Principal and Group ACL Entries

When a security mechanism applies ACLs, the ACL entries are chosen in a particular order. The most specific ones are chosen before the less specific.

In using the ACL entry types for principals and groups, think of the **user_obj**, **group_obj**, and **other_obj** types as being similar to the POSIX file permissions of **user**, **group** and **other**. Use the **user** and **group** types to specify permissions for a specific principal or group.

The **user_obj, group_obj**, **other_obj, user**, and **group** entry types apply to principals and groups in the default cell of the ACL. To set permissions for specific principals and groups in a foreign cell, use the **foreign_user** and **foreign_group** entries. These entries set permissions in a foreign cell in the same way that **user** and **group** entries do in the default cell. Use **foreign_other** to set permissions for others in the foreign cell, in the same way that **other_obj** does for others in the default cell.

The **any_other** entry type sets permissions for all local and foreign principals to which the other entry types do not apply. If any of the other types of entries are set for a local or foreign principal either explicitly or implicitly, the **any_other** entry will not be applied. This is because once the manager finds a match between a principal and an entry, it stops examining the ACL list and applies the found entry (or in the case of groups, entries). All other ACL entry types, except for mask types (described below), are examined by the ACL manager to see if a match exists before the ACL manager examines the **any_other** entry type. See Section 28.2.7 for details of the order of ACL checking.

28.2.5 ACL Entry Types for Masks

Masks in ACL entries establish maximum permissions that can be granted to a principal. There are two masks: the **mask_obj mask** and the **unauthenticated mask**. Only permissions given in an ACL entry and the mask are granted. For example, if the ACL entry specifies **rwx** permissions and the mask specifies only the **x** permission, the permissions are ANDed with the mask, and only the **x** permission is granted.

The **mask_obj** mask, if it exists, applies to all entry types except **user_obj** and **other_obj**. The **unauthenticated** mask is applied to all unauthenticated principals. As the ACL manager derives the permissions from the ACL entries, it filters each one through the **mask_obj** mask (if one exists), and finally through the **unauthenticated** mask. The manager grants only those permissions that are in the first matching entry, the **mask_obj** mask, and the **unauthenticated** mask.

> **Note:** If you do not create an **unauthenticated** mask, unauthenticated principals are denied all access to objects. If a user is unauthenticated because that user has no DCE credentials, then the only entry that the user matches is the **any_other** entry type, which is then masked by the **unauthenticated** mask. This means that, for such unauthenticated users to have any access to an object, the object's ACL must contain an **any_other** type entry and an **unauthenticated** mask entry.

An example of mask usage follows. For a particular object, there are a great number of ACL entries specifying **rw** access to that object. You need to restrict the access to read-only, temporarily, but do not want to change all the ACL entries. Simply creating a **mask_obj** mask of **r**, and then removing it when you are done, provides the temporary restriction.

28.2.6 ACL Entry Types for Dissimilar DCE Releases

The **extended** entry type provides a generic format for ACL entries that allows future DCE releases to implement new ACL entry types. Because the new types are "packaged" in the generic format of the **extended** entry, earlier DCE releases can copy, display, and print the new entry types even if they cannot interpret their meaning.

Section 28.4 tells how to copy extended entries. Note that extended entries cannot be modified; however, they can be deleted.

An **extended** ACL entry has the following form:

{**extended** *uuid.ndr.ndr.ndr.ndr.number_of_bytes.data permissions*}

where:

uuid   A UUID that identifies the entry type of the extended ACL entry. (This UUID can identify one of the ACL entry types described in this document or an as-yet-undefined ACL entry type.)

ndr.ndr.ndr.ndr A Network Data Representation (NDR) format label (in hexadecimal format and separated by dots) that identifies the encoding of data.

number_of_bytes   A decimal number that specifies the total number of bytes in *data.* It is followed by a dot.

data   The ACL data in hexadecimal format. (Each byte of ACL data is two hexadecimal digits.) The ACL data includes all of the ACL entry specification except the permissions. The ACL data is not interpreted; it is assumed that the ACL manager to which the data is being passed can understand that data.

permissions   The permissions to be granted by the entry.

28.2.7 The Checking Sequence for ACL Entries

An ACL manager reads through a list of ACL entries to find the particular entry that applies to an individual who is trying to perform a particular operation. The ACL manager first looks for a match between the privilege attributes of the principal or process desiring access and the privilege attributes listed in the ACL. When the ACL manager finds a match, it examines the permissions in the matching ACL entry and applies the **mask_obj** mask to it (unless it is an entry of type **user_obj** or **other_obj**) if a **mask_obj** mask exists. Finally, the ACL manager applies the **unauthenticated** mask (if it exists) if the principal is not authenticated. If the permissions that result grant the requested access, the manager grants it to the principal. If not, access is denied.

Because an ACL manager stops checking the ACL entries when it finds a match, it is important to understand the order in which the ACLs are checked. Figure 28-3 shows the order of checking and the masks applied. ACL managers check entries in the following order, with the exception that the initiator principal is not checked against **..._delegate** entries. Delegate principals are checked against all entries.

1. First, the ACL manager checks the user ACL entries, in the following order:

   - **user_obj**

   - **user_obj_delegate**

   - **user**

   - **user_delegate**

   - **foreign_user**

   - **foreign_user_delegate**

   The ACL manager stops all entry checking at the first matching user entry it finds and applies the permissions in the entry. The user entries are checked in order as shown in the previous list from most specific to least specific.

2. If the ACL manager does not find a match in the user entries, it checks *all* of the following group entries:

   - **group_obj**

   - **group_obj_delegate**

   - **group**

   - **group_delegate**

   - **foreign_group**

   - **foreign_group_delegate**

   If any group ACL entries match the principal's project list, and the logical OR of permissions from these entries grants access, then access is granted and no further checking is performed.

   Because principals accrue permissions from all groups listed in the ACL of which they are a member (and for which they are in the project list), *all* the groups are checked and *all* the principal's group permissions are logically ORed. The order of group entry checking is not important. See Section 28.2.3 for more information on project lists.

3. If the ACL manager does not find a match between the principal requesting permission and a member of a group in the group entries, it checks the **other_obj** and **other_obj_delegate** entries. If the ACL manager finds a match, it stops checking ACL entries.

4. If the ACL manager does not find a match between the principal requesting permission and the **other_obj** or **other_obj_delegate** entries, it checks the **foreign_other** and **foreign_other_delegate** entries. If the ACL manager finds a match, it stops checking ACL entries.

5. If the ACL manager does not find a match between the principal requesting permission and the **foreign_other** or **foreign_other_-delegate** entries, it checks the **any_other** and **any_other_delegate** entries. If it does not find a match in the **any_other** or **any_other_-delegate** entries, it denies all access to the object.

The final permission is the intersection of the permission of the initiator principal and of each delegate.

Figure 28-3 shows these steps as they apply to the ACL entries. The two columns distinguish between ACL entries that are not masked by **mask_obj** and those that are masked by it.

Figure 28–3. Order of Checking ACLs and Applying Masks

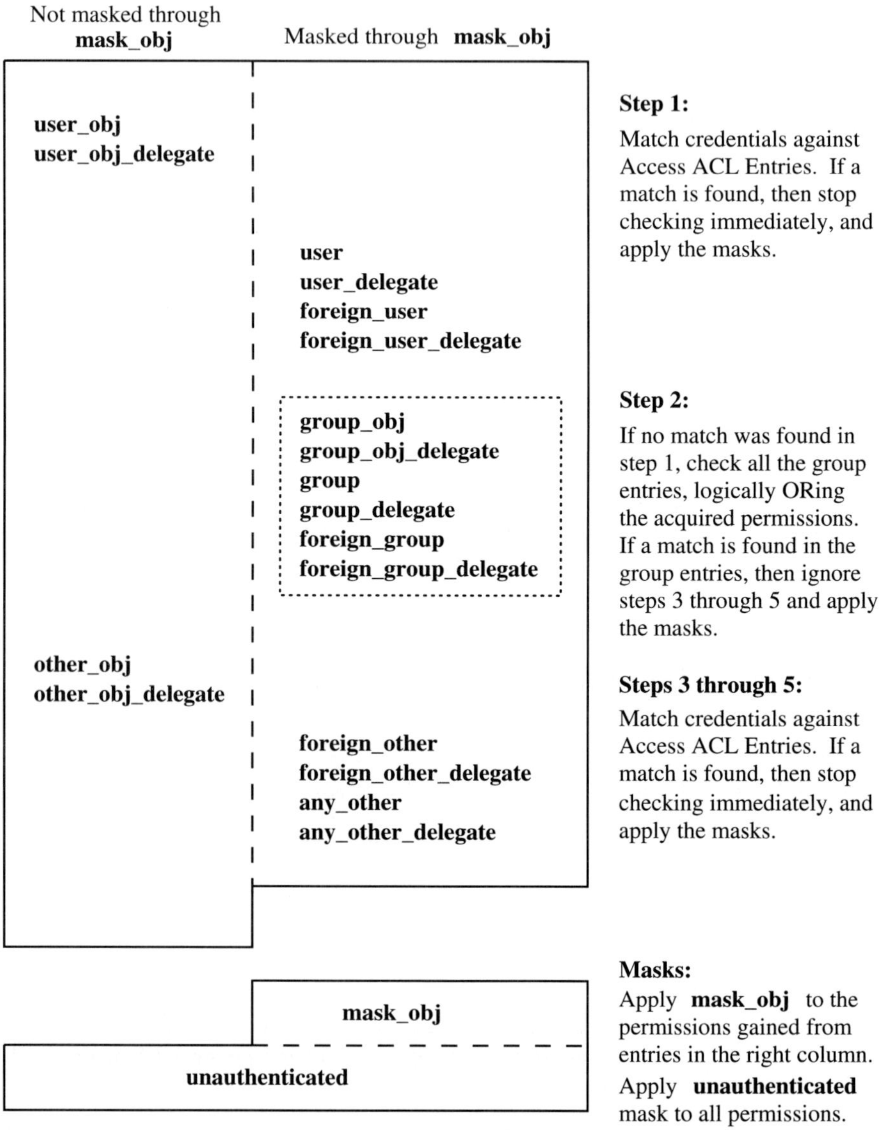

Not masked through **mask_obj**

Masked through **mask_obj**

user_obj
user_obj_delegate

user
user_delegate
foreign_user
foreign_user_delegate

group_obj
group_obj_delegate
group
group_delegate
foreign_group
foreign_group_delegate

other_obj
other_obj_delegate

foreign_other
foreign_other_delegate
any_other
any_other_delegate

mask_obj

unauthenticated

Step 1:

Match credentials against Access ACL Entries. If a match is found, then stop checking immediately, and apply the masks.

Step 2:

If no match was found in step 1, check all the group entries, logically ORing the acquired permissions. If a match is found in the group entries, then ignore steps 3 through 5 and apply the masks.

Steps 3 through 5:

Match credentials against Access ACL Entries. If a match is found, then stop checking immediately, and apply the masks.

Masks:

Apply **mask_obj** to the permissions gained from entries in the right column. Apply **unauthenticated** mask to all permissions.

28.2.7.1 The **mask_obj** Mask and ACL Checking

Before the ACL manager grants any permissions derived from checking the ACL entries, it filters the entry permissions through the **mask_obj** mask. Only those permissions named in the ACL entry and in the mask are granted. For example, if an ACL entry grants **rwx** permissions and the **mask_obj** entry specifies only **r** and **w** permission, only **r** and **w** are granted. The **x** permission named in the ACL entry is ignored.

28.2.7.2 The Unauthenticated Mask and ACL Checking

If an ACL manager receives an access request from an unauthenticated principal, it checks the ACL entries and applies the **mask_obj** mask, if available, as described previously. It then filters the resulting permissions through the mask for unauthenticated principals (entry type of **unauthenticated**). Only those permissions specified in the **unauthenticated** mask, in the ACL entry, and in the **mask_obj** mask (if it exists) are granted.

28.2.7.3 The Effect of the Checking Order on Granting Permissions

You can think of the order in which the ACL entries are checked as going from most specific to least specific. For example, assume an ACL contains the following entries:

```
{user mahler r}
{group composers rwx}
```

If the principal named **mahler**, who is a member of the group **composers**, requests execute (**x**) access, it is denied. This happens because the order of checking specifies that all user entries (**user_obj**, **user**, and **foreign_user**) are checked before all group (**group_obj**, **group**, and **foreign_group**) entries. Therefore, the first match found by the ACL manager is the match between user **mahler** and the ACL entry for user **mahler**. Once a matching user entry is found, checking stops and the found permissions are applied. In this case, checking stops before the **group** entry, the entry with the more liberal permissions.

28.2.8 Denying Access

When you create an ACL entry for a principal or group, you grant only the permissions you specify in the ACL entry. To deny a principal all access to an object, create an ACL entry that contains a dash in place of the permissions. For example, to deny all access to user **mozart**, the entry would be

{user mozart -}

If you choose to deny access to a specific principal or group, select the most specific entry type available. Generally for principals this is an entry type of **user** or **foreign_user**; for groups, it is an entry type of **group** or **foreign_group**. Note that, if the principal is the object's owner or a member of the object's group, you must use the **user_obj** or **group_obj** entry types to ensure that access is denied.

To deny access to all unauthenticated users, do not create the **unauthenticated** mask. If this mask is not created (ACL entry type of **unauthenticated**), only authenticated principals can access the object. The same behavior is achieved by creating an **unauthenticated** mask with no permissions (or a dash in place of the permissions). This method also has the additional advantage of illustrating graphically that unauthenticated users have no access rights.

28.3 ACL Management Tasks

ACL management involves creating, modifying, and deleting the entries for the ACLs on DCE entities. You can use the DCE control program to do all of these tasks. The control program's **acl** commands perform the following operations on ACLs:

- Create and modify ACL entries for DCE objects in the local cell and foreign cells. (Note that when objects are created they are associated with initial ACL entries. See Section 28.5 for more information.)

- Display the permissions implemented for an object by the object's ACL manager.

- Create and modify masks used to restrict allowable permissions.

Note: Standard UNIX tools that display and manipulate UNIX modes have an effect only on the ACLs established for the file system.

For a detailed description of the DCE control program's **acl** commands, see the **acl(8dce)** reference page.

28.4 Copying ACLs

To copy an ACL from one DCE object to another, use the DCE control program **acl replace** command with the **-acl** option as shown here:

dcecp> **acl replace /.:/hosts/hermes -acl [acl show /.:/hosts/cyclops]**

The example command replaces the ACL for the host **hermes** with the ACL for the host **cyclops** whose name is specified in the **acl show** command invoked by the **-acl** option. Note how the **-acl show** command in the **-acl** option is enclosed in [ ] (brackets). This is required when the **-acl** option value is a command invocation.

If you are copying between cells, use the **acl replace** command's **-cell** option, as well as its **-acl** option. For example:

dcecp> **acl replace /.:/hosts/hermes -acl [acl show /.:/hosts/cyclops] \
        -cell [acl show /.:/hosts/cyclops -cell]**

To copy an **extended** entry type from the domain of one ACL manager to the domain of another ACL manager, use the output of the **dcecp acl show** command as the input to an **acl replace** command. To copy **extended** entries this way, both ACL managers must support the **extended** entry type.

28.5 Generating ACLs from Files

A convenient way to create an ACL is to create and edit a text file so that it contains the desired ACL entries, and then generate the ACL from it by using an **acl replace** operation.

For example, assume the file **std_acl** contains the following entries:

```
mask_obj:crwxid-
user_obj:crwxid-
group_obj:crwx---
other_obj:-r-----
user:lizt:crwx---
group:composers:-r-----
user:bach:crwx---
user:mozart:crwx---
```

The following **acl replace** operation adds the entries in **std_acl** to an ACL named **/.../dresden.com/my_filesystem/opus**:

```
dcecp> acl replace /.../dresden.com/my_filesystem/opus -acl [cat std_acl]
```

The **acl replace** operation overwrites all ACL entries with the ones from the file **std_acl**. Regardless of what they were before, the ACLs for **opus** now look like this:

```
mask_obj:crwxid-
user_obj:crwxid-
user:lizt:crwx---
user:bach:crwx---
user:mozart:crwx---
group_obj:crwx---
group:composers:-r-----
other_obj:-r-----
```

28.6 Container ACLs

The Object ACL controls access to the object itself. A container object has, in addition to its Object ACL, an Initial Container ACL and an Initial Object ACL. These two ACLs are not used for access control as such, but instead for cloning initial ACLs for objects or containers created within the initial container. The Initial Container ACLs and the Initial Object ACLs can be edited in the same way as the usual ACL by using the **-ic** and **-io** options to the **dcecp acl** commands.

28.6.1 Objects and Containers

The type of ACL used for an object depends on whether the object is a simple object or a container. Containers are objects that hold other objects. The objects they hold can themselves be either simple objects or container objects. Simple objects do not hold other objects. Although any DCE component can have objects and containers, the simplest and most common illustration is the file system. In the file system, there are files and directories. The files are simple objects, and the directories are containers. The directories can hold simple objects (files) and other containers (subdirectories).

The Object ACL is associated with simple and container objects. The Initial Container and Initial Object ACLs are associated only with container objects.

28.6.2 Initial ACLs for Objects and Containers

Initial ACL entries and the ACL that contains them are applied automatically when an object is created. The entries can be modified at any time with the DCE control program. The types of DCE ACLs used as Initial ACLs for containers and objects are as follows:

- The Initial Container ACL determines the default ACL for containers created within a container. For example, the file system Initial Container ACL for a directory specifies the default ACL for subdirectories created within that directory.

- The Initial Object ACL determines the default for objects created within a container. For example, the file system Initial Object ACL for a directory specifies the default ACL for files created within that directory.

28.6.2.1 Default ACLs for Objects

When a simple object is created in a container, it inherits the container's Initial Object ACL as its Object ACL. Figure 28-4 illustrates how the default ACL is assigned to simple objects created in containers.

Figure 28–4. Initial ACLs for Objects Created in Containers

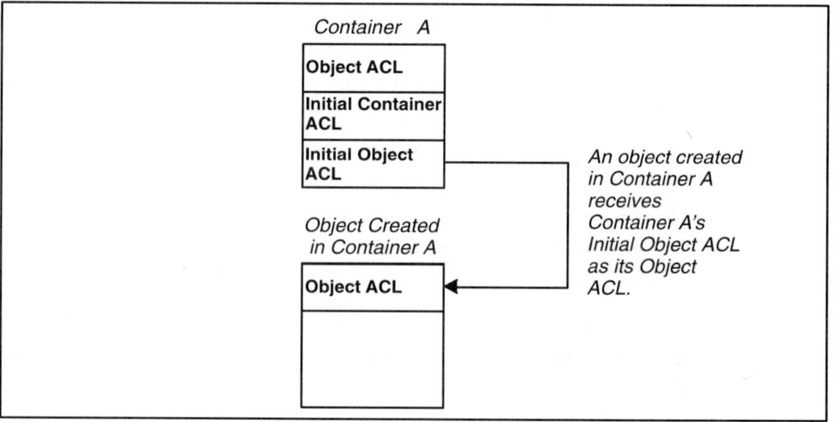

28.6.2.2 Default ACLs for Containers

When a container is created within a container (a subdirectory within a directory, for example), it inherits the parent container's

- Initial Container ACL as its Object ACL and as its Initial Container ACL

- Initial Object ACL as its Initial Object ACL

OSF DCE Administration Guide—Core Components

For example, if you create a file named **report** in the directory **marketing**, the system assigns **report** the Initial Object ACL of the directory **marketing**. If you create a subdirectory in **marketing**, the system assigns the new subdirectory the Initial Container ACL of **marketing**. New subdirectories also receive a set of initial ACLs that match the parent directory's initial ACLs. In this example, the new subdirectory also receives **marketing**'s initial ACLs as its own ACLs. Figure 28-5 illustrates how the default ACLs are assigned to objects created in containers.

Figure 28–5. Initial ACLs for Containers Created in Containers

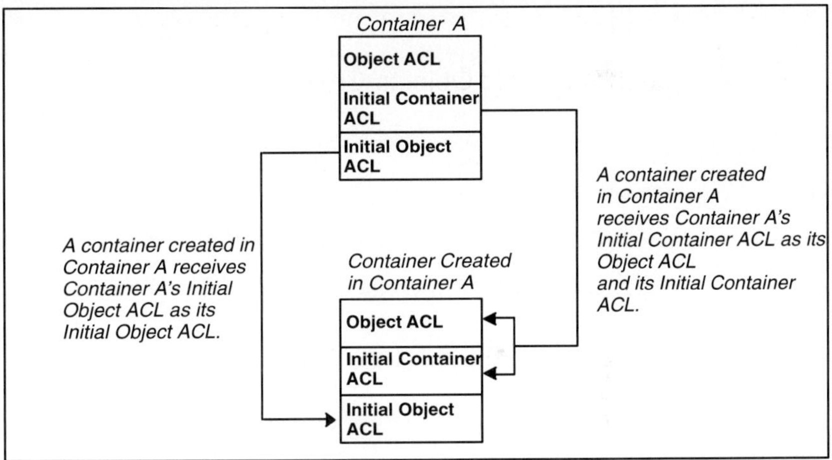

28.6.2.3 Default Container ACL Example

The following example shows how ACLs are initially assigned to containers created within containers.

Assume Container A has the following ACLs:

Object ACL

```
{user_obj crwxid}
{group_obj crwxid}
{other_obj r}
```

Initial Container ACL

```
{user_obj crwxid}
{group_obj rw}
{other_obj r}
```

Initial Object ACL

```
{user_obj crwxid}
{group_obj r}
{other_obj r}
```

When Container B is created in Container A, it has the following default ACLs:

Object ACL (Container A's Initial Container ACL)

```
{user_obj crwxid}
{group_obj rw}
{other_obj r}
```

Initial Container ACL (Container A's Initial Container ACL)

```
{user_obj crwxid}
{group_obj rw}
{other_obj r}
```

Initial Object ACL (Container A's Initial Object ACL)

```
{user_obj crwxid}
{group_obj r}
{other_obj r}
```

28.6.3 Effect of Masks When Editing ACLs

If the user specifies a new **mask_obj** ACL entry, then **acl modify** uses it. Otherwise, the **acl modify** command recalculates the mask, using the algorithm shown in the following paragraph, unless the user has specified one of the **-mask calc**, **-mask nocalc**, or **-purge** options. Therefore the mask can change, granting more or fewer permissions, on every **acl modify** command.

Here is the algorithm that the **acl modify** command uses when calculating the mask:

1. Retrieve the existing ACL of the file.

2. Perform all requests to remove entries and to reduce the permissions of existing entries.

3. Calculate the union of the actual permissions of all remaining entries.

4. Determine which permissions differ between the actual and effective rights. (This is the logical XOR of the results of steps 3 and 4.)

5. Perform all requests to add new entries to the ACL and all requests to increase the permissions of existing entries.

6. Calculate the union of these newly granted permissions and the old effective permissions (from step 4). This is the candidate new mask value.

7. If there are any permissions in the candidate new mask that are also in the permissions that differ between the original actual and effective rights (from step 5), applying the candidate new mask would unexpectedly grant some new right that the user did not intend. Unless the user specified one of the options **-mask calc**, **-mask nocalc**, or **-purge**, this condition is an error, and the ACL is not modified. Otherwise, the candidate new mask is applied as the new mask.

For the vast majority of ACL operations, such automatic recalculation is safe. In certain rare cases, the recalculation of the mask can grant additional rights that the user did not expect; for instance, a permission granted to an entry that the user did not specify and that was not among the entry's previous effective rights.

The following example shows the way mask recalculation works, as well as the effect of the options.

Observe that the ACL contains an entry granting **rwx** permission to some user, but the mask allows an effective permission of **r-x**. Adding a new **rwx** ACL entry and recalculating the mask (according to step 6) to **rwx** is unsafe because the first user's effective access rights are unexpectedly changed from **r-x** to **rwx**. If the **acl modify** command detects such an unsafe condition, its default action is to issue an error message and not change the ACL.

The initial state, showing the permissions and the effective permissions, is

```
dcecp> acl show /.:/concertos
{user vivaldi rwx effective r-x}
{mask_obj r-x}
```

Adding a user as shown results in an error because the mask recalculation would give **vivaldi** an effective permission of **rwx**:

```
dcecp> acl modify /.:/concertos -add {user telemann rwx}
Error: Unintended permissions not granted.
```

Explicit use of the **-mask calc** option allows the recalculated mask to be applied in spite of the new permission granted to **vivaldi**. The mask is set to the union of the permissions granted to the file group class entries on the ACL. This option can result in the inadvertent granting of extra permissions.

```
dcecp> acl modify /.:/concertos -add {user telemann rwx} -mask calc
dcecp> acl show /.:/concertos
{user vivaldi rwx effective rwx}
{user telemann rwx effective rwx}
{mask_obj rwx}
```

Using the **-mask nocalc** option explicitly retains the **r-x** mask, resulting in reduced effective permissions for **telemann**. The ACL is modified exactly as specified by the user, and no mask calculation or purging of permissions occurs.

```
dcecp> acl modify /.:/concertos -add {user telemann rwx} -mask nocalc
dcecp> acl show /.:/concertos
{user vivaldi  rwx effective r-x}
{user telemann rwx effective r-x}
{mask_obj  r-x}
```

Using the **-purge** option replaces the actual permissions with the effective permissions in all entries. More precisely, if the command detects an unsafe condition, then the condition intersects the current value of the mask with all of the existing, unmodified entries in the file group class, replacing all ACL entries (except **user_obj**, **other_obj**, **mask_obj** and **unauthenticated**) with their effective permissions.

```
dcecp> acl modify /.:/concertos -add {user telemann rwx} -purge
dcecp> acl show /.:/concertos
{user vivaldi  rwx effective r-x}
{user telemann rwx effective rwx}
{mask_obj  rwx}
```

Chapter 29

Control Programs for Managing the DCE Security Service

You can perform most of the management tasks for the DCE Security Service by using the DCE control program (**dcecp**). However, some of the components of this service require you to use other control programs provided in DCE.

This chapter provides information about the commands that the DCE control program offers for DCE Security Service management. The chapter also describes the commands that the registry editor program (**rgy_edit**) provides for maintaining local registries. In addition, the chapter describes the commands that the **sec_admin** program supplies for reorganizing the registry replica set in a cell.

Control programs that you use for security-related management tasks from time to time, such as **password_export** and **sec_create_db**, are not covered in this chapter. These programs are described in subsequent chapters of this guide along with the instructions for performing the tasks.

Table 29–1. DCE Control Program Operations for the DCE Security Service

Operation	Description
add	Adds a principal to a group or organization to a registry replica.
catalog	Displays the names of all the principals, groups, and organizations in a registry replica. For the registry itself, displays the master and slave replicas existing in a DCE cell.
check	Displays the permissions that a DCE ACL currently grants to a security principal.
create	Creates a new principal, group, organization, or account in a registry replica. Also, creates a new entry for an ERA schema.
delete	Deletes a principal, group, organization, or account from a registry replica. For the registry itself, deletes a slave replica. For an ERA schema, deletes entries. For a DCE ACL, removes ACL entries.
disable	Disables the master replica of the registry for updates.
dump	Displays information on each replica of the registry existing in a cell.
enable	Enables the master replica of the registry for updates.
help	Displays help information about a principal, group, organization, account, ERA schema, or DCE ACL in a registry replica, or about the registry replica itself.
list	Displays the names of the principals belonging to a group or organization in a registry replica.
modify	Modifies the attribute information in a registry replica for a principal, group, account, ERA schema entry, DCE ACL entry, or for the registry itself. For an organization, also modifies the policy information.
operations	Displays the operations that can be performed by or on a principal, group, organization, account, ERA schema, DCE ACL, or registry replica.

Operation	Description
permissions	Displays the permissions granted by a ACL on a protected DCE component.
remove	Removes one or more principals from a group or organization in a registry replica.
rename	Changes the name of a principal, group, organization, or ERA schema in a registry replica.
replace	Replaces the entire ACL on a DCE component.
show	Displays information about the attributes of a principal, group, ERA schema entries, or DCE ACL entries. Also displays information about the policies for an organization, account, or registry replica.
stop	Stops a security server process.
synchronize	Instructs the slave replica of the registry to update its contents from the master replica.
verify	Checks if all of the registry's replicas are up-to-date.

29.2 Using the Registry Editor

Although you can use the DCE control program to maintain the network-wide registry, you can only use the registry editor to maintain the local registries located on the hosts in a cell.

The following subsections explain how to start, stop, and get help for the registry editor and describe the commands to use for local registry maintenance. Specific instructions for using the registry editor to maintain the local registry are given in Chapters 30 and 31.

For detailed descriptions of all of the registry editor commands, see the **rgy_edit(8sec)** reference page.

- Reserved Principals:

  - **dce-ptgt**

  - **krbtgt/***cell_name*

  - **dce-rgy**

  - *host_principal_name*

- Reserved Accounts:

  - **dce-ptgt none none**

  - **krbtgt/***cell_name* **none none**

  - **dce-rgy none none**

  - *host_principal_name* **none none**

30.3 Object Creation Quotas

You can assign an object creation quota to each principal. This assignment allows you to control the number of registry objects that can be created by the principal. If you allow users to create their own groups, for example, you can use this quota to limit the total number of groups they can create. The default for the object creation quota is **unlimited**, meaning that no limits are placed on the number of objects the principal can create. A value of 0 (zero) prohibits the principal from creating any registry objects.

Each time a principal creates a registry object, the principal's object creation quota is decremented by 1. When the object creation quota reaches 0, the principal is prohibited from creating registry objects unless you reset the object creation quota to a number other than 0 by using the **dcecp principal modify** command. Note that, when an object that is created by a principal is deleted, the principal's object creation quota is *not* incremented.

Use the **dcecp principal show** command to view principals' current object creation quotas. This command displays the total number of objects that the principal is allowed to create at the current time; that is, the original quota minus the number of objects created by the principal.

30.4 Universal Unique Identifiers and UNIX IDs

The DCE Security Service automatically associates a principal's, group's, or organization's primary name with a UUID. UUIDs identify objects, which is a function performed by UNIX numbers (UNIX IDs) in UNIX systems. (The registry database also contains UNIX numbers, but they are used solely for compatibility with UNIX programs.)

Normally, you do not have to be aware of UUIDs. They are created and maintained automatically. However, be aware that, although the DCE Security Service prints names and you can access objects by name, it identifies all objects internally by UUID. If you delete a principal from the registry, you also delete the principal's UUID. Any objects (files, programs) that are owned by the principal are associated with an ''orphaned'' UUID; that is, a UUID with no corresponding name. This means that the object is now owned by a deleted principal. If no other principals were previously given access to the object, the object cannot be accessed.

To solve this problem, use the **dcecp principal create** command with the **-uuid** option to associate the UUID with a name and thus ''adopt'' the orphaned object. UUIDs are assigned automatically when the object is created by using the DCE control program's **principal create** command. Therefore, you cannot simply add a new user and acquire a previously used UUID. You must execute the **dcecp principal create** command with the **-uuid** option for this purpose.

UNIX numbers in the registry must fall within the range of numbers you set as a registry property. When you supply a UNIX number in the command line for creating or modifying an account, you should avoid numbers under 100 since these are generally reserved for system accounts.

30.5 Adding and Maintaining Principals

Use the **dcecp principal create** command to create principals. A principal must exist before you can create an account for the principal. When you use the **dcecp principal create** command, you must supply the principal's primary name as an argument. In addition, you can supply the attribute options summarized in Table 30-1.

Table 30–1. Attribute Options to Create Principals

Option	Meaning
-fullname *namestring*	An optional name that is used to more fully describe a primary name. To include spaces, enclose the full name in braces. The default is blank.
-uid *integer*	The required UNIX ID that is associated with the principal. You can enter this number explicitly or allow it to be generated automatically. If you enter it, the number you enter cannot exceed the maximum allowable UNIX number (the **maxuid** attribute) set with the **registry modify** command; however, you can enter a number lower than the low UNIX number (the **minuid** attribute) set for principals with the **registry modify** command. If you allow the number to be assigned automatically, it falls in the range defined by the low UNIX number and maximum UNIX number.
-quota *quota*	The number of registry objects that can be created by the principal, known as the principal's object *creation quota*. To allow a principal to create an unlimited number of registry objects, enter the text string **unlimited** to set no quota. To prevent a principal from creating any registry objects, enter a 0. The *quota* argument defaults to **unlimited**.

Note: In addition to these standard principal attributes, you can also attach ERA instances to principals to control such aspects of DCE security as preauthentication, password strength and password generation, and handling of invalid logins. See Section 30.6 for information on these ''well-known'' ERAs. See Chapter 32 for information on ERAs in general.

30.5.1 Adding Principals

To add principals to the registry, use the **principal create** command. For example, the following sample command creates a principal with a primary name of **mahler** and a full name of **gustav mahler**:

dcecp> **principal create mahler -fullname {gustav mahler} -quota 5**

In the example, the UNIX number defaults to one that is generated automatically. Notice that, because the full name (**gustav mahler**) assigned to the principal contains a space, it is enclosed in braces.

Note that it is possible to create multiple principals with one **principal create** command. To do so, enclose the principal names in braces, separated by spaces. For example, to create the principals **bach**, **britten**, **mahler**, and **satie**, you could enter the following:

dcecp> **principal create {bach britten mahler satie}**

If you create multiple principals, you must allow the principal's UNIX ID to default to the system assigned ID. This is because, if you include an attribute option in the command line, that attribute value is assigned to each principal. For example, the following sample command creates the principals **bach**, **britten**, **mahler** and assigns each an object creation quota of 5.

dcecp> **principal create {bach britten mahler satie} -quota 5**

30.5.2 Changing Principals

You can change a principal's primary name and other information related to the principal. Additionally, you can change a primary name to an alias and an alias to a primary name. If you change a primary name to an alias and do not make an alias the primary name, operations that return names choose one of the aliases at random.

30.5.2.1 Changing Primary Names

Use the **dcecp principal rename** command to change a primary name. Enter the command in the following form:

principal rename *old_name* **-to** *new_name*

where:

old_name   Is the primary name of the principal to be changed.

new_name   Is the new primary name of the principal.

The following example shows the **principal rename** command used to change a full name from **mahlar** to **mahler**:

dcecp> **principal rename mahlar -to mahler**

Note that, if you change a primary name, that change is reflected in the membership lists of all the groups and organizations in which the principal is a member.

In the unusual case where you are changing a host's principal name while the host is logged into a DCE cell, the existing host credentials will become invalid unless you perform extra steps to update the host credentials with the new principal name.

Host credentials are managed by the **secval** process, which performs security client functions on a DCE host. Normally, just after the host starts, the **secval** process logs the host into the DCE cell, getting the host credentials and storing them on the host. Deactivate and reactivate the **secval** process to update these credentials after changing the principal name. The following illustrates these operations on remote host **persephone**:

```
dcecp> secval deactivate /.:/hosts/persephone/config/secval
dcecp> secval activate /.:/hosts/persephone/config/secval
```

30.5.2.2 Changing Principal Information

Use the **dcecp principal modify** command to change any principal
information except the UNIX ID and user ID. The following example shows
the **principal modify** command used to change principal **mahler**'s object
creation quota to 10.

```
dcecp> principal modify mahlar -quota 10
```

30.5.3 Deleting Principals and Aliases

If you delete a principal or an alias, the system automatically deletes any
accounts for that principal or alias. For example, if you delete the principal
mahler, the **mahler composers classic** account is also deleted. If you
delete the principal alias **gustav**, you also delete the **gustav music_admin
classic** account. If you delete the group alias **music_admin**, you also delete
the **gustav music_admin classic** account. Be aware that deleting a
principal or a principal's alias could orphan the objects that are owned by
the principal/UUID.

The following example shows the **principal delete** command used to delete
the principal named **mahler**:

```
dcecp> principal delete mahler
```

You can delete multiple principals or aliases with one **principal delete**
command. To do so, enclose the principal names in braces, separated by
spaces. For example, to delete the principals **bach**, **britten**, and **mahler**,
you would enter the following:

```
dcecp> principal delete {bach britten mahler}
```

30.6 Extended Security Attributes for Principals

You can attach ERA instances to principals to manage several aspects of DCE login and password security. ERAs are available to control

- The level of authentication security required for principal login requests

- Handling of invalid logins

- Strength of principals' passwords as well as generation of passwords for principals

- Handling of login attempts by principals with expired passwords

These ERAs are introduced and explained in the following sections. See Chapter 32 for information on how to use **dcecp** to attach these ERAs to principals.

30.6.1 DCE Version 1.1 Authentication

With the addition of user preauthentication, DCE Version 1.1 authentication addresses certain security deficiencies in the Kerberos V5 authentication protocols, used as the basis for the DCE authentication protocol in versions previous to DCE Version 1.1. These deficiencies result from

- The security server responding to client login requests without verifying that the user knows the password

- The use of user passwords, which are notoriously weak, to encrypt plaintext data that is then sent across the network

These practices are subject to attacks in which the attacker obtains network transmissions and proceeds to attack them offline to elicit user's passwords. These kinds of attacks, if successful, can compromise the security of a DCE cell (and of all other cells in a trust relationship with that cell.)

DCE Version 1.1 reduces the likelihood of such attacks succeeding by providing for

- Preauthentication of principals making login requests (that is, by having the DCE Security Service verify the identity of the requestor before responding to the request)

- The use of strong keys to encrypt all network transmissions involving validation between security clients and servers

There are three levels of authentication, ranging from most to least secure, and representing decreasingly strict preauthentication protocols. By attaching an instance of the *pre_auth_req* era (described in the following section) to the principal, administrators can control the minimum level of preauthentication that the security server will accept when authenticating the principal.

The preauthentication protocols are the following:

- The *third-party* protocol, which provides the highest level of security. No lesser level of preauthentication should be specified for any principal unless there is a compelling reason to do so. (See the comment on **cell_admin** in the next bullet.) DCE Version 1.1 clients always construct authentication requests with this protocol, except in cases where they are unable to do so because the machine session key, which is required to construct third-party requests, is unavailable (for example, at cell startup, or when the **secval** process is down.)

- The *timestamps* protocol, which provides an intermediate level of security. Timestamps preauthentication should be specified only for principals (such as cell administrators and noninteractive principals) who must be able to operate when the client is unable to construct a third-party authentication request as previously described.

  In these cases, the client constructs and forwards a timestamps login request.

  In particular, the cell administrator *must* have timestamps login capability, since **cell_admin** must be able to log in to set up the initial machine key during initial configuration of the cell.

- The DCE Version 1.0 (Kerberos V5) protocol, which is used to authenticate pre-DCE Version 1.1 clients only, and provides no preauthentication security.

30.6.1.1 Managing User Authentication

You manage preauthentication for a given principal by attaching an instance of the *pre_auth_req* ERA to the principal and specifying a value to indicate *the lowest level protocol* the DCE Security Service should accept for the principal, as follows:

0   **(NONE)** Specifies that the DCE Security Service should accept, from this principal, login requests using any of the three protocols (including the pre-DCE Version 1.1 protocol.) This is the least secure level and is provided only in order to enable DCE Version 1.1 servers to accept login requests from pre-DCE Version 1.1 clients. It is most vulnerable to the type of attack previously described.

> **Warning:** Failing to attach an instance of the *pre_auth_req* ERA to a principal is equivalent to specifying **0** (NONE).

1   **(PADATA-ENC-TIMESTAMPS)** Specifies that the DCE Security Service should accept, from this principal, login requests using either the timestamp or third-party protocol. The timestamp protocol protects against attackers masquerading as a security client and attacking replies from the DCE Authentication Service, but is still vulnerable to attacks by processes capable of monitoring the network.

2   **(PADATA-ENC-THIRD-PARTY)** Specifies that the only login requests the DCE Security Service will accept from this principal are those using the third-party protocol. This is the highest level of DCE preauthentication and provides the most protection against the attacks previously described. With third-party preauthentication, all authentication data sent over the network is encrypted with a "strong" random key known only to the local machine principal and the DCE Security Service.

When the authentication service receives a login request for a principal, it always attempts to respond using the same protocol as the request, unless the *pre_auth_req* ERA value for that principal "forbids" it to do so. Table 30-2 provides a matrix describing the actions taken by the authentication service under the various combinations of login (authentication) request type and *pre_auth_req* ERA value.

For complete information on the details of DCE authentication (including the operation of the preauthentication protocols), see the *OSF DCE Application Development Guide—Core Components*.

The following is an example of a **dcecp** command to create a principal and attach a *pre_auth_req* ERA specifying third-party preauthentication:

dcecp> **principal create smitty -attribute {pre_auth_req 2}**

For further information on how to use **dcecp** to attach ERAs to principals, see Chapter 32.

30.6.1.2 Preauthentication Interoperability Between DCE Versions

Table 30-2 describes how login requests are handled when DCE Version 1.1 clients/servers interoperate with pre-DCE Version 1.1 clients/servers in a single cell.

Table 30–2. DCE Version 1.1/Pre-DCE Version 1.1 Authentication Interoperation

Login Request Type	Pre-1.1 Server Response	1.1 Server Response
DCE Version 1.0 From pre-DCE Version 1.1 clients only.	No preauthentication. Returns DCE Version 1.0 (unpreauthenticated) response.	Supports preauthentication. Checks for *pre_auth_req* ERA instance: If no ERA exists, or existing ERA has *value=*0 (**NONE**), returns DCE Version 1.0 (unpreauthenticated) response. Otherwise, rejects login request.
TIMESTAMPS From DCE Version 1.1 clients only.	No preauthentication. Server ignores preauthentication data in request and returns pre-DCE Version 1.1 (unpreauthenticated) response.	Supports preauthentication. Checks for *pre_auth_req* ERA instance: If no ERA exists, or existing ERA has *value=*0 (**NONE**) or *value=*1 (**PADATA-ENC-TIMESTAMPS**), returns DCE Version 1.1 **TIMESTAMPS** response. If existing ERA has *value=*2 (**PADATA-ENC-THIRD-PARTY**), rejects login request.
THIRD-PARTY From DCE Version 1.1 clients only.	No preauthentication. Server ignores preauthentication data in request and returns pre-DCE Version 1.1 (unpreauthenticated) response.	Supports preauthentication. Returns DCE Version 1.1 **THIRD-PARTY** response.

30.6.2 Managing Invalid Login Handling

When you specify a preauthentication level of **2 (PADATA-ENC-THIRD-PARTY)** for a principal, the security server is able to detect and track invalid login attempts for that principal. This makes it possible for administrators to limit the possible impact of password guessing attacks by

- Setting a limit to the number of successive invalid login attempts before the principal's account is disabled. (A successful login resets the counter.)

- Specifying the period of time the principal's account will be disabled once that limit is reached.

You do this by attaching instances of two ERAs (*max_invalid_attempts* and *disable_time_interval*) to the principal. Specify values for these ERAs as follows:

max_invalid_attempts Specifies an integer indicating the number of successive invalid login attempts the security server should accept before marking the principal's account as disabled.

disable_time_interval Specifies an integer indicating the number of minutes the principal's account should be disabled from login attempts.

The following is an example of a **dcecp** command to create a principal and attach *max_invalid_attempts* and *disable_time_interval* ERAs:

```
dcecp> principal create smitty -attribute {{max_invalid_attempts 7}\
          {disable_time_interval 60}}
```

Note: At DCE Version 1.1, the invalid login handling functionality accurately tracks login activity in a cell with one master and no replicas, but does not keep accurate counts in replicated cells. This is because

- Login attempts in a replicated cell are randomly assigned to either a master or replica.

- There is at present no mechanism for replicas to communicate to the the master and, therefore, no way for the master to maintain an accurate count.

For further information on how to use **dcecp** to attach ERAs to principals, see Chapter 32.

30.7 Adding and Maintaining Groups and Organizations

A group or organization must have been added to the registry before it can be used in an account. When you add groups by using the **dcecp group create** command, you can set a project list inclusion property that controls whether individual groups are included in project lists. (Project lists do not apply to organizations.)

30.7.1 Project Lists

A principal's project list is a list of all the groups in which a principal or alias is a member. When a principal tries to access an object, the principal has the access rights that accrue from membership in every group that is named in the object's ACL. (See Chapter 28 for a description of ACLs.) For example, assume the ACL for file X contains two entries: one permits group A write access and one permits group B read access. Then, any principal who is a member of both groups A and B can read and write to file X.

30.7.1.1 Project Lists and Rights

Principals accrue project list access rights only from the groups that are associated with the name or alias with which they log in. They do not accrue rights from their names and all of their aliases. For example, assume that a principal named **gustav** is a member of groups A and B. Under the alias **gus**, **gustav** is also a member of groups C and D. When the principal logs in as **gustav**, the principal accrues access rights from groups A and B only. When the principal logs in with the alias **gus**, the principal accrues access rights from groups C and D only.

To display the groups in which a principal (or its alias) is a member, use the **principal show** command described in Chapter 34.

30.7.1.2 Prohibiting Inclusion on Project Lists

If a group is prohibited from inclusion in a project list, its rights are not accrued. For example, assume again that file X's ACL includes two entries: one that permits group A read access to file X and one that permits group B write access to file X. Assume that the project list inclusion property is set to disallow group B from project lists. A principal who is a member of both groups A and B who tries to access file X is allowed only read permissions, not write permissions. If the project list inclusion property allows group B to be on project lists, a member of groups A and B receives both read and write access.

You may decide to prohibit some groups from inclusion on the list. You may, for example, want to prohibit any reserved groups with access rights similar to root from inclusion on any project lists.

30.7.2 Adding Groups and Organizations

Use the **dcecp group create** command to add groups and the **dcecp organization create** command to add organizations. When you add a group or organization, you must specify the group's or organization's primary name. In addition, you can supply the attribute options listed in Table 30-3.

Note that, when you use the **dcecp group create** command and **dcecp organization create** command, you can create multiple groups or organizations with one command in the same way that you can create multiple principals. See Section 30.5.1 for details.

Table 30–3. Attribute Options to Create Groups and Organizations

Information	Meaning
-gid	The required UNIX ID that is associated with the group or organization. You can enter this number explicitly or allow it to be generated automatically. The number that is entered cannot exceed the maximum allowable UNIX number (the **maxuid** attribute) set with the **dcecp registry modify** command; however, you can enter a number lower than the low UNIX number (the **minuid** attribute) set for groups or organizations with the **registry modify** command. If you allow the number to be assigned automatically, it falls in the range defined by the low UNIX number and the maximum UNIX number.
-fullname *string*	An optional name that is used to more fully describe a primary name. To include spaces, enclose the full name in braces. The default is blank.
-inprojlist *value*	For groups only, whether the group can be on project lists. The default is **yes**.

30.7.2.1 Adding a Group

The following example shows how to add a group named **symphonists** to the **registry**:

```
dcecp> group create symphonists
```

In the example, the group UNIX ID is generated automatically, no full name is supplied, and the group is included on project lists.

30.7.2.2 Adding an Organization

The following example shows how to add an organization named **classic** to the registry:

dcecp> **organization create classic**

In the example, the organization UNIX ID is generated automatically and no full name is supplied.

30.7.3 Changing Groups and Organizations

For groups and organizations, you can change the primary name and full name. In addition, for groups you can change whether or not the group can appear in project lists, and for organizations you can change policy. (See Chapter 35 for details on changing organization policy.)

Use the **dcecp group modify** command to modify change groups. The following example shows the use of this command with the **-inprojlist** option to change the group **symphonist**'s project list inclusion property from **yes** (include on project lists) to **no** (prohibit from project lists).

dcecp> **group modify symphonists -inprojlist no**

Use the **dcecp group rename** command to change a group's primary name or the **dcecp organization rename** command to change an organization's primary name. These commands have the following form:

group rename *old_name* **-to** *new_name*

organization rename *old_name* **-to** *new_name*

where:

old_name   Is the primary name of the group or organization to be changed.

new_name   Is the new primary name of the group or organization.

The following example shows the **group rename** command used to change a full name from **symphonists** to **symphonists7**:

dcecp> **group rename symphonists -to symphonists7**

Note that, if you change a primary name, that change is reflected in the membership lists of all the groups and organizations in which the group or organization is listed as a member.

30.7.4 Deleting Groups and Organizations

If you delete a group or organization, you also automatically delete any accounts that use the group or organization. For example, if you delete the group **symphonists**, you also automatically delete the accounts **vivaldi symphonists baroque** and **mozart symphonists classic**.

Use the **dcecp group delete** to delete groups and the **dcecp organization delete** command to delete organizations. The following example shows the **group delete** command being used to delete the group **symphonists**:

dcecp> **group delete symphonists**

The next example shows the **organization delete** command being used to delete the organization **classic**:

dcecp> **organization delete classic**

Note that you can delete multiple groups or organizations with a single **group delete** or **organization delete** command by including the names to delete in braces and separated by spaces just as you would to delete multiple principals.

30.8 Maintaining Membership Lists

Each group or organization has a membership list, which lists the principals that are members of the group or organization. Use the **dcecp group add** command to add members to the membership list and the **dcecp group remove** command to remove members from the list.

If you delete a member from a group or organization, any accounts for the deleted member that are associated with the group or organization are also deleted. For example, if you delete the principal **mahler** from the group **symphonists**, the account **mahler symphonists classic** is also deleted.

Note that the deleting of a principal from a group or organization can affect the principal's rights to objects. This change takes effect only when the principal's ticket-granting ticket is renewed. See Chapter 31 for more information on ticket renewals.

30.8.1 Effects of Account Creation on Membership Lists

When you create accounts, the principal for whom the account is created must be a member of the group or organization that is named in the account. For example, if you create the account **mahler symphonists classic**, the principal **mahler** must be a member of the **symphonists** group and the **classic** organization.

The **dcecp** command recognizes this requirement and, if you have the permissions to add to the group or organization, tries to add the principal to the group and organization. For example, assume that the principal **mahler** is not a member of either the group **symphonists** or the organization **classic**. If you have the proper permissions when you create the account **mahler symphonists classic**, the **account create** command automatically adds **mahler** to the **symphonists** and **classic** membership lists so that you can create the account in one step.

However, if you do not have the required permissions, the command fails and displays a message like the following:

```
Not authorized to perform operation
```

30.8.2 Adding and Deleting Group Members

The following example shows the use of the **dcecp group add** command with the **-member** option to add **mahler** to the group **symphonists** and delete **strauss** from the group **symphonists**:

```
dcecp>  group add symphonists -member mahler
dcecp>  group remove symphonists -member mahler
```

You can add and remove mutiple members with one **group add** or **group remove** command. To do so, enclose the member names in quotes, separated by spaces. For example, to add the principals **bach**, **britten**, and **mahler** to the group **symphonists**, you would enter the following:

```
dcecp>  group add symphonists -member {bach britten mahler}
```

In the unusual case where you are changing a host's group name information while the host is logged into a DCE cell, the existing host credentials will become invalid unless you perform extra steps to update the host credentials with the new group name information.

Host credentials are managed by the **secval** process, which performs security client functions on a DCE host. Normally, just after the host starts, the **secval** process logs the host into the DCE cell, getting the host credentials and storing them on the host. Deactivate and reactivate the **secval** process to update these credentials after changing the group name information. The following example illustrates these operations on remote host **persephone**:

```
dcecp>  secval deactivate /.:/hosts/persephone/config/secval
dcecp>  secval activate /.:/hosts/persephone/config/secval
```

30.9 Creating and Maintaining Aliases for Principals or Groups

Use the **dcecp principal create** command to create an maintain aliases for principals and groups. Organizations cannot be given aliases.

30.9.1 Creating Aliases

To create an alias for a principal, enter the **dcecp principal create** command in the following form:

principal create *name* **-uid** *unix_ID* **-alias**

where:

name　　　　　Is the alias name for the principal or group.

unix_ID　　　Is the UNIX ID that is associated with the principal for which you are creating the alias.

-alias　　　Indicates that *name* is an alias.

To create an alias for a group, enter the **dcecp group create** command in the following form:

group create *name* **-gid** *groupunix_ID* **-alias**

where:

name　　　　　Is the alias name for the principal or group.

groupunix_ID　Is the UNIX ID that is associated with the group for which you are creating the alias.

-alias　　　Indicates that *name* is an alias.

30.9.2 Changing Primary Names to Aliases and Vice Versa

To change an alias to a primary name or a primary name to an alias, use the
dcecp principal modify command for a principal or the **dcecp group
modify** command for a group. These commands have the following form:

principal modify *name* **-alias {yes|no}**
group modify *name* **-alias {yes|no}**

where:

name   Is the primary name to be changed to an alias or the alias to
                 be changed to a primary name.

-alias   Specifying **-alias yes** changes the primary name identified
                 by *name* to an alias; specifying **-alias no** changes the alias
                 identified by *name* to the primary name.

A principal or group can have only one primary name at a time. Before you
change an alias to a primary name, first change the primary name to an alias.

Chapter 31

Creating and Maintaining Accounts

All principals have two identities: a network identity that provides the ability to access DCE objects on machines across the network, and a local identity that provides the ability to access objects on the local machine. The two identities exist in tandem, but independently of each other. A principal's network identity is defined by an account in the network registry. A principal's local identity is defined by local data, such as entries in the **/etc/passwd** and **/etc/group** files that are stored on the local machine. If the **passwd_export** command is used to update the **/etc/passwd** and **/etc/group** files with data that is stored in the local registry, local identity data is derived from information that is stored in the network registry.

Registry accounts define a network identity by associating a principal with a group, an organization, and related account information, such as the password that is used to authenticate a principal's identity. You must create a registry account for any principal that engages in communications across the network, regardless of whether the communications are authenticated. The principals for which you must create registry accounts are as follows:

- Each human user who accesses objects across the network; this probably includes all human users unless you are specifically restricting a user to the local machine.

- Each server that accesses objects across the network and runs under its own identity, not the identity of the principal who started it.

- Each machine in the network.

- Any cell with which you engage in authenticated cross-cell communications. (Accounts for cross-cell authentication are special types of accounts that are described in Chapter 33.

This chapter describes

- Each type of account and how to create and maintain it

- How accounts are authenticated and how to display privilege attributes and tickets

- How to create and maintain the keytab file that stores keys for server principals

- How to maintain the local registry

31.1 User Accounts

User accounts are associated with the user's password and information that is used when the user logs into DCE. Account information includes such things as the principal's home directory and login shell, and authentication policy, which defines parameters that help control a principal's access to DCE. Use the **dcecp account create** command to create accounts for human users, the **dcecp account modify** command to modify them, and the **dcecp account delete** command to delete them.

31.2 Server Accounts

Servers, which can also be called *applications*, that engage in communications across the network can run under their own network identity or the network identity of the principal who started them. To run under their own identity, servers must be programmed to perform a login and authenticate that identity. Therefore, you must use the **dececp account create** command to create registry accounts for these servers.

31.2.1 Passwords for Server Accounts

During login, all principals (human, server, and machine) must pass their password to the DCE Authentication Service, which uses these passwords to generate authentication keys. The most common method for human users is to simply enter their password. A different method must be provided for server principals. The recommended method, which is based on APIs that are supplied with DCE, is to store server keys in a locally protected key table. The default implementation of the DCE-supplied API stores the key table in a keytab file on the server's local machine and protects the file so that only a principal's local identity can read or write the file.

You can access the keytab files remotely. On the local machine, store the keytab files in a partition of the machine's disk that is not exported by any file system.

Except for servers running as root or under the identity of the local machine, a separate keytab file needs to be used for each server. During login, the server can access this file to obtain its key, pass its key to the authentication service, log in, and be authenticated.

Use the **dcecp keytab add** command to add keys for servers to the keytab file and the **dcecp keytab remove** command to delete server keys.

31.2.2 Steps for Creating Server Accounts

To create an account for a server, first run the **dcecp account create** command to create the account and then run the **dcecp keytab add** command to add an entry to the keytab file. The server's password in the registry and the server's key in the keytab file must match. You can ensure that these passwords are the same by manually entering the same passwords in both commands, or you can specify that the **keytab add** command should reset the server's registry password at the same time that it sets the server's password in the keytab file.

31.3 Machine Accounts

All machines must also have accounts in the registry. Machine accounts, like server accounts, are created by first running the **account create** command to create the account and then running the **keytab add** command to add the server's password to the keytab file. Like server accounts, the password for a machine account in the registry and in the keytab file must match. Principal names in machine accounts must be the same as the machine's name in the cell namespace. (See the *OSF DCE Administration Guide—Introduction* for more information on names in the cell namespace.)

31.4 How Identities Represented by Accounts Are Authenticated

When principals log into the DCE, the security client uses the password they supply (or that is supplied for them in the case of a server or machine principal) to derive the principal's authentication key. A copy of the principal's authentication key exists also in the registry database, having been stored there when the principal's account was created (or when the password was changed.) It is thus available to the authentication service.

This key is used by the authentication service to authenticate the principal (that is, to guarantee the principal's identity) as follows:

1. The security client does the following:

   a. Queries the user for the password and uses it to derive the principal's authentication key

   b. Prepares a login request, part of which is encrypted using the authentication key

   c. Forwards the request to the authentication service

2. The authentication service does the following:

    a. Receives the login request

    b. Obtains the registry's copy of the principal's authentication key

    c. Attempts to decrypt the login request with this key

If the decryption succeeds, the keys are the same; the principal is therefore authenticated and the login is successful.

If the decryption fails, then the password supplied by the principal and used by the security client to derive its version of the principal's authentication key is invalid (that is, different from the password used to derive the registry's copy of the principal's authentication key), and login is denied.

This is a very general introductory description; see the *OSF DCE Application Development Guide—Core Components* for a detailed discussion of principal authentication.

31.4.1 Privilege Attributes

After a principal is authenticated, the DCE Security Service helps obtain the principal's privilege attributes. Privilege attributes consist of UUIDs that represent the principal's network identity, the groups in which the principal is a member, and any extended attributes associated with the principal. They are used when principals request access to objects to determine their rights to those objects. Privilege attributes that are provided by the DCE Security Service are authenticated. Authenticated privileges are accepted by network services. Unauthenticated privilege attributes may not be accepted. This means that the kinds of access to DCE objects that principals are allowed can differ, depending on whether or not a principal's privilege attributes are authenticated. (DCE ACLs, which are used to control access to DCE objects based on a principal's privilege attributes, are described in Chapter 28.)

31.4.2 Ticket-Granting Tickets and Tickets to Services

A ticket-granting ticket allows a principal to request and receive tickets to DCE services, such as to a Distributed File System server, to read a file. The tickets that let principals access DCE services are called *service tickets*.

Both ticket-granting tickets and service tickets have lifetimes that are determined by the settings for individual accounts and registry policies and properties. When a principal's ticket-granting ticket expires, the principal is no longer considered an authenticated user. An unauthenticated principal's access to objects other than those on the local machine is severely curtailed, and the principal's ability to use DCE services becomes extremely limited. To remedy this, the principal must reauthenticate by running the **kinit** command (see the **kinit(8sec)** reference page) or by logging out and logging in again to DCE.

If you flag an account as able to renew service tickets, the principal's service tickets are renewed automatically by the authentication service, requiring no action on the principal's part. Note, however, that the lifetime allocated to a service ticket can never exceed the time remaining on the principal's *ticket-granting ticket* (TGT).

31.4.3 Displaying Privilege Attributes and Tickets

DCE cell administrators can use the **klist** command to display a principal's current tickets and privilege attributes. The **klist** command displays three types of information: privilege attributes, expiration information, and service ticket information. DCE users can also run **klist** to display their current and expired tickets. The **klist** command is described on the **klist(8sec)** reference page.

31.4.3.1 The First Part of the **klist** Display—Privilege Attributes

The **klist** command displays a principal's privilege attributes. This display first lists the fully qualified principal name, followed by the UUIDs and names of the cell, the principal name (without the cell name and DCE global identifier), and all the groups of which the principals is a member. A sample of this section of the **klist** display follows:

```
DCE Identity Information:
   Global Principal: /.../dresden.com/music/mozart
   Cell: 5ad96550-80c4-11ca-b26c-08001e039431 /.../dresden.com
   Principal:       00000066-80c5-11ca-b600-08001e039431 music/mozart
   Group: 00000003-80c4-11ca-b201-08001e039431 composers
```

31.4.3.2 The Second Part of the **klist** Display—Expiration Dates and Times

The second part of the **klist** display shows the dates and time that the principal's ticket-granting ticket, account, and password expire:

- The first line shows the date and time the ticket-granting ticket expires. Before this happens, the principal should reinitialize it by running **kinit** or logging in again to DCE.

- The second line shows when the principal's account expires. If the account expires, the principal will be unable to log into DCE. To remedy this, DCE administrators must change the principal's account expiration date in the registry.

- The third line shows the date the principal's password expires. Before this happens, the principal should change the password by using the **dcecp** command. If the password expires, the principal will be unable to log into DCE. To remedy this, DCE administrators must change the principal's password in the registry.

A sample of the second part of the **klist** display follows:

```
Identity Info Expires:  91/10/03:12:07:18
Account Expires:        91/12/31:12:00:00
Passwd Expires:         91/10/31:12:00:00
```

31.4.3.3 The Third Part of the **klist** Display—Tickets

The third and final part of the **klist** display shows the principal's ticket information and the name of the principal's ticket cache. The first three tickets labeled **Server** in the following display are the tickets used after the principal logged in and obtained privilege attributes. The display for all principals has these entries.

The remaining tickets labeled **Client** show the principal's ticket-granting ticket and service tickets. In the listing for each ticket after the word **Client**, the display shows the name of the privilege server, a server that grants privilege attributes after the principal's identity has been authenticated by the DCE Security Service. The name of the server to which the principal has tickets is shown after the **Server** entry, and the dates and times these tickets are valid are shown on the following line. For example, in the following sample display, the last line shows that the principal has a ticket to the server named **file_server**. The lifetime of this ticket is from 1:24 and 2 seconds p.m. on 10/2/91 to 12:07 and 18 seconds p.m. on 10/3/91. (The time is shown in 24-hour format.)

```
Kerberos Ticket Information:
Ticket cache: /tmp/dcecred_17a80000
Default principal: music/mozart@dresden.com
Server: krbtgt/dresden@dresden.com
    valid 91/10/02:12:07:18 to 91/10/03:12:07:18
Server:dce/rgy@dresden.com
    valid 91/10/02:12:07:20 to 91/10/03:12:07:18
Server:dce/ptgt@dresden.com
    valid 91/10/02:12:07:49 to 91/10/03:12:07:18
Client:dce/ptgt@dresden          Server:krbtgt/dresden@dresden.com
    valid 91/10/02:12:07:50 to 91/10/03:12:07:18
Client:dce/ptgt@dresden.com      Server:dce/rgy@dresden.com
    valid 91/10/02:12:07:53 to 91/10/03:12:07:18
Client:dce/ptgt@dresden.com      Server:file_server@dresden.com
    valid 91/10/02:13:24:02 to 91/10/03:12:07:18
```

31.4.4 Destroying a Principal's Tickets

Use the **kdestroy** command to invalidate the tickets that a principal has
acquired. When the principal logs out, the principal's tickets are not
destroyed; they remain valid until they expire. DCE users may want to use
kdestroy just before they log out to ensure that no valid tickets remain.
However, if the principal has the kernel-resident ticket cache, the
principal's tickets are destroyed when the principal's last process
terminates. This means that it is generally not necessary to run **kdestroy** at
logout.

The **kdestroy** command is described on the **kdestroy(8sec)** reference page.

31.5 Adding Accounts

Use the **dcecp account create** command to add accounts to the registry.
Information that is associated with accounts falls roughly into the following
two categories:

- User information similar to that typically found in the **/etc/passwd** file.

- Authentication policy that lets you control the account's access to the
  network. Authentication policy establishes account and password
  validity, account expiration policy, and ticket expiration policy. The
  tighter you control authentication policy, the more secure your cell is,
  but the more processing overhead you can accrue.

Both types of information are supplied as attributes in standard **dcecp**
attribute lists or as attribute options.

Note that authentication policy can also be set for the registry. If the registry
policy differs from the policy that you enter for an account, the stricter
policy applies. (See Chapter 35 for more information on contradictory
policy.)

Table 31-1 lists the attribute options used to create accounts. Note that the
options described in this table can also be supplied without the dashes in
attribute lists.

Table 31–1. Attribute Options to Create Accounts

Option	Meaning
-acctvalid {yes|no}	A flag that determines account validity. If you set this flag to **no**, the account is invalid and the account principal cannot log into the account. The default is **yes**.
-client {yes|no}	A flag that indicates whether or not the account is for a principal that can act as a client. If you set this flag to **yes**, the principal is able to log into the account and acquire tickets for authentication. The default is **yes**.
-description *string*	A text string in Portable Character Set (PCS) format that is typically used to describe the use of the account. No default.
-dupkey {yes|no}	A flag that determines if tickets issued to the account's principal can have duplicate keys. The default is **no**.
-expdate	The date (in ISO timestamp format *YY-MM-DD-hh:mm:ss*) on which the account expires. To renew a account after it expires, change the date. The default is **none**, meaning the account never expires.
-forwardabletkt {yes|no}	A flag determining whether a new ticket-granting ticket with a network address that differs from the present TGT's network address can be issued to the account's principal. (The **-proxiabletkt** attribute performs the same function for service tickets.) The default is **yes**.

Option	Meaning
-goodsince *date*	The date and time (in ISO timestamp format *YY-MM-DD-hh:mm:ss*) that the account was last known to be in an uncompromised state. Any tickets granted before this date are invalid. Control over this date is especially useful if you know that an account's password was compromised. Changing the password can prevent the unauthorized principal from accessing the system again by using that password, but does not prevent the principal from accessing the system components for which tickets were obtained fraudulently before the password was changed. To eliminate the principal's access to the system, the tickets must be canceled. Set the **-goodsince** attribute to the date and time the compromised password was changed to invalidate all tickets issued before that time and eliminate the unauthorized principal's system access. When the account is created, the **-goodsince** attribute is set to the current date.
-group *group_name*	The name of the group that is associated with the account. This attribute must be supplied to create an account; there is no default.
-home *dir_name*	The directory in which the principal is placed at login. No default.
-organization *org_name*	The name of the organization that is associated with the account. This attribute must be supplied to create an account; there is no default.

Option	Meaning
-password *password*	The required password for the account in plaintext. The system encrypts the password you supply. No default.
-postdatedtkt {yes|no}	A flag that determines whether or not tickets with a start time in the future can be issued to the account's principal. The default is **no**.
-proxiabletkt {yes|no}	A flag determines whether or not a new ticket with a different network address than the present ticket can be issued to the account's principal. (The **-forwardabletkt** attribute option performs the same function for ticket-granting tickets.) The default is **no**.
-pwdvalid {yes|no}	A flag that determines whether the current password is valid. If this flag is set to **no**, the account password has expired and the principal will be prompted to change it the next time that the principal logs into the account. The default is **yes**.
-renewabletkt {yes|no}	The Kerberos V5 renewable ticket feature is not currently used by DCE; any use of the renewable ticket attribute is unsupported at the present time.
-server {yes|no}	A flag that indicates whether or not the account is for a principal that can act as a server. If the account is for a server that engages in authenticated communications, set this flag to **yes**. The default is **yes**.

Option	Meaning
-shell *path_to_shell*	The shell that is executed when a principal logs in.
-stdtgtauth {yes|no}	A flag that determines whether or not tickets issued to the account's principal can use the ticket-granting-ticket authentication mechanism. The default is **yes**.
-maxtktlife *hours*	The maximum ticket lifetime. This is the maximum amount of time in hours that a ticket can be valid. When a client requests a ticket to a server, the lifetime granted to the ticket takes into account the **maxtktlife** attribute value for both the server and the client. In other words, the lifetime cannot exceed the shorter of the server's or client's maximum ticket lifetime. If you do not specify a **maxtktlifetime** attribute value for an account, the **maxtktlifetime** attribute value defined for the registry authorization policy is used. (See Chapter 35.)

Option	Meaning
-maxtktrenew *hours*	The maximum ticket renewable. This is the amount of time in hours before a principal's ticket-granting ticket expires and that principal must log into the system again to reauthenticate and obtain another ticket-granting ticket. The lifetime of the principal's service tickets can never exceed the lifetime of the principal's ticket-granting ticket. The shorter you make Maximum Certificate Renewable, the greater the security of the system. However, since principals must log in again to renew their ticket-granting ticket, the time needs to take into consideration user convenience and the level of security required.
	If you do not specify a **maxtktrenew** attribute value for an account, the **maxtktrenew** attribute value defined for the registry authorization policy is used. (See Chapter 35.)

Note: The maximum ticket lifetime and maximum ticket renewable can be set as registry properties for the registry as a whole with the **dcecp registry modify** command. When they are set with the **dcecp account create** or **account modify** commands, they apply only to a specific account.

31.5.1 Setting Ticket Lifetimes

You should be aware of two other options set by the **dcecp registry modify** command: default ticket lifetimes and minimum ticket lifetime.

- Minimum Ticket Lifetime—The shortest possible lifetime that can be assigned to a ticket. Note that the actual effective value of Minimum Ticket Lifetime is affected by Default Certificate Lifetime.

- Default Ticket Lifetime—The lifetime granted for tickets, unless the principal specifically requests a different lifetime. Although principals can request a specific lifetime for a ticket, the majority accept the default lifetime. (If a principal requests a ticket lifetime of 0 (zero), the default lifetime is assigned to the ticket.)

  Note that the actual effective value of Default Ticket Lifetime is affected by Maximum Certificate Lifetime.

The actual lifetimes assigned to tickets depends on rules enforced by the DCE Security Service regarding the settings of Maximum Ticket Lifetime, Default Ticket Lifetime, and Minimum Ticket Lifetime. These rules are as follows:

- The maximum ticket lifetime can never be larger than the renewable ticket lifetime (in other words, **max_life = min (max_life, renewable_life)**) or less than 60 seconds. If the maximum ticket lifetime is larger than the renewable ticket lifetime, then the renewable ticket lifetime is used as the maximum ticket lifetime. For example, suppose an account's is set to 15 hours. If you set the renewable ticket lifetime to 20 hours, the effective maximum ticket lifetime is not 20, but 15 hours.

- The default ticket lifetime can never be larger than the maximum ticket lifetime (in other words, **default_life = min (default_life, max_life)**) or less than 60 seconds. If the default ticket lifetime is larger than the maximum ticket lifetime, then the maximum ticket lifetime is used as the default ticket lifetime. For example, suppose registry policy specifies a default ticket lifetime of 25 hours. If you set the registry's maximum ticket lifetime to 15 hours, the registry's effective default certificate lifetime is not 25, but 15 hours.

- The minimum ticket lifetime can never be larger than the default certificate lifetime (in other words, **min_life = min (min_life, default_life)**) or less than 60 seconds. If the minimum ticket lifetime is larger than the default certificate lifetime, then the default ticket lifetime is used as the minimum ticket lifetime. For example, suppose registry policy specifies a default ticket lifetime of 10 hours. If you set an account's minimum ticket lifetime to 15 hours, the account's effective minimum ticket lifetime is not 15, but 10 hours.

where:

none Indicates the attribute is not associated with a trigger server. (This is the default.)

query Indicates that the attribute is associated with a query trigger. Query trigger servers can perform only queries.

update Indicates the attribute is associated with an update trigger. Update trigger servers can perform queries and updates.

> **Note:** Update trigger servers are not supported in this release.

Once set the **-trigtype** option cannot be modified.

32.3.2 The -trigbind Option

The **-trigbind** option defines authentication information for the trigger server and the trigger binding itself.

The **-trigbind** option has the following format.

-trigbind {{*auth_info*} {*binding_info*}}

The following sections describe how to specify the authentication type and the binding.

32.3.2.1 Specifying the Authentication Type

The *auth_info* parameter has the following syntax:

{*auth_serv_type name prot_level authentication_service authorization_service*}

where:

auth_serv_type Specifies the authentication type, which can be

- **none**—No authentication is performed.

- **dce**—Standard DCE authentication is performed.

If you are using no authentication, no other information except the binding itself is required. If you are using the standard DCE authentication type, you must specify all the remaining parameters.

name Specifies the principal name of the trigger server.

prot_level Specifies the protection level that determines the degree to which authenticated communications between the client and the server are protected by the authentication service. The possible protection levels are

- **default**—Uses the default protection level of **pkt**.

- **none**—Performs no authentication: tickets are not exchanged, session keys are not established, client EPACs or names are not certified, and transmissions are in the clear. Note that although uncertified EPACs should not be trusted, they may be useful for debugging, tracing, and measurement purposes.

- **connect**—Authenticates only when the client establishes a relationship with the server.

- **call**—Authenticates only at the beginning of each remote procedure call when the server receives the request.

  This level does not apply to remote procedure calls made over a connection-based protocol sequence (that is, **ncacn_ip_tcp**). If this level is specified and the binding handle uses a connection-based protocol sequence, the routine uses the **pkt** protection level instead.

- **pkt**—Ensures that all data received is from the expected client.

- **pktinteg**—Ensures and verifies that none of the data transferred between client and server has been modified. This is the highest protection level that is guaranteed to be present in the RPC runtime.

- **pktprivacy**—Authenticates as specified by all of the previous levels and also encrypts each RPC argument value. This is the highest protection level, but it is not guaranteed to be present in the RPC runtime.

authentication_service   Specifies the authentication service. The exact level of protection provided by the authentication service is specified by the protection level. The supported authentication services are as follows:

- **default**—DCE shared-secret key.

- **none**—No authentication: no tickets are exchanged, no session keys established, client EPACs or names are not transmitted, and transmissions are in the clear. Specify **none** to turn authentication off for remote procedure calls made using this binding.

- **secret**—DCE shared-secret key authentication.

authorization_service   Specifies the authorization service. The validity and trustworthiness of authorization data, like any application data, is dependent on the authentication service and protection level specified. The supported authorization services are as follows:

- **none**—Server performs no authorization. This is valid only if the authorization service is set to **none**, specifying that no authentication is being performed.

- **name**—Server performs authorization based on the client principal name. This value cannot be used if the authorization service is **none**.

- **dce**—Server performs authorization by using the client's DCE EPAC sent to the server with each remote procedure call made with this binding. Generally, access is checked against DCE ACLs.

32.3.2.2 Specifying the Binding Information

The *binding_info* parameter specifies the binding, which can be a string binding, a server entry name, or a list containing one or more string bindings or server entry names. The following example shows a server entry name binding:

./.:/hosts/host_name/dce_entity_name

The following example shows a string binding in standard syntax:

ncadg_udp_ip:130.105.96.3[1234]

The following example shows a string binding in TCL syntax:

ncarn_ip_tcp 10-29.58.00 2001

32.3.2.3 Sample Value for the **-trigbind** Option

The following sample shows the value for a **-trigbind** option. In the sample, the binding has the principal name **MVS_server**, is authenticated with packet-privacy protection level, uses a shared secret key and an authorization service of DCE. The binding is supplied as a server entry name.

**-trigbind {{dce MVS_server pktprivacy secret dce} \
   {/.:/hosts/host_name/dce_entity_name}}**

32.4 Creating and Maintaining Attribute Instances

Using **dcecp**, operations you can attach extended registry attributes to objects, modify the values assigned to those attributes, and delete the attachement just as you would any attribute attached to an object.

You can attach extended registry attributes to any of the following registry objects using the **dcecp create** and **modify** commands:

- **principal**

- **group**

- **organization**

- **policy**

  Note: In DCE Version 1.1, you cannot attach attributes to the policy object.

- **directory**

- **replist**

- **xattrschema**

32.4.1 Attaching Attribute Instances to Objects

You can attach attributes to object when you create the objects with the **dcecp principal -attribute** operation, or you can attach attributes to existing objects with the **dcecp modify -add** operation.

For example, to create the principal **delores** and at the same time attach the **MVSname** attribute with a value of **admin**, use the following **principal create** command:

```
dcecp> principal create delores -attribute {MVSname admin}
```

To attach the **MVSname** attribute with a value of **admin** to the principal named **delores**, use the following **principal modify** command:

```
dcecp> principal modify delores -add {MVSname admin}
```

To add instances of a multivalued extended attribute, include each value, separated by a space after the attribute name. For example, to attach the **multi_name** attribute with values of **value1**, **value2**, **value3**, and **value4** to the principal named **delores**, use the following command:

```
dcecp> principal modify delores -add {multi_name value1 value2 \
          value3 value4}
```

32.4.2 Modifying Attribute Instances

Use the **dcecp modify -change** operation to change the values of attribute instances. Whether an attribute is modifiable is determined by the application that uses the attribute. For example, the following command changes the value assigned to the **MVSname** from **admin** to **cell_admin** for the principal named **delores**.

```
dcecp> principal modify delores -change {MVSname cell_admin}
```

If you use the **dcecp modify -change** command as shown in the previous paragraphs to change the value of a multivalued attribute, all instances of the multivalued attribute are deleted and replaced by the new values specified in the command. For example, to change only a specific value, you must enter all the values. For example, assume that the **multi_name** attribute has the following four values: **value1**, **value2**, **value3**, and **value4**. To change **value4** to **value5** you must enter the following command:

```
dcecp> principal modify delores -change {multi_name {value1 value2 \
          value3 value5}}
```

However, you can add and remove individual values from a multivalued attribute. Use the **-add** option to add values. For example, assume that the **multi_name** attribute has values of **value1**, **value2**, **value3**, and **value5**. The following sample command adds **value6** to the **multi_name** attribute.

```
dcecp> principal modify delores -add {multi_name value6}
```

(Use the **remove** option described in the following subsection to delete specific values in a multivalued attribute.)

Note that the following command replaces all instances of the attribute named **multi_name** attached to the principal named **delores** with a single instance with a value of **value1**:

dcecp> **principal modify delores -change {multi_name value1}**

For example, if the **multi_name** attribute had the following values:

```
{multi_name value1 value2 value3}
```

then the previous command would change the values as follows:

```
{multi_name value1}
```

32.4.3 Deleting Attribute Instances

Use the **dcecp modify** command with the **-remove** option to delete attribute instances attached to an object. To delete all instances of an attribute from an object, supply the attribute name to the **-remove** option. For example, the following command deletes all instances of the **MVSname** attribute from the principal named **delores**:

dcecp> **principal modify delores -remove MVSname**

To remove a single instance of a multivalued attribute, supply the attribute name and the attribute value. For example, the following command deletes only the instance **value5** from the multivalued attribute named **multi-value**. All other values and the attribute itself remain intact.

dcecp> **principal modify delores -remove {multi-value value5}**

However, if you delete the last instance of a multivalued attribute, **dcecp** will also delete the attribute from the object because an attribute without a value cannot be attached to an object. Note that you cannot combine deleting multivalued attributes and values from multivalued attributes with the same command.

To delete more than one attribute from an object, you must use the **-types** option. This option tells **dcecp** that all the values supplied are the names of attribute types, not attribute values. For example, the following sample command uses the **-types** option to delete the attributes named **MVSname** and **MVSinteger** from the principal **delores**:

dcecp> **principal modify delores -remove {MVSname MVSinteger} -types**

Without the **-types** option, **dcecp** will assume that **MVSinteger** is the value for the **MVSname** attribute and, because no such value exists, the command will fail.

32.4.4 Using Attribute Sets

At attribute set is a collection of attribute UUIDs that identify the attribute instances that are members of the set. Attribute sets let you group related attributes instances on an object for easier access. For example, if you use the **dcecp show** operation to display an attribute set, the display expands the attribute set and includes all members of the set in the display output. This attribute expansion works only for **dcecp** commands that display information. The commands to create and modify attribute instances work only on the specific attribute named in the command. Since the attributes that are set members exist independently of the attribute set, they can be manipulated directly like any other attribute.

Each attribute set is attached to an object and, although the system does not enforce it, each attribute that is a member of a set should also be attached to the same object. Attribute sets cannot be nested; a member of an attribute set cannot itself be an attribute set.

To create, modify, and delete members in an attribute set, follow the instructions to create, modify, and delete mutli-valued attributes. The attribute instances that are members of the set are identified by UUIDs.

Chapter 33

Administering a Multicell Environment

Previous chapters in this guide described the DCE administration tasks that are performed within individual cells. The administration of a multicell environment, which is one in which principals from foreign cells access objects in the local cell, has additional tasks and considerations that arise from the interaction of principals across different cells.

In fact, you can have two types of system administrators: one for local cell administration and one for intercell administration of the multicell environment. If you set up groups for the two types of administrators, you can set the ACL for the **krbtgt** directory, which contains cell principals, in the registry database to allow updating only by the group of intercell administrators. Be sure, however, to allow all other users read access to the **krbtgt** directory or intercell access will be denied to those users. Note that, if you protect the **krbtgt** directory in this way, ensure that all directories below the **krbtgt** directory also have the proper ACLs. The easiest way to accomplish this is to change the Object ACL and the Initial Creation ACLs on the **krbtgt** directory after the registry is created.

This chapter describes the trust relationships between cells that allow principals from foreign cells access to objects in your cell and vice versa.

33.1 Trust Relationships

Note: *The DCE Version 1.1. code does not provide support for the transitive trust relationships discussed in this section.*

To give explicit permission for principals in other cells to engage in authenticated access to objects in your cell, you must establish a trust relationship with that cell. You do this using the **dcecp registry connect** command to create two special accounts: one in your cell's registry to represent the foreign cell and one in the foreign cell's registry to represent your cell. Establishing these accounts indicates that you trust the foreign cell's authentication service to correctly authenticate foreign users, and, therefore, you consider all users from this cell to be authenticated if they are marked as authenticated by the foreign cell's authentication service.

Once the trust relationship is established, you can control foreign principals' access to specific objects with ACL entries, just as you do for principals in the local cell. The trust relationship also allows users in the foreign cell to log into accounts in the local cell and vice versa.

Two kinds of trust relationships allow principals in other cells to engage in authenticated access to objects in your cell. These relationships are *direct trust relationships* and *hierarchical transitive trust relationships.* Throughout this chapter the term *transitive trust relationship* is used to indicate the DCE implementation of hierarchical transitive trust relationships.

33.1.1 Direct Trust Relationships

In a direct trust relationship, two cells' authentication service share authentication keys and trust each other to authenticate principals from their respective cells. Therefore, both cells consider all users from each cell to be authenticated if they are marked as authenticated by their respective authentication services. The shared authentication keys are derived from a single password (one for each cell) that is used by all principals from one cell to be authenticated to the other cell. A direct trust relationship involves only two cells.

33.1.2 Transitive Trust Relationships

A transitive trust relationship comes about as a result of a direct trust relationship. In this relationship, cells in a direct trust relationship trust (with some constraints) each other's authentication service to authenticate principals not only from their respective cells but also from the cells with which they have direct trust relationships. A transitive trust relationship can involve three or more cells. A transitive trust relationship is illustrated in Figure 33-1.

Figure 33–1. Transitive Trust Relationships

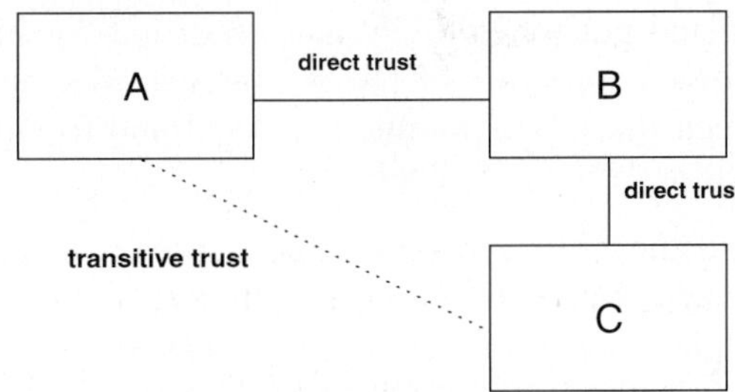

In this figure, cell A trusts peer cell B (the cell with which it has a direct trust relationship) to authenticate the principals in cell B and to guarantee the authentication of the principals in cell B/C (the cell with which it has a transitive trust relationship).

Because cell A trusts cell B's authentication service, it allows authenticated access to all principals whose authentication is guaranteed by cell B's authentication service. These authenticated principals include principals from cell B and principals from cell B/C.

33.1.3 Establishing Trust Relationships

Use the **registry connect** command to establish direct trust and transitive trust relationships. Note that, although you can create a direct trust relationship between any two cells, you can create a transitive trust relationship only for those cells connected by a transitive trust path.

This command creates two special accounts: one in your cell's registry to represent the foreign cell, another in the foreign cell's registry to represent your cell. The command creates the accounts' principals at the same time. Once the trust relationship is established, users in the foreign cell can log into accounts in the local cell and vice versa. You control foreign principals' access to specific objects with ACL entries, just as you do for principals in the local cell.

When the accounts are created, the **registry connect** command performs two tasks that you should be aware of. First, it automatically generates *one* password that is shared by both accounts. This means that users who log into a cell with which their cell has a trust relationship are seen as the same principal and share the same password. Second, the **registry modify** command generates a UNIX number that is shared by all principals that are in a given foreign cell. This shared UNIX number helps prevent collision between the UNIX numbers of local and foreign principals when objects on a local machine are accessed.

Within the registry and for the purposes of network access, principals are identified by a UUID that represents their fully qualified names; for example, **/.../dresden.com/dce/users/mahler** for the principal **mahler**. However, the local operating system on a local machine identifies principals by UNIX number. Because UNIX numbers are not required to be unique across cells, it is possible for two principals from different cells to have the same UNIX number. Thus, a foreign principal that is accessing files in the local cell could have the same UNIX number as the local principal and be seen by the local system as the owner of the local user's files on the local machine.

Creating a UNIX number that is applied to every principal from a given cell that accesses the local cell prevents this from occurring. However, you need to be aware that, because the foreign users all have the same UNIX number, the very feature that prevents them from accessing the local user's files allows them to access each other's files. Because each user from the same foreign cell is seen as the same user, every file on the local machine that is owned by a foreign user can be accessed by every other foreign user from the same foreign cell.

33.1.4 Constraints on Transitive Trust Relationships

To prevent the widespread proliferation of trust relationships that could result in unwieldy administrative burdens and weakened security, the DCE Security Service imposes the following three rules on transitive trust relationships:

1. Any number of descendent cells can be traversed by a transitive trust relationship, and any number of ancestor cells can be traversed by a transitive trust relationship.

2. No more than one direct trust peer relationship can be traversed by a transitive trust relationship. (A direct trust peer relationship is a direct trust relationship between cells that are neither ancestors nor descendants of each other in the naming hierarchy.)

3. Once a hierarchical trust relationship traverses a direct trust ancestor and an optional direct trust peer, it cannot traverse to an ancestor of the peer cell. In other words, once a transitive trust path goes up and across, it can't go up.

The ramifications of these rules are explained in the following paragraphs.

Rule 1:

Any number of descendent cells can be traversed in a hierarchical trust relationship, and any number of ancestor cells can be traversed by a transitive trust relationship.

For example, in Figure 33-2, peer Cells A and B have a direct trust relationship. Cell A has a transitive trust relationship with cells B/C and B/C/D.

Figure 33–2. Direct and Transitive Trust Relationships

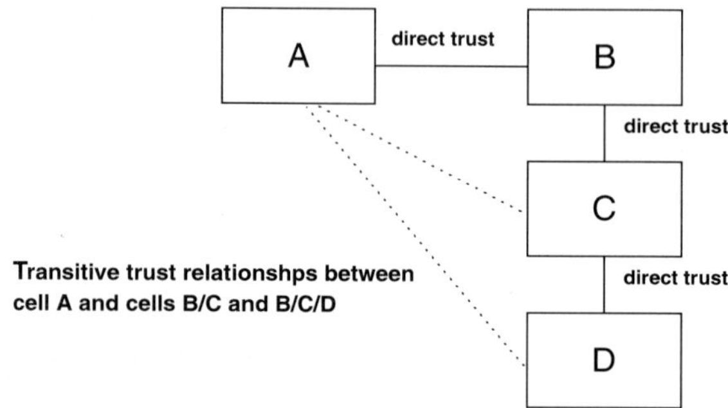

The previous configuration also makes possible the transitive trust relationship between B and cell B/C/D shown in Figure 33-3.

Figure 33–3. Cell Traversal in Transitive Trust Relationships

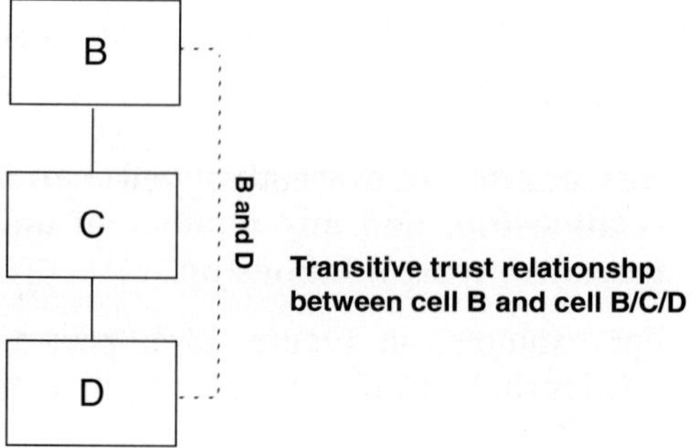

Rule 2:

No more than one direct trust peer relationship can be traversed by a transitive trust relationship.

For example, in Figure 33-4, cells A, B, and C are peer cells. Cell A has a direct trust peer relationship with cell B, and cell B has a direct trust peer relationship with cell C. Cell A does not have a transitive trust relationship with cell C because to do so would traverse more than one direct trust peer relationship (A to B and B to C).

Figure 33–4. Limited Direct Trust Peer Traversal in Transitive Trust

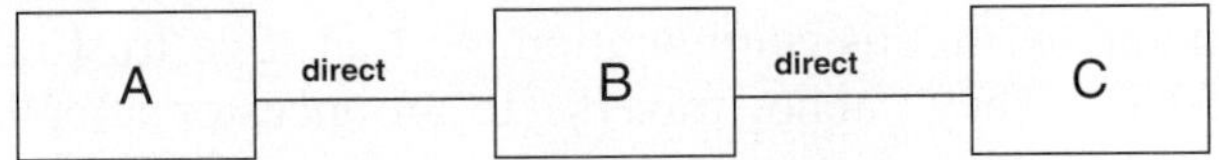

Note that it is not required to traverse a direct trust peer relationship to have a transitive trust relationship. In Figure 33-5, no direct trust peer relationships are traversed. In the figure, a transitive trust relationship exists between the following:

- B_Division and C_Division and C_organization

- C_Division and B_Division and B_organization

Figure 33–5. Transitive Trust Without Direct Trust Peer Traversal

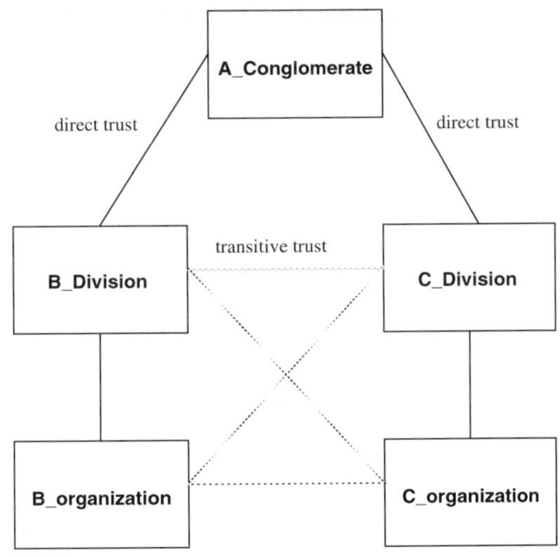

Rule 3:

Once a hierarchical trust relationship traverses a direct trust ancestor and a direct trust peer, it cannot traverse to an ancestor of the cell.

For example, consider Figure 33-6. The A_Conglomerate cell hierarchy and the B_Conglomerate cell are connected by direct trust relationships. Additionally, there is a direct trust relationship between A_product in the A_Conglomerate hierarchy and B_product in the B_Conglomerate hierarchy. In this configuration, no transitive trust relationships are possible because they cannot traverse to an ancestor after traversing a direct trust peer.

Figure 33–6. Limited Trust Traversal to Cell Ancestors

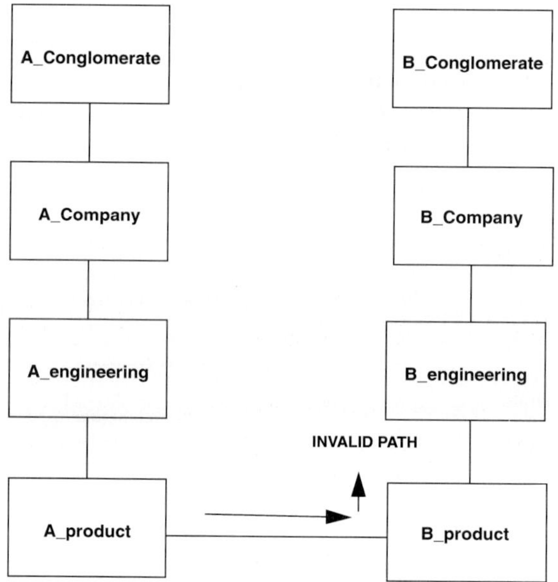

The type of trust relationship shown in this figure might be used by two companies that have a very limited agreement to cooperate on product development.

Figure 33-7 shows another transitive trust path.

Figure 33–7. Alternate Trust Traversal to Cell Ancestors

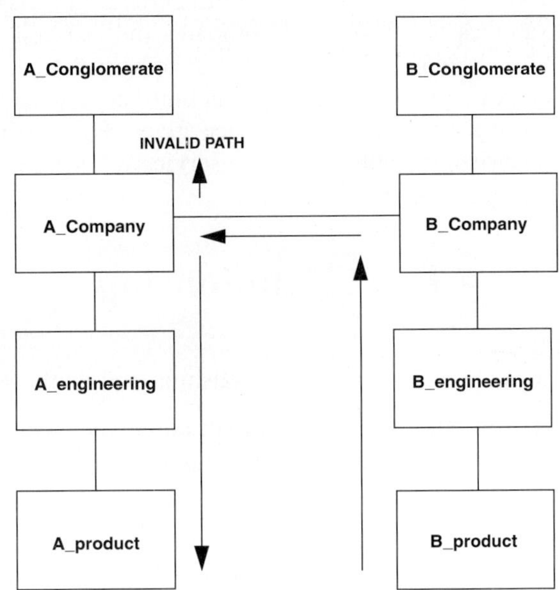

In the path, the B_product cell has a transitive trust path up to its ancestor, B_Company, and from B_Company to A_Company. But from A_company, the transitive trust path cannot continue up to A_Company's ancestor, although it can continue down to A_Company's descendants. Because this transitive trust relationship has traversed up to a trust ancestor (B_Company) and across to a trust peer (A_Company), it cannot then continue by going up to A_Company's ancestor (A_Conglomerate). This type of relationship might be used by two companies that have decided to combine operations at a very high level.

Note that a principal accessing a foreign cell through transitive trust relationships is not authenticated by each cell transited in the trust path, but only by the target cell itself. The authentication Service in a transited cell simply gives the principal a ticket to the next cell in the path, stamping the ticket with the hierarchical name of the transited cell, until the principal acquires a ticket to the target cell.

To determine whether or not to give a principal a ticket to the next cell in a transitive trust path, the authentication service in each transited cell examines the ticket and compares the last cell transited to the next cell in the path and applies the rules of transitive trust described in this section. If the next cell to be transited is consistent with a valid transitive trust path, then the authentication service gives the principal a ticket to the next cell; otherwise, the authentication service refuses to issue a ticket.

33.2 Creating Trust Relationships

To create peer-to-peer relationships, follow these steps:

1. Run the **registry connect** command to create cross-cell authentication accounts (an account in your cell's registry and another account in the foreign cell's registry).

2. Optionally, use the **account modify** command to fine tune the attributes of the account, which were assigned by default when the account was created. For example, the account's expiration date (**expdate** attribute) defaults to **none**. You may want to enter a date to ensure that the account will be actively renewed after a period of time.

3. Ensure that the system administrator in the foreign cell changes the **acctvalid** flag of the account that represents your cell to **yes** in order to indicate that the account is valid. If one or both accounts are invalid, no cross-cell communications can take place.

33.2.1 Command Options for the registry connect Command

When you use the **registry connect** command, you must supply the fully qualified name of the foreign cell with which you will establish a peer-to-peer relationship. This name is stripped of the full pathname, prefixed with **krbtgt**, and used as the primary name of the account's principal. For example, if you enter a cell name of **/.../dresden.com**, the principal name is **krbtgt/dresden.com**. The unchanged cell name is stored as the principal's full name.

Note that **registry connect** uses your local cell name for the primary name of the local cell's account principal. This name is stripped of the full pathname and prefixed with **krbtgt**, just as the foreign cell name is.

The following outlines additional information that you can supply to the **registry connect** command:

-mypwd

The **registry connect** command does not prompt you for a password for the accounts that you are creating; it generates this password randomly. However, you must supply your password with the **mypw** option as to validate your identity.

-facct, -facctpw

The system administrator in the foreign cell must provide you with the name and password of an account in the foreign cell. The foreign account must have the permissions that are required to create principals and accounts. You need the account to access the foreign registry in order to create the account that represents your cell in the foreign account's registry. The lifetime and creation quota of this account should be limited to only that necessary to complete the task.

-group, -fgroup

The group name to be associated with the account in the local cell (**-group**) and the foreign cell (**-fgroup**). These groups have no meaning for the accounts and are not associated with any users in the foreign or local cell. You must enter them because it is a requirement of the registry that all accounts be associated with groups. If the group does not exist, it will be created.

-org, -forg

The organization name to be associated with the account in the local cell (**-org**) and the foreign cell (**-forg**). These organizations have no meaning for the accounts and are not associated with any users in the foreign or local cell. You must enter them because it is a requirement of the registry that all accounts be associated with organizations. If the organization does not exist, it will be created.

-expdate   The time and date that both the local and the foreign cell's account expires, and the peer-to-peer relationship is ended, prohibiting any further authenticated communications between principals in the two cells. To renew the account, change the date in this field. The default is **none**.

33.2.2 Creating Cross-Cell Authentication Accounts Example

The following sample **registry connect** command is used to create an account for the foreign cell identified by **/.../dresden.com**. The local account is associated with the group named **cell_group_local**, the organization named **cell_group_dres**, and the organization named **cell_org_dres**. The expiration date for the accounts is allowed to default to **none**.

```
dcecp>  registry connect /.../dresden.com -facct cell_log -facctpw music \
            -group cell_group_local -fgroup cell_group_dres \
            -org cell_org_local -forg cell_org_dres -mypwd cell_admin
```

33.2.3 The Accounts Created by the registry connect Command

The accounts and principals that are created by the **registry connect** command are given default attribute values listed in Table 33-1. These attributes apply to all foreign princpals when they access objects in your cell. Likewise, the attributes of the account created for your cell in the foreign cell apply to all principals in your cell when they access objects in the foreign cell.

Table 33–1. Default Attribute Values of Cross-Cell Authorization Principals and Accounts

Information	Meaning
Account Principal Name	The local cell name for the local cell's account, or foreign cell name for the foreign cell's account stripped of its full pathname and prefixed with **krbtgt**.
fullname	The cell's pathname.
quota	Set to **none**. This quota applies to all principals who use the cross-cell authentication accounts to access objects in foreign cells. For example, if you change the object creation quota to 10, the total number of objects that can be created in your cell's registry by all foreign users who use the account to access your cell cannot exceed 10. It is not 10 per foreign principal. The object creation quota that is set for your cell's account in the foreign cell places the same restriction on the number of objects that your cell's principals can create in the foreign cell's registry.
description, **home**, **shell**	Set to blank.
server	Set to **yes**; that is, the account is a server that can engage in authenticated communications.
client	Set to **no**.
pwdvalid	Set to **yes** (valid).
acctvalid	Set to **no** (not valid).
postdatedtkt	Set to **yes**; that is, the account can be issued tickets with a start time in the future.
forwardabletkt	Set to **yes**; that is, the account can be issued a new ticket-granting ticket with a network address that is different than the present ticket-granting ticket.

Information	Meaning
renewabletkt	Set to **yes**; that is, the account's tickets can be renewed.
proxiabletkt	Set to **yes**; that is, the account can be issued tickets with a different network address than the present tickets.
dupkey	Set to **yes**; that is, the account's ticket can have duplicate keys.
goodsince	Set to the date that the account was created.
maxtktlife	Set to the registry policy.
maxtktrenew	Set to the registry policy.

33.3 Modifying Cross-Cell Authentication Accounts

You can change the account that is created by the **registry connect** command at any time using the standard **dcecp account** operations. However, you should be aware of the following cautions.

Never set the account's **pwdvalid** attribute to **no** (invalid). For standard accounts, setting the attribute to **no** causes the user to be prompted to change their passwords at the next login. Passwords for cross-cell authentication accounts, however, are shared by the authentication services in two cells. If you change one, this synchronization is destroyed and cross-cell communications end. If you want to change the passwords that are shared by the authentication services, you must rerun the **registry connect** command to recreate the accounts and create the properly synchronized passwords.

Generally, do not delete the accounts or the account's principals unless you are breaking the peer-to-peer relationship with the cell. If one of the accounts is deleted, you must run the **registry connect** command to recreate both accounts and restore the peer-to-peer relationship.

Chapter 34

Viewing Registry Information

Using **dcecp**, you can display information about the following security objects:

- Principals
- Groups
- Organizations
- Accounts
- The registry
- The **xattrschema** object
- ACLs
- Keytab files

The following **dcecp** operations provide these displays:

- The **catalog** command displays the names of all the specified objects.
- The **list** command displays the names of the members of the specified groups or organizations or of the specified key table.
- The **show** command displays information about a specific instance of an object.

This chapter describes how to display operation available for all security objects except the registry object, which is described in Chapter 36.

34.1 Displaying Account Information

Use the **dcecp account catalog** and **account show** commands to display information about accounts. When you use the **account show** command, you must supply the name of the account's principal to specify the account to display. You can supply multiple principal names by enclosing them in braces and separating them with spaces.

To display all accounts in the registry database in alphabetic order with names prefixed by the cell name, enter

account catalog

To display all accounts in the registry database in alphabetic order with names *not* prefixed by the cell name, enter

account catalog -simplename

To display all attributes for a named principal's account, enter

account show *principal_name*

To display all policies for a named principal's account, enter

account show *acct_name* **-policy**

To display all attributes and all policies for a named principal's account, enter

account show *acct_name* **-all**

The following example shows the **account catalog** command used without the **-simplename** option:

```
dcecp> account catalog
/.../dresden.com/bach
/.../dresden.com/bin
/.../dresden.com/brahms
/.../dresden.com/britten
/.../dresden.com/cell_admin
/.../dresden.com/daemon
/.../dresden.com/dce-ptgt
/.../dresden.com/dce-rgy
/.../dresden.com/mahler
/.../dresden.com/nobody
/.../dresden.com/root
/.../dresden.com/uucp
/.../dresden.com/hosts/pmin17/cds-server
/.../dresden.com/hosts/pmin17/gda
/.../dresden.com/hosts/pmin17/self
/.../dresden.com/krbtgt/dresden.com
```

The following example shows the **account show** command used to display
the attributes and associated with the account for **mahler**:

```
dcecp> account show mahler
{acctvalid yes}
{client yes}
{created /.../dresden.com/cell_admin 1994-06-15-18:31:08.000+00:00I-----}
{description {}}
{dupkey no}
{expdate 1995-06-16-00:00:00.000+00:00I-----}
{forwardabletkt yes}
{goodsince 1994-06-15-18:31:05.000+00:00I-----}
{group users}
{home /}
{lastchange /.../dresden.com/cell_admin 1994-06-16-12:21:07.000+00:00I-----}
{organization users}
{postdatedtkt no}
{proxiabletkt no}
{pwdvalid yes}
{renewabletkt yes}
{server yes}
{shell {}}
{stdtgtauth yes}
```

Note that, if the policy defined for the account is not actually in effect
because it is overridden by the registry policy, the policy is followed by the
effective tag and the actual value in effect.

34.2 Displaying Group and Organization Information

Use the **dcecp group catalog**, **group show**, and **group list** commands to display information about groups and the **dcecp organization catalog**, **organization show**, and **organization list** commands to display information about organizations. When you use the **group list**, **group show**, **organization list**, and **organization show** commands, you must supply the name of the group or organization to display. You can supply multiple names by enclosing them in braces and separating them with spaces.

To display all groups or organizations in the registry database in alphabetic order with names prefixed by the cell name, enter

group catalog

or

organization catalog

To display all groups or organizations in the registry database in alphabetic order with names *not* prefixed by the cell name, enter

group catalog -simplename

or

organization catalog -simplename

To display all members of a specified group or organization in alphabetical order with names prefixed by the cell name, enter

group list *group_name*

or

organization list *group_name*

To display all members of a specified group or organization in alphabetical order with names *not* prefixed by the cell name, enter

group list *group_name* **-simplename**

or

group list *group_name* **-simplename**

To display all attributes for a group or organization, enter

group show *group_name*

or

organization show *group_name*

To display all extended attribute instances attached to a group or organization, enter

group show *group_name* **-xattrs**

or

organization show *group_name* **-xattrs**

To display all regular attributes and all extended attributes for a group or organization, enter

group show *group_name* **-all**

or

organization show *group_name* **-all**

The following example shows the **group catalog** command used without the **-simplename** option:

```
dcecp> group cat
/.../dresden.com/nogroup
/.../dresden.com/system
/.../dresden.com/daemon
/.../dresden.com/uucp
/.../dresden.com/bin
/.../dresden.com/kmem
/.../dresden.com/mail
/.../dresden.com/tty
/.../dresden.com/none
/.../dresden.com/tcb
/.../dresden.com/acct-admin
/.../dresden.com/subsys/dce/sec-admin
/.../dresden.com/subsys/dce/cds-admin
/.../dresden.com/subsys/dce/dts-admin
/.../dresden.com/subsys/dce/cds-server
/.../dresden.com/subsys/dce/dts-servers
/.../dresden.com/users
```

The following example shows the attributes of the group named **users_temporary**:

```
dcecp> group show users_temporary
{alias no}
{gid 5211}
{uuid 0000145b-9362-21cd-a601-0000c08adf56}
{inprojlist no}
{fullname {temporary users}}
```

Note, in the preceding example, the line that says **{alias no}**. This indicates that the name **users_temporary** is the primary name, not an alias name. For an alias, this line would read **{alias yes}**.

The following **group list** command displays the members of the group **symphonists**:

```
dcecp> group list symphonists
/.../dresden.com/bach
/.../dresden.com/britten
/.../dresden.com/mahler
```

34.3 Displaying Principal Information

Use the **dcecp principal catalog** and **principal show** commands to display information about principals. When you use the **principal show** command, you must supply the name of the principal to display. You can supply multiple principal names by enclosing them in braces and separating them with spaces.

To display all principals in the registry database in alphabetic order with names prefixed by the cell name, enter

principal catalog

To display all principals in the registry database in alphabetic order with names *not* prefixed by the cell name, enter

principal catalog -simplename

To display all attributes for a named principal, enter

principal show *principal_name*

To display all extended attribute instances attached to a principal, enter

principal show *principal_name* **-xattrs**

To display all regular attributes and all extended attributes for a principal, enter

principal show *principal_name* **-all**

The following example shows the **principal catalog** used with the **-simplename** option:

```
dcecp> principal catalog -simplename
bach
bin
brahms
britten
cell_admin
daemon
dce-ptgt
dce-rgy
mahler
nobody
root
uucp
cds-server
```

The following example shows the **principal show** command used to display
information about the principal **mahler**:

```
dcecp> principal show /.:/mahler
{fullname {Gustav Mahler}}
{uid 30014}
{uuid 0000753e-f51f-2e0e-b000-0000c08adf56}
{alias no}
{quota unlimited}
{groups {{symphonists composers}}
```

All the information listed by the **principal show** command is information
created when the principal was added to the registry, except the line for
groups. This line lists the groups in which the principal is a member.

34.4 Displaying xattrschema Information

Use the **dcecp xattrschema catalog** and **xattrschema show** commands to
display information about the extended attribute types. Note that, to see
instances of an extended attribute attached to a principal, use the **-xattr**
option with the **principal**, **group**, or **organization show** commands.

The **xattrschema catalog** command displays the names of the extended attribute instances defined in a named schema. When you use this command, you must specify the name of the schema for which to display extended attributes. For the registry database, this name is **/.:/sec/xattrschema**. Your site must supply you with the name of the schema.

The **xattrschema show** command displays the attributes of named schemas in either the registry schema or a schema in use at your site. When you use this command , you must specify the name of the extended attribute type for which to display information. You can supply multiple names by enclosing them in braces and separating them with spaces.

To display the names of all attribute types in the registry database in alphabetic order with names prefixed by the cell name, enter

xattrschema catalog /.:/sec/xattrschema

To display all attribute types in the registry database in alphabetic order *not* prefixed by the cell name, enter

xattrschema catalog /.:/sec/xattrschema

To display attributes in a schema other than the registry, replace **/.:/sec/xattrschema** with the fully specified name of the other schema.

To display the attributes of a named extended attribute type, enter

xattrschema show *attr_name*

The following example, lists the names of all extended attributes in the registry prefixed by the cell name:

dcecp> **xattrschema catalog /.:/sec/xattrschema**
```
/.../dresden/sec/xattrschema/pre_auth_req
/.../dresden/sec/xattrschema/pwd_val_type
/.../dresden/sec/xattrschema/pwd_mgmt_binding
/.../dresden/sec/xattrschema/X500_DN
/.../dresden/sec/xattrschema/X500_DSA_Admin
/.../dresden/sec/xattrschema/disable_time_interval
/.../dresden/sec/xattrschema/max_invalid_attempts
/.../dresden/sec/xattrschema/passwd_override
/.../dresden/sec/xattrschema/test_integer
```

The following example, list the attributes of the extended registry attribute named **test_integer**:

dcecp> **xattrschema show /.:/sec/xattrschema/test_integer**
```
{aclmgr {principal {{query r} {update r} {test r} {delete r}}}}
{annotation {test_integer: encoding type integer}}
{applydefs yes}
{encoding integer}
{intercell reject}
{multivalued yes}
{reserved no}
{scope {}}
{trigbind {none {}}}
{trigtype none}
{unique no}
{uuid 5f439154-2af1-11cd-8ec3-080009353559}
```

34.5 Displaying ACL Information

Use the **dcecp acl show** commands to display ACL entries for a named object. When you use this command, you must specify the name of the object for which to display ACL entries. You can supply multiple names by enclosing them in braces and separating them with spaces.

If this command is not able to determine the name of the object, it will display the object's UUID.

To display the ACL entries for a specified object, enter

acl show *object_name*

To display the ACL's default cell, enter

acl show *object_name* **-cell**

To display the ACL managers supported by an object, enter

acl show *object_name* **-managers**

The following example displays ACL entries for the object named **hosts**:

```
dcecp> acl show /.:/hosts
{unauthenticated r--t---}
{user cell_admin rwdtcia}
{user hosts/absolut/cds-server1 rwdtcia}
{user root rwdtcia}
{group subsys/dce/cds-admin rwdtcia}
{group subsys/dce/cds-server rwdtcia}
{any_other r--t---}
```

34.6 Displaying keytab Information

Use the **dcecp keytab catalog, keytab list**, and **keytab show** commands to display information about accounts. When you use the **keytab catalog** command, you must supply the name of the host for which to display keytab files. When you use the **keytab list** or **keytab show** command, you must supply the name of the **dced** object for which to display keytab information. You can supply multiple names to either command by enclosing them in braces and separating them with spaces.

To display the names of all keytab files on a specified host with names prefixed by the cell name, enter

keytab catalog *host_name*

If you do not supply *host_name*, the display lists keytab files on the current host.

To display the names of all keytab files on a specified host with names *not* prefixed by the cell name, enter

keytab catalog *host_name* **-simplename**

To display a list of all principals for which there are entries in a specified keytab file, enter

keytab list *file_name*

To display all principals for which there are entries in a named keytab file, enter

keytab show *file_name*

The information displayed includes only the principal name.

To display the local names of a specified key file, enter

keytab show *dced_object_name* **-entry**

To display all entries in a key file, including the keys, enter

keytab show *dced_object_name* **-members**

The following example shows the entries in the keytab file named **svr_3**:

```
dcecp> keytab show /.:/hosts/music/config/keytab/svr_3 -members
{brahms des 1}
{britten plain 3}
{mahler des 2}
```

Chapter 35

Maintaining Policies and Properties

Registry polices are attributes that can be set registry wide. To provide a finer lever of control, policies can also be set for individual organizations and accounts. An organization's or account's policies can override the registry default policies if the organization's or account's policies are more restrictive.

Registry properties are attributes that apply to the principals, groups, and organizations created in the registry. They cannot be set for individual organizations or accounts. Properties regulate such things as the range of numbers that can be used for UNIX IDs and whether encrypted passwords are displayed.

You can set both polices and properties with the **dcecp registry modify** command. In addition, you can set policies for an individual organization or account with the **dcecp organization modify** and **dcecp account modify** commands. In all commands, policies and properties to be set are supplied as attributes in standard **dcecp** attribute lists with the **-change** option or as attribute options.

This chapter first describes policies and then properties.

35

Chapter 36

Performing Routine Maintenance

This chapter describes security maintenance procedures that should be performed on a regular basis, such as

- Adding new users to the registry

- Creating overrides for individual machines

- Changing the master key

- Backing up and restoring the database

- Updating the **/etc/passwd** and **/etc/group** files so that they are consistent with the registry

36.1 Adding Accounts

To add new user accounts to the registry, you must have the appropriate
permissions to the registry (see Chapter 41). Once you have the appropriate
permissions, you can proceed as follows to add accounts:

1. If the principal to be used in the account does not already exist,
   execute the **principal create** command to add the principal.

2. Execute the **group create** command to add the group to be used in the
   account if this group does not already exist.

3. Execute the **organization create** command to add the organization to
   be used in the account if this organization does not already exist.

4. Finally, execute the **account create** command to add the account.

36.2 Overriding Entries in the Local Registry

You can override registry entries for local machines. By using overrides,
you can, for example, prevent individuals and groups from logging into a
particular machine, establish local root passwords, and tailor local user
environments. The override information is in effect for the local machine
only and has no effect on the account information that is stored in the
registry.

The override mechanism provides a high level of local autonomy and allows
individual users to control their own machines. For example, an
administrator who is responsible for a group of machines can use the
override facility to restrict access to those machines. The administrator can
allow access to specific groups, or the administrator can allow access to
everyone except specific groups or principals.

36.2.1 How Overrides Work

The **passwd_override** administrative file that is stored in the local machine's *dcelocal*/**etc/security** directory contains override information. By using this file, you can enter overrides for the following:

- Passwords

- GECOS information

- Home directories

- Login shells

- Group memberships

- UNIX IDs for principals

The override information that you enter is in effect only for the local machine, which is the machine on which the **passwd_override** file is stored. When a user logs into a machine with an override file, any information for the user's account in the override file replaces the pertinent information obtained from the registry.

For example, assume that the registry account for **bach** specifies a Korn shell at login. Since **bach** normally logs into a machine that can run a Korn shell, this is fine for a majority of situations. However, **bach** occasionally works for another department and logs into a machine that cannot run a Korn shell. To accommodate **bach**'s needs, you can create an override file on the machine that cannot run the Korn shell. The override can specify a Bourne login shell. Then, if **bach** logs into the machine that can run a Korn shell, registry data is used and a Korn shell is invoked. When **bach** logs into the machine that cannot run a Korn shell, override data is used and a Bourne shell is invoked.

36.2.2 The passwd_override File Format

Entries in the **passwd_override** file have the following format:

principal_name:*passwd*:*principal_uid*:*group_uid*:*GECOS*:*home_dir*:*shell*

36.2.3 The group_override File Format

This section explains the **group_override** file.

36.2.3.1 Description

The **/opt/***dcelocal***/etc/group_override** administrative file lets you override the UNIX group ID for a group similar to the way in which the **passwd_override** file permits overriding information in the network registry database.

The **group_override** file is stored on each machine. Any changes you make to it are in effect for the local machine only; they have no effect on the centralized registry. You might find working with file **group_override** especially useful in overriding the default group definitions supplied with the registry if they do not match your local UNIX system.

36.2.3.2 File Format

The format of the entries in file **group_override** is similar to the format of the entries in the UNIX **group** file. This format is

group_name:passwd:group_uid:members

In this entry, *group_name* and *group_uid* are keyfields. You must enter one to identify the group to which the override applies. The keyfield is used to perform a lookup in the override file when you use the **passwd_export** command. The lookup is performed in order as the entries are specified in an override file: first by group name, then by group UNIX ID. If you specify both keyfields in an override entry, the group name is used as the lookup key; subsequent fields are used as overrides.

36.2.3.3 Field Descriptions

The following list describes each entry in the file **group_override**:

group_name   A keyfield that contains the name that identifies the group to which the override applies.

passwd   This field specifies the encrypted password. If you specify an override in this field, the password you enter is in effect for this local machine only.

The use of **OMIT** along with an option to the **passwd_export** command prevents the inclusion of this group in the group file created by the **passwd_export** command. This effectively disallows **newgrp** commands to this group on the local machine. (See Section 36.2.3.5 for details.)

group_uid   A UNIX group ID. This field can function as a keyfield when no other keyfields are entered. It can also function as a field containing an override when entered along with *group_name*. The *group_uid* value specifies the local override of the group ID supplied by the network registry server.

members   This field specifies a comma-separated list of members of the group. The contents of this field will override information in the registry when the **passwd_export** command creates an **/etc/group** file. Note that, to specify a null membership, as opposed to indicating that no override is required, use a * (asterisk) for this field.

36.2.3.4 Leaving Fields Blank

If you do not want to override an item, leave its field blank, separating each blank field with a : (colon). Note that, to override a group with a null membership list, enter an asterisk for the *members* field.

36.2.3.5 Using **OMIT**

If you specify **OMIT** and issue a **passwd_export** command with the **-x** option, then the named group will not appear in the **/etc/group** file produced by the **passwd_export** command. Subsequent to this, users will not be able to issue a **newgrp** command to this group on the local machine.

The **ls** command is likewise affected. For example, the following command accesses the group file to obtain additional information about a group:

ls -lg

If the group is omitted, no group entry will exist and no information will be available. For this reason, you should use **OMIT** to omit groups from file **/etc/group** only if your user community is very large and either of the following conditions occur:

- The group file is taking up too much space.

- Group ID-to-name mapping is too slow (during an **ls -lg** command, for example).

36.2.3.6 Examples

To override the group ID of group **kmem** to be **3**, use the following entry:

kmem::3:

To override the group password and membership for group **system** to the single account **root**, use the following entry:

system:*::root

36.2.4 Creating Override File Entries

To create override file entries, edit the **passwd_override** file and supply the override entries. The entry must identify the account (or accounts) to which the override applies by specifying one of the following keyfields:

principal_name The name of the specific principal to which to apply the overrides. The override applies only to the account for the principal's primary name. For example, if you specify **mahler** as the principal name in an override entry, the overrides apply only to principal **mahler**'s account, and not to any accounts for **mahler**'s aliases.

principal_uid A UNIX ID that identifies the accounts to which to apply the override if *principal_name* is not specified. The override is applied to all accounts for the principal that is identified by *principal_uid*, including any accounts for the principal's aliases. For example, suppose that principal **mahler** has a UNIX ID of **2195**. If you specify **2195** as the key of the entry, the overrides apply to all accounts that are associated with that UNIX ID. Because a principal's primary name and aliases carry the same UNIX ID, this means that the overrides apply to accounts for the principal's primary name and all aliases.

group_uid A UNIX ID that identifies the group to which to apply the overrides if neither *principal_name* nor *principal_uid* are specified. The overrides are applied to all accounts for all principals that are members of the identified group.

The *principal_name* field always acts as the keyfield and cannot be overridden. If you enter *principal_name*, it identifies the specific account to be overridden. The *principal_uid* or the *group_uid* field can act as the keyfield or they can act as override fields. Only one of the possible keyfields is used as a key for any one entry; the others (if entered) are used as override fields. The *principal_name* field takes precedence, followed by *principal_uid*, and finally *group_uid*.

For example, if you enter *principal_uid* and *do not* enter *principal_name*, *principal_uid* is used as the keyfield. If you enter *principal_uid* and *principal_name*, *principal_name* is used as the keyfield and *principal_uid* is used as an override field.

If you enter the *group_uid* field and *do not* enter any other keyfields (*principal_name* or *principal_uid*), *group_uid* is used as the keyfield, and the overrides apply to the accounts of all members of the group. If you enter *principal_name* and *group_uid*, *principal_name* is used as the keyfield, and the group affiliation of the named principal is overridden by the group that is identified by the group UNIX ID.

36.2.5 Leaving passwd_override File Fields Blank

If you do not want to override an item in the **passwd_override** file, leave its field blank, separating each blank field with a : (colon). You must enter one of the keyfields, however, to identify the principal or group for which you are creating overrides. For example, an entry to override the home directory for the account identified by **mozart** looks like this:

```
mozart:::::/aria/wolfgang:
```

You must enter the colons that are associated with any blank trailing fields. In the preceding example, a colon is required for the shell field, which is the remaining field after the home directory field.

36.2.6 Specifying Passwords for a Specific Machine

Manually edit the password entry in the **passwd_override** file on the local machine to create an entry in the override file to override passwords on the local machine. The password that you enter must be encrypted, but you can copy the encrypted password from the **/etc/passwd** file or you can write a program that generates encrypted passwords.

When you override a principal's password, only the principal's local credentials are obtained at login, not the principal's network credentials. Without network credentials, the principal cannot access the network registry and obtain the information that is normally provided at network login. Therefore, you must supply all of this information in the **password_override** file entry. For overrides to passwords, you must enter all of the fields in the override entry, including all keyfields.

The following example shows a **passwd_override** file entry that changes a specific machine's password for user **mozart**'s account:

```
mozart:sq1Rc1Urrb1L6:678:893:Wolfgang A.  Mozart:/aria/wolfgang:/bin/csh
```

Note: If your password is overridden and you then use **rlogin** or **rsh** to log in remotely to the machine with the overrides, you are prompted for a password, regardless of what is in either the **/etc/hosts.equiv** or **.rhosts** file.

36.2.7 Preventing Login to a Machine

To prevent users from logging into a machine, create an override entry with an invalid string in the **passwd** field. Because the **passwd** field contains an encrypted password, any character string that is not exactly 13 characters in length can be used as an invalid password. For example, the following entry in the **passwd_override** file supplies **exclude** as a password. This string of less than 13 characters prevents members of the group that is identified by a UNIX ID of **25** from logging in.

```
:exclude::25:::
```

36.2.8 Omitting Users from the Local Password Files

An invalid password entry in the **passwd_override** file prohibits users from logging into the machine on which the file exists. However, the invalid entry **OMIT** has a special meaning. Just as with any other invalid password, if you enter **OMIT**, the user cannot log in. Additionally, however, if you maintain the standard **/etc/passwd** and **/etc/group** files and used the **passwd_export** command to keep these files consistent with the registry database, you can specify that users with a password of **OMIT** be excluded from the **/etc/passwd** file. (See Section 36.7 for more information on the **passwd_export** command.)

Also, be aware that, if you have omitted users from the **/etc/passwd** file, information about those users is not available to any programs that use the password file. For example, the **ls -l** and the **finger** commands both access the password file to obtain further information about a user identified by a UNIX ID. If the user is omitted, no password entry exists and no information is available on that user.

36.2.9 Specifying a Home Directory and Login Shell for a Machine

To change an account's home directory and login shell for a specific machine, create an override entry with a home directory name and a login shell name. For example, the following entry changes the home directory and login shell for user **mozart**'s account:

```
mozart:::::rondo/mozart:/bin/ksh
```

36.2.10 Overriding a Principal's Group Affiliation

To override a principal's group affiliation, create an override entry that contains the principal's name or UNIX ID as a key and the UNIX ID of the group that is to be used as the override. Use the principal's name as a key to apply the overrides only to the account for the principal's primary name. Use the principal's UNIX ID as a key to apply the overrides to all of the principal's accounts, including any accounts for the principal's aliases. For example, the following entry overrides the group that is normally associated with the account for principal **mozart**:

```
mozart:::356:::
```

This override does not apply to any accounts for any of **mozart**'s aliases. To apply the overrides to those accounts, the entry must be keyed by **mozart**'s UNIX ID (**567**), as follows:

```
::567:356:::
```

36.2.11 Applying Overrides to All Members of a Group

To apply overrides to all members of a specific group, create an override entry that contains the group's UNIX ID as a key and the items to override. For groups, you can override passwords, GECOS information, home directories, and shells. For example, the following entry makes **/sonata/piano** the home directory for all members of the group that is identified by UNIX ID **356**:

```
:::356::/sonata/piano:
```

Be sure not to include the *principal_name* or *principal_uid* keyfields. If you do, the principal name or UNIX ID that you supply will be used as a keyfield, and the group UNIX ID will be used to override that principal's group affiliations.

36.2.12 How passwd_override Handles Multiple Override Entries

When more than one override entry applies to an account, the entry with the most specific account identifier (that is, either a principal UNIX ID, a group UNIX ID, or a principal name) is selected. Principal names are the most specific, followed by the principal UNIX ID and group UNIX ID.

For example, assume that the override file contains the following two entries that override the login shells:

```
mozart::::::/bin/ksh
:::25:::/bin/csh
```

If a principal logs in as **mozart**, the override that is keyed by **mozart** is in effect. In this case, the principal (**mozart**) is more specific than the group (**25**).

36.3 Changing the Registry's Master Key

All passwords stored in a registry are encrypted by a master key. Note that the master key is created when you create the registry database during system configuration.

You can use the **dcecp registry modify** command with the **-key** option to change the registry's master key and to reencrypt all passwords with the new master key. Each replica (master and slave) maintains its own master key to access the data in its copy of the registry.

You should change each replica's master key on a regular basis. Before you run either program to do this, ensure that you are logged into an administrative account.

The following command line changes the master key and reencrypts all the passwords for the replica **art_server_1**:

```
dcecp>  registry modify /.../giverny.com/subsys/dce/sec/art_server_1 -key
```

36.4 Validating the Authenticity of the DCE Security Service

The **secval** process within the DCE daemon can confirm that the DCE security server is an authentic server. An illegitimate DCE security server could give a malicious user root access on a machine by returning a counterfeit local system identity. A **secval ping** operation confirms the authenticity of the DCE security server by performing an authenticated RPC to the **secval** process. A successful return (**1**) indicates that the security server used all of the correct passwords needed for the authenticated RPC to succeed.

You can perform a **secval ping** operation on the local host or you can supply an argument to operate on a remote host. Because remote hosts might use different security servers, performing **secval ping** operations on remote hosts provides a way to test the authenticity of other security servers operating in a cell.

The following example illustrates a **secval ping** operation to the **secval** process on remote host **charon**:

```
dcecp>  secval ping /.:/hosts/charon/config/secval
1
```

36.5 Backing Up and Restoring the Registry Database

Use the exact procedures that are described here to back up the registry database to prevent backups from arriving at the master during the backup.

Only the master replica database and its master key file need to be backed up. Use the procedures that are described in the following subsections when you back up the entire disk on which the master replica and its master key are stored, and when you back up only the master's database files and its master key file.

36.5.1 Procedures for Backing Up the Registry Database

To run the backup procedures, ensure that you are logged into DCE via an administrative account. Then, run the DCE control program to do the backup. The backup steps are as follows:

1. Enter the **registry disable** command to set the master replica to the maintenance state. The following command sets the master registry in the cell **giverny.com** to maintenance state:

   dcecp> **registry disable /.../giverny.com/subsys/dce/sec/master**

   Setting the master replica to the maintenance state causes the master to save its database to disk and refuse all updates.

2. Back up the master registry by backing up either the entire volume or the *dcelocal***/var/security/rgy_data** tree (the registry) and the *dcelocal***/var/security/.mkey** file, which is the file that contains the master key used to encrypt all keys in the registry. Note that, because the *dcelocal***/var/security/.mkey** file contains the master key, restoring a backup of the registry database is useless unless the *dcelocal***/var/security/.mkey** file is also restored.

   The exact commands that are used for the backup are a matter of personal preference. However, if you write both the database and the master key file to the same tape, store the tape in a locked area with restricted access. Alternatively, you can write the database and the key file to separate tapes and store each tape in a different location.

3. When the backup completes, take the master replica out of maintenance state, as follows:

   dcecp> **registry enable /.../giverny.com/subsys/dce/sec/master**

   The security server resumes accepting updates.

Note that the previous examples supplied the name of the registry master site to the **registry enable** and **registry disable** commands. If you do not supply a registry site name, the commands use the site named in the **_s(sec_)** variable. If this variable is not set, the commands use the master registry of the machine's default cell. See Section 36.6 for more information.

36.5.2 Procedure for Restoring the Registry Database

This section provides instructions for restoring the master replica's database files and master key file. The procedure assumes that the database is being restored to the same machine from which it was backed up, and that you are using the DCE control program. If you are moving the database to a different machine, follow the instructions in Chapter 37.

To restore the registry database to a machine, perform the following steps:

1. Log in as **root** at the master registry site.

2. If **secd** is running, stop it by issuing the **registry stop** command. When you use this command, you must supply the fully qualified name of a specific replica as an argument. The followng sample command stops the **secd** named **master**:

   dcecp> **registry stop /.../giverny.com/subsys/dce/sec/master**

3. Copy the backup files from the backup media to the machine. If you have backed up only the registry data files and the master key files, be sure to copy the registry database to *dcelocal*/**var/security/rgy_data** and the master key file to *dcelocal*/**var/security/.mkey**. Note that, because the *dcelocal*/**var/security/.mkey** file contains the master key, restoring a backup of the registry database is useless unless the *dcelocal*/**var/security/.mkey** file is also restored.

4. Restart the server by invoking **secd** with the **-restore_master** option, as follows:

   dcelocal/**bin/secd -restore_master &**

   This command will start **secd** and cause the master to mark all slaves to be reinitialized.

5. Verify that **secd** starts automatically at system startup.

Note: If you are restoring *only* a master key file and have not changed the master key, you can simply copy the master key file from the backup media without performing all of the other steps that are in the restore procedures.

36.6 Setting the _s(sec) Variable

You can supply the name of the registry site to bind to as an argument to the **dcecp** commands that operate on the registry. If you do not supply a name, the command binds to the replica named in the _s(sec) variable. If this variable is not set, the command binds to the cell's master replica. You can set the _s(sec) variable and then use that replica as the default replica for **dcecp registry** commands. To do so, use the **set** command as shown in the following sample that sets the default replica to the master replica (named **slave_3**) in the cell **giverny.com**:

dcecp> **set _s(sec) /.../giverny.com/subsys/dce/sec/slave_3**

The name of the new default replica that you supply as an argument to the **set** command can be in any of the following forms:

- A cell name (for example, **/.../dresden.com**)

  If you enter a cell name, the named cell becomes the default cell. The DCE control program randomly chooses a replica to bind to in the named cell, and that replica becomes the default replica.

- The global name given to the replica when it was created (for example, **/.../dresden.com/subsys/dce/sec/rs_server_250_2**)

  A global name identifies a specific replica in a specific cell. That cell becomes the default cell, and that replica becomes the default replica.

- The replica's name as it appears on the replica list of the current default replica (that is, its cell-relative name; for example, **subsys/dce/sec/rs_server_250_2**)

  That replica becomes the default replica, and the cell in which the replica exists becomes the default cell.

- The network address of the host on which the replica is running (for example, **ncadg_ip_udp:15.22.144.248**)

  The replica on that host becomes the default replica, and the cell in which the host exists becomes the default cell.

Some of the **dcecp** commands can act only on the master replica and thus require binding to the master. If you execute a command that acts only on the master and the master is not the default replica, **dcecp** automatically attempts to bind to the master replica in the current default cell. If this attempt is successful, **dcecp** displays a warning message, informing you that the default replica has been changed to the master registry. The master registry will then remain the default replica until you change it. If the attempt to bind is not successful, **dcecp** displays an error message, and the command fails.

36.7 Ensuring Consistent Local Files

The **passwd_export** command makes the standard **/etc/passwd** and **/etc/group** files on the local machine consistent with the registry database. Run the **passwd_export** command on a regular, but staggered, basis preferably as part of **cron** processing. If **passwd_export** succeeds in creating the new password and group files, it saves the current files as backups that are named **passwd.bak** and **group.bak**. If it fails, it leaves the current files as is.

The **passwd_export** command has the following syntax:

passwd_export [-n][-d *directory_name*] [-x] [-m *max_entries*] [-s] | [-h[elp] [-v]

where:

-n Specifies that **passwd_override** and **group_override** file entries should be ignored. Without this flag, **passwd_export** applies the override entries from both files to the local password and group files that it creates.

-d *directory_name* Specifies the name of a directory in which to store the local password and group files that are created by **passwd_export**. If you do not enter this option, the files are stored by default in the **/etc** directory on the local node.

For example, to store the files in the directory that is called **/etc/locals**, enter the command in the following form:

dceshared/**bin/passwd_export -d/etc/locals**

-x

Prohibits the creation of entries for users with password or group overrides (on the local machine) that specify **OMIT** as their encrypted password. Use the **-x** option to exclude ''omitted'' users or groups from the password and group files that are created by **passwd_export**. To omit a user, you must create an override entry for the user and enter the word **OMIT** as the user's password field entry. Omitted users are unable to log into the local machine. (See Section 36.2.8.) To omit a group, create an override entry for the group and enter the word **OMIT** as the group's password field entry.

-m *max_entries*

Sets the maximum number of registry entries that are put in the **/etc/passwd** and **/etc/group** files.

-s

Sorts the entries in the **/etc/passwd** and **/etc/group** files by UNIX number. If this option is not specified, the entries are in the random order in which they are retrieved from the registry.

-h[elp]

Displays help information.

-v

Runs in verbose mode.

Chapter 37

Handling Network Reconfigurations

This chapter describes the procedures to handle network reconfigurations that change the locations of registry replicas. Specifically, this chapter covers the following:

- Changing the master registry site

- Removing a node from the network

- Handling network address changes

To perform the procedures in this chapter, you must be logged into the network registry account via an administrative account.

37.1 Changing the Master Replica Site

The machine that runs the master replica server must be available at all times. If you are planning to remove this machine from your network or to shut it down for an extended period, you need to change the site of the master replica.

The preferred method for changing the master registry site is to use the **dcecp registry set** command to reverse the roles of the master server and a slave server. In other words, make the master the slave and the slave the master.

When you invoke the **dcecp registry set** command, the following occurs:

1. The current master sends all pending updates and its propagation queue to the replica designated as the new master.

2. The designated new master reads the current master's replica list to obtain information required for it to manage propagation to the slaves.

3. When the designated new master has obtained all necessary information from the current master, it becomes the new master, and the current master becomes a slave.

Because this orderly and complete transfer of information ensures that no data is lost, the **dcecp registry set** command is the preferred method to move the master registry to another machine when the registry servers at the master and slave sites are operating normally. Note that the **dcecp registry set -master** command is also available to change a replica from a slave to the master. However, because the **dcecp registry set -master** command can cause data to be lost, use it *only* when the current master has been destroyed. It is not recommended in instances when the master is unreachable because of a network failure or because the master has gone down temporarily. See Chapter 40 for more information on the **dcecp registry set -master** command.

Follow these steps to change the site of a master replica:

1. Choose the new master site. A slave replica must exist at this site. If necessary, use the **dce_config** command or your platform's equivalent to configure a slave machine.

2. Issue the **set** command to set the default replica to the current master replica. In the following example, the master replica is set to the replica named **master** in the cell **giverny.com**:

    dcecp> **set _s(sec) /.../giverny.com/subsys/dce/sec/master**

3. Issue the **registry set** command to reverse the roles of the master and slave. This command takes the name of the replica to be made the new master as an argument. The following example makes the replica named **/.../giverny.com/subsys/dce/sec/music** the new master:

   dcecp> **registry set /.../giverny.com/subsys/dce/sec/music**

4. Verify that the master site changed. Do this by issuing the **registry catalog** command.

37.2 Removing a Server Machine from the Network

If you are planning to remove a machine that runs a slave replica from the network or to shut the machine down for an extended period, delete the replica at that site.

If you are removing a node running the master server, you must change the master server site as described previously before you remove the node.

Use the **dcecp registry delete** command to delete a slave replica. When execute this command, the master performs the following actions:

1. Marks the replica as deleted

2. Propagates the deletion to all replicas on its replica list

3. Delivers the delete request to the replica

4. Removes the replica from its replica list

The following sample command deletes the slave replica named **/.../giverny.com/subsys/dce/sec/art_1**:

dcecp> **registry delete /.../giverny.com/subsys/dce/sec/art_1**

When you issue this command, **dcecp** binds to the master replica that is in the current cell, if necessary; then the master replica instructs the slave replica to delete itself.

To verify that the slave is deleted, issue the **dcecp registry catalog** command. When the master has received the request to delete the slave, the slave appears on the replica list as marked for deletion. When the replica has actually been deleted, it no longer appears on the list.

37.3 Handling Network Address Changes

When **secd** starts, master and slave replicas can detect address changes and can perform the necessary updates to the master's replica list and to the cell namespace. Generally, all that is required on your part to handle network address changes is to update the **pe_site** file. However, if the network address of the master and a slave replica change simultaneously, your intervention is required. This subsection describes how to update the **pe_site** file and how to handle simultaneous address changes.

37.3.1 Updating the pe_site File

Whenever the master's or a slave's network address changes, you must update the **/opt/***dcelocal***/etc/security/pe_site** file on that host before restarting **secd**. This file, which exists on each machine in the cell, is required for binding by the DCE Security Service to itself. For the master replica, the file contains the cell name and the name of the master. For slave replicas, the file contains the cell name, the name of the master replica, and the name of the replica itself.

If the master replica address changes, update the **pe_site** file on every node in the cell that runs a security server (including the master) with the new address for the master. If a slave address changes, update only that slave's **pe_site** file to reflect its changed address.

37.3.2 Handling Simultaneous Address Changes

If an address change occurs simultaneously for the master replica and a slave replica, the master and slave will not be able to reach each other while both are trying to notify the other of the changed address. To avoid this problem, make sure the address change of one replica (either master or slave) is propagated to all replicas before the other address is changed. Make one address change. Then, use the **dcecp registry show -replica** command to view the replica list at both the master site and the slave replica site. When the new address is displayed, on both replica lists, it is safe to proceed with the next network address change.

If you are unable to prevent simultaneous network address changes for the master and a slave, the only way to restore communication between the master and slave is to delete the slave, then recreate it. Delete the slave by using one of the following methods, depending on your circumstances:

- If you anticipate a simultaneous address change, while the master and slave are still communicating, use the **dcecp set** command to bind to the master and then the **dcecp registry delete** command to delete the slave replica.

- If **secd** is running at the master and slave sites, but the master and slave are not communicating, first use the **dcecp set** command to bind to the slave and then the **registry delete -only** command to destroy the slave. Then use **dcecp set** to bind to the master and the **registry delete -force** command to remove the replica list entry for the slave.

- If **secd** is not running at the slave site or if you are unable to bind to the slave site, use the procedure for recreating a replica described in Chapter 40.

-k[eyseed] *keyseed*

> This is a character string that you enter to seed the random key generator in order to create the master key for the database that you are creating. It should be a string that cannot be easily guessed. The master key is used to encrypt all account passwords. Each instance of a replica (master or slave) has its own master key. You can change the master key by using the **dcecp registry modify** command or **sec_admin master_key** command. (See Chapter 36 for information on the use of the **dcecp registry modify** command for modifying the master key. If you do not enter this option, **sec_create_db** prompts you for it.

-cr[eator] *creator_name*

> This is the name of the registry creator. The registry creator is the initial privileged user of the registry database. Note that you can give equivalent privileges to another user at any time by using the **dcecp acl modify** command or **acl_edit modify** command to change the registry database ACL. When the registry is created, default ACL entries for registry objects are also created. These entries give the most privileged permissions to the principal that is named in the **-cr** option. If the principal that is named as the registry creator is not one of the reserved names, **sec_create_db** adds the principal and an account for that principal. If you do not enter this option, the initial privileged user of the registry database is **root**.

-cu[nix_id] *creator_unix_id*

> This is a UNIX number that you specify to be assigned to the registry creator. If you do not enter this option, the registry creator's UNIX number is assigned dynamically.

-u[uid] *cell_uuid*

> This is the cell's UUID. If you do not enter this UUID, it is assigned dynamically.

-p[erson_low_unix_id] *unix_id*

> This is the starting point for UNIX IDs that are automatically generated when a principal is added by using the **dcecp registry modify** command or **rgy_edit properties** command. Note that you can explicitly assign a lower UNIX ID than this number; this lower limit applies only to automatically generated UNIX IDs.

-g[roup_low_unix_id] *unix_id*

This is the starting point for UNIX IDs that are automatically generated when a group is added by using the **dcecp registry modify** command or **rgy_edit properties** command. Note that you can explicitly enter a lower UNIX ID than this number; this lower limit applies only to automatically generated UNIX IDs.

-o[rg_low_unix_id] *unix_id*

This is the starting point for UNIX IDs that are automatically generated by the security service when an organization is added by using the **dcecp registry modify** command or **rgy_edit properties** command. Note that you can explicitly enter a lower UNIX ID than this number; this lower limit applies only to automatically generated UNIX IDs.

-ma[x_unix_id] *unix_id*

This is the highest number that can be assigned as a UNIX ID when a principal, group, or organization is added. No UNIX IDs higher than this number are assigned automatically, and you cannot specifically enter numbers higher than this number. The maximum UNIX ID stays in place until you change it with the **dcecp registry modify** command or **rgy_edit properties** command.

-pa[ssword] *default_password*

This is the default password that is assigned to the accounts created by **sec_create_db**. If you do not specify a default password, **-dce-** is used. Note the accounts **hosts/**local_host_name/principal_name **none none**, **krbtgt/**cell_name **none**, and **nobody none none** are not assigned the default password, but instead a randomly generated password.

-v[erbose] Runs in verbose mode and generates a verbose transcript of all activity.

38.2.2 A sec_create_db Run Example

The following example shows the **sec_create_db** command that is run to create the master database and the information that **sec_create_db** displays as it runs. Note that, because the **-k** option is not entered, **sec_create_db** prompts you for the master key seed string. This string is not displayed as it is entered.

/work/krb/sec_create_db -v -myname /.../dresden.com/subsys/dce/sec/master -master

```
Enter keyseed for initial database master key: <enter up to
        1024 characters>

SECD Checkpoint on Tue Sep 27 11:44:12 1994
....   saving rgy
....   saving acct
....   saving person
....   saving group
....   saving org
....   saving replicas
....   saving acl
End SECD Checkpoint on Tue Sep 27 11:44:13 1994
SECD Checkpoint on Tue Sep 27 11:44:15 1994
....   saving rgy
....   saving acct
....   saving person
....   saving group
....   saving org
....   saving acl
End SECD Checkpoint on Tue Sep 27 11:44:17 1994
```

38.2.3 The Results of sec_create_db

The master registry database that is created by **sec_create_db** contains the principals, groups, and organizations listed in Table 38-1.

Table 38–1. Initial Persons, Groups, and Organizations

Principal	Group	Organization
bin	bin	none
daemon	daemon	-
dce-ptgt	kmem	-
dce-rgy	mail	-
krbtgt/*local_cell_name*	nogroup	-
hosts/*local_host*/self	none	-
mail	system	-
nobody	tcb	-
root	tty	-
sys	uucp	-
tcb	-	-
uucp	-	-
who	-	-

The accounts that are created by the **sec_create_db** command are as follows:

- **bin bin none**

- **daemon daemon none**

- **dce-ptgt none none**

- **dce-rgy none none**

- **hosts/***local_host***/self none none**

- **krbtgt/***cell_name*** none none**

- **nobody nogroup none**

- **root system none**

- **uucp uucp none**

Some of the objects that were initially created by **sec_create_db** are reserved and cannot be deleted. These are indicated in the following list.

- The reserved principals are as follows:

  — **dce-ptgt**

  — **krbtgt/***cell_name*

  — **dce-rgy**

- The reserved group is **none**.

- The reserved organization is **none**.

- The reserved accounts are as follows:

  — **dce-ptgt none none**

  — **krbtgt/***cell_name* **none none**

  — **dce-rgy none none**

When you run the **sec_create_db** command to create the master registry database, you can name the principal who has the most privileged access to the registry. This person is known as the registry creator. If the registry creator you name is not one of the default principals, **sec_create_db** adds the account *rgy_creator* **none none**, where *rgy_creator* is the principal you named as the registry creator. If you do not name a registry creator, **sec_create_db** assigns the most privileged registry access to the **root system none** account.

With one exception, all of the accounts created by the **sec_create_db** command are assigned randomly generated passwords and are marked as invalid. Before these principals can log into these accounts, you must change the account passwords and mark the accounts as valid. You can do this by using the **dcecp account modify** command or **rgy_edit change** command. Chapter 31 provides instructions for using the **dcecp account modify** command to change all of the attributes for a principal's account in the registry, including the principal's password. Also, both commands have options to randomly generate new passwords.

However, the exception is that the account created for the registry creator is valid and is assigned the DCE default password (**-dce-**). Change the default password to ensure the security of the registry creator account.

In addition to the group memberships implied by the accounts that are created by **sec_create_db**, the principals are also made members of the groups listed in Table 38-2.

Table 38–2. Group Memberships Created by sec_create_db

The principal...	Is a member of the group...
who	bin
root	system kmen tty
sys	kmem
mail	mail
tcb	tcb

Chapter 30 provides instructions for adding principals to groups.

38.3 Starting the Master Replica

After **dce_config** creates the master replica, it starts the master replica. To start the master replica (**secd**) explicitly, use the following steps:

1. Log in as **root** on the machine that will run the master replica.

2. Use **ps** to ensure that a **dced** is running on the machine. If one is not, start one. To do so, ensure you are **root** and enter

    dceshared/**bin/dced**

3. Start the master replica by entering

    dcelocal/**bin/secd**

    Set up **secd** so that it starts automatically when the machine is rebooted.

38.4 Populating the New Registry Database

Once the master replica has been created and started, you must populate the database by setting policies and procedures and adding accounts.

38.4.1 Setting Policies and Properties

Use the **dcecp registry show** and **dcecp registry modify** commands to view policies and properties and to change them as desired. The **rgy_edit properties**, **policy**, and **authpolicy** commands perform the same functions.

38.4.2 Adding Accounts

After a new registry database is created, it contains only the principals, groups, organizations, and accounts that were added as initial information by **sec_create_db**. Use the **dcecp account create** command or **rgy_edit add** command to add any other names and accounts that your site requires. You can do this now or at any time later. See Chapter 31 for information about adding accounts by using **dcecp**.

38.5 Creating Slave Replicas

After the master replica database has been created and started and its database has been populated, you run **dce_config** at the slave sites to create the slave replicas and start them. To create and start a slave replica, **dce_config** first ensures that the sites are running **dced**, and the appropriate CDS servers. It then executes the following **sec_create_db** command:

*dcelocal/***bin/sec_create_db -slave -myname** *my_server_name*

First, the command creates a database for the new slave replica. The database consists of only stub files. The command then locates the master replica and adds the new slave to the master's replica list. The master marks the new replica for initialization. Finally, the **dce_config** script starts **secd** and ensures that it starts automatically each time the machine reboots.

You must run **dce_config** to configure a slave replica at each machine where you want to run a slave replica.

38.6 Verifying That the Replicas Are Running

After the master and slave replicas are in place and started, perform the following steps to ensure that they are running:

1. Invoke **sec_admin**, as follows:

dceshared/**bin/sec_admin**

```
Default replica:/.../giverny.com/subsys/dce/sec/art_server_master
Default cell:/.../giverny.com
sec_admin>
```

2. Issue the **lrep** command with the **-state** option to display all security servers and their status, as follows:

sec_admin> **lrep -state**

```
Default cell:/.../giverny.com
Default replica:/.../giverny.com/subsys/dce/sec/art_server_master

subsys/dce/sec/art_server_master (master)
        State:                 in service - master
        Last update time: Tue Feb  8 14:39:57 1994
subsys/dce/sec/mk
        State:                 in service - slave
        Last update time: Tue Feb  8 14:39:57 1994
```

Chapter 39

Importing UNIX Accounts to DCE

The **passwd_import** command creates entries in the registry that are based on information in the **/etc/passwd** and **/etc/group** files. It provides a method of ensuring account consistency between machines that use the DCE Security Service and those that do not, and a means of adding an existing UNIX user base to the registry.

39.1 How passwd_import Works

When **passwd_import** processes entries, it compares group and password file entries to registry entries. It can find two types of conflicts:

Name Conflicts   These conflicts arise when the same name string is defined in the registry and the group or password files. The names **joe 102** and **joe 555** exemplify such a conflict. The duplicate name can represent the same user or two different users.

UNIX ID Conflicts — These conflicts arise when the same UNIX ID is defined in the registry and the group or password files for users with different names. The names **joe 102** and **ann 102** exemplify such a conflict.

These conflicts can be found separately, as in the preceding examples, or together. For example, a registry entry of **joe 102** and a UNIX entry of **joe 102** are in conflict. When a conflict is found, you must either supply the information that is used to change the password and group file entries or inform **passwd_import** not to import that entry. The **passwd_import** command makes no changes to existing registry principals, groups, or accounts; but, if you so specify, it will create new principals, groups, and accounts in the registry that are based on the group and password files.

39.1.1 The passwd_import Processing Steps

As **passwd_import** processes entries, it performs the following steps in sequence:

1. It opens the group and password files and establishes a connection to the registry.

2. It compares the group file entries to groups in the registry. If there are no conflicts, it creates groups in the registry that correspond to the groups in the group file.

3. It compares the entries in the password file to principals in the registry. Again, if there are no conflicts, it

   - Creates principals in the registry that correspond to the entries in the password file.

   - Adds the newly created principals to the appropriate groups.

   - Creates accounts for the newly created principals.

4. It reexamines the group file and adds the principals as members of any additional groups that it finds there.

The changes to the registry are made individually as each step is processed. If you specify the **-o** option, **passwd_import** adds all newly created registry principals to the specified organization. If you do not specify the organization, the principals are added to the organization **none**.

39.1.2 Registry Entries Created by passwd_import

If an entry exists in the password or group file but does not exist in the registry, **passwd_import** creates a new registry entry. For additional registry information, **passwd_import** takes the following values:

- For Principal and Group Entries:

  - **Alias/Primary Name** = If the password file contains two entries with the same UNIX number, **passwd_import** creates a primary name entry for the first UNIX number it finds and an alias for each occurrence of the same UNIX number.

  - **Full Name** = A blank string; no full name is added for the entry.

  - **Membership List** = For new groups only, all principals that are listed in the group file and all principals with registry accounts that are associated with that group.

  - **Project List** = Yes (for groups only).

- For Account Entries:

  - **Account Expiration Date** = None.

  - **Account-Valid Flag** = No. Use the **dcecp acount modify** command to change this flag to **y** after the password is set.

  - **Client Flag** = Yes.

  - **Duplicate Certificate Flag** = No.

  - **Forwardable Certificate Flag** = Yes.

  - **GECOS** = The same value as the entry in the principal's GECOS field in the **etc/passwd** file.

  - **Good Since Date** = Time of the account creation.

  - **Home Directory** = The same value as the principal's home directory entry in the **/etc/passwd** file.

  - **Login Shell** = The same value as the principal's login shell entry in the **/etc/passwd** file.

  - **Maximum Certificate Lifetime** = Set to the registry authentication policy.

- **Maximum Certificate Renewable** = Set to the registry authentication policy.

- **Password** = Randomly generated. Note that you must modify or reset randomly generated passwords before user authentication is possible.

- **Password Date and Time Modified** = Set to the date and time **passwd_import** was run.

- **Password-Valid Flag** = No.

- **Postdated Certificate Flag** = No.

- **Proxiable Certificate Flag** = No.

- **Renewable Certificate Flag** = Yes.

- **Server Flag** = Yes.

- **TGT Authentication Flag** = Yes.

Note that **passwd_import** does not set usable passwords for the accounts it creates. You must use the **dcecp account modify** command to set passwords before authentication is possible.

39.2 The passwd_import Command Syntax

The **passwd_import** command has the following syntax:

dceshared/**bin/passwd_import** [**-h**] [**-c**] **-d** *pathname* [**-i**] [**-o** *org*] \
   [**-p** *password*] [**-u** *username*] [**-v**]

where:

-h

Displays usage information.

-c

Runs in check mode; processes the command showing conflicts, but makes no changes to the registry.

-d *pathname*

The path to the directory containing the password and group files to be imported.

-i

Specifies that identical name strings are not in conflict, but represent the same identity.

-o *org*	The name of the organization to be assigned to all principals that are added to the registry. The default is the organization named **none**.
-p *password*	The password for the account with whose privileges **passwd_import** will run. If you do not use the **-i** option, **passwd_import** prompts you to resolve the name conflict.
-u *username*	The principal name of the account with whose privileges **passwd_import** will run. This account must have the privileges to access the registry and add principals, groups, accounts and organizations, and members to groups and organizations. The principal name and password are used to obtain network authentication. If you do not supply them, **passwd_import** prompts you for them, even if you have already performed a network login.
-v	Runs in verbose mode, generating a verbose transcript of all activity.

39.3 Using passwd_import

To use **passwd_import**, the security server must be running. The following subsections describe how to use the **passwd_import** command and its options.

39.3.1 Using the Identical User Option

The **-i** option lets you specify that duplicate names are not in conflict but, instead, represent the same identity. When **passwd_import** finds duplicate name entries, it processes them as though they are the same user and skips to the next entry.

39.3.2 Using Check Mode

Run **passwd_import** first in check mode by using the **-c** option. In this mode, **passwd_import** attempts to simulate the results of a processing run, showing the conflicts that are encountered when **passwd_import** is run without the **-c** option.

Check mode gives you a good idea of the quantity and complexity of the potential conflicts. However, check mode does not make any changes to the registry. When you run **passwd_import** without the **-c** option and make changes to resolve conflicts, these changes can in turn create further conflicts not readily apparent in check mode.

If you encounter numerous conflicts in check mode, it is more efficient to manually edit either the registry or the UNIX group and password files to resolve some obvious conflicts before you run **passwd_import**.

39.3.3 Resolving Conflicts

The **passwd_import** command prompts you for instructions on how to resolve the conflicts it finds. You have the following choices:

- You can create an alias to resolve a UNIX ID conflict. This action creates an alias for the registry object that is in conflict. This alias is assigned the same name as the conflicting entry in the group or password file. For example, if the entry **joe 555** exists in the registry and the entry **tim 555** exists in the password file, this option creates the alias **tim** for **joe 555**.

- You can generate a new UNIX ID automatically or enter a new one explicitly to resolve a UNIX ID conflict. For example, if there is a conflict between the entry **joe 555** in the registry and **tim 555** in the password file, you can generate a new UNIX ID for **tim**.

- You can enter a new name to resolve a name conflict. For example, if there is a conflict between the entry **joe 555** in the registry and **joe 383** in the password file, you can generate a new name for **joe 383**. This new name will be added to the registry.

In addition, you are given the option of ignoring the conflict and skipping the entry.

39.3.4 Answering Prompts

When you run **passwd_import**, you can be prompted for names and numbers (UNIX IDs). Names can contain any characters or digits except the @ (at sign) and : (colon) characters, and they must not exceed 1024 characters in length.

If you enter a name or number in an incorrect format, **passwd_import** ignores your entry and prompts you again.

39.4 Sample passwd_import Session

This section shows a simplified **passwd_import** session. The sample session uses the following registry group and password entries and the UNIX group file and password file entries. For convenience, the registry entries are shown in the password and group file format, although they are not stored that way in the registry database.

Registry Group and Password Entries

- **Group Entries**

```
wheel::0:
daemon::1:
none::2:
backup::3:user
locksmith::4:
login::5:
mail::6:bin
bin::7:root
server::8:
sys::9:root
staff::10:
sys_admin::11:user
sys_proj::12:
tgroup::35:
```

- **Password Entries**

```
root:sq1RclUrrb1L6:0:10::/:
daemon:sq1RclUrrb1L6:1:2::/:
none:sq1RclUrrb1L6:2:2::/:
user:sq1RclUrrb1L6:3:2::/:
lp:sq1RclUrrb1L6:4:7::/:
sys_person:sq1RclUrrb1L6:5:2::/:
admin:sq1RclUrrb1L6:6:2::/:
uucp:sq1RclUrrb1L6:7:2::/usr/spool/uucppublic:
bin:sq1RclUrrb1L6:8:7::/:
```

UNIX Group and Password File Entries

- **Group File Entries**

```
system::0:root
other::1:
bin::2:root,bin,daemon
sys::3:root,bin,sys,adm
adm::4:root,adm,daemon
mail::6:root
rje::8:rje,shqer
daemon::12:root,daemon
tgroup::35:
diags::48:brown,smith,jones
cheetah::50:root,daemon
mkt_dev::52:roberts,anderson,hill
```

- **Password File Entries**

```
root::0:1:0000-Admin(0000):/:
daemon::1:1:0000-Admin(0000):/:
bin::2:2:0000-Admin(0000):/bin:
sys::3:3:0000-Admin(0000):/usr/src:
adm::4:4:0000-Admin(0000):/usr/adm:
uucp::5:5:0000-uucp(0000):/usr/lib/uucp:
rje::18:18:0000-rje(0000):/usr/rje:
trouble::70:1:trouble(0000):/usr/lib/trouble:
lp::71:2:0000-lp(0000):/usr/spool/lp:
setup::0:0:general system administration:/usr/admin:/bin/rsh
powerdown::0:0:general system administration:/usr/admin:/bin/rsh
sysadm::0:0:general system administration:/usr/admin:/bin/rsh
checkfsys::0:0:check diskette file system:/usr/admin:/bin/rsh
makefsys::0:0:make diskette file system:/usr/admin:/bin/rsh
mountfsys::0:0:mount diskette file system:/usr/admin:/bin/rsh
umountfsys::0:0:unmount diskette file system:/usr/admin:/bin/rsh
```

39.4.1 Invoking passwd_import

In the sample session, the following **passwd_import** command is entered at the shell prompt:

passwd_import -d sys5.3_tapes/adm -i -v -u cell_admin

This command specifies that

- Identical names represent the same identity (**-i**).

- The UNIX group and password files are in the **sys5.3_tapes/adm** directory.

- The command will not run in check mode (**-c** is not specified).

- The command will run in verbose mode (**-v** is specified).

- The principal whose account should be used for authentication is **cell_admin**.

- The command prompts you for the **cell_admin** account's password because the **-p** option is not used.

After the command is invoked, the system prepares for **passwd_import** processing by displaying the following:

```
Preparing import files. (dce / sad)
Setting up registry information. (dce / sad)
Verifying that the necessary Organization exists. (dce / sad)
Creating group objects from group file. (dce / sad)
```

As **passwd_import** reads the UNIX group and password files, it informs you of any conflicts and prompts for their resolution.

39.4.2 Examining the Group File

The **passwd_import** command first checks the group file for name and then UNIX ID conflicts. When you resolve the conflict by answering the prompt, **passwd_import** creates the groups in the registry if it is so directed.

The following steps show how UNIX ID group conflicts are handled:

1. The **passwd_import** command first finds a conflict between UNIX
    IDs, as shown in the preceding sections. The name **wheel** in the group
    file and the name **system** in the registry both have UNIX IDs of **0**.
    The **passwd_import** command prompts you for how to resolve the
    conflict, as follows:

    ```
    CONFLICT: (wheel 0) - Import Group's UNIX id exists in registry.
             (dce / sad)
             (system 0) is the conflicting entry from the registry.
    Do you wish to resolve the conflict (y) or skip this entry (n):
    ```

2. If you enter an **n** to skip the entry, **passwd_import** continues
    processing. If you enter a **y** to resolve the conflict, **passwd_import**
    prompts you for how to resolve the conflict. In the following
    example, the conflict is resolved by creating an alias of **wheel** for the
    system entry in the registry:

    ```
    Do you wish to resolve the conflict (y) or skip this entry (n): y
    Select one of: (a)lias, (g)enerate, (e)nter, (s)kip entry, (h)elp: a
    >> Adding Group entry for: wheel 0
    ```

    Because it is running in verbose mode, **passwd_import** describes the
    actions it is taking. Each action description is prefaced with the **>>**
    (redirection symbols).

    If you are running **passwd_import** in check mode, you are not
    prompted to resolve the conflict. Instead, you are informed of the
    conflict and processing continues. The message looks like the
    following display:

    ```
    CONFLICT: (wheel 0) - Import Group's UNIX id exists in registry.
             (dce / sad)
             (system 0) is the conflicting entry from the registry.
    Would need new UNIX id to resolve conflict. (dce / sad)
    ```

3. If **passwd_import** does not find conflicts that you must resolve, it
    displays the group entries as it processes them and, because it is
    running in verbose mode, the actions it is taking. In the following
    example, you are not prompted to resolve the name conflict because
    passwd_import was invoked with the **-i** option.

```
CONFLICT: (tgroup 35)
            - Group name exists in registry and UNIX ids match.
            (dce / sad)
>> Import Group:  - Ignoring name conflict, as instructed
            (dce / sad)
>> Adding Group entry for: diags 48
>> Adding Group entry for: cheetah 50
>> Adding Group entry for: mkt_dev 52
```

As **passwd_import** continues through the UNIX group file, it finds two other UNIX ID conflicts: UNIX entries **adm 4** and **rje 8**, which are in conflict with registry entries **locksmith 4** and **server 8**, respectively.

39.4.3 Examining the Password File

The **passwd_import** command then proceeds to examine the password file for conflicts. As it begins, it displays the following:

```
Creating principal entries and accounts from password file.
        (dce / sad)
```

When an entry is processed with no conflicts, **passwd_import** creates the principal in the registry, adds the principal to the appropriate group and organization, and creates an account for the principal. As it does this, it displays the following:

```
>> Adding Principal entry for: rje
>> Adding account for rje none.
```

The following example shows the warning message that is displayed when **passwd_import** finds a conflict:

```
CONFLICT: (bin 2)
            - Principal name exists in registry and UNIX ids match.
            (dce / sad)
>> Import Principal:  - Ignoring name conflict, as instructed
            (dce / sad)
```

This message notifies you that the account for **bin** exists in the registry. Both accounts remain unchanged even though the UNIX password file entry contains information that differs from the registry account.

Because the **-i** option is specified in the command used in the sample session, name conflicts are ignored. The following example shows the prompt from a name conflict that was found when **passwd_import** was run without the **-i** option:

```
CONFLICT: (daemon 1)
           - Principal name exists in registry and UNIX ids match.
             (dce / sad)
Do you wish to resolve the conflict (y) or skip this entry (n):
```

If you enter an **n**, the entry is skipped and processing continues. If you enter a **y**, **passwd_import** prompts you for the new name for the foreign principal, as follows:

```
Enter new name for principal "daemon" "1":
```

39.4.4 Adding Members to Groups

When **passwd_import** completes the processing of the UNIX password file, it reexamines the group file and adds the newly created principals to any additional groups that it finds there. As it does, it displays the following:

```
Add memberships from imported group file. (dce / sad)
>> Add root as member of group with UNIX id: 0
>> Add root as member of group with UNIX id: 2
>> Add daemon as member of group with UNIX id: 2
```

39.4.5 Completing Processing

When **passwd_import** completes processing, it displays the following:

```
Closing import files. (dce / sad)
Closing connection to registry. (dce / sad)
```

Chapter 40

Troubleshooting Procedures

This chapter contains procedures for troubleshooting the security servers. Use these procedures only when network or hardware failures disrupt operation of the registry, or when you encounter problems that can be remedied in no other way. These procedures tell you how to

- Restart a security server

- Restart a security server in locksmith mode

- Restore replicas from a backup

- Forcibly delete a slave replica

- Adopt a registry object that was orphaned because its owner was deleted

Before you run the procedures, ensure that you are logged in via an administrative account.

40.1 Restarting Security Servers

To restart a security server (master or slave), enter the following command:

dcelocal/**bin/secd &**

For convenience, set up the server to start automatically whenever the machine reboots.

40.2 Restarting the Master Server in Locksmith Mode

The **secd -locksmith** option starts **secd** in locksmith mode. This option can be used only on the master replica. In locksmith mode, the principal name that you specify to **secd** becomes the locksmith principal. As the locksmith principal, you can repair malicious or accidental changes that prevent you from logging in with full registry access privileges.

When you bring up a security server in locksmith mode, **secd** automatically creates a locksmith account or, if the locksmith account exists, it lets you supply a new password for that account. Once the security server is running, you can log into the locksmith account by using the newly changed password, if you changed it, and access the registry to change the account or policy information that may have prevented you from accessing the registry by using your normal credentials.

In locksmith mode, all principals with valid accounts can log in and operate on the registry with normal access checking. The locksmith principal, however, is granted special access to the registry: no access checking is performed for the authenticated locksmith principal. This means that, as the locksmith principal, you can operate on the registry with full access.

40.2.1 Automatic Changes to the Locksmith Account

If the locksmith account exists when you start the security server in locksmith mode, the security server checks certain account and registry policy information and makes the changes shown in Tables 40-1 and 40-2. These changes ensure that, even if account or registry policy was tampered with, you will now be able to log into the locksmith account. For example, if an intruder changes the Account Lifespan registry policy to 1 minute, the locksmith account will never be valid long enough to be used. Therefore, if the security server finds that the Account Lifespan registry policy is set to less than what is required for the locksmith account to be valid for at least 1 hour, it changes the Account Lifespan policy to be the time difference between the creation time of the locksmith account and the time 1 hour from the current time.

Table 40–1. Locksmith Account Changes Made by the Security Server

If the security server finds the...	It changes the....
Password-Valid Flag is set to **no**	Password-Valid Flag to **yes**
Account Expiration Date is set to less than the current time plus 1 hour	Account Expiration Date to the current time plus 1 hour
Client Flag is set to **no**	Client Flag to **yes**
Account-Valid Flag is set to **no**	Account-Valid Flag to **yes**
Good Since Date is set to greater than the current time	Good Since Date to the current time
Password Expiration Date is set to less than the current time plus 1 hour	Password Expiration Date to the current time plus 1 hour

Table 40–2. Registry Policy Changes Made by the Security Server

If the security server finds the...	It changes the....
Account Lifespan is set to less than the difference between the locksmith account creation date and the current time plus 1 hour	Account Lifespan to the current time plus 1 hour minus the locksmith account creation date
Password Expiration Date is set to greater than the time the password was last changed but less than the current time plus 1 hour	Password Expiration Date to the current time plus 1 hour

40.2.2 Starting a Security Server in Locksmith Mode

Use the following form of the **secd** command to start a security server in locksmith mode:

dcelocal/**bin/secd** [**-locksm[ith]** *pname* [**-lockpw**] [**-rem[ote]**]]]

where:

-locksm[ith]   Starts a security server in locksmith mode.

pname   Specifies the name of the locksmith principal. If no registry account exists for this principal, **secd** creates one.

-lockpw   Prompts for a new locksmith password. This option allows you to specify a new password for the locksmith account when the old one is unknown.

-rem[ote]   Allows the locksmith principal to log in remotely. If this option is not used, the principal must log in from the local machine on which **secd** will be started.

40.2.3 Restarting a Security Server in Locksmith Mode

To restart a security server in locksmith mode, perform the following steps on the node on which the master replica is running. You must have **root** access to this node.

1. Shut down the security server.

    a. If you cannot log in with administrative privileges and access **dcecp** to shut down the server, log in as **root** on the machine on which the server is running and kill the security server process.

    b. If you are able to log in with administrative privileges, use the **dcecp registry stop** command to shut down the security server. When you use this command, you must supply the fully qualified name of the replica to stop as an argument. The following sample command stops the replica named **slave_3**:

        dcecp> **registry stop /.../giverny.com/subsys/dce/sec/slave_3**

2. Start the security server in locksmith mode. The following example shows the security server started with the locksmith account that was created for the principal named **master_admin**. The **-remote** option is also supplied to allow **master_admin** to log in from a remote node; otherwise, **master_admin** must log in from the node on which the security server was started.

    dcelocal/**bin/secd -locksmith master_admin -remote**

    If the locksmith account exists but you have lost its password, use the **-lockpw** option to cause **secd** to prompt you for a new locksmith password and replace the existing password with the one you enter.

The security server normally runs in the background. When you start a security server in locksmith mode, it runs in the foreground so that you can answer prompts.

Once the security server is started in locksmith mode, you can use the **dcecp registry modify** command to change the registry so that the standard privileged account can access it. After these changes are made, you should do the following:

1. Shut down the security server that is running in locksmith mode.

2. Restart a security server according to your standard procedures.

40.3 Recovering the Master Replica

To recover a master replica because the master's database is damaged, you can use either of the following methods:

- Use the **dcecp registry set master** command to make a slave replica the master replica and create a slave replica on the host of the former master. This method is described in the following subsection.

- Restore the master from a backup. This method is described in Chapter 36.

The method you choose depends on whether the master replica's backup database or the slave replica's database is more current.

40.3.1 Determining the Most Current Database

To determine whether the backup of the master replica's database or a slave replica's database is more current, run the **dcecp registry show -replica** command for the replica. The output of this command lists the last update sequence number and the update date and time. Compare the replica's last update sequence number and the update date and time with the sequence number and date and time of the master's backup. If the replica is more current, make the replica the new master as described in the following section. If the master's backup is more current, restore the master from the backup as described in Chapter 36.

40.3.2 Turning a Slave into the Master

This subsection describes how to use the **dcecp registry set -master** command to turn a slave into the master. Be aware that, because the **registry set -master** command can cause data to be lost, the **registry set** command without the **-master** option is the preferred means of designating a different master replica. Use the **registry set -master** command only if the master replica is irrevocably damaged and you are unable to use the **registry set** command without the **-master** option.

Follow these steps to turn a master replica into a slave replica:

1. Choose the slave replica that will become the new master.

2. If necessary, issue the **set _s(sec)** command to set the chosen slave to the default replica. The following example sets the default replica to **/.../musee.com/subsys/dce/sec/art**:

   dcecp> **set _s(sec) /.../musee.com/subsys/dce/sec/art**

3. Issue the following **registry set -master** command to change the default host to the master registry:

   dcecp> **registry set -master**

4. Use the **registry show -replica** command to verify the change.

5. Use standard UNIX commands to delete the old master replica's database and **.mkey** file by deleting the directory *dcelocal***/var/security/rgy_data** and the file *dcelocal***/var/.mkey**.

6. Use the **registry delete** command with the **-force** option to remove the old master from the replica list. The following example deletes the old master named **history** from the replica list:

   dcecp> **registry delete -force /.../musee.com/subsys/dce/sec/history**

40.4 Recovering Slave Replicas

Because slave replicas are not backed up, you must recreate a replica to restore a replica that is corrupted. To do so, use the following procedure:

1. Use standard UNIX commands to manually delete the replica's database files and master key file. To do this, delete all the files in **/opt/***dcelocal***/var/security/rgy_data**, as well as the file in **/opt/***dcelocal***/var/security/.mkey**.

2. Use the **set _s(sec)** command to bind to the master and then the **dcecp registry delete -force** command to delete the replica from the master's replica list. The following commands first bind to the master **/.../musee.com/subsys/dce/sec/master** and then delete the replica **/.../musee.com/subsys/dce/sec/art**.

    dcecp> **set _s(sec) /.../musee.com/subsys/dce/sec/master**
    dcecp> **registry delete /.../musee.com/subsys/dce/sec/art -force**

3. Use standard UNIX commands to copy the file **/opt/dcelocal/etc/security/pe_site** from the machine running the master to the machine that will run the replica.

4. Use **/etc/dce_config** (or your provider's equivalent) on the replica machine to do the following:

    a. Stop DCE daemons.

    b. Start DCE daemons.

    c. Configure a security server replica. This configuration creates the replica's database and starts **secd**.

5. When you configure the replica in the previous step, you assign it a name. If you did not give this replica the same name that it previously had, the old name must be deleted from CDS by performing the following steps:

    a. Deleting the replica's server entry name from **/.:/subsys/dce/sec**

    b. Deleting the replica's name from the CDS group **/.:/sec**

40.5 Turning a Master into a Slave

Use this procedure to turn a master replica into a slave. Use this procedure only if you have more than one master running on your network or the Internet, which is a highly unusual condition.

1. Choose the master replica that will become a slave.

2. If necessary, issue the **dcecp set _s(sec)** command to to set the chosen master to the default host. The following example sets the default host to **/.../dublin.com/subsys/dce/sec/lit:**

    dcecp> **set _s(sec)/.../dublin.com/subsys/dce/sec/lit:**

3. Issue the following **registry set -slave** command to change the chosen master to a slave:

    dcecp> **registry set -slave**

4. Use the **registry show -replica** command to verify the change.

40.6 Forcibly Deleting a Slave Replica

The procedure described in this section explains how to forcibly delete a slave replica. Use this drastic method only when the ordinary method of deletion described in Chapter 37 fails.

To forcibly delete a slave replica, use the **dcecp registry delete** command with the **-force** option. This command deletes the slave replica from the master's replica list. The master then propagates the delete request to the other replicas. Since this operation never communicates with the deleted replica, use the **-force** option only when the replica dies and cannot be restarted. If a forcibly deleted replica continues operation, use the **registry delete** command with the **-only** option to stop the server and delete its database. You can also simply stop **secd** (by using the **dcecp registry stop** command) and delete or rename its database.

The **-uuid** option creates a principal, group, or organization and lets you specify the UUID with which it should be associated instead of assigning it automatically. Except for the manner in which it is created, a principal, group, or organization created by these commands is no different from any other principal, group, or organization. The following examples show how to use this option to create a principal, group, or organization to adopt an orphaned registry object.

To create a principal associated with the UUID that owns the orphaned object, use the following command:

principal create *name* **-uuid** *uuid* [**-fullname** *fullname*] \
   [**-quota** *object_creation_quota*] [**-uid** *UNIX_number*]

To create a group associated with the UUID that owns the orphaned object, use the following command:

group create *name* **-uuid** *uuid* [**-fullname** *string*] \
   [**-inprojlist** [**yes** | **no**]] [**-gid** *UNIX_number*]

To create an organization associated with the UUID that owns the orphaned object, use the following command:

group create *name* [**-fullname** *string*] [**-gid** *UNIX_number*]

where:

name
   The principal's, group's, or organization's primary name.

uuid
   The UUID number to be assigned to the principal, group, or organization. This UUID should be the one that owns the orphaned object (that is, the one that was associated with the deleted registry object). The UUID is specified in RPC print string format as 8 hexadecimal digits, a hyphen; 4 hexadecimal digits, a hyphen; 4 hexadecimal digits, a hyphen; 4 hexadecimal digits, a hyphen; and 12 hexadecimal digits. The format is as follows:

nnnnnnnn-nnnn-nnnn-nnnn-nnnnnnnnnnnn

string The principal's, group's, or organization's full name.

UNIX_number For cell principals *only,* the UNIX number to be associated with the name. If you do not enter this option, the next sequential UNIX number is supplied. For all principals other than cells, the UNIX number is extracted from information that is embedded in the principal's UUID and cannot be specified here.

object_creation_quota For principals *only*, the principal's object creation quota. If you do not enter this option, the default is **unlimited**.

-inprojlist For groups *only*, **yes** turns off the project list inclusion so that groups are not included in project lists. If you enter **no**, the group is included in project lists.

Note: In the current implementation of DCE, UNIX numbers are embedded in UUIDs. If you try to create a group or organization to adopt an orphaned object and fail, it could be because the embedded UNIX number is invalid because it does not fall within the range of valid UNIX numbers set for the cell as a registry property. If this is the case, you must reset the range of valid UNIX number to include the UNIX number embedded in the UUID and then try again to adopt the object. See Chapter 35 for information on setting the valid range of UNIX numbers.

Accessing Registry Objects

This chapter describes the permissions that apply to objects in the registry. Because the permissions that are granted are based on the way the registry database is structured, this chapter first briefly describes the structure of the registry database. It then describes the permissions for each object in the registry database, the registry ACL managers, and the initial registry ACLs.

Both **dcecp** and the **acl_edit** command have functions for creating, modifying, and deleting ACL entries for registry objects. See each command's reference page in the *OSF DCE Command Reference* for a description of the operations it performs on ACL entries.

41.1 The Registry Database

The registry is structured into the following main directories:

- The **principal** directory—Contains information about principals

- The **group** directory—Contains information about groups

- The **org** directory—Contains information about organizations

In addition to the directories, the registry contains the **policy** object, the **replist** object, and the **xattrschema** object, all of which are created when the registry is created during machine configuration. The **policy** object contains information that applies to registry properties and policies and organization policies; the **replist** object contains information about the replicas in the DCE cell; and the **xattrschema** object contains information about extended registry attributes (ERAs). You can modify **policy** and **replica** information at any time by using the **dcecp registry** commands. The **xattrschema** object is modified by using the **dcecp xattrschema** commands.

When you create simple objects in the **principal**, **group**, or **org** directory, subdirectories are created as needed. For example, if you add a principal such as **preludes/villa/lobos**, the subdirectories **preludes** and **villa** are created. You can use these subdirectories to help organize your data. When you delete all objects in a subdirectory, the subdirectory itself is deleted. (You cannot delete the **principal**, **group**, or **org** directory.)

The permissions that are granted to objects in the registry depend on where the object fits in the structure of the registry database. Figure 41-1 illustrates the registry database. The boxes represent container objects (directories). The ovals represent simple objects. Figure 41-1 shows only the top level **principal**, **group**, and **org** directories. Your registry can have subdirectories if you create them.

Figure 41–1. The Registry Database Structure

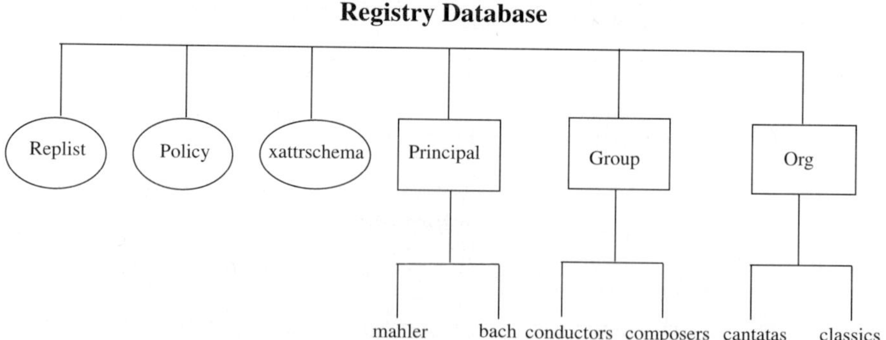

41.2 Registry Permissions

Table 41-1 lists the permissions that can be granted for the object types found in the registry.

Table 41–1. Permissions for Registry Objects

Permission	Meaning
A	Execute commands that act on replicas (**sec_admin**).
a	Modifies authentication information.
c	Modifies ACLs on objects. All registry ACLs must have one entry that specifies c (control) permission.
d	Deletes from an object's contents.
D	Deletes an object from the registry.
f	Modifies a principal's, group's, or organization's full name.
g	Adds a principal to a group.
i	Adds to a object's contents.
m	Modifies management information.
M	Adds and deletes members from this group or organization. To add a member to a group, you must also have **g** permission for the principal to be added.
n	Modifies the name of a directory, a principal, a group, or an organization.
u	Modifies user information.
r	Views management, authentication, and user information.
t	Tests the group or organization membership of a named principal.

41.2.1 Management, Authentication, and User Information

The registry contains three different kinds of information about the objects in it: management information, authentication information, and user information. The specific items of information that are kept for each object type are summarized in the following subsections.

41.2.1.1 Management Information

Management information includes the following categories:

- For registry policies and properties

  — The account lifespan

  — The password minimum length

  — The password lifespan

  — Whether or not passwords can contain spaces

  — Whether or not passwords can consist of all nonalphanumeric characters

  — The password expiration date

  — The minimum ticket lifetime

  — The default ticket lifetime

  — A number that defines the lowest UNIX ID that is supplied automatically when principals, groups, or organizations are created

  — A number that defines the highest number that can be supplied (either automatically or manually) as a UNIX ID when principals, groups, or organizations are created

  — Whether or not encrypted passwords are displayed (the shadow password property)

- For principals

  — The account, group, and organization names

  — Text string showing the full name of the principal

- — Object creation quota for the principal

- — Whether the principal can change primary names to aliases and aliases to primary names

- — User Identifier (UID) of the principal

- — Unique User Identifier (UUID) of the principal

- — The expiration date for the principal's account

- — The Account-Valid Flag for the principal's account

- — Flags that indicate whether the account is for a principal that can act as a client or as a server

- For groups

  - — Primary name of the group

  - — Text string showing the full name of the group

  - — Whether the group's primary name can be changed to an alias and its aliases to its primary name

  - — Group Identifier (GID) for the group

  - — The project list inclusion property

  - — UUID of the group

- For organizations

  - — Primary name of the organization

  - — Whether the organization's primary name can be changed to an alias and its aliases to its primary name

  - — Text string showing the full name of the organization

  - — Organization Identifier (ORGID) for the organization

  - — UUID of the organization

  - — The account lifespan

  - — The password minimum length

  - — The password lifespan

  - — The password expiration date

— Whether or not passwords can contain spaces

— Whether or not passwords can consist of all nonalphanumeric characters

- For the **xattrschema** object

— Whether or not the xattrschema can be modified

41.2.1.2 Authentication Information

Authentication information includes the following categories:

- For registry policies and properties

— The maximum ticket lifetime

— The maximum time for which tickets can be renewed

- For principals

— The maximum ticket lifetime for the principal's account

— The maximum time for which tickets that are issued to the principal's account can be renewed

— The date and time that the principal's account was last changed (Good Since Date)

— The date and time that the principal's account was enabled (Last Changed Date)

— The creator of the principal's account and account creation date

— Description of the account's use

— Whether the principal's account can be issued postdated tickets, forwardable tickets, renewable tickets, or proxiable tickets

— Whether the DCE Authentication Service can issue tickets to the principal's account based on ticket-granting ticket authorization or whether principals must obtain tickets directly for the service

— Whether the principal's account can be issued duplicate session keys

41.2.1.3 User Information

User information includes the following information pertaining to a principal's account:

- Password

- Home directory

- Miscellaneous information (GECOS information)

- Login shell

- Password-Valid Flag

41.2.2 Permission Required to Create Principals, Groups, or Organizations

Figure 41-2 shows the permission that is required to create principals, groups, or organizations.

Figure 41–2. Permission Required to Create Principals, Groups, or Organizations

Parent Directory

i permission

To create a principal, group, or organization, you must have **i** permission on the directory in which you create the principal, group, or organization. For example, to create the principal **preludes/villa/lobos**, you must have **i** on **villa**.

41.2.3 Permissions Required to Delete Principals, Group, or Organizations

Figure 41-3 shows the permissions that are required to delete principals, groups, or organizations.

Figure 41–3. Permissions Required to Delete Principals, Groups, or Organizations

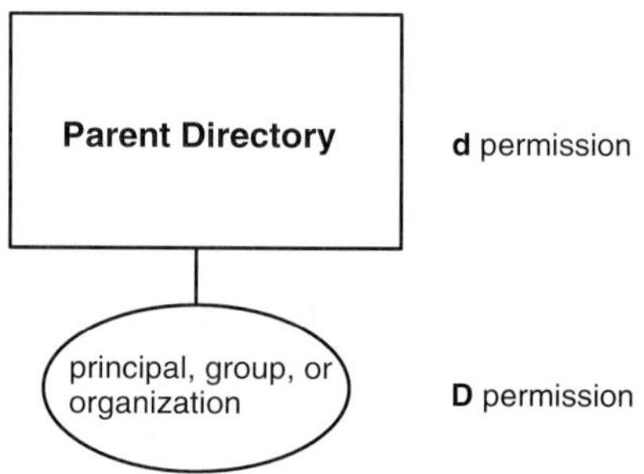

To delete principals, groups, or organizations, you must have the following permissions:

- The **d** permission on the directory in which the principal to be deleted exists

- The **rD** permission on the principal, group, or organization to be deleted

For example, to delete the principal **preludes/villa/lobos**, you must have the **d** permission for the **preludes/villa** directory, and **rD** permissions for the principal **preludes/villa/lobos**.

41.2.4 Permissions Required to Add Accounts

When you add accounts, **dcecp** or the **rgy_edit** command add the principal to the group or organization that is named in the account, if the principal is not already a member of the group and/or organization. For this reason, the permissions that are required to add an account may include the permissions that are required to add a member to a group or organization. The following topics are covered in the discussion of the permissions required to add accounts:

- The permissions that are required to add an account and at the same time add the principal as a member of the group and organization that is named in the account. (See Section 41.2.4.1.)

- The permissions that are required to add an account for which the principal is already a member of the named group and organization. (See Section 41.2.4.2.)

- The permissions that are required to add an account and add the principal only to the group that is named in the account (because the principal is already a member of the organization). (See Section 41.2.4.3.)

- The permissions that are required to add an account and add the principal only to the organization that is named in the account (because the principal is already a member of the group). (See Section 41.2.4.4.)

41.2.4.1 Adding an Account and the Account Principal to the Group and Organization

Figure 41-4 shows the permissions required to add an account and the account principals to the group or organization.

Figure 41–4. Permissions Required to Add an Account and the Account Principal to the Group and Organization

To add an account and add the account's principal to the group and the organization named in the account automatically, you must have the following permissions:

- The **maug** permissions on the account's principal

Figure 41–10. Permissions Required to Add Members to Organizations

To add members to organizations, you must have the following permissions:

- The **rM** permissions on the organization to which the principal is being added

- The **r** permissions on the principal to be added

For example, to add the principal **preludes/villa/lobos** to the organization **pianists**, you must have the following permissions:

- The **rM** permissions on the organization **pianists**

- The **r** permission on the principal **lobos**

41.2.8 Permissions to Delete Members from Groups or Organizations

Figure 41-11 shows the permissions that are required to delete members from groups or organizations.

Figure 41–11. Permissions to Delete Members From Groups or Organizations

To delete members from a group or organization, you need the **rM** permissions on the group or organization from which the principal is being deleted and the **r** permission on the principal being deleted.

For example, to delete the principal **preludes/villa/lobos** from the group **composers**, you must have the following permissions:

- The **rM** permissions on the group **composers**

- The **r** permission on the principal **lobos**

41.2.9 Permissions Required to Change a Principal's, Group's, or Organization's Full Name

Figure 41-12 shows the permissions that are required to change a principal's, a group's, or an organization's full name.

Figure 41–12. Permissions Required to Change a Principal's, Group's, or Organization's Full Name

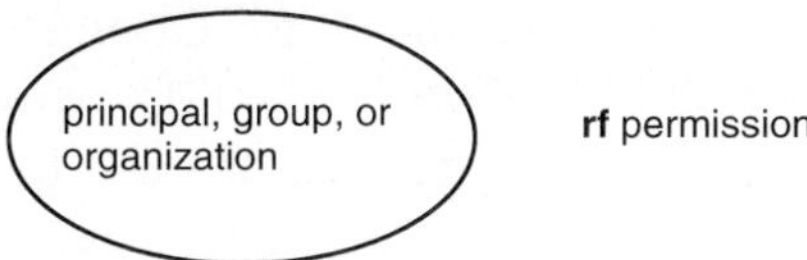

To change a principal's, group's, or organization's full name, you must have the **rf** permissions for the principal, group, or organization for which you are making the change.

41.2.10 Permissions Required to Change Management Information for Principals, Groups, or Organizations

Figure 41-13 shows the permissions that are required to change management information for principals, groups, or organizations.

Figure 41–13. Permissions Required to Change Management Information For Principals, Groups, or Organizations

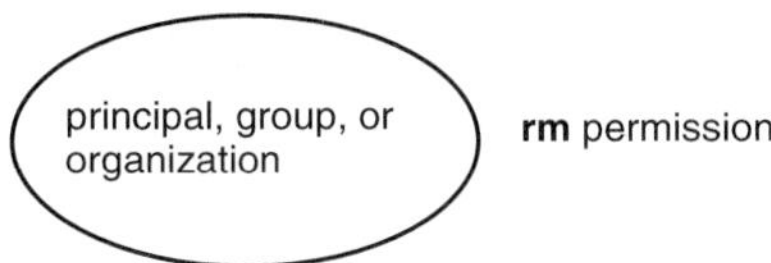

To change management information for a principal, a group, or an organization, you must have the **rm** permissions for the object for which you are changing management information.

41.2.11 Permissions Required to Change Management, Authentication, and User Information (Except Passwords) for Accounts

Figure 41-14 shows the permissions that are required to change management, authentication, and user information (except passwords) for accounts.

Figure 41–14. Permissions Required to Change Management, Authentication, and User Information (Except Passwords) For Accounts

To change all management, authentication, and user information (except passwords) for accounts, you must have the following permissions for the principal that is named in the account:

- The **ra** permission to change authentication information

- The **rm** permission to change management information

- The **ru** permission to change user information

41.2.12 Permissions Required to Change Passwords for Accounts

Figure 41-15 shows the permissions that are required to change passwords for accounts.

Figure 41–15. Permissions Required to Change Passwords For Accounts

To change passwords for accounts, you must have the following permissions for the principal that is named in the account:

- The **ru** permissions on the account's principal

- The **r** permission on the registry **policy** object

41.2.13 Permissions Required to Change Authentication and Management Information for Registry Policies and Properties

Figure 41-16 shows the permissions that are required to change authentication and management information for registry policies and properties.

Figure 41–16. Permissions Required to Change Authentication and Management Information For Registry Policies and Properties

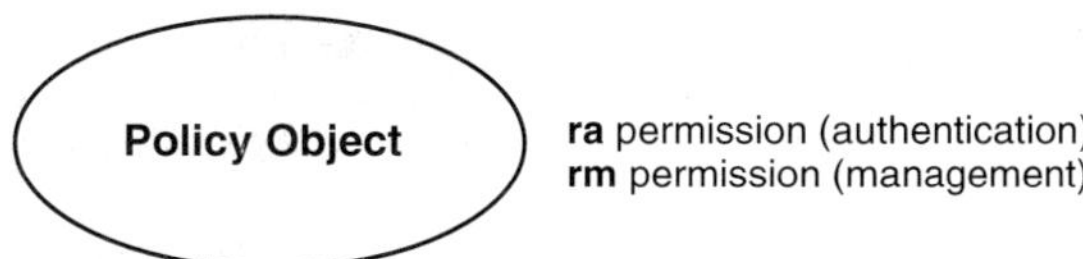

To change management or authentication information for the registry by using the **dcecp registry modify** command or the **rgy_edit prop**, **po**, and **auth** commands, you must have the **ra** permissions to change authentication information or the **rm** permissions to change management information for the registry **policy** object.

41.2.14 Permissions Required to Execute Commands That Act on Replicas

Figure 41-17 shows the permissions that are required to execute commands that act on replicas.

Figure 41–17. Permissions Required to Execute Commands That Act on Replicas

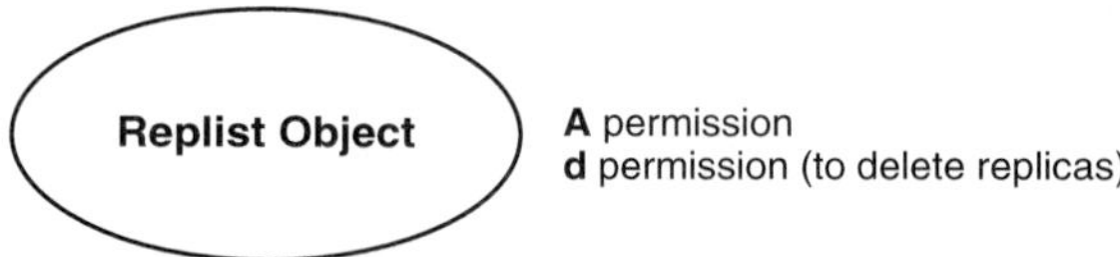

To execute any of the commands that act on replicas, you must have the following permissions on the **replist** object:

- The **A** permission to execute all commands except for those that display replica information, which require no permissions on the **replist** object.

- The **d** permission to execute the commands that delete replicas.

41.2.15 Permissions Required to Create Extended Registry Attribute Types

Figure 41-18 shows the permission that is required to create ERA types.

Figure 41–18. Permissions Required to Create Extended Registry Attribute Types

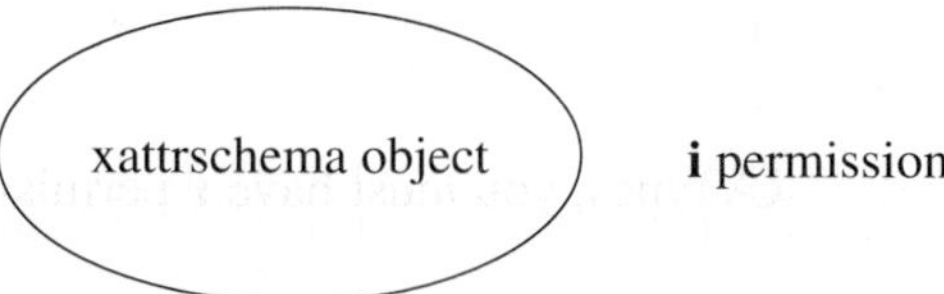

To create an ERA type in the registry schema, you must have **i** permission on the **xattrschema** object.

41.2.16 Permissions Required to Delete Extended Registry Attribute Types

Figure 41-19 shows the permissions that are required to delete ERA types.

Figure 41–19. Permissions Required to Delete Extended Registry Attribute Types

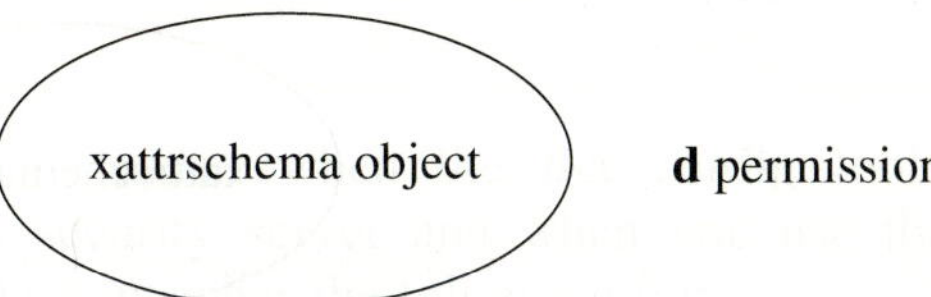

To delete ERA types, you must have **d** permission on the **xattrschema** object.

41.2.17 Permissions Required to View Extended Registry Attribute Types

Figure 41-20 shows the permission that is required to view one or more ERAs in the registry's schema database (with the **dcecp schema show** command).

Figure 41–20. Permissions Required to View Extended Registry Attributes

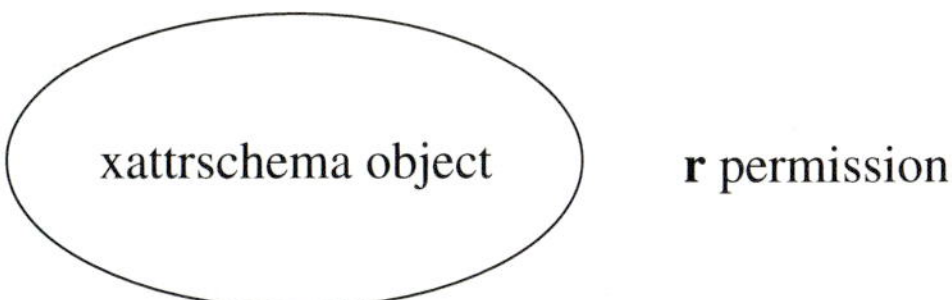

To view ERA types, you must have **r** permission on the **xattrschema** object.

Table 41–2. ACL managers and Valid Permissions and ACL Entry Types

Manager Type	Controls	Valid Permissions	Invalid ACL Entry Types
dir	**directory** objects	**rcidDn**	**user_obj, group_obj**
policy	the **policy** object	**rcma**	**user_obj, group_obj**
principal	**principal** objects	**rcDnfmaug**	**group_obj**
group	**group** objects	**rctDnfmM**	**user_obj**
org	**org** objects	**rctDnfmM**	**user_obj, group_obj**
replist	replica lists	**cidmlA**	**user_obj, group_obj**
xattrschema	ERA types	**rcidm**	**user_obj, group_obj**

41.4 Initial Registry ACLs

When the registry database is created, the **principal**, **group**, and **org** directories and the **policy**, **replist**, and **xattrschema** objects are given initial ACLs. As new objects are created in the registry, they inherit their ACLs from the **principal**, **group**, and **org** directory ACLs. The ACL entry key for those initial ACL entries that require a key is the name of the principal that creates the registry database (supplied to the **sec_create_db** command as the registry creator), or **root** if no name is supplied. (See Chapter 38 for more information on **sec_create_db** and the registry creator.)

The initial ACLs that are created when the registry database is created are described in the following list. In the list, *rgy_creator* signifies the principal that is named as the registry creator.

Note: You platform's configuration tool may update these initial ACLs.

- For **principal** objects

```
unauthenticated:r--------
user_obj:r---f--ug
user:rgy_creator:rcDnFmaug
other_obj:r-------g
any_other:r--------
```

- For **group** objects

```
unauthenticated:r-t-----
user:rgy_creator:rctDnfmM
group_obj:r-t-----
other_obj:r-t-----
any_other:r-t-----
```

- For **org** objects

```
unauthenticated:r-t-----
user:rgy_creator:rctDnfmM
other_obj:r-t-----
any_other:r-t-----
```

- For the **policy** object

```
unauthenticated:r----
user:rgy_creator:rcma
other_obj:r----
any_other:r----
```

- For **directory** objects

```
unauthenticated:r-----
user:rgy_creator:rcidDn
other_obj:r-----
any_other:r-----
```

- For the **replist** object

```
user:cell_admin:cidmA-
```

- For the **xattrschema** object

```
unauthenticated:r-----
user:cell_admin:rcidm
other_obj:r-----
any_other:r-----
```

Chapter 42

DCE Audit Service

Auditing plays a critical role in distributed systems. Adequate audit facilities are necessary for detecting and recording critical events in distributed applications.

Auditing, a key component of DCE, is provided by the DCE Audit Service. This chapter provides an introduction to the DCE Audit Service.

42.1 Features of the DCE Audit Service

The DCE Audit Service has the following features:

- An audit daemon (**auditd**) performs the logging of audit records based on specified criteria.

- Application programming interfaces (APIs) can be used as part of application server programs to record audit events. These APIs can also be used to create tools that can analyze the audit records.

- An administrative command interface to the audit daemon directs the daemon in selecting the events that are going to be recorded based on certain criteria. This interface is accessed through the DCE control program (**dcecp**).

- An event classification mechanism allows the logical grouping of a set of events for ease of administration.

- Audit records can be directed to logs or to the console.

42.2 Components of the DCE Audit Service

The DCE Audit Service has three basic components:

- Application programming interfaces (APIs)

  Provide the functions that are used to detect and record critical events when the application server services a client. The application programmer uses these functions at certain *code points* in the application server program to actuate the recording of audit events. Other APIs can be used to create tools that examine and analyze the audit event records.

- audit daemon

  The audit daemon provides the following services:

  — Maintains the filters and the central audit trail file.

  — Exports an RPC interface with which it can be controlled by the DCE control program (**dcecp**).

- DCE control program

  The DCE Audit Service's management interface to the audit daemon. As an administrator, you can use it to specify how the audit daemon will filter the recording of audit events.

42.3 DCE Audit Service Concepts

This section describes some of the concepts that are relevant to the administration of the DCE Audit Service.

42.3.1 Audit Clients

All RPC-based servers are potential audit clients; DCE servers and user-written application servers. The DCE Security Service and the Distributed Time Service are auditable. That is, code points (discussed in the next section) are already in place in these services.

The audit daemon can also audit itself.

Audit clients should have the **log** permission to the audit daemon object to be able to use the central audit trail file. Permissions to the audit daemon are discussed in Chapter 43.

42.3.2 Code Points

A code point is a location in the application server program where DCE audit APIs are used. Code points generally correspond to operations or functions offered by the application server that requires audit. For example, if a bank server offers the cash withdrawal function **acct_withdraw( )**, this function may be deemed to be an auditable event and be designated as a code point.

Code points are already in place in the DCE Security Service, Distributed Time Service, and Audit Service code. Code points and their associated events for the DCE Security Service are documented in the **sec_audit_events(5sec)** reference page. Code points and their associated events for the DCE Distributed Time Service are documented in the **dts_audit_events(5sec)** reference page. Code points and their associated events for the DCE Audit Service are documented in the **aud_audit_events(5sec)** reference page.

42.3.3 Audit Events

An audit event is any event that an audit client wishes to record. Generally, audit events involve the integrity of the system. For example, when a client withdraws cash from his bank account, this can be an audit event because it can involve a possible security violation on the bank account.

An audit event is associated with a code point in the application server code.

42.3.4 Event Numbers

Every audit event is assigned an event number by the application programmer. The event number is a 32-bit integer, such as 0xC0000000. Event numbers are discussed in more detail in the *OSF DCE Application Development Guide—Core Components*.

42.3.5 Event Classes

Audit events can be logically grouped together into an event class. Event classes provide an efficient mechanism by which sets of events can be specified by a single value. Generally, an event class consists of audit events with some commonality. For example, in a bank server program, the cash transactions (deposit, withdrawal, and transfer) may be grouped into an event class. Event classes are also discussed in Chapter 43.

42.3.5.1 Event Class Files

Event classes are defined in *event class files*. All event class files must be created in the *dcelocal*/**etc/audit/ec** directory.

Default event class files are provided to classify auditable events from the DCE Security Service, Time Service, and Audit Service. They are installed on the host system when any of these services is installed.

The name of an event class is the same as its filename. Each event class is defined within an event class file.

You can define new event classes by removing or adding event numbers in the event class files, or by creating new event class files.

42.3.5.2 Event Class Names

Each event class has a symbolic name assigned to it. Following is the suggested name format of event classes that vendors should follow:

ec_*org_product_class*

where:

org   Is the name of the organization or company that defines the event class.

product Is the name of the product for which the event class is defined.

class   Is the characterization of the event class.

The following are two examples of event class names:

- **ec_osf_dce_authentication**—Defines an authentication event class for OSF's DCE core components.

- **ec_transarc_encina_update**—Defines an update event class for Transarc's Encina.

You can also define event classes to meet your own auditing needs. The following is the suggested name format for these event classes:

dce_*server-name_class*

where *class* is a characterization of the event class.

42.3.5.3 Event Class Numbers

If you define your own event classes, you must associate it with an event class number. Event class numbers are 32-bit integers. Each event class number is a tuple made up of a *set ID* and the *class ID*. The set ID corresponds to a set of event classes and is assigned by OSF to an organization or vendor. The class ID identifies an event class within the set of event classes. The organization or vendor manages the issuance of the class ID numbers to generate an event class number.

The structure and administration of event class numbers can be likened to the structure and administration of IP addresses. Recall that an IP address is a tuple of a network ID (analogous to the set ID) and a host ID (analogous to the class ID).

42.3.5.4 Event Class Number Formats

Event class numbers follow one of five formats (A to E), depending on the number of event classes in the organization. The format of an event class number can be determined from its four high-order bits.

Format A can be used by large organizations (such as OSF or major DCE vendors) that need more than 16 bits for the class ID. This format allocates 7 bits to the set ID and 24 bits to the class ID. Format A event class numbers with zero (0) as its set ID are assigned to OSF. That is, all event class numbers used by OSF have a zero in the most significant byte.

Format B can be used by intermediate-sized organizations that need 8 to 16 bits for the class ID.

Format C can be used by small organizations that need less than 8 bits for the class ID.

Format D is not administered by OSF and can be used freely within the cell. These event class numbers cannot be unique across cells and should not be used by application servers that are installed in more than one cell.

Format E is reserved for future use.

The numbers with 110 in the most significant bits (that is, 0xC0000000 to 0xDFFFFFFF) are reserved to be used locally within a cell.

The event class number formats are illustrated in Figure 42-1.

Figure 42–1. Event Class Number Formats

	0 1 2 3 4	8	16	24	31
Format A	0 set–id		event–id		
Format B	1 0 set–id			event–id	
Format C	1 1 0 set–id				event–id
Format D	1 1 1 0 event–id				
Format E	1 1 1 1 reserved				

The cell administrator is responsible for administering and assigning local event class numbers and their names.

42.3.6 Filters

Once the code points are identified and placed in the application server, all audit events corresponding to the code points will be logged in the audit trail file, irrespective of the outcome of these audit events. However, recording all audit events under all conditions may neither be practical nor necessary. Filters provide a means by which audit records are logged only when certain conditions are satsified. The administrator defines filters using the DCE control program.

A filter is composed of filter guides that specify these conditions. Filter guides also specify what action to take if the condition (outcome) is met.

A filter answers the following questions:

- Who will be audited?

- What events will be audited?

- What should be the outcome of these events before an audit record is written?

- Will the audit record be logged in the audit trail file, or displayed on the system console, or both?

For example, for the bank server program, you can impose the following conditions before an audit record is written:

''Log audit records on all withdrawal transactions (the audit events) that fail because of access denial (outcome of the event) that are performed by all customers in the DCE cell (who to audit).''

42.3.6.1 Filter Subject Identity

A filter is associated with one filter subject, which denotes *to whom* the filter applies. The filter subject is the client of the distributed application who caused the event to happen. The filter subject has two parts: the filter type and the key.

There are eight filter types:

- **principal**—DCE principal in the local cell.

- **foreign_principal**—DCE principal in a foreign cell.

- **group**—DCE group in the local cell.

- **foreign_group**—DCE group in a foreign cell.

- **cell**—DCE cell in the network.

- **cell_overridable**—DCE cell in the network. This type can be overriden by a more specific filter type.

- **world**—All clients of the distributed application.

- **world_overridable**—All clients of the distributed application. This type can be overriden by a more specific filter type.

The key is the specific name of the **principal**, **foreign_principal**, **group**, **foreign_group**, **cell**, and **cell_overridable** filter types. The **world** and **world_overridable** filter types have no keys.

42.3.6.2 Filter Guides

A filter contains one or more guides. A filter guide contains three elements: audit condition, audit action, and event class.

An audit condition specifies the required outcome (or outcomes) of the event before an audit record is written to the audit trail. These outcomes are not mutually exclusive. The audit conditions are

- **success**—Records only if event succeeds.

- **failure**—Records only if event fails.

- **denial**—Records only if event failed because of access denial.

An audit action specifies where the audit record is written. The audit actions are

- **alarm**—Displays the audit record on system console

- **log**—Logs the audit record through an audit daemon or directly to an audit trail file.

The audit actions are not mutually exclusive; you can specify both.

The third element of the filter guide specifies the event class or event classes to which the filter will apply (for the specific filter subject identity).

42.3.6.3 Example of Filter Guides

The following is an example of a filter with two guides:

```
filter type: foreign_principal
key: /.../cell_x/foo
guide 1:
        audit conditions - denial
        audit actions - log
        event classes - Confidential
guide 2:
        audit conditions - denial
        audit actions - alarm, log
        event classes - Restricted
```

Guide 1 specifies that an audit record will be logged for any event in event class **Confidential** if the user is the foreign principal **/.../cell_x/foo** and the event failed because of access denial. Guide 2 specifies that an audit record will not only be logged but also be displayed on the system console for any event in event class **Restricted**, for the same user and event outcome.

42.3.6.4 Filter Rules

Filter rules are used to resolve overlapping guides from different filters. There are two filter rules: the override and the high-water-mark.

Under the override rule, filters that are overridable (that is, **cell_overridable** and **world_overridable** types) are nullified by more specific filters. The override rule serves as a mechanism that allows for complementary filters. A filter for a principal or a group is more specific than a filter for a cell or for the world.

The high-water-mark rule is applied after the override rule. If multiple filters are applicable to a client, the union of the actions (log or alarm) specified by these filters is applied.

A filter is applicable to a client if its principal, groups, or cell identity matches the key of the filter. The **world** and **world_overridable** filters have no keys and are applicable to all clients. If there are multiple filters that are applicable to a client, then the union of the actions (log or alarm) specified by these filters is taken.

42.3.6.5 Example of Using Filter Rules

The use of overridable filters is described in the following scenario:

Alice in Company (cell) X is responsible for activating some operations (event class **critical_transactions**). Other principals in the company are also authorized to activate the same operations, but only under certain conditions; for example, when Alice is not available. The system administrator wants to log an audit record regardless of the event outcome (that is, audit conditions = all) or who activates these operations. The administrator also wants to generate an alarm if the activator is not Alice. This specification is implemented by the following two filters:

```
Filter 1:

        filter type: principal
        key: Alice
        guide 1:
                audit conditions - all
                audit actions - log
                event classes - critical_transactions

Filter 2:

        filter type: cell_overridable
        key: X
        guide 1:
                audit conditions - all
                audit actions - log, alarm
                event classes - critical_transactions
```

When Alice invokes events in the **critical_transactions** event class, the principal filter (filter 1) is applicable because its key matches Alice's identity. The principal filter is more specific than the cell filter. Although the cell filter (filter 2) is also applicable to Alice (Alice belongs to cell X), it is overridden by the principal filter because the cell filter is overridable. For other principals in Company (cell) X, the only applicable filter is the cell filter (filter 2). Thus, these same events will cause an audit record to be logged and also raise an alarm.

Nonoverridable world and cell filters are also useful. Without them, an administrator, for example, would have to delete all filters for groups and principals of a cell in order to make a cell-wide filter effective to the whole cell. (System administrators may want to introduce a *temporary* nonoverridable cell filter when a cell is suspected to be the source of a security problem.)

The following figure illustrates the override relations between different types of filters. An arrow from filter type X to filter type Y means that X overrides Y.

Figure 42–2. Override Relations Between Filter Types

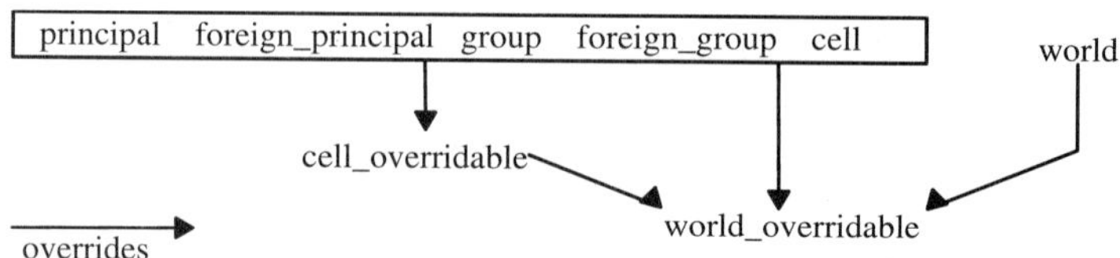

DCE groups are generally defined for the purpose of granting access permissions. A group filter specifies *auditing the intent to use the group's privileges*, instead of specifying *auditing the principals that belong to the group*. That is, a group filter would not have auditing effects on a member principal of the group unless the principal has the intent to use the group's privileges (by including the group in the PAC). Because group filters are defined to audit the intention of using a group's privileges, they are independent of other filters and are not overridable.

42.3.7 Audit Trail File

The audit trail file contains all the audit records that are written by the audit daemon. You can specify either a *central audit trail file* or a *vocal audit trail file*.

The central audit trail file is created by the audit daemon when it is started. By default, if the **dce_aud_open( )** function does not specify a name for an audit trail file, all audit records are sent to the audit daemon, which stores them in the central audit trail file.

If the **dce_aud_open( )** function is invoked with a name for the trail file, this name becomes the pathname to the local audit trail file and all audit records are sent to that file.

42.4 Administration and Programming in DCE Audit

Many of the DCE Audit Service administrative tasks are related to the tasks performed by the application programer. To understand these administrative tasks, you should be familiar with some programming aspects of the DCE Audit Service. This section describes a typical DCE Audit Service programming and administrative scenario and their tasks.

A banking server example illustrates this scenario.

42.4.1 Programmer Tasks

The application programmer uses the DCE audit APIs to enable auditing in the application server program. Specifically, the programmer performs the following tasks:

1. Identifies the code points corresponding to the audit events in the application server program.

   For example, a banking server program can have these functions: **acct_open()**, **acct_close()**, **acct_withdraw()**, **acct_deposit()**, and **acct_transfer()**. Each of these functions can be designated as a code point, meaning that these are possible audit events that can be recorded (depending on the filter):

   ```
   acct_open()              /* first code point */
   acct_close()             /* second code point */
   acct_withdraw()          /* third code point */
   acct_deposit()           /* fourth code point */
   acct_transfer()          /* fifth code point */
   ```

2. Assigns an event number to each code point. The event numbers are used as parameters by the **dce_aud_open()** API, which opens an audit trail, and the **dce_aud_start()** API, which initializes the audit record for the code point. The programmer may want to define these event numbers in the server's header file.

For example:

```
/* event number for the first code point, acct_open() */
#define evt_vn_bank_server_acct_open        0x01000000

/* event number for the second code point, acct_close() */
#define evt_vn_bank_server_acct_close       0x01000001

/* event number for the third code point, acct_withdraw() */
#define evt_vn_bank_server_acct_withdraw  0x01000002

/* event number for the fourth code point, acct_deposit() */
#define evt_vn_bank_server_acct_deposit     0x01000003

/* event number for the fifth code point, acct_transfer() */
#define evt_vn_bank_server_acct_transfer  0x01000004
```

3. Adds a call to the **dce_aud_open**( ) API to the application server's
    initialization routines. This opens the audit trail file. This function
    uses the event number of the lowest numbered event, (in this case
    acct_open( )) as one of its parameters. For example:

```
main()
/* evt_vn_bank_server_acct_open is the lowest event number */
dce_aud_open(aud_c_trl_open_write, description,
             evt_vn_bank_server_acct_open,
             5, &audit_trail, &status);
```

4. Adds Audit event logging functions to every code point in the
    application server code. These functions perform the following at
    each code point:

    - Initializes an audit record by using the **dce_aud_start**( ) API.
      This function "assigns" the event number to the code point
      representing an event. Thus, this function uses the event number
      as one of its parameters.

    - Adds event-specific information to the audit record by using the
      dce_aud_put_ev_info( ) API.

    - Commits the audit record using the **dce_aud_commit**( ) API. This
      function writes the audit record to the audit trail file.

    Following is an example of how these APIs are used on the code
    points of the bank server program:

```
acct_open()        /* first code point */

/* Uses the event number for acct_open(), */
/*                          evt_vn_bank_server_acct_open */

dce_aud_start(evt_vn_bank_server_acct_open,
             binding,options,outcome,&ard, &status);
 if (ard) /* If events need to be logged */
     dce_aud_put_ev_info(ard,info,&status);
 if (ard) /* If events were logged */
     dce_aud_commit(at,ard,options,format,&outcome,&status);
acct_close()    /* second code point */

/* Uses the event number for acct_close(), */
/*                          evt_vn_bank_server_acct_close */

dce_aud_start(evt_vn_bank_server_acct_close,
             binding,options,outcome,&ard, &status);
 if (ard) /* If events need to be logged */
     dce_aud_put_ev_info(ard,info,&status);
 if (ard) /* If events were logged */
     dce_aud_commit(at,ard,options,format,&outcome,&status);
```

5. Closes the audit trail file when the server shuts down, using the
    dce_aud_close( ) API in the main server routine. For example:

```
dce_aud_close(audit_trail, &status);
```

42.4.2 Administrator Tasks

The administrator uses the event numbers representing the different code
points in the audit client application server program to create event class
files and filter guides in the following manner:

1. The administrator obtains the event numbers of the code points
    (representing each audit event) from the application server
    programmer. In our example, these code points were assigned the
    following event numbers:

acct_open( )   0x01000000

acct_close( )   0x01000001

acct_withdraw( )   0x01000002

acct_deposit( )   0x01000003

acct_transfer( )   0x01000004

(Note that event numbers should be entirely sequential. That is, no missing members of the sequence are allowed.)

2.   The administrator decides to create two event classes: the **account_creation_operations** class comprised of **acct_open( )** and **acct_close( )**, and the **account_balance_operations** class comprised of **acct_withdraw( )**, **acct_deposit( )**, and **acct_transfer( )**. The administrator assigns the event class **account_creation_operations** the event class number 0xC0000006. Event class **account_-balance_operations** is assigned the event class number 0xC0000007.

To create the event classes, the administrator creates and edits two files, one for each event class. The name of each of these files will be the same as the event class that each represents. Each file will contain the numbers of the events in each event class.

The file with the name **account_creation_operations** is edited as follows (lines that begin with # (number sign) are comment lines):

```
# Event class number of account_creation_operations
ECN = 0xC0000006

# Event number of acct_open()
0xC1000000

# Event number of acct_close()
0xC1000001
```

The file with the name **account_balance_operations** is edited as follows:

```
# Event number of acct_withdraw()
0xC1000002


# Event number of acct_deposit()
0xC1000003


# Event number of acct_transfer()
0xC1000004
```

The administrator stores both files in the *dcelocal*/**etc/audit/ec** directory.

3. The administrator decides to create two filters: one for all users within the cell (for the cell **/.:/torolabcell**), and the other for all other users.

    The filter for all users within the cell has the following guides:

    - Audit the events in the event class **account_balance_operations** only, subject to the next condition.

    - Write an audit record only if an operation in that event class failed because of access denial.

    - If the first condition is fulfilled, write the audit record in an audit trail file only.

    - The administrator then uses the DCE control program's **audfilter create** command to create this filter:

    > dcecp> **audfilter create {cell /.../torolabcell} -attribute **
    >   **{account_balance_operations denial log}**

    The filter for all other users has the following guides:

    - Audit the events in both event classes, subject to the next condition.

    - Write an audit record if an operation in that event class succeeded, failed, or failed because of access denial.

    - Write the audit record both in an audit trail file and the console.

The first entry allows any unauthenticated user only **read** access to the filters. The second entry allows the host principal (**hosts/**<hostname>**/self**) to query and modify the filters, control the audit daemon, and to write to the audit trail file. The third entry allows the members of the group **subsys/dce/audit-admin** the same access rights as the host principal. The last entry allows all other principals only **read** access to the filters. You can modify this ACL to suit your security requirements by using **dcecp**.

43.3.3 Giving Permissions to Audit Clients and Administrators

Using **dcecp**, you can add entries to the ACL of the audit daemon that will grant audit clients the **log** permission to the audit trail file. You can create a DCE security group that consists of the servers on the host that are authorized to generate audit records. For example:

group/hosts/<hostname>**/audit-clients**

Give this group the **log** permission to the audit daemon. For example:

dcecp> **acl modify /.:/hosts/machine1/audit-server \\
        -add {group hosts/machine1/audit-clients l}**

All audit clients can then be made members of this group and inherit its permssions to the audit daemon.

ACL entries must also be added to grant designated administrators the read, query, and control permissions to the audit daemon. For example, for the administrator's group **group/hosts/machine1/audit-admin**:

dcecp> **acl modify /.:/hosts/machine1/audit-server \\
        -add {group hosts/machine1/audit-admin rwc}**

43.4 Defining Event Classes

Individual audit events can be grouped together to form event classes. The event class provides an efficient mechanism by which sets of events can be logically grouped and selected using a single value.

DCE audit event classes are configurable. You can add or remove events of an existing event class or define new event classes.

The ability to define local event classes is useful in simplifying the management of audit services in multiple DCE applications. Administrators can design their own audit event classes reflecting their security requirements and trail storage resource constraints.

Temporary event classes can also be created to track down security violations.

43.4.1 Steps in Defining an Event Class

To define an event class, follow these steps:

1. Obtain an event class number for the event class from your cell administrator. A range of event class numbers should have been allocated to your organization by OSF. If not, contact OSF.

2. Create an event class file in the *dcelocal***/etc/audit/ec** directory. Edit the file as follows:

   a. Declare the *event class number* (ECN) by adding a line with the following format:

      ECN=_*event_class_number*

   b. Optionally, you can add a *server event prefix* (SEP) line in the file. The SEP line contains the event number prefixes of each server. The event number prefix is the lowest event number in each server. The SEP line has the following format:

      SEP=_*event_number1 event_number2 event_number3* ...

You can put the SEP line anywhere in the file. The SEP line speeds up the scanning of audit clients by skipping irrelevant event class files.

c. From the application, obtain the event numbers for the code points that you want to include in the event class.

d. Add the event numbers corresponding to the events that you want to include in the event class, one number per line.

In the event class file, empty lines are ignored and comments are designated by a # (number sign) preceding the comment text.

43.4.2 Example Event Class File

Following is a sample event class file named **ec_local_cell_critical_events**:

```
ECN = 0xC0000005


# Server Event Number Prefixes
# 0x000001 Security Service Events
# 0x000002 Time Service Events
# 0x000003 Audit Service Events


SEP = 0x00000100 0x00000200 0x00000300


# Security Service Critical Events
# evt_osf_dce_rs_properties_set_info (sets registry properties)
0x0000011f
# evt_osf_dce_rs_policy_set_info (sets registry policy)
0x00000121
# evt_osf_dce_rs_rep_admin_stop (stops the registery service)
0x00000127
# evet_osf_dce_rs_rep_admin_mkey (changes master key)
0x00000129


# Time Service Critical Events
# evt_osf_dce_dts_create (creates a server or a clerk)
0x00000201
# evt_osf_dce_dts_delete (deletes a server or a clerk)
0x00000202
# evt_osf_dce_dts_enable (enables the time service)
0x00000203
# evt_osf_dce_dts_disable (disables the time service)
0x00000204
```

```
# Audit Service Critical Events
# evt_osf_dce_aud_enable (enables audit-record logging service)
0x00000301
# evt_osf_dce_aud_disable (disables audit-record logging service)
0x00000302
# evt_osf_dce_aud_stop (terminates the execution of the audit daemon)
0x00000303
```

43.5 Creating and Maintaining Filters

After starting the audit daemon and creating the event class file, you can run **dcecp** to create, modify, or display the filters maintained by the audit daemon. Use the **audfilter create**, **audfilter modify**, and **audfilter delete** commands to create, modify, and delete the filters. Use the **audfilter catalog** and **audfilter show** commands to display the existing filters.

43.5.1 Creating Filters

The following is an example **audfilter create** command for creating a filter:

dcecp> **audfilter create {group trust}** \
        -attribute {ec_local_bank_audit denial log}

The example command specifies that a filter type **group** be created for the DCE group named **trust** in the local cell.

The **-attributes** option is required. The argument to the option is a *filter guide* or list of guides. Each filter guide is made up of three elements: an *event class name* or list of names, an *audit condition* or list of conditions, and an *audit action* or list of actions.

The event class name corresponds to the name of the event class file for which your are creating a filter.

The audit condition is the condition required for the event to be audited. Valid conditions are **success**, **denial**, **failure**, **pending**, and **all**.

The audit action is the action to take if the event being generated matches the audit condition specified. Valid actions are **log**, **alarm**, and **all**.

43.5.2 Modifying Filters

You can modify an existing audit filter by adding or deleting one or more of the filter's guides. The following is a sample **dcecp** command for modifying an existing filter:

dcecp> **audfilter modify world -add {Monetary_Transfers denial log}**

The example command adds a guide with an event class of **Monetary_Transfers**, an audit condition of **denial**, and an audit action of **log** to the existing filter type **world**. Note that the filter type **world** does not take a key.

The DCE control program does not use commas. Multiple guides and multiple filters are specified in the standard **dcecp** list format: **{x y}** for single arguments or **{{x y} {a b}}** for multiple arguments.

In order to execute the **audfilter modify** command, you must have write (**w**) permission to the audit daemon's ACL.

43.5.3 Deleting Filters

You can delete one or more of the audit filters for a DCE client by using the **audfilter delete** command. The following is an example **audfilter delete** command:

dcecp> **audfilter delete {foreign_principal /.../foreign_cell_name/jedwards}**

The example command deletes the audit filter for the DCE principal **jedwards** in the foreign cell **/.../foreign_cell_name**.

You can specify more than one filter to be operated on in the **audfilter delete** command. As with the previous example of modifying filters, when deleting multiple filter, you must use the standard **dcecp** syntax.

In order to execute this command, you must have write (**w**) permission to the audit daemon's ACL.

43.5.4 Default Filters

During the configuration of the host (using **dce_config**), the following **audfilter create** commands (using **dcecp**) are executed to create filters for the security daemon, the DTS daemon, and the audit daemon:

```
audfilter create world -at {dce_sec_modify success log}

audfilter create world -at {dce_sec_modify {failure denial} all}

audfilter create world -at {dce_sec_server success log}

audfilter create world -at {dce_sec_server {failure denial} all}

audfilter create world -at {dce_sec_authent {failure denial} all}

audfilter create world -at {dce_sec_query denial all}


audfilter create world -at {dce_dts_mgt_modify success log}

audfilter create world -at {dce_dts_mgt_modify {failure denial} all}

audfilter create world -at {dce_dts_mgt_query {failure denial} all}


audfilter create world -at {dce_audit_admin_modify success log}

audfilter create world -at {dce_audit_admin_modify {failure denial} all}

audfilter create world -at {dce_audit_filter_modify success log}

audfilter create world -at {dce_audit_filter_modify {failure denial} all}

audfilter create world -at {dce_audit_admin_query {failure denial} all}

audfilter create world -at {dce_audit_filter_query {failure denial} all}
```

43.5.5 Enabling Audit Filters

If you want to enable the audit filters, you must first set the **DCEAUDITFILTERON** environment variable. You must set this variable before starting the server (that is, the audit client).

43.5.5.1 Removing the Update Binding File

If a server (audit client) is running with filters enabled (that is, **DCEAUDITFILTERON** was set), **libaudit** (which is linked to the server) obtains the server's binding information and stores it in the following:

/opt/dcelocal/var/audit/client/*pid-of-server***/update_binding_file**

where *pid-of-server* is the process ID of the server.

If the server ends abnormally, this file must be removed manually. If this is not removed, you will receive an error message the next time you restart the server with **DCEAUDITFILTERON**. The message indicates that the audit daemon is unable to inform the audit client of filter updates:

```
unable to inform process
/opt/dcelocal/var/audit/client/pid-of-server/update_binding_file
about esl update.
```

You can also check for stale update binding files by checking what servers are running (for example, using **ps -e**) and comparing their process IDs with the pathnames of the update binding files. Because the pathname of these files contain a *pid-of-server* component, you can determine what files correspond to nonexistent servers.

Both the binding information file and the directory containing it (*pid-of-server*) must be removed.

43.5.5.2 Buffering of the Audit Trail

The operating system buffers the audit trail data while it is written before writing it to disk. For this reason, the growth of the audit trail file will not become apparent until the data is flushed to disk.

43.6 Enabling and Disabling the Audit Logging Service

Use **dcecp** to enable or disable the audit record logging service of the audit daemon. The **aud enable** command enables the logging service, and the **aud disable** command disables it.

You may want to disable the logging service when the audit trail file becomes too large, and then enable it again after the audit trail has been backed up and rewound (using the **aud rewind** command).

Using the enable or disable commands enable or disable audit record logging to the central audit trail file. Applications such as the security server and the time server use their own audit trail files and are not affected by use of enable or disable.

The **aud stop** command stops the audit daemon.

43.7 Modifying and Querying Audit Daemon Attributes

The DCE audit daemon has two attributes that relate to the audit trail file:

- **stostrategy**—Specifies the storage strategy when the size of the audit trail file has reached its limit. You can specify either of the following storage strategies:

save   If the specified trail size limit is reached, the audit daemon saves the current trail file to a new file (renaming it to its original name with a timestamp appended at the end of the name). The audit daemon then deletes the contents of the original trail file and continues auditing from the beginning of this file. This is the default value for **stostrategy**.

wrap   The audit daemon will overwrite the old audit trails.

- **state**—Indicates whether the audit daemon is servicing audit record logging requests from audit clients. The possible values for this attribute are **enabled** (default value) or **disabled**.

You can use **dcecp** to see the value of these settings, as follows:

```
dcecp> aud show
{state enabled}
{stostrategy save}
```

Use the **aud modify** command to change these attributes.

43.8 Controlling and Displaying Audit Trails

Audit daemons log audit records sent from audit clients into an audit trail file. If the audit daemon is started without any argument, then the default audit trail file used is *dcelocal*/**var/audit/adm/central_trail**. You can also direct the audit trail to another file by using the **-t** option of the **auditd** command when starting daemon; the *trail* argument to the **-t** option specifies the pathname of the file to which the logs should be written.

43.8.1 Displaying Audit Trail Files

Use the **dcecp auditrail show** command to examine the contents of an audit trail file. You can display the contents of either the central or local audit trail file.

For example, you can use the following command to see the contents of the audit trail file **central_trail**:

dcecp> **audtrail show /opt/dcelocal/var/audit/adm/central_trail**

--- Start of an event record --- Event Number: 259
Client: /.../stp.gburg.ibm.com/hosts/drinkernisti/self
Event Outcome: success
Authorization Status: Authorized with a pac
Local Time: 1994-12-19-19:02:27.037-05:00I-----
--- End of an event record ---

--- Start of an event record --- Event Number: 256
Client: /.../stp.gburg.ibm.com/hosts/drinkernisti/self
Event Outcome: success
Authorization Status: Authorized with a pac
Local Time: 1994-12-19-19:02:28.819-05:00I-----
--- End of an event record ---

If you prefer to have the audit trail data put into a file instead of displayed on your screen, include the **-to** option in the **audtrail show** command line. This option prints the audit trail file's contents to a specified filename. Using this option is strongly recommended for large trail files.

43.8.2 Controlling the Audit Trail Size

By default, audit trail files are limited to a size of 2 MB. When the audit service detects that the trail file will grow larger than this value, it closes the file, creates a new unique name for the file by using timestamp information, and then opens a new trail file with the original name. It then proceeds to write new audit logs to this file. When this file grows too large, this process is repeated.

If you wish to change the size of the audit trail file, you must set the environment variable **DCEAUDITTRAILSIZE** to the size you require before starting the application that is using the audit service. Setting this environment variable overrides the default 2 MB size limit.

For example, if you wish to use a trail file size of 5 MB, the value of **DCEAUDITTRAILSIZE** should be as follows:

```
DCEAUDITTRAILSIZE 5000000
```

You can also allow the audit daemon to ''wrap'' around the central trail file when its limit (the default 2 MB or set by **DCEAUDITTRAILSIZE**) is reached. To do this, you should start the audit daemon with the **-wrap** option:

auditd -wrap

You may also want to use this option if old audit records have little or no value and you want to keep only relatively recent records.

A trail size limit can also be set using the **-s** option of the **auditd** command. The limit set using this method overrides the default 2 MB limit.

If for any reason you desire to take a snapshot of the audit trail before it reaches the limit, you can use the **dcecp aud disable** command to disable logging and then copy the file. You can then use the **dcecp aud rewind** command to rewind the central audit trail file. (Note that, if required, you can back up this audit file at this time. But, if backup is desired, it is best to let the audit service automatically create new trail files and back these up.) Then use the **aud enable** command to enable the audit daemon's logging service again.

43.8.3 Changing the Audit Trail File Storage Option

The storage strategy option can be changed while the audit daemon is running. This can only be performed on the central audit trail file.

The following example shows how the **aud modify** command is used to cause the audit trail to wrap when it reaches the limit of the file:

dcecp> **aud modify -stostrategy wrap**

This example command changes the value of the audit daemon's storage strategy attribute to **wrap**.

Appendix A

Valid Characters and Naming Rules for CDS

This appendix discusses the valid character sets for the DCE Directory Service names as used by CDS interfaces. It also explains some characters that have special meaning and describes some restrictions and rules regarding case matching, syntax, and size limits. It is not a comprehensive reference for CDS, GDS, and DNS, but instead gives an overview of some key points to remember about each service. For specific information on valid characters in GDS and DNS names, see the documentation for each technology.

The use of names in DCE often involves more than one directory service. For example, CDS interacts with either GDS or DNS to find names outside the local cell.

Note: Because CDS, GDS, and DNS all have their own valid character sets and syntax rules, the best way to avoid problems is to keep names short and simple, consisting of a minimal set of characters common to all three services. The recommended set is the letters A to Z, a to z, and the digits 0 to 9. In addition to making directory service interoperations easier, use of this subset decreases the probability that users in a heterogeneous hardware and software environment will encounter problems in creating and using names.

B.1 Origin of Object Identifiers

The purpose of object identifiers is to ensure uniqueness among the attribute types that many different applications generate and use. Object identifiers are typically obtained from a hierarchy of allocation authorities, the highest being the International Organization for Standardization (ISO) and the International Telegraph and Telephone Consultative Committee (CCITT). Individual application developers do not usually have to contact ISO or CCITT directly to obtain unique numbers. Application developers are more likely to request object identifiers from a person within their company who is in charge of allocating them. The company authority would in turn contact a higher authority to obtain a unique company prefix.

The hierarchy of allocation authorities is indicated by dots that separate portions of an object identifier. Each string of numbers delineated by dots represents a level of the allocation hierarchy, going left to right from the highest authority down. For example, the object identifier **1.3.22.1.1.2** consists of the following levels:

1	ISO
3	Identified organization
22	Open Software Foundation
1	Distributed Computing Environment
1	Remote Procedure Call
2	RPC Object UUIDs

B.2 The cds_attributes File

The **cds_attributes** file contains object identifiers for CDS attributes and object classes. The following is a sample portion of the default contents of the file:

```
#      OID            LABEL                   SYNTAX
#
1.3.22.1.3.10        CDS_Members             GroupMember
1.3.22.1.3.11        CDS_GroupRevoke         Timeout
1.3.22.1.3.12        CDS_CTS                 Timestamp
1.3.22.1.3.13        CDS_UTS                 Timestamp
1.3.22.1.3.15        CDS_Class               byte
1.3.22.1.3.16        CDS_ClassVersion        Version
1.3.22.1.3.17        CDS_ObjectUUID          uuid
1.3.22.1.3.19        CDS_Replicas            ReplicaPointer
1.3.22.1.3.20        CDS_AllUpTo             Timestamp
1.3.22.1.3.21        CDS_Convergence         small
1.3.22.1.3.22        CDS_InCHName            small
1.3.22.1.3.23        CDS_ParentPointer       ParentPointer
1.3.22.1.3.24        CDS_DirectoryVersion    Version
1.3.22.1.3.25        CDS_UpgradeTo           Version
1.3.22.1.3.27        CDS_LinkTarget          FullName
1.3.22.1.3.28        CDS_LinkTimeout         Timeout
1.3.22.1.3.30        CDS_Towers              byte
1.3.22.1.3.32        CDS_CHName              FullName
1.3.22.1.3.34        CDS_CHLastAddress       byte
1.3.22.1.3.36        CDS_CHState             small
1.3.22.1.3.37        CDS_CHDirectories       CHDirectory
1.3.22.1.3.40        CDS_ReplicaState        small
1.3.22.1.3.41        CDS_ReplicaType         small
1.3.22.1.3.42        CDS_LastSkulk           Timestamp
1.3.22.1.3.43        CDS_LastUpdate          Timestamp
1.3.22.1.3.44        CDS_RingPointer         uuid
1.3.22.1.3.45        CDS_Epoch               uuid
1.3.22.1.3.46        CDS_ReplicaVersion      Version
1.3.22.1.3.48        CDS_NSCellname          char
1.3.22.1.3.52        CDS_GDAPointers         gdaPointer
1.3.22.1.3.53        CDS_CellAliases         GroupMember
1.3.22.1.3.54        CDS_ParentCellPointers  ReplicaPointer
1.3.22.1.1.1         RPC_ClassVersion        byte
1.3.22.1.1.2         RPC_ObjectUUIDs         byte
1.3.22.1.1.3         RPC_Group               byte
1.3.22.1.1.4         RPC_Profile             byte
1.3.22.1.1.5         RPC_Codesets            byte
1.3.22.1.5.1         SEC_RepUUID             byte
```

The first column contains the OID, the second column contains a label (the name to which the identifier is mapped), and the third column indicates the data type. Descriptions of the CDS data types are in the **cdsclerk.h** header file. (See the *OSF DCE Administration Guide—Introduction* and the *OSF DCE Porting and Testing Guide* for the full pathnames of all CDS files.)

Application programmers should never need to modify, except for the purpose of foreign language translation, the CDS labels associated with the unique OIDs in the **cds_attributes** file. However, programmers can obtain new OIDs from the appropriate allocation authority, create new attributes for their own object entries, and then append them to the existing list.

B.3 The cds_globalnames File

The **cds_globalnames** file contains a copy of data that is stored in a Directory Service Agent (DSA) schema for use by GDS. CDS uses this file to interpret the GDS portion of global names that it handles. The file contains only naming attributes; that is, attributes that constitute a distinguished name. The following is a sample portion of the **cds_globalnames** file:

```
# OID           LABEL   ASN.1-IDENTIFIER              SYNTAX  MATCHING
#
# Reference: X.520 (Selected Attribute Types for the Directory)
2.5.4.0         OC      objectClass                   -       -
2.5.4.1         AO      aliasedObjectName             -       -
2.5.4.2         KI      knowledgeInformation          CIS     CIM
2.5.4.3         CN      commonName                    CIS     CIM
2.5.4.4         S       surname                       CIS     CIM
2.5.4.5         SN      serialNumber                  PS      PM
2.5.4.6         C       countryName                   PS      CIM
2.5.4.7         L       localityName                  CIS     CIM
2.5.4.8         SP      stateOrProvinceName           CIS     CIM
2.5.4.9         SADR    streetAddress                 CIS     CIM
2.5.4.10        O       organizationName              CIS     CIM
2.5.4.11        OU      organizationalUnitName        CIS     CIM
2.5.4.12        T       title                         CIS     CIM
2.5.4.13        D       description                   CIS     CIM
#2.5.4.14       SG      searchGuide                   Guide   -
2.5.4.15        BC      businessCategory              CIS     CIM
#2.5.4.16       POST    postalAddress                 PostalAddress
2.5.4.17        PC      postalCode                    CIS     CIM
2.5.4.18        POB     postOfficeBox                 CIS     CIM
```

The first column contains the object identifier, and the second column contains the string name to which it is mapped. The third column is the ASN.1 identifier for the attribute type, as defined in the appropriate CCITT recommendation (X.500 or X.400). The fourth column is the ASN.1 label for the syntax of the attribute type. The fifth column contains the ASN.1 identifier of the matching rule to be applied to the attribute type. Possible syntax abbreviations are as follows:

CES	Case Exact String
CIS	Case Ignore String
PS	Printable String
NS	Numeric String
-	Unspecified

Matching rules are defined as follows:

CEM	Case Exact String Matching—Leading and trailing spaces are ignored and multiple consecutive internal spaces are reduced to one; otherwise, the strings must be the same length and corresponding characters must be identical.
CIM	Case Ignore String Matching—Same as CEM, except that characters differing only in case are considered to match.
PM	Printable String Matching—Same as CEM.
NM	Numeric String Matching—Same as CEM, except that all spaces are ignored.
-	Unspecified.

The **cds_globalnames** file contains additional comments and descriptive information about attribute types and case-matching rules. (See the X.500 recommendation for details on the ASN.1 identifiers and their meaning.)

B.4 Modifying the Files

When a programmer develops an application that uses the directory service, the directory service manager or the application developer needs to obtain unique identifiers for any new CDS attribute names or GDS attribute types that the new application uses and then update the appropriate file.

If the application stores names in CDS, edit the **cds_attributes** file. (Refer to the **cdsclerk.h** file for the list of appropriate data type descriptors.) If the application stores names in GDS, edit the **cds_globalnames** file and use the appropriate ASN.1 identifiers to describe the data type, syntax, and case-matching rules for the name.

Note: If you modify the OID values for standard attributes in the **cds_attributes** and **cds_globalnames** files, you may encounter problems interoperating with other directory service implementations.

B.5 Modifying a CDS Entity's Attributes

Every CDS entity has attributes, which are pieces or sets of data that are associated with that entity. Attributes can reflect or affect the operational behavior of an entity, record the number of times a particular event or problem occurred since the entity was last enabled, and uniquely distinquish an entity for any other entity.

CDS attributes are identified by ISO OIDs. Every CDS attribute name maps to an OID and a corresponding data type. Usually, client applications define the name of an attribute and its data type. Application programmers should never need to modify (except for the purpose of foreign language translation) the existing CDS labels associated with the unique OIDs in the **cds_attributes** file. However, programmers can obtain new OIDs from the appropriate authority, create new attributes for their own object entries, and then append them to the existing list. The OID and data type of each attribute are stored in the file **cds_attributes**. Descriptions of the CDS data types that applications can use are in the **cdsclerk.h** file.

B.5.1 Adding a New Attribute

Use the **dcecp modify** command with the **-add** option to add a new attribute to an object entity.

To add a new attribute, you must have previously added the new attribute to the **cds_attributes** file on each host in the cell. You must also have write permission to the entity to which you are adding new attributes.

For example, the following command adds the single-valued attribute (**owner**) to a directory (**/.:/admin**) and assigns a value of **Leland** to the new attribute:

```
dcecp> directory modify /.:/admin -add {owner Leland}
```

The following command adds a new multivalued attribute (**vegetables**) to an object (**/.:/admin/garden**) and assigns values of **carrots** and **lettuce** to the new attribute:

```
dcecp> object modify /.:/admin/garden -add {vegetables {carrots} {lettuce}}
```

B.5.2 Modifying the Value of an Existing Attribute

Use the **dcecp modify** command with the **-change** option to modify the value of an existing attribute.

To modify the value of an attribute, you must have write permission to the name whose attributes you are modifying.

For example, the following command changes the value of the owner attribute of the **/.:/admin** directory from **Leland** to **Peters**:

```
dcecp> directory modify /.:/admin -change {owner Peters}
```

B.5.3 Removing an Attribute

Use the **dcecp modify** command with the **-remove** option to remove an attribute from an object entity.

To remove an attribute, you must have write permission to the name whose attribute you are removing.

To remove an attribute, use the **modify** command with the **-remove** and **-types** options. For example, the following command removes the owner attribute from the **/.:/admin** directory:

dcecp> **directory modify /.:/admin -remove owner -types**

To remove a single value from a multivalued attribute, use the **-remove** option and specify the value to be removed. For example, the following command removes the carrots value of the vegetables attribute from the **/.:/admin/garden** object:

dcecp> **object modify /.:/admin/garden -remove {vegetables carrots}**

Appendix C

Time-Providers and Time Services

This appendix explains the criteria to use when selecting a time-provider, and describes time dissemination services, time-providers (hardware and software) and their interaction with DTS. The appendix also contains a world time zone map.

C.1 Criteria for Selecting a Time Source

Before you select a time source for your network, ask the following questions:

- How accurate is the time that is provided?

  Accuracy is affected by the time source itself, as well as the transmission media. As long as the inaccuracy is known, it can be compensated for.

- How reliable is the time source?

  The time source must be available. If it is not , the server connected to the time-provider uses times from other servers and compensates for any time difference when the source again becomes available.

- What is the extent of coverage?

  The time source must be available in the geographical area where the time-provider server is located.

- What is the level of known inaccuracy?

  If this is known, DTS can compensate for it. Most sources have known inaccuracy levels.

- What is the cost?

- Does the source conform to the operating environment?

  The available power supply and physical conditions must be compatible with the source; consult the supplier for the specifications.

Table C-1 summarizes the selection criteria for each type of time source.

Table C–1. Time-Provider Selection Criteria

Type	Coverage	Inaccuracy	Cost
Telephone			
NIST	Regional	10 msec.	Variable fee per call
Radio			
MSF	Europe	10 msec.	$1K to 2K
WWV	North America	100 msec.	$1K to 2K
WWVB	North America & Europe	10 msec.	$1K to 2K
WWVH	Eastern & Central North Pacific	100 msec.	$1K to 2K
Satellite			
GOES	Worldwide	1 msec. corrected	$2K to $20K
GPS	Worldwide	< 100 nsec.	$15K to $20K

C.2 Sources of Coordinated Universal Time

There are several sources of UTC time, including telephone, radio, and satellite, as described in the following subsections.

C.2.1 Telephone Services

Telephone time-provider services require the time-provider to dial a centralized UTC time source through a modem. Modem speeds and line delays can affect the accuracy of the time returned.

Telephone services are usually provided by standards agencies. For example, in the United States this service is offered by the National Institute of Standards and Technology (NIST). There is a per-call fee for the service in addition to the cost of the modem software.

C.2.2 Radio Transmissions

DTS can obtain time from a radio time source. Commercial receivers that monitor time and frequency broadcasts can return time values through the Time-Provider Interface (TPI) to the DTS server. The NIST operates the following U.S. time and frequency stations:

- WWV

  Transmits at 2.5, 5.0, 10.0, 15.0 MHz to North America and South America.

- WWVB

  Transmits at 60 kHz primarily to the United States, providing high-quality frequency information because atmospheric propagation effects are relatively minor.

- WWVH

  Transmits at 2.5, 5.0, 10.0, 15.0 MHz to Alaska, Hawaii, Australia, New Zealand, Japan, and Southeast Asia.

The following stations are available in Europe:

- MSF

  Broadcasts from England at 60 kHz.

- DCF77

  Broadcasts from Germany at 77.5 kHz.

In addition to the stations previously listed, more than 30 radio stations worldwide provide UTC time. Consult the national standards organization in your country for further information.

C.2.3 Network Time Protocol

Nodes that have Internet access can use the Network Time Protocol (NTP) as a source of UTC time for DTS. (See Chapter 26 for an explanation of how to use NTP as a time-provider.)

C.2.4 Satellite

Satellites have worldwide availability; they can provide relatively precise times if their delays are known and compensated for. See the following list for satellite sources of UTC:

- GOES

  Geostationary Operational Environment Satellite

- TRANSIT

  A U.S. Navy satellite system consisting of four tracking systems and two ground satellite communications sites

- GPS

  Global Positioning System, a satellite receiver

C.3 World Time Zone Map

Figure C-1 shows a map of the world time zones, including the following:

- UTC reference zone

- Odd-numbered and even-numbered zones

- Half-hour zones

- Countries and areas that have not adopted the zone system or where time differs other than a half hour from the neighboring zone

Figure C–1. World Time Zone Map

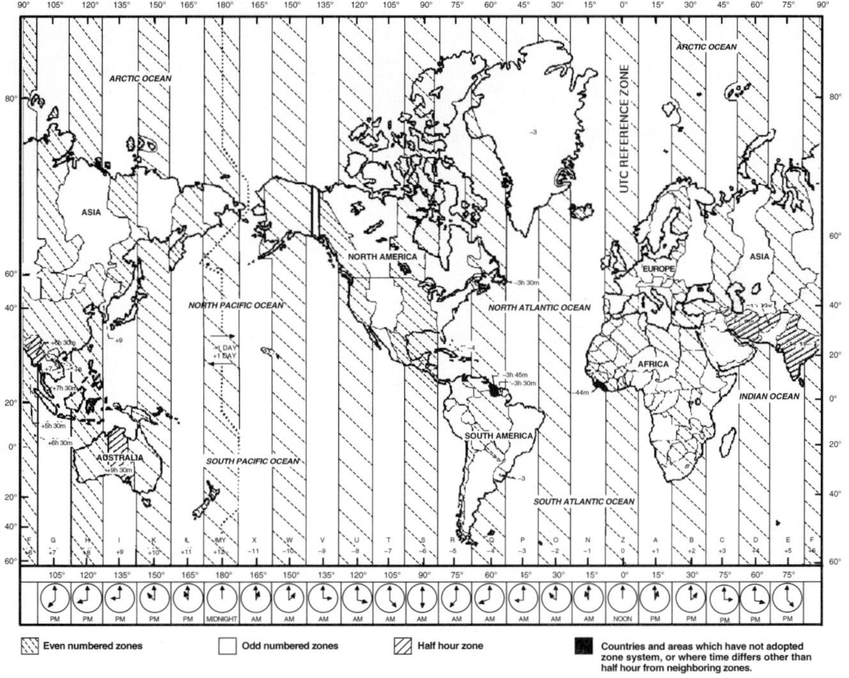

DTS Extended BNF

This appendix defines the Distributed Time Service (DTS) syntax in extended Backus Naur Format (BNF) notation.

The BNF for DTS time conversion has four parts: *year*, *day*, *tdf*, and *inaccuracy*. For any part whose value is not explicitly expressed, the conversion default value is taken as that of the current day. The BNF for the DTS time conversion is as follows:

```
dts_time :  year_part day_part tdf_part inacc_part
         |  year_part day_part tdf_part
         |  year_part day_part
         |  year_part day_part inacc_part
         |  year_part inacc_part
         |  year_part
         |  day_part  tdf_part inacc_part
         |  day_part  tdf_part
         |  day_part inacc_part
         |  day_part
         |  year_part Z
         |  year_part Z inacc_part
         |  year_part day_part Z inacc_part
         |  day_part  Z inacc_part
         |  day_part  Z
;

year_part : number - number - number -
          | number - number - number T
          | number - number T
          | number T
;

day_part  : partial : partial : partial
          | partial : partial
          | partial
;

tdf_part  : sign number : number
          | sign number
;

sign      : -
          | +
;

partial   : number
          | number frac
          | number frac number
          | frac number
;
```

```
frac        : .
        | ,
;

inacc_part : I
        | I partial
        | I infinity
;

infinity   : 'i''n''f'
        | - -
        | - - - - -
;

number      : DIGIT
        | number DIGIT
;
```

OSF DCE Administration Guide—Core Components

access between, 33–1,
33–14
backing up servers, 5–5
changing names in
hierarchical, 21–23
changing the names of, 6–3
contacting foreign, 22–6 to
22–11
creating hierarchical, 21–18
extending the **cell** task
object, 5–6
managing the names of, 6–1
managing with **cell** task
object, 5–1
naming environments, 11–7
testing operation of, 5–4

child

cells
and child pointers,
12–7
naming, 11–8
pointers
about, 12–7
and child cells, 12–7
how they work, 13–5
to 13–7

clearinghouses
about, 12–3, 12–4
communications with CDS
clerks, 17–3
deleting, 21–16 to 21–18
object entries, 12–6, 13–3 to
13–4
preserving after server
upgrades, 17–7
relocating, 21–14 to 21–16
viewing contents, 17–3

viewing counters, 17–2
clients, showing in a cell, 5–2
clocks
adjusting. *See* system time

adjustment mechanism,
23–12
correcting malfunctions,
25–18 to 25–20
errors, 23–7
forcing synchronization,
25–29
restricting synchronization
cycles, 25–17
synchronizing, 23–9 to
23–11
clock set command, 25–26, 25–27
code point, 42–3
command-line editing, 1–13
commands, **dcecp**, 16–15, 25–2,
25–3
command substitution, used in
dcecp, 2–4
comments, in **dcecp** scripts, 2–9
computed time, 23–10
configuration, password
management server, 30–17
containers, definition of, 28–23
control programs. *See* DCE control
program
convenience variables
current cell name, 2–12
current host name, 2–12
current principal name,
2–11
DCE server names, 2–16
in **dcecp** scripts, 2–10
last security server used,
2–18

OSF DCE Administration Guide—Core Components

L

M

N

O

OSF DCE Administration Guide—Core Components

OSF DCE Administration Guide—Core Components

U